WORLD AFFAIRS
National and International Viewpoints

WORLD AFFAIRS
National and International Viewpoints

The titles in this collection were selected
from the Council on Foreign Relations' publication:
The Foreign Affairs 50-Year Bibliography

Advisory Editor
RONALD STEEL

THE EQUALITY OF STATES
IN
INTERNATIONAL LAW

BY

EDWIN DeWITT DICKINSON

ARNO PRESS
A NEW YORK TIMES COMPANY
New York • 1972

341.26
D553e

Reprint Edition 1972 by Arno Press Inc.

Reprinted from a copy in The Newark Public Library

World Affairs: National and International Viewpoints
ISBN for complete set: 0-405-04560-3
See last pages of this volume for titles.

Manufactured in the United States of America

~~~~~~~~~~~~~~~~~~

Library of Congress Cataloging in Publication Data

Dickinson, Edwin De Witt, 1887-1961.
    The equality of states in international law.

    (World affairs: national and international
viewpoints)
    Original ed. issued as v. 3 of the Harvard studies
in jurisprudence.
    Originally presented as the author's thesis, Harvard,
1918.
    Bibliography: p.
    1. Equality of states. I. Title. II. Series.
III. Series: Harvard studies in jurisprudence, v. 3.
JX4003.D5 1972   341.26   72-4270
ISBN 0-405-04566-2

HARVARD STUDIES IN
JURISPRUDENCE

VOLUME III

THE EQUALITY OF STATES
IN
INTERNATIONAL LAW

THE EQUALITY OF STATES
IN
INTERNATIONAL LAW

BY

EDWIN DeWITT DICKINSON
Ph.D., J.D.

PROFESSOR OF LAW IN THE UNIVERSITY OF MICHIGAN. SOMETIME OZIAS GOODWIN
MEMORIAL FELLOW IN INTERNATIONAL LAW IN THE GRADUATE SCHOOL
OF ARTS AND SCIENCES OF HARVARD UNIVERSITY

CAMBRIDGE
HARVARD UNIVERSITY PRESS
LONDON: HUMPHREY MILFORD
OXFORD UNIVERSITY PRESS
1920

81-7853

TO

M. H. D.

LOYAL COMPANION

IN RESEARCH

PREFACE

THE author has attempted in this volume to present the equality of states as it appears in the theory of international law and also as it is affected by common usage. Theoretical aspects of the subject are considered in chapters dealing with the sources of the principle, its origin, and its significance in the writings of modern publicists and in illustrative documents. The opinion that Grotius first established the principle in international law is examined and evidence is adduced which indicates that the opinion is erroneous. The equality of states as affected by common usage is really their inequality or status. It involves the study of internal and external factors which limit the capacity of the state as an international person in a variety of ways. Attention has been given to certain features of the organic constitution of the state and also to certain external relationships with other states which are regarded as limitations upon international legal capacity. Political capacity has been viewed as a distinct problem and the limitations of which international relationships afford illustrations have received separate consideration.

Everything in the volume except the Supplementary Chapter was written during the World War and the manuscript was in the printer's hands before the Peace Conference assembled. The materials on the work of the Peace Conference which have since become available are considered in the Supplementary Chapter. This chapter is of necessity incomplete, but it is believed that the relevancy of the subject matter justifies its inclusion.

The investigation of an underlying legal principle is never an easy undertaking. It is peculiarly difficult in international law where so much is ill-defined and unsettled and where there is such an extraordinary divergence between accepted theories and common practice. The author entertains no illusions as to his own success in meeting the difficulties inherent in his undertaking. The late John Chipman Gray once remarked that "on no subject of human interest, except theology, has there been so much loose writing and nebulous speculation as on International Law." The author would like to feel that a realistic outlook and the application to the subject matter of established principles of legal analysis have at least saved him from the pitfalls of "loose writing and nebulous speculation." Beyond that he will feel amply repaid if his effort contributes something to the understanding of an important subject which has been too casually treated hitherto. It will be especially gratifying if the volume stimulates further research.

The bibliography, it should be noted, is not what the accepted meaning of the term implies. Perhaps it would be better to call it a guide to the materials used. A bibliography in the accepted sense is impossible. On the one hand, there is next to nothing on the subject of equality in the literature of international law which purports to be the result of special study. On the other hand, almost every modern writer on international law has had something to say about equality and almost everything written is more or less relevant. The bibliography printed with the present volume includes everything that has been of any use in connection with the study undertaken. It is, as suggested, a guide to sources rather than a bibliography.

This volume was written originally as a doctoral dissertation under the direction of Professor George Grafton Wilson of Harvard University. The author takes this occasion to express his immeasurable debt to Professor Wilson for arousing interest in the subject, encouraging at every stage with kindly criticism and helpful suggestion, and inspiriting with the generous enthusiasm of a great teacher. The author is deeply indebted also to Dean Roscoe Pound of the Harvard Law School for an opportunity to attend his lectures on Roman Law in 1917–18, while the present volume was in preparation, and for assistance in seeing the book through the press. Further acknowledgments are due to Professor Frank M. Anderson of Dartmouth College for helpful suggestions in connection with the revision of the manuscript, to Miss Elizabeth C. Roth of Ann Arbor for a critical reading of several of the translations from the French and the German, to Mr. Stephen Scatori of the University of Michigan for a critical reading of certain passages translated from the Italian, to Dr. Hessel E. Yntema of the University of Michigan for reading the proof of the earlier chapters, to Mr. Harold G. Rugg of Dartmouth College for assistance in procuring books and verifying references, to Mr. George E. Osborne of Cambridge for assistance in verifying references, and to Miss May M. McCarthy of Cambridge, whose services have been generously placed at the author's disposal by Dean Pound, and who has read the proof and verified a host of references which could not be conveniently verified outside the Harvard libraries. A generous share of credit for any merit which the book may have belongs to the author's wife, whose untiring assistance in the assembling of materials, the preparation of manuscript, and the reading of proof has made her an indispensable copartner in the enterprise and companion in research.

E. D. D.

ANN ARBOR, MICHIGAN,
    April 20, 1920.

CONTENTS

CHAPTER IV

CHAPTER V

CHAPTER VI

CHAPTER VII

CHAPTER VIII

CHAPTER IX

SUPPLEMENTARY CHAPTER

THE EQUALITY OF STATES IN
INTERNATIONAL LAW

THE EQUALITY OF STATES IN INTERNATIONAL LAW

CHAPTER I

THE SOURCES OF THE PRINCIPLE OF STATE EQUALITY

EQUALITY AS A PRINCIPLE OF LAW

THE word " equality " has been used in so many different senses in the literature of politics, philosophy, and law that it seems essential, in a study having equality for its theme, to begin by laying down certain definitions and limitations. When the word is used with reference to the law of nations, particularly when it is used as a term of juridical significance, it indicates commonly either of two important legal principles. In the first place, it may mean what is perhaps best described as the equal protection of the law or as equality before the law. International persons are equal before the law when they are equally protected in the enjoyment of their rights and equally compelled to fulfil their obligations. This would seem to have been the significance of the remark, made by the first French delegate at the Second Hague Conference in 1907, that " each nation is a sovereign person, equal to others in moral dignity, and having, whether small or great, weak or powerful, an equal claim to respect for its rights, an equal obligation in the performance of its duties." [1] Equal protection of the law is not inconsistent with the grouping of states into classes, each of which the law regards differently. The legal condition of each class is its status,

---

[1] Bourgeois, *La Deux. Confér.*, II, 88. See also his declaration before the First Hague Conference, *La Confér. Int.*, Pt. IV, p. 76, quoted *infra*, p. 181. Cf. Kent, *Commentaries*, I, 21.

and that status is shared by each member of the class and
becomes the measure of each member's capacity for rights.
It should be noted that the word " rights " in the law of nations is used very loosely to comprehend what scientific jurisprudence would distinguish as natural, legal, and political
rights. In the second place, the word " equality " may be
used to mean an equal capacity for rights. This is commonly described in the law of nations as an equality of
rights and obligations, or more often simply as an equality
of rights. Here again the unscientific comprehensiveness of
the word " rights " must be noted, for it may include, not
only all that was indicated above, but the conception of
legal transactions and of legal acts as well. The equality of
states in this sense means, not that all have the same rights,
but that all are equally capable of acquiring rights, entering
into transactions, and performing acts. When used in this
significance equality may be said to constitute the negation
of status.[1]

It will be observed at once that there is a fundamental
difference between these two conceptions, not only in their
meaning, but also in their importance. Equal protection of
the law or equality before the law is essential to any legal
system. In municipal law it is the alternative to an unguarded tyranny of magistrates. In the law of nations it is
the necessary consequence of the denial of universal empire,
and of the claim of separate states to live together in an
international society controlled by law. An equality of capacity for rights, on the other hand, is a postulate by no
means essential to the rule of law. Within reasonable limitations it is commonly regarded as a desideratum, as an ideal
toward which the law should seek to develop, assuming that

[1] Status and capacity are discussed in *Digest*, I, 5, and in Austin, *Jurisprudence*,
II, 683–725, and *passim;* Ehrlich, *Die Rechtsfähigkeit;* Holland, *Jurisprudence*,
pp. 135–145, 351–357, 395; Markby, *Elements*, §§ 168–180, 300; Planiol, *Traité
élémentaire de droit civil*, I, §§ 419–432; Poste, *Gai institutiones*, Bk. I.

there is a certain homogeneity of characteristics among the persons included in the number of its subjects. In systems of municipal law history reveals that such an equality is never present in the rudimentary stages, and is only attained imperfectly as the law develops. It is a curious circumstance that in the law of nations what would seem to be the natural course of development has been turned about. Through the powerful influence of certain theories, to be considered presently, an absolute equality of capacity for rights among international persons was established as a fundamental postulate when the science was still in a primitive stage. The subsequent history of international relations shows a continuous struggle to impose limitations upon that equality. The primary cause for this inversion of what seems to be a normal course of development is found in the extraordinary influence of text-writers upon the law of nations in its formative period.

There is a remarkable confusion of thought and of statement with reference to these two principles. Writers and statesmen refer frequently to equality before the law, equal protection of the law, and equality of rights as though they meant the same thing.[1] It is rare that the distinction is drawn clearly and with logical precision. Notwithstanding this unfortunate confusion it is evident enough that when publicists refer to the equality of states they usually mean an equality of capacity for rights. Unless otherwise indicated, equality is to be understood in this significance throughout the following pages.

Sources: The Law of Nature in Antiquity

The principle that states have an equal capacity for rights in the law of nations is a creation of the publicists.[2]

---

[1] See *infra*, p. 104, note 2.

[2] It is frequently said that equality was established by the Peace of Westphalia. On this see *infra*, pp. 231–233, 247–248.

It had its inception in four important sources or formulating agencies used by writers of the sixteenth and seventeenth centuries: (*a*) the law of nature, (*b*) the idea of natural equality, (*c*) the conception of the state of nature, and (*d*) the analogy between natural persons and separate states in the international society. Of these sources, the first three had a very ancient history. The last was one of the major premises upon which the law of nations was founded in the sixteenth and seventeenth centuries.

The law of nature [1] was a very important part of the common stock of mediaeval learning. It derived popularity from the opportunities which it afforded for nice and abstract speculation, and authority from the respectable antiquity of its conceptions. Its place in the theory of a great legal system had been taken for granted since the age of the classical Roman jurists. In philosophy its history could be traced to the sages of ancient Greece. Heraclitus and Socrates suggested the theory of natural right. Its essential idea was recognized in the writings of Plato. Among the Sophists, and from the Sophists until the time of Aristotle, it provided a favorite subject for disputation. [2] Aristotle distinguished natural justice from that which is conventional:

[1] On the law of nature, see Brini, *Jus naturale;* Bryce, *Studies,* pp. 556–606; Carlyle, *Med. Pol. Theory,* I, 4–6, 19–20, 36–44, 71–76, 82–83, 102–110, and *passim,* II, 28–33, 102–113, and *passim,* III, *passim;* Dunning, *Political Theories, Ancient and Mediaeval,* and *Political Theories from Luther to Montesquieu, passim;* Hély, *Étude,* pp. 207 ff.; Holland, *Jurisprudence,* pp. 31–40; Korkunov, *General Theory of Law,* pp. 116–138; Maine, *Ancient Law,* chs. 3 and 4, and Pollock's Notes E, G, and H; Muirhead, *Law of Rome,* pp. 270–273; Phillipson, *Int. Law and Custom,* I, ch. 3, and *passim;* Pollock, in *J. S. C. L.* (1900) N.S., II, 418–433, and (1901) N.S., III, 204–213; Reeves, in *A. J. I. L.* (1909), III, 547–561; Ritchie, *Natural Rights,* pp. 20–47; Salmond, in *L. Q. R.* (1895), XI, 121–143; Vaunois, *De la notion du droit naturel chez les Romains;* Voigt, *Das jus naturale;* Walker, *History, passim.*

[2] On the Hellenic conception of universal law, see Bonucci, *La legge comune nel pensiero greco;* Bryce, *Studies,* pp. 562–569; Phillipson, *Int. Law and Custom,* I, ch. 2; Ritchie, *Natural Rights,* pp. 21 ff.; Voigt, *Das jus naturale,* I, §§ 17–34.

Political justice is partly natural and partly conventional. The part which is natural is that which has the same authority everywhere, and is independent of opinion; that which is conventional is such that it does not matter in the first instance whether it takes one form or another, it only matters when it has been laid down, . . .[1]

He divided law into that which is common, being in accordance with nature and admitted among civilized men, and that which is particular because settled by each community for itself:

Law, now, I understand, to be either peculiar or universal; peculiar to be that which has been marked out by each people in reference to itself, and that this is partly unwritten, partly written. I call that law universal, which is conformable merely to dictates of nature; for there does exist naturally an universal sense of right and wrong, which, in a certain degree, all intuitively divine, even should no intercourse with each other, nor any compact have existed; . . .[2]

Aristotle's conception of nature included more than the mere notion of principles of conduct admitted wherever there was settled government; it implied a rational design for the universe, a design which is manifested though never perfectly realized in the material world.[3]

These theories were widely discussed and diffused in the following centuries. They were taken up and developed, especially on the ethical side, by the Stoics.[4] This school of philosophers conceived of nature in a pantheistic sense as the embodiment of supreme universal law. They presented the law of nature as the sum of those principles which

---

[1] *Nicomachean Ethics*, V, 10 (Welldon's transl.).

[2] *Rhetoric*, I, 13, 2 (Buckley's transl.). Cf. *ibid.*, I, 10, 3.

[3] On Aristotle's conception of nature and universal law, see Bryce, *Studies*, p. 567; Cope, *Introduction to Aristotle's Rhetoric*, pp. 239–244; Pollock, in *J. S. C. L.* (1900) N. S., II, 418; Ritchie, *Natural Rights*, pp. 27 ff.; Voigt, *Das jus naturale*, I, §§ 24–25.

[4] On the law of nature in Stoic philosophy, see Arnold, *Roman Stoicism;* Bryce, *Studies*, p. 568; Pollock, in *J. S. C. L.* (1900) N. S., II, 419; Ritchie, *Natural Rights*, pp. 33 ff.; Voigt, *Das jus naturale*, I, §§ 27–28.

are founded in human nature, and which determine the conduct befitting man as a rational and social being. The ideal life was the life in conformity with these principles. From the practical point of view such conformity was to be sought through the cultivation of human reason. The Stoics recognized the difference between the ideal character of society and its actually existing institutions. Their ideal continued to be valid; but they realized that human life would be impossible without the existence of institutions and rules of law which, although far from perfect, were necessary if men were to lead an orderly life and progress towards the ideal.

The conception of natural right founded upon reason attained a mature development in the teachings of Stoicism. During the last days of the Republic it found its way to Rome, where Cicero,[1] pupil of Posidonius, made it the source and foundation of the highest law.[2] Although Cicero would hardly have described himself as a Stoic, the appeal to the feelings implanted by God and nature in the heart of every man, to the common sense or the universal opinion of mankind, was the very essence of his teaching. In Greek philosophy the emphasis had been placed upon the metaphysical and moral aspects of the idea of nature. In Roman thought, as represented by Cicero, the notion was brought into more intimate relationship with law in the sense of rules of human conduct. Cicero's law of nature came from God,[3] and was inborn in men.[4] It was older than the ages,[5] was everywhere the same,[6] and was permanent and immutable.

---

[1] " Cicero is a political writer of great interest, not because he possesses any great originality of mind, or any great power of political analysis, but rather because, in the eclectic fashion of an amateur philosopher, he sums up the commonplaces of the political theory of his time." Carlyle, *Med. Pol. Theory*, I, 3.

[2] *De legibus*, I, 6-16; *De república*, III, 22. Among secondary authorities, see Bryce, *Studies*, p. 575; Carlyle, *Med. Pol. Theory*, I, ch. 1; Gasquy, *Cicéron jurisconsulte*; Ritchie, *Natural Rights*, p. 36; Voigt, *Das jus naturale*, I, §§ 27-28.

[3] *De legibus*, I, 7.   [4] *Ibid.*, I, 10.   [5] *Ibid.*, I, 6.   [6] *Ibid.*, I, 12.

In a passage in *De republica*, preserved by Lactantius, Cicero is quoted as having said:

True law is, indeed, right reason, conformable to nature, pervading all things, constant, eternal; it incites to duty by commanding, and deters from crime by forbidding; it does not by its behest command or deter good men, nor appeal to bad men, in vain. It is not lawful to alter this law, to derogate from it, or to repeal it. Nor can we possibly be absolved from this law, either by the senate or the people; nor is any other explanation or interpretation of it to be found; nor will it be one law for Rome and another for Athens; one thing today and another tomorrow; but it is a law eternal and unchangeable for all people and in every age; and it becomes as it were, the one common god, master and governor of all. Reason is the author, publisher, and proposer of this law; he who does not share this sentiment flies from himself and nature as a man despised; and deserves the severest punishments, even if he escape the penalty of death which may be deserved.[1]

Here is the first distinct formulation of the idea of natural law in the very form in which it survived in mediaeval thought. For Cicero it furnished the basis of all morality and the ideal for positive law. It was an ethereal principle, beyond all the actual laws and customs of men, a supreme and permanent law to which all human order should strive to conform.

The Law of Nature in the Legal System of Rome

This idea of the law of nature as the source of morality and the true ideal for all civil laws came to pervade the minds of thinking men, whatever their philosophy might be. Similar doctrines were taught by Seneca at the beginning of the Christian era.[2] It was his opinion that

no *good* can be without reason; and reason always follows nature. *What then is reason ?* The imitation of nature. And what is the sum-

---

[1] *De republica*, III, 22 (Hardingham's transl.).

[2] *De beneficiis*, III, 18; IV, 7–8, and *passim; Ad Lucilium epistularum moralium,* Epist. 25, 48, 50, 72, 120.

mum bonum, or *chief good* of man ?   The behaving himself agreeably
to the dictates of nature.[1]

It was chiefly through Cicero's graceful Latin and the teaching of Seneca that the conception of the law of nature passed
from philosophy into Roman juristic speculation.   The
greatest of the Roman jurists were of Stoic tendencies.
They gave the characteristic doctrines of the Stoic philosophy a juristic application as well as a clearness and precision which had been wholly lacking in the days of Cicero.[2]
And so the universal law of the philosophers became the
speculative *jus naturale* of the Roman jurists, a body of ideal
principles supposed to be characterized by universal applicability to all men, among all peoples, and in all ages, and
by their correspondence with an innate conviction of right.[3]

This transition from Stoic philosophy to juristic speculation was made easier by the existence at Rome of the *jus
gentium,*[4] an important body of case law which had been
growing up in the praetorian edicts for more than two centuries before the Christian era.   Originally the *jus gentium* had been the practical outcome of the necessity that
pressed upon the Romans to provide rules of law for the
settlement of disputes between Roman citizens and aliens,
and between aliens and aliens.   Some of its principles were
influenced by usages prevailing among other peoples, particularly among the Greeks, but for the most part it was

---

[1] Epist. 66 (Morell's transl.).

[2] See Laferrière, *L'influence du stoicisme sur la doctrine des jurisconsultes romains*,
in Mémoires de l'académie des sciences moral et politiques (1860), X, 579–685.

[3] Voigt, *Das jus naturale*, I, § 59.

[4] On the *jus gentium*, see Bryce, *Studies*, pp. 570–575; Clark, *Practical Jurisprudence*, pp. 353–363; Cuq, *Les institutions juridiques des Romains*, I, 487–491;
Karlowa, *Römische Rechtsgeschichte*, I, 451–458; Mitteis, *Römisches Privatrecht*,
pp. 62–72; Moyle, *Institutes*, pp. 26–43; Muirhead, *Law of Rome*, pp. 215 ff.;
Nettleship, in *Journal of Philology* (1885), XIII, 169–181; Phillipson, *Int. Law
and Custom*, I, ch. 3; Poste, *Gai institutiones*, pp. 1–4; Sherman, in *A. J. I. L.*
(1918), XII, 56–63; Sohm, *Institutes*, pp. 64 ff.; Voigt, *Das jus naturale*, I, §§ 13–
15, 79–98, and *passim;* Westlake, *Collected Papers*, pp. 18–21.

pure Roman law mitigated by the praetor's idea of what was equitable and just. Long before the notion of natural law was borrowed from the philosophers the *jus gentium* had attained a high stage of development, and had commenced to influence the old law of Rome and the administration of Roman courts in the provinces. While the edict of the alien praetor made its liberal principles law for aliens, its precepts were gradually transferred to regulate the mutual inter-course of citizens by means of the city praetor's edict and the writings of the jurists. Because of its equitable char-acter, compared with the stricter rules of the *jus civile*, the *jus gentium* came to be regarded as a kind of universal law for all mankind, a law established by natural reason among all men. Thus, according to Gaius,

The laws of every people governed by statutes and customs are partly peculiar to itself, partly common to all mankind. The rules established by a given state for its own members are peculiar to itself, and are called jus civile; the rules constituted by natural reason for all are observed by all nations alike, and are called jus gentium.[1]

This did not alter the character of the *jus gentium* as a part of the positive and private law of Rome. It was simply as-sumed that because of its inherent reasonableness it must be in accord in its fundamental conceptions with the positive and private law of other peoples.

It was easy for jurists, in the course of this progressive liberalization of the Roman Law, to see a relationship be-tween the working system with which they were familiar and the theoretical law of nature of the philosophers.[2] What

---

[1] Gaius, *Institutes*, I, 1 (Poste's transl.). Cf. Justinian's *Institutes*, I, 2, 2; *Digest*, I, 1, 1, 4; I, 1, 5; I, 1, 9.

[2] On the relation between *jus naturale* and *jus gentium*, see Bryce, *Studies*, pp. 575–586; Carlyle, *Med. Pol. Theory*, I, 36–54, 71–77; Dunning, *Political Theory, Ancient and Mediaeval*, pp. 126–129; Nettleship, in *Journal of Philology* (1885), XIII, 179–181; Phillipson, *Int. Law and Custom*, I, ch. 3; Pollock, in *J. S. C. L.* (1900) N. S., II, 420; Ritchie, *Natural Rights*, p. 36; Voigt, *Das jus naturale*, I, §§ 42, 89–96, and *passim*; Walker, *History*, p. 152, and *passim*.

could be more natural than that the latter should furnish
the ideal foundation for the former. The substance of the
jus gentium, when actually applied in practice, was thought
to harmonize in greater part with the precepts of natural
justice. It is easy to see how its theory would tend to co-
alesce with that of the *jus naturale*, once the latter had
found its way from Greek philosophy into the minds of
Roman lawyers. The *jus naturale* came to represent the
ideal, what ought to be established; the *jus gentium* represented the real, what was universally established. The
principles of the former could hardly be expected to exist
in universal practice, but they were in any case to be desired.
The latter was positive law, enforced everywhere in the
Roman Empire, and conceived of as common to all mankind. As the two systems apparently converged towards
the same goal there was a tendency to call one by the name
of the other. Cicero came very near to suggesting such an
identity. Gaius in the second century impliedly recognized
it as complete.[1] A group of jurists at the beginning of the
third century, however, denied a complete identification.
It is a significant circumstance that the appearance in
Roman juristic writings of this disposition to distinguish
us gentium and *jus naturale* corresponds in point of time
with the appearance of certain new phrases about human

---

[1] *Institutes*, I, 1, incorporated in Justinian's *Digest*, I, 1, 9. This passage from
Gaius has been taken frequently as authority for the proposition that there was no
real distinction between the *jus gentium* and the *jus naturale* in Roman Law. See
Barbeyrac's Grotius, II, 8, 1, notes 1 and 4; Barbeyrac's Pufendorf, II, 3, 23,
note 3; Blackstone, *Commentaries*, Introd., I, 43; Taylor, *Summary of Roman
Law*, p. 53. Sir Henry Maine gave popular currency to this interpretation in the
nineteenth century, particularly among English and American writers. *Ancient
Law*, p. 55. See Lawrence, *Essays*, p. 196; Lawrence, *Int. Law*, p. 39; Salmond, in
L. Q. R. (1895), XI, 129; Taylor, *Int. Pub. Law*, pp. 2, 22, 76; Westlake, *Collected
Papers*, pp. 22, 47. More recent investigation has discredited this interpretation
and has done much to clear up one of the most difficult points in Roman legal theory.
See Bryce, *Studies*, pp. 583–585; Carlyle, *Med. Pol. Theory*, I, 36–54; Voigt, *Das
jus naturale*, I, §§ 42, 89–96, 100, and *passim*. See the explanation for the above
passage from Gaius in Kniep, *Gai institutionum*, I, 90 ff.

nature and with the dogmatic assertion of the natural liberty
and equality of men.[1]

THE IDEA OF NATURAL EQUALITY IN ANTIQUITY

The origin of the idea of natural equality is lost in the
obscurity that prevails with reference to the period between
Aristotle and Cicero. Somewhere in that period there occurred at least one decisive change in political thinking, a
change that is of profound significance in connection with
the present subject. Aristotle taught the natural inequality
of human nature. "But is there a slave by nature," he
queried, and his answer was affirmative:

> But is there any one thus intended by nature to be a slave, and
> for whom such a condition is expedient and right, or rather is not
> all slavery a violation of nature?
> There is no difficulty in answering this question, on grounds both
> of reason and of fact. For that some should rule, and others be
> ruled is a thing, not only necessary, but expedient; from the hour of
> their birth, some are marked out for subjection, others for rule.
> . . . It is clear, then, that some men are by nature free, and others
> slaves, and that for these latter slavery is both expedient and right.[2]

Cicero, on the other hand, proclaimed the natural equality of mankind:

> For there is no one thing so like or so equal to another, as in every
> instance man is to man. And if the corruption of customs, and the
> variation of opinions, did not induce an imbecility of minds, and turn
> them aside from the course of nature, no one would more nearly re-
> semble himself than all men would resemble all men. Therefore,
> whatever definition we give of man, will be applicable to the whole
> human race. And this is a good argument that there is no dissimi-
> larity of kind among men; because if this were the case, one defini-
> tion could not include all men.
> In fact, reason, which alone gives us so many advantages over
> beasts, by means of which we conjecture, argue, refute, discourse, and

---

[1] Carlyle, *Med. Pol. Theory*, I, 45.
[2] *Politics*, I, 5 (Jowett's transl.).

accomplish and conclude our designs, is assuredly common to all men; for the faculty of acquiring knowledge is similar in all human minds, though the knowledge itself may be endlessly diversified. By the same senses we all perceive the same objects, and those things which move the senses at all, do move in the same way the senses of all men. And those first rude elements of intelligence which, as I before observed, are the earliest developments of thought, are similarly impressed upon all men; and that faculty of speech which is the interpreter of the mind, agrees in the ideas which it conveys, though it may differ in the words by which it expresses them. And therefore there exists not a man in any nation, who, if he adopts nature for his guide, may not arrive at virtue.[1]

Thus Cicero distinguished the true or ideal character of man from the actual. He maintained the theory of natural human equality, but realized that account must be taken of the actual facts of human diversity and corruption.[2]

Under the early Empire Seneca developed Cicero's conception of natural equality in somewhat greater detail.[3] *Unus omnium parens mundus est,* he declared, and those who denied the natural capacity of slaves he denounced as ignorant of human right. To the notion of natural equality, Seneca added the conception of a primitive state of nature in which men were innocent and happy.[4] This enabled him to draw out somewhat more sharply the distinction between the conditions suitable to man in a state of natural equality and those made necessary by the actual corruption of human nature. He regarded the great institutions of society — property, slavery, and government — as the consequences of and remedies for human corruption. They were good as remedies, but not properly to be considered as good in themselves. "It can scarcely be doubted," remarks Mr. A. J. Carlyle of the theories represented by Cicero and Seneca,

---

[1] *De legibus,* I, 10 (Barham's transl.). See Carlyle, *Med. Pol. Theory,* I, ch. 1.
[2] *De legibus,* I, 12.
[3] *De beneficiis,* III, 18; III, 20; III, 28; *Ad Lucilium epistularum moralium,* Epist. 47. See Carlyle, *Med. Pol. Theory,* I, ch. 2.
[4] *Epist.,* 90.

" that we have here presented to us the foundation of those dogmatic statements of the lawyers like Ulpian and Florentinus, in which all men are presented to us as being by nature free, by nature equal." [1] It seems equally certain that we are here very close to the origin of that conception of natural equality which writers of the seventeenth century were to translate into the theory of the law of nations and apply to separate states.

THE IDEA OF NATURAL EQUALITY IN THE LEGAL SYSTEM OF ROME

The idea of natural equality followed the conception of the law of nature into the speculations of the Roman jurists and ultimately became one of the fundamental postulates of the *jus naturale*. It helped to accentuate the essentially ideal character of that body of principles, and checked the tendency which had appeared in some of the earlier jurists to identify those principles with the rules of the *jus gentium*. Later jurists clearly opposed the *jus gentium* to the *jus naturale* on at least one point of profound importance. Slavery was universal in the ancient world and so must be regarded as part of the *jus gentium;* but it was contrary to the *jus naturale*, for by the law of nature all men should be free and equal. The distinction was stated explicitly by Ulpian, who declared that " by natural law all were born free," while " slavery came in through the *jus gentium*." [2] Florentinus said:

Slavery is a creation of the *jus gentium*, by which a man is subjected, contrary to nature, to ownership on the part of another.[3]

And Tryphoninus made the same distinction:

Liberty we know exists in virtue of natural law and command over men was introduced by the law of the world (*jus gentium*), . . .[4]

[1] *Med. Pol. Theory*, I, 9.   [3] *Ibid.*, I, 5, 4 (Monro's transl.).
[2] *Digest*, I, 1, 4.   [4] *Ibid.*, XII, 6, 64 (Monro's transl.).

In Ulpian's famous phrase, *quod ad jus naturale attinet, omnes homines æquales sunt.*[1] Through Ulpian, Tryphoninus, and Florentinus, at the beginning of the third century, the theory of the natural equality of men passed into the system of the Roman Law.[2] It became the goal of the law's development, an ideal never perfectly attained but still to be desired.

The maxim of equality had never been defined with any great precision by the philosophers. In a general way they seem to have had in mind an equality of capacity for learning, virtue, or natural rights. For the lawyers of Rome the idea had a significance which can be stated somewhat definitely; their ideal of equality was an equality of capacity for legal rights. The old *jus civile* had contained many arbitrary distinctions between classes of persons.[3] When the later jurists declared that *omnes homines æquales sunt* they intended to affirm that under the ideal *jus naturale*, and in so far as positive law approximated to it, these arbitrary distinctions were swept away. The conflict which they discovered on the subject of slavery illustrates the point. Inequalities of condition like slavery were contrary to the law of nature and could only be justified by positive law. The opinions held by the later jurists were embodied in the Corpus Juris Civilis. So also were certain confusing extracts from Gaius. By the time of Justinian, however, equality in the Roman Law had acquired that significance which it retained throughout the Middle Ages. The *jus naturale* had come to mean a body of ideal principles which men could rationally apprehend and which included the perfect standards of

---

[1] *Digest*, L, 17, 32. " Quod attinet ad jus civile, servi pro nullis habentur; non tamen et jure naturali, quia, quod ad jus naturale attinet, omnes homines æquales sunt."

[2] *Institutes*, I, 2, 2. On slavery in Roman Law, see Bryce, *Studies*, p. 583; Buckland, *Roman Law of Slavery;* Carlyle, *Med. Pol. Theory*, I, 36–54, 71–77.

[3] See Poste, *Gai institutiones*, §§ 9 ff.

right conduct and justice. Equality by the *jus naturale* was an ideal norm of theoretical perfection meaning an equality of capacity for rights. From Rome the idea of natural equality passed to the cloistered scholars of the Middle Ages.

THE LAW OF NATURE AND NATURAL EQUALITY IN PATRISTIC WRITINGS

Similar conceptions in slightly different guise were transmitted to the Middle Ages by the Fathers of the Christian Church.[1] The Greek theory of natural law obtained a prominent place in theology at the very beginning of the Christian era. St. Paul's conception of law written in the hearts of men [2] was not unlike Cicero's law universal. At any rate his words were taken in that sense by the early Fathers. The theories of Cicero and the later philosophers were adopted by the Fathers with only such changes of detail as were convenient for the teaching of Christianity. Nature was identified with God, and the law of nature with the unwritten law of God. The theory of natural law became a commonplace of patristic thought.[3]

The early Church held also a conception of human equality which was quite similar to that of contemporary philosophy. Faith in Jesus was made the primary test, and in this faith there were no distinctions of rich or poor, high or low, free or slave. So there developed among the lowly classes a notion of equality which coincided in many respects with the theory which Stoicism was propagating at the social apex. As Christianity spread upward its way was made easier by the Stoic conception of the identity of human nature over all the world. The prevalence of this theory is suggested by the treatment of slavery in the New Testa-

---

[1] The best secondary account in English is in Carlyle, *Med. Pol. Theory*, I, 82–89, 102–124. The author is indebted to this work for many valuable references.

[2] Romans, II, 12 ff.

[3] See St. Isidore of Seville, *Etymologiarum*, V, 2 and 4.

ment.[1] Distinctions of condition were regarded as belonging to the outer man. Whether slave or free, all men were considered equal in capacity for the moral and spiritual life.

The same idea was developed by the Christian Fathers, who simply restated in their own fashion the theories of Cicero, Seneca, and the lawyers. The transition to the patristic conception of natural equality is well illustrated by Lactantius, who said:

For God, who produces and gives breath to men, willed that all should be equal, that is, equally matched. He has imposed on all the same condition of living; He has produced all to wisdom; He has promised immortality to all; no one is cut off from His heavenly benefits. For as He distributes to all alike His one light, sends forth His fountains to all, supplies food, and gives the most pleasant rest of sleep; so He bestows on all equity and virtue. In His sight no one is a slave, no one a master; for if all have the same Father, by an equal right we are all children.[2]

Salvian referred to slaves *quos etsi nobis servitutis conditio inferiores, humana tamen sors reddit æquales*.[3] St. Augustine declared that men as created by God were free and equal.[4] St. Gregory the Great insisted upon the same conception, and his phrase *omnes namque homines natura æquales sumus* [5] was the patristic parallel of Ulpian's *quod ad jus naturale attinet, omnes homines æquales sunt*. The Fathers discussed the idea of equality in greatest detail in connection with slavery. Adopting Seneca's suggestion, they argued that coercion had been unnecessary in the state of nature and perfect equality had been the rule, but when sin came into the world men required discipline and coercion to make them observe the principles of justice and right. Hence much which was

---

[1] See I Corinthians, XII, 13; Galatians, III, 26–28; Colossians, III, 11.
[2] *Divinarum institutionum*, V, 15 (Fletcher's transl.).
[3] *De gubernatione Dei*, III, 7.
[4] *De civitate Dei*, XIX, 15.
[5] *Moralium libri*, XXI, 15. Cf. his *Regulæ pastoralis liber*, Pt. III, c. 5, "Quomodo admonendi servi et domini."

contrary to nature in the primitive state became necessary in the actual conditions of human life, and slavery became a legitimate and useful institution. This explanation of the contrast between actual institutions and the ideal of equality was stated clearly by St. Augustine:

Sin therefore is the mother of servitude, and first cause of man's subjection to man: which notwithstanding comes not to pass but by the direction of the highest, in whom is no injustice, and who alone knows best how to proportionate his punishment unto man's offences: . . . But take a man as God created him at first, and so he is neither slave to man nor to sin. But penal servitude had the institution from that law which commands the conservation, and forbids the disturbance of nature's order: for if that law had not first been transgressed, penal servitude had never been enjoined.[1]

The theory of the Fall deprived the idea of equality of much of the practical significance which it had for the lawyers. So far from being a goal toward which mankind could hope to progress on earth, it became an ideal condition from which mankind had long since fallen. An equality of capacity for the moral and spiritual life was all that remained of the perfect equality of the age of innocence.

Thus far attention has been directed briefly to the rise of the idea of natural law in Greek philosophy, its further development in Stoicism, its influence at Rome in the age of Cicero, and its incorporation into the theory of Roman Law by the classical jurists and into the theory of the Church by the Christian Fathers. The ideal character of natural law has been emphasized both in relation to Roman Law and to patristic theory. An important change has been indicated between the time of Aristotle and the age of Cicero with reference to the conception of natural equality; and it has been pointed out that this conception became one of the principles of the Roman *jus naturale* and one of the postu-

[1] *De civitate Dei*, XIX, 15 (XV, 15, Healey's transl.). Cf. St. Ambrose, *De Joseph patriarcha*, c. 4.

lates of patristic speculation. It is important to remember
that these ideas had a perfectly continuous history down to
the period of the classical writers on the law of nations in the
sixteenth and seventeenth centuries. The philosophers of
the ancient world, the Roman jurists, and the Christian
Fathers were the fount and inspiration of mediaeval thought.

THE LAW OF NATURE IN THE MIDDLE AGES

The history of the law of nature illustrates this essential
continuity of ideas throughout the Middle Ages. The mediaeval civilians were certain to adhere closely to the lines
laid down by their classical predecessors, if for no other reason because of the extraordinary value which they attached
to the letter of written texts.[1] It never occurred to them to
challenge the existence of an immutable law of nature which
could be ascertained by reason. The canonists repeated the
tripartite classification of law, and in addition identified the
immutable law of nature with the law of God revealed in
human reason. The definitions formulated by St. Isidore
of Seville at the beginning of the seventh century were taken
over almost literally in Gratian's *Decretum:*

> All laws are either divine or human. Divine laws are in accord
> with nature, human laws with custom; and therefore the latter vary,
> since some are suited to one nation, some to another. . . .
> Law, moreover, is either natural, or civil, or of nations.
> Natural law is common to all nations in that it is adhered to every-
> where by an instinct of nature without legislation.[2]

These conceptions were blended into a single system in
the theory of law presented by St. Thomas Aquinas in the

---

[1] See Accursius, *Institutionum juris civilis* . . . *cum Accursiana interpretatione,*
I, 2; Azo, *Summa Azonis, Inst.,* I, 2; *Brachylogos totius iuris civilis,* p. 6; Irnerius
De æquitate, III, and *Questiones de iuris subtilitatibus,* II; Rogerius, *Summa codicis,*
I, 14.

[2] *Decretum,* Distinctio prima, cc. 1, 6, and 7. Cf. St. Isidore, *Etymologiarum,*
V, 2-4. See Legnano, *Tractatus,* chs. 11, 80, 171, and *passim.*

thirteenth century. His fourfold classification had an enduring influence. Law according to St. Thomas was eternal, natural, human, and divine.[1] The eternal law was the expression of the reason of God the supreme Lawgiver. That part of the eternal law which was not revealed, but was made known to man by his own reason was the law of nature.[2] Throughout the thirteenth, fourteenth, and fifteenth centuries there was a tendency to recur to the ancient philosophers and to such ecclesiastical authorities as Gratian and Aquinas, with the result that the law of nature was more commonly used in an ethical or theological significance.[3] In the course of the Reformation, however, there was a reversion to Roman texts.[4] Protestant writers did not acknowledge the authority of the Church or the Canon Law. Catholic disputants were anxious to meet them on their own ground, and so the tendency was to bring the classical Roman Law into greater prominence. Thus a more secular and legal cast was given to the whole discussion of natural law, and the way was prepared for the great writers on the modern law of nations.

Among the schoolmen a great deal of controversy about the law of nature turned upon the question which asks whether the essence of law is will or reason.[5] According to one view the law of nature was an intellectual act independent of will. It was the dictate of reason as to what is right, and though grounded in the being of God it was unalterable even by him. The other opinion saw in the law of nature a divine command which was right and binding because willed by God the supreme lawgiver. According to either view God was the ultimate cause of natural law. The prevailing

[1] *Summa theologica*, II, 1, 91.
[2] *Ibid.*, II, 1, 91, 1-2; II, 1, 94.
[3] Bryce, *Studies*, p. 595.
[4] Pollock, in *J. S. C. L.* (1900) N. S., II, 429.
[5] Gierke, *Political Theory*, p. 172.

opinion seems to have been of a mediating kind. It regarded the substance of natural law as the dictate of reason flowing from the divine being and unalterably determined by the nature of things which is comprised in God. Its binding force, and that alone, was traced to God's will. Thus St. Thomas Aquinas defined law as

an ordinance of reason for the general good, emanating from him who has the care of the community, and promulgated.[1]

According to this definition,

Every law emanates from the reason and will of the lawgiver: divine and natural law from the reasonable will of God; human law from the will of man regulated by reason.[2]

The same opinion was presented later by Suarez.[3]

Another difficulty common to all speculation on the law of nature was concerned with its immutability. Throughout the Middle Ages it was described as supreme and immutable law; and yet it was always recognized that the rules of natural law must be amplified or restricted to suit the world of realities. So a distinction was often drawn between the immutable first principles and the mutable secondary rules. This distinction was stated clearly by St. Thomas Aquinas:

A change in the natural law may be understood in two ways. One way is the way of addition; and in that way there is nothing to hinder the natural law being changed: for many enactments useful to human life have been added over and above the natural law, as well by the divine law as by human laws. Another conceivable way in which the natural law might be changed is the way of subtraction, that something should cease to be of the natural law that was of it before. Understanding change in this sense, the natural law is absolutely immutable in its first principles: but as to secondary precepts, which

[1] *Summa theologica*, II, 1, 90, 4 (Rickaby's transl.).
[2] *Ibid.*, II, 97, 3 (Rickaby's transl.).
[3] *Tractatus de legibus*, II, 5-16.

are certain detailed conclusions closely related to the first principles, the natural law is not so changed as that its dictate is not right in most cases steadily to abide by: it may, however, be changed in some particular case, and in rare instances, through some special causes impeding the observance of these secondary precepts, as has been said above.[1]

In the next century William of Ockham offered a classification of *jus naturale* into (*a*) the universal rules of conduct dictated by natural reason, (*b*) the rules binding on a society governed by natural reason without any positive or customary law, and (*c*) the rules which, while deduced from the precepts of natural justice, are not concerned with fundamentals and hence may be modified by positive authority.[2] The " Secondary law of nature " could be referred to either the second or third category in Ockham's classification.

Whatever disputes arose with respect to its attributes, the ground of its obligatory force, or its immutability, all were agreed that there was a law of nature which was true and perfectly binding law. Bodin, in the second half of the sixteenth century, accepted without question or discussion the existence of a law of nature apart from all positive law.[3] His opinion was simply added evidence of that widespread and deeply rooted conviction which was already receiving a new application among the forerunners of Hugo Grotius.

THE IDEA OF NATURAL EQUALITY IN THE
MIDDLE AGES

There is a similar continuity in the mediaeval development of the idea of natural equality. The opinions of the Roman jurists on equality and slavery were repeated many times by the civilians of the Middle Ages, and never with any important variation from classical texts. It was uni-

---

[1] *Summa theologica*, II, 1, 94, 5 (Rickaby's transl.).
[2] *Dialogus*, III, 2, 3, 6.
[3] *De la republique*, I, 8, and *passim*.

formly held that all men were equal by the *jus naturale*, but that slavery had been introduced by the *jus civile* and the *jus gentium*.[1] For the glossators, as for the classical jurists, equality by the *jus naturale* was an ideal norm rather than a practical rule.

Similarly, the patristic theory of natural equality, and of slavery as a disciplinary check upon the license and disorder of sinful men, was repeatedly affirmed in the writings of the canonists and theologians of the Middle Ages. St. Isidore's assertion that by the law of nature there is *omnium una libertas* reappeared in Gratian's *Decretum*[2] in the twelfth century and was frequently repeated thereafter. Rufinus, one of the most important twelfth century commentators on Gratian, explained the conflict between the *jus naturale* and the *jus gentium* in regard to equality by dividing the former into commands, prohibitions, and demonstrations.[3] Included in the demonstrations were those things which natural law neither commands nor forbids, but simply shows to be good and therefore desirable. The commands and prohibitions were unalterable; but the demonstrations could be changed by positive law. Rufinus thought, in fact, that they must be changed on occasion in order that the true ends of natural law might be realized. Natural liberty was included among the demonstrations, and the conclusion was reached that institutions like slavery, which appeared to violate natural law, were really the means by which men were trained to obey it. Along with their assertion of the dogma of equality, the canonists tolerated slavery and even justified it. No more convincing proof is needed than the

---

[1] Cf. a commission of manumission granted by Queen Elizabeth of England, in Howell, *State Trials*, XX, 1372; and the opinion of Chief Justice Marshall, in The Antelope, 10 Wheaton 66, 120 (1825).

[2] Cf. St. Isidore's *Etymologiarum*, V, 4, and the *Decretum*, Distinctio, I, c. 7.

[3] Rufinus, *Summa decretorum*, Distinctio I. Cf. Stephen of Tournai, *Summa decretorum*, Distinctio I.

provision which the Canon Law made for the position of the Church as a slave-owner.[1]

It was common learning throughout the Middle Ages that there were no natural distinctions in human nature, but that differences of condition had been introduced by positive law. St. Thomas Aquinas argued that all men were equal by the law of nature, but that the natural law had been changed by addition in this respect " by the reason of men for the utility of human life." [2] He justified slavery, not only as a punishment for sin, but also as an incentive to bravery on the part of soldiers who might be enslaved if vanquished.[3] Traditional theories were presented by William of Ockham,[4] Wycliffe,[5] and countless others after Aquinas. It is unnecessary to multiply illustrations. Civilians, canonists, theologians, and mediaeval law writers generally [6] affirmed the natural equality of all mankind.

The heritage of mediaeval learning from which classical writers on the modern law of nations derived the materials for their treatises contained few conceptions of greater importance than that of the equality of men by the natural law. This natural equality was not immutable. It had been seriously restricted by the positive *jus gentium*. It was essentially an ideal equality, whether the ideal was posterior as with the theologians, or anterior as with the lawyers. It was an equality of capacity, among the theologians a residuary equality of capacity for the moral and spiritual life, and among the lawyers an ideal equality of capacity for rights.

[1] Gratian, *Decretum*, Distinctio LIV.
[2] *Summa theologica*, II, 1, 94, 5.
[3] *De regimine principum*, II, 10.
[4] *Dialogus*, III, 2, 3, 6.
[5] *De civili dominio*, I, 32–34.
[6] See *Britton*, I, 32, 1; and *Des Sachsenspiegels erster Theil*, III, 42, 1, " Gleichheit der Menschen vor Gott."

THE CONCEPTION OF A STATE OF NATURE

The conception of an original state of nature was the third important agency constantly relied upon by the publicists who translated the idea of natural equality into the law of nations. This conception had no necessary connection with natural law or natural equality, although historically it was closely associated with them both. The literature of antiquity abounds in allusions to the condition of man prior to the institution of human government and indeed prior to any social life. This natural condition was of no great interest to philosophers like Aristotle or Cicero, who held that man was by nature adapted to political society. For later philosophers, however, it had an absorbing interest. It occupied an important place in the political theories of Seneca at the beginning of the Christian era. One of the most important differences between the political theories of Cicero and of Seneca is to be found in the latter's conception of the primitive state of innocence. According to Seneca's opinion there was a golden age antedating the age of conventional institutions:

> But the first men and their immediate descendants followed Nature; pure and uncorrupt; and held the same both for their leader and the law; by an orderly submission of the worse to the better: for this was ever the rule of simple Nature. . . . Exquisitely happy then must the people have been, among whom none could obtain power but he that was a good man: for he may do whatever he pleases, who thinks he can do no more than what he ought to do. *Posidonius* therefore judgeth, that wise men only ruled in the age that was called *the golden.* . . .
>
> What could be happier than the race of man ? They enjoyed all Nature in common; she as a kind parent was the protectress of all men; and gave them secure possession of the public wealth.[1]

The contrast which Seneca drew between primitive and conventional institutions probably represented a tradition

---

[1] *Ad Lucilium epistularum moralium*, Epist. 90 (Morell's transl.).

which was current among at least some of the Stoic thinkers
of his time.

Apparently this tradition had no great influence on the
Roman jurists. Mr. Carlyle thinks that he has detected a
disposition in Ulpian, Tryphoninus, and Florentinus to contrast the primitive with the conventional state of society
in connection with the institution of slavery; he suggests
that this disposition may have had something to do with the
rise of the distinction between the *jus gentium* and the *jus
naturale*.[1] The evidence is not very conclusive. In general
it may be said that the *jus naturale* of the Roman lawyers
had no connection with the primitive state of nature. The
jurists were not troubled about primitive man, nor did they
believe that in the *jus naturale* they had discovered a " lost
code of nature." They were content to leave such speculations to the poets and the philosophers.

The Fathers, on the other hand, were very much under
the influence of this conception. They conceived of the
state of man before the Fall much as Seneca conceived of the
Golden Age. They professed to believe that there had been
a time when men were free and equal, goods were possessed
in common, and government was not necessary. " And this
is not to be regarded as a poetic fiction, but as the truth,"
declared Lactantius.[2] They held that because of sin man
passed out of this primitive state and into that condition in
which the conventional institutions of society became necessary.[3] The patristic view of slavery, property, and government turned upon this distinction between the primitive
and the conventional.

The theory of a state of nature was reproduced in a variety of forms by writers of the Middle Ages. Although it

[1] *Med. Pol. Theory*, I, 36–44. Cf. *Digest*, I, 1, 4; I, 1, 5; I, 5, 4; XII, 6, 64;
Institutes, I, 2, 2.

[2] *Divinarum institutionum*, V, 5.

[3] St. Augustine, *De civitate Dei*, XIX, 15.

was not a subject of great interest to the civilians, they frequently accounted for the existence of institutions contrary to natural law by assuming that the law of nature was appropriate to a natural or primitive condition of mankind, while the actual institutions of society had perforce been accommodated to other and less perfect conditions. The idea found occasional expression in the treatises of other mediaeval lawyers. There is a passage in *Britton*, in the chapter on villenage, which illustrates the conception's influence:

This condition was of ancient time changed from freedom to bondage by the constitution of nations, and not by the law of nature, as it stood at the time of the flood and earlier, when all things were common to every one, and all men were entirely free, and lived according to the law of nature.[1]

The canonists did not occupy themselves to any great extent with speculation about the state of nature, but they apparently held an opinion of the Golden Age of innocence and of the Fall which was based upon the theory developed by Seneca and the Fathers. In the scholastic literature of the later Middle Ages there is a great deal of speculation about the primitive state of man. Marsilius of Padua's account of the origin of civil communities began with the state of nature.[2] The conception was presented with unusual literary grace in the fifteenth century by Æneas Sylvius, who blended the Biblical description of paradise and the fancies of pagan philosophy to produce a complete account of the state of nature previous to the formation of political society.[3] The anti-monarchic writers found a new

---

[1] I, 32, 1 (Nichols' transl.). Cf. Beaumanoir, *Coutumes de Beauvaisis*, § 1453, II, 235. A commission of manumission granted by Queen Elizabeth of England states that in the beginning God created all men free by nature, and that afterwards the law of nations placed some under the yoke of slavery. See Howell, *State Trials*, XX, 1372.

[2] *Defensor pacis*, I, 3 ff.

[3] *De ortu et authoritate Imperii Romani*, in Goldast, *Monarchia*, II, 1558-1566.

use for the conception in the sixteenth century; [1] and by this time the idea had become well established in the common tradition of political speculation. There was always considerable diversity of opinion as to the character and significance of the state of nature. The present importance of the notion does not depend upon the particular forms in which men held it, but in the prevalence everywhere of the notion of a primitive condition of mankind in which natural equality prevailed, and in which men were subject to no law beyond the precepts of the law of nature. Such a concept was pregnant with possibilities for the seventeenth century jurist, seeking an explanation for the new international society which was gradually taking shape in the polity of Europe.

The Analogy between Natural Persons and the State

The conception of natural equality was introduced into the law of nations by drawing an analogy between natural persons and separate states or international persons.[2] This analogy made its appearance, of course, only with the rise of the modern law of nations; but it had its roots in certain habits of thought which were characteristic of the Middle Ages. Mediaeval thought proceeded from the idea of a single whole. It was a common practice, under the influence of biblical allegories and the models adopted by Greek and Roman writers, to compare mankind at large and indeed every human organization to an animate body.[3] So not only

[1] See Buchanan, *De jure regni apud Scotos*, § 8; and the *Vindiciæ contra tyrannos*, Q. III, 108.

[2] The author has discussed the subject of the analogy in an article in *Y. L. J.* (1917), XXVI, 564–591.

[3] On the organic conception of society in the Middle Ages, see Gierke, *Political Theory*, pp. 22–30. On pp. 129–137 there are excellent bibliographical notes from which the following illustrations have been selected. See also evidence of anthropomorphism in Legnano, *Tractatus*, chs. 10, 79, 123, 125, and *passim*.

the universal Church and the universal Empire, but also every particular church and every particular state, were compared to the natural body. They were thought of and commonly described as mystical bodies.

The comparison with the natural body was frequently spun out into amusing detail. One of the earliest attempts to find some member of the natural body which would correspond to each part of the state was made by John of Salisbury. He represented the servants of religion as the soul of the state, the prince as the head, the senate as the heart, officers and judges as the eyes, ears, and tongue, the executive as the unarmed and the army as the armed hand, the financial department as the belly and intestines, and land folk, handicraftsmen, and the like as the feet, so that the state exceeded the centipede *numerositate pedum*, while protection of the people became the shoeing and their distress the state's gout.[1] Ptolomaeus of Lucca based state life upon a harmony analogous to that harmony of organic forces which obtains in the natural body, and he argued that it is reason in the one body as in the other that brings those forces into correlation and perfects their unity. Engelbert of Volkersdorf based his whole exposition of the well ordered state upon the assumption that there is a complete analogy between state and individual. Marsilius of Padua founded his theory of the state upon the proposition *civitas est velut animata seu animalis natura quaedam*.[2] Prominent writers of the fourteenth and fifteenth centuries found a variety of uses for this analogy; but it was never more elaborately developed than by Nicholas of Cues, who utilized all of contemporary medical knowledge in perfecting his comparison between the state and the natural body.

[1] *Polycraticus*, V, 1 ff. Webb's recent edition of this work is the most satisfactory. The above summary is from Gierke's note 76, p. 131.

[2] *Defensor pacis*, I, 2, in Goldast's *Monarchia*, II, 156. The analogy is developed in I, 15.

The organic conception of the state did not develop into the legal idea of state personality during the Middle Ages, but that consummation was not far in the future. Nor was it a far cry to the principles soon to be proclaimed by Hobbes and Pufendorf that *civitates semel institutae induunt proprietates hominum personales* and are therefore the subjects of that identical law of nature which controls natural individuals. It was through such principles as these that the idea of the analogy was soon to have an influence of far reaching significance.

THE RECEPTION OF THE SOURCES BY THE CLASSICAL PUBLICISTS

This preliminary sketch of the four main sources from which the principle of state equality was derived should make it somewhat easier to understand the use that was made of them by the classical publicists. The ideas were accepted by the publicists substantially as they had come down from antiquity, through mediaeval thought, to the modern age. The law of nature was regarded as a body of ideal principles grounded in the being of God, ascertained by reason, and distinct from the *jus gentium* and all positive law. Its reality was in no way qualified by its somewhat ethereal attributes. That it was permanent and immutable was emphasized with tiresome reiteration; but it was agreed also that it consisted of primary or fundamental principles which were immutable and principles which were secondary or less than fundamental and therefore mutable. So the hypothetical immutability lost most of its practical significance. The concept of natural equality was accepted by everyone; and with equal unanimity it was included, either expressly or by implication, among the demonstrations or secondary principles of the law of nature. The most important distinction between the rules of the *jus naturale* and the *jus gentium* turned on the principle of equality. By the latter conventional differences of status had been instituted. The state of nature in which there was no law but nature's law and in which uncorrupted natural equality prevailed was common tradition. It was accepted by some as an historical condition antedating civil society, by others as a useful analytical conception in distinguishing natural from conventional institutions. Finally, there was a deeply rooted disposition to draw analogies between corporate and natural bodies and to apply to states theories and principles which had their origin in the relations of human beings.

A new use for these conceptions was discovered after the Reformation.[1] The old theory of a common superior had decayed on account of the incapacity of either Emperor or Pope to command universal obedience. The notion of a society of states supplanted the idea of universal empire. It was the task of the early publicists to find an explanation for this society, its members, and its law. There were differences of opinion among them on some of the most important points, and divergent tendencies appeared which produced different schools of thought. Certain of these differences were of very great importance in connection with the principle of state equality. Viewing the work of the early publicists as a whole, however, it may be said that they derived the law applicable to the relations between separate states from two sources. In the first place, finding some rules already in existence, especially in connection with diplomacy and warfare, they referred to established customs, usages, and understandings. Finding that large parts of the field of international relations were not covered

---

[1] On the use made of these sources by the classical publicists, see Bryce, *Studies*, p. 602; Franck, *Réformateurs*, p. 276; Mackintosh, *Discourse*; Maine, *Ancient Law*, pp. 99–114; Nys, *Le droit int.*, II, 235–237, and *Les origines*, p. 8; Olney, in *A. J. I. L.* (1907), I, 420; Pollock, in *C. L. R.* (1902), II, 511–524; Pollock, in *J. S. C. L.* (1901) N.S., III, 204–207; Westlake, *Collected Papers*, p. 10.

by established custom, they sought a more general and permanent basis whereon to build a system of positive rules. They recurred, in the second place, to the law of nature, a law grounded on reason and valid for all mankind, and applied it to the relations between separate states. There was a tendency to reason that men in a state of nature were controlled by natural law, that since there was no common superior to control the relations of separate states they must be in a state of nature with respect to each other, and that by analogy with men in a state of nature they must be controlled by natural law. From such premises it was an easy step to the conclusion that the principle of natural equality applied to separate states in the international society. This conclusion to be sure was not a logical necessity. Even if accepted it did not need to have great practical significance. Both the conclusion and its significance were contingent upon the use which the publicists made of the ideas whose evolution has been sketched briefly in this chapter. What was the significance of these ideas in the classical treatises on the law of nations? Before attempting to answer this question it is necessary to examine the great treatises written in the sixteenth, seventeenth, and eighteenth centuries, beginning with the system initiated by the forerunners of Grotius and established in the work of the great Dutch jurist.

CHAPTER II

THE PRINCIPLE OF STATE EQUALITY IN THE SYSTEM OF GROTIUS

The Tradition that Grotius Established State Equality

THERE is a widespread tradition that the principle of state equality, as formulated in most modern textbooks and treatises, had its inception in the *De Jure Belli ac Pacis* of Hugo Grotius.[1] The influence of the principle has been greatly enhanced, particularly in England and America, by the common assumption that it was supported by his opinion. Now the truth is that his opinion did not support it at all. Grotius never applied the theory of natural equality to the society of separate states, except in certain particular instances and for a limited purpose. The idea of a general principle of state equality was never developed by him, either expressly, or by necessary implication. He did not base his system upon any such postulate.

There are several factors which contribute to explain the contrary tradition, and among them the following should be particularly noted. In the first place, there is a common tendency to attribute to Grotius the origin of almost everything that is regarded as in any way fundamental in the modern law of nations. This undiscriminating disposition

---

[1] See Figgis, *Gerson to Grotius*, pp. 190, 216, 220, 242; Hershey, *Essentials*, pp. 58, 148; Hicks, in *A. J. I. L.* (1908), II, 531–532; Hicks, in *A. S. I. L. Proceedings* (1909), III, 239; Lawrence, *Essays*, pp. 194–204; Lawrence, *Int. Law*, pp. 52, 268; Maine, *Ancient Law*, p. 103; Moore, *Principles of American Diplomacy*, p. 197; Olney, in *A. J. I. L.* (1907), I, 418; Reeves, in *The University Record* (1917), III, 254; Scott, *The Hague Peace Conferences*, I, 456; Taylor, *Int. Pub. Law*, §§ 51, 69, pp. 75, 98; Twiss, *Law of Nations*, p. xvii; *Venez. Arbit.* (Cohen's argument), p. 1259; Vreeland, *Hugo Grotius*, pp. 241–242; White, *Seven Great Statesmen*, p. 77.

has occasionally been the cause of serious error, and rarely more conspicuously than with reference to the idea of state equality. In the second place, there has been a good deal of confusion with reference to the meaning of state equality. If all that is meant is the equal protection of the law, then of course equality was a fundamental principle of the Grotian system. Grotius did not state the principle in so many words; he took it for granted. It was absolutely prerequisite to his assumption that there existed a society of separate states controlled by law. It is another matter, however, if equality is taken to mean equality of capacity for rights. Such a principle was not an essential prerequisite to the system of Grotius. Indeed, the tendencies of his age would have been much more accurately reflected by another principle. So far from assuming equality in this significance as a fundamental postulate, there is evidence that Grotius would have repudiated it. In the third place, Grotius drew freely from all those sources from which later writers derived the general doctrine of state equality; he made use of everyone of those ideas which were his heritage from ancient and mediaeval learning. Therefore, it is not infrequently inferred, he must have reached the conclusion that the theory of natural equality was applicable to states. What later writers have too often failed to understand is the fact that such a conclusion was contingent upon the use made of the premises. About his use of the premises there has been a great deal of misunderstanding. In general, in his application of the law of nature, the idea of natural equality, the conception of the state of nature, and the analogy between the natural person and the state, Grotius followed the broad lines laid down by his predecessors. Before investigating the system of Grotius it will be profitable to consider briefly certain of the leading principles announced by his forerunners of the sixteenth century.

The Leading Principles of Grotius' Forerunners

There is no statement of the principle that states have equal rights by the law of nations in the treatises of Victoria,[1] Vasquez,[2] Ayala,[3] or Suarez,[4] four of the most illustrious of the Catholic precursors of Grotius.[5] Neither is there any satisfactory evidence that the premises which these writers defended made the principle of equality a necessary conclusion. They accepted the common conception of a law of nature. Thus Victoria referred to natural law grounded upon reason;[6] Ayala cited the law of nature in support of the right of defense, and declared it immutable and paramount to the authority of all kings and princes;[7] while Suarez developed in considerable detail the theory of natural law presented by St. Thomas Aquinas.[8] The Catholic writers referred occasionally to what Victoria described as the beginning of the world " when everything was in common," [9] and Ayala as " that primitive time which pagans

---

[1] Victoria lived 1480–1546. His *Relectiones theologicæ* was published in 1557. The Salamanca edition of 1565, and Relectiones V and VI, published in the Classics of International Law, have been consulted. Page references are to J. P. Bate's transl. in the latter edition. See Barthélemy, in Pillet, *Les fondateurs*, pp. 1–36; Walker, *History*, pp. 214–230; Wright, *Francisci de Victoria*.

[2] Vasquez lived 1509–1566. His *Controversiarum illustrium* was published in 1564. References are to the first edition. See Walker, *History*, *passim*.

[3] Ayala lived 1548–1584. His *De jure et officiis bellicis et disciplina militari* was published in 1582. References are to the edition in the Classics of International Law, and page references are to J. P. Bate's transl. in Vol. II. See Walker, *History, passim*.

[4] Suarez lived 1548–1617. His *Tractatus de legibus ac Deo legislatore* was published in 1612. References are to the Mayence edition of 1619. See Dunning, *History of Political Theories from Luther to Montesquieu*, pp. 135–149; Rolland, in Pillet, *Les fondateurs*, pp. 95–124.

[5] The following secondary authorities have also been consulted: Figgis, *Gerson to Grotius*, pp. 190–217; Hallam, *Introduction to the Literature of Europe*; Kaltenborn, *Vorläufer des Hugo Grotius*, pp. 124–190; Nys, *Le droit int.*, I, 224–244, and *Les origines;* Ompteda, *Litteratur;* Wheaton, *History*.

[6] Rel. V, *De Indis*, §§ 2–3, *passim;* Rel. VI, *De iure belli, passim*. Cf. Vasquez, I, 27, 11.

[7] I, 2, p. 10; I, 5, p. 41; I, 7, p. 81.

[8] II, 5–16.   [9] Rel. V, § 3, p. 151.

used to call the Golden Age."[1] They were agreed that by
nature men were equal, and they were just as unanimous in
holding that natural equality had been restricted by positive
law.[2] They distinguished the ideal *jus naturale* from positive
jus gentium according to the common tradition. Vasquez
distinguished *jus gentium primævum*, which was natural law,
from *jus gentium secundarium*, which was positive law derived
from custom.[3] Suarez worked out a similar distinction at
great length, and thereby was able to adapt the immutable
jus naturale to the practical life of men.[4]

The *jus gentium* with these writers began to take on a
modern aspect. To the ancient conception of a law common to many peoples, they added the modern conception of
a law between separate states.[5] One and all they rejected
the notion of universal sovereignty,[6] and represented Christendom as a society of separate states with rights and obligations *inter se*.[7] Their conception of the separate state was
that of a perfect political community acknowledging no
temporal superior; their law between nations was in part
natural and in part positive as founded on usage. No one
of these writers ever completely identified the law of nature
and the law of nations. They all believed in a state of nature antecedent to the state of corruption; but they did not
develop the thesis that the relation between separate states
was natural and analogous to the relation between men in a
state of nature. Now it was precisely the identification and

[1] I, 5, p. 41.
[2] Victoria, Rel. V, § 1, p. 128, § 2, p. 131, § 3, p. 161; Rel. VI, p. 181; Ayala, I, 5, pp. 40-42.
[3] I, 10, 18; I, 41, 30; I, 46, 12; II, 53, 3; II, 54, 4.
[4] II, 17-20.
[5] Victoria, Rel. V, § 3, pp. 151-153; Rel. VI, pp. 169, 172, 183; Ayala, I, 2, p. 8; Suarez, II, 19, 9; Walker, *History*, pp. 154, 214. See also Legnano, *Tractatus*, chs. 59, 60, 123, 124.
[6] Victoria, Rel. V, § 2, pp. 131, 135; Vasquez, I, 20-22; Ayala, I, 2, p. 20.
[7] Victoria, Rel. V, § 2, p. 133; Rel. VI, pp. 169, 172; Ayala, I, 2, pp. 9, 15, 22; Suarez, II, 19, 9.

analogy suggested above that made the principle of state equality a necessary conclusion for certain publicists of the following century.[1] The Catholic writers of the sixteenth century were under no such necessity and drew no such conclusion. The theory of the natural equality of men was common learning, but it still awaited the innovator bold enough to translate it into the law of nations.

The leading principles announced by the Protestant writers who preceded Grotius appear to have accorded in all essential points with those of their Catholic contemporaries.[2] They, too, conceived of a new international order composed of separate states. They, too, applied to that order a law between nations derived partly from natural reason and partly from custom. Of all those who wrote before Grotius Albericus Gentilis was probably the most distinctly modern in his tendencies.[3] Gentilis was thoroughly familiar with all those conceptions which have already been considered in other writers, but he made few *a priori* deductions from them. His *jus gentium* was a law between states that acknowledged no superior.[4] Even infidel and barbarian communities might be included in this international society.[5] He found the sources of the law of nations in custom and nature.[6] While he was always ready to appeal to natural reason to explain the origin of this law, or to provide an additional sanction for a particular rule, the emphasis was

---

[1] See *infra*, pp. 75 ff.

[2] See Kaltenborn, *Vorläufer des Hugo Grotius*, pp. 190–246; and works cited *supra*, p. 36, note 5.

[3] Gentilis lived 1552–1608. His *De legationibus* was published in 1585, *De jure belli* in 1588–1589, and *Hispanicæ advocationis* in 1613. References are to the Hanover edition of *De legationibus* of 1594, and to Holland's edition of *De jure belli*. The following secondary works have been consulted; Abbott, in *A. J. I. L.* (1916), X, 737–748; Balch, in *ibid.* (1911), V, 665–679; Holland, *Studies*, pp. 1–39; Nézard, in Pillet, *Les fondateurs*, pp. 37–93; Phillipson, in Macdonell and Manson, *Great Jurists*, pp. 109–143; Walker, *History*, pp. 249–276.

[4] *De jure belli*, I, 3; I, 16; III, 15.   [6] *Ibid.*, I, 1; III, 9.

[5] *De legationibus*, II, 11; *De jure belli*, I, 25; III, 19.

constantly upon the positive aspects of his subject. Gentilis avoided dogmatic methods, undiscriminating adoration of the law of nature, and fallacious presumptions of an analogy between rules suited to natural persons and rules suited to separate states. In many respects he anticipated the positivist tendencies of Zouche, Rachel, and Bynkershoek. So far from deducing the principle of state equality from abstract premises, he left evidence that he was aware of the practical significance of another principle.[1]

THE SOURCES OF THE GROTIAN SYSTEM

The learning of his predecessors, the common traditions of the Middle Ages, and the wisdom of antiquity, all blended into a single system under the hand of Hugo Grotius. If there was little that was original in either the matter or the arrangement of his *De Jure Belli ac Pacis*,[2] certainly there was almost nothing of any value in the vast literature of his field that he neglected. He called Aristotle, Cicero, Seneca, the classical jurists, and the Christian Fathers to testify to the soundness of his conclusions. He ransacked

---

[1] See, for example, *De legationibus*, I, 4; *De jure belli*, I, 3; III, 10.

[2] Grotius lived 1583–1645. The *De jure belli ac pacis* was published in 1625. The following editions have been consulted: the text of 1646 reproduced in the Classics of International Law, the text and abridged translation in Whewell's edition, the French translation of Barbeyrac, the French translation of Pradier-Fodéré, and an English translation of 1738. *Mare liberum* was published in 1609. References are to R. V. D. Magoffin's transl., ed. by J. B. Scott. Among secondary authorities, see Basdevant, in Pillet, *Les fondateurs*, pp. 125–267; Burginy, *Vie de Grotius;* Butler, *Life of Grotius;* Caumont, *Étude sur la vie et les travaux de Grotius;* Dunning, *Political Theories from Luther to Montesquieu*, ch. 5; Franck, *Réformateurs*, pp. 253–332; Hallam, *Introduction to the Literature of Europe*, II, 141–162; Hély, *Étude sur le droit de la guerre de Grotius;* Lawrence, *Essays*, pp. 163–207; Luden, *Hugo Grotius nach seinen Schicksalen und Schriften;* Ompteda, *Litteratur*, pp. 174–248; Pradier-Fodéré, *Essai biographique*, in the first volume of his transl. of *De jure belli ac pacis;* Rattigan, in Macdonell and Manson, *Great Jurists*, pp. 169–184; Taylor, *Int. Pub. Law*, pp. 73–92; Vreeland, *Hugo Grotius;* Walker, *History*, pp. 278–329; Walker, *Science*, pp. 91–111; Westlake, *Collected Papers*, pp. 36–51; Wheaton, *History*, pp. 54–60; White, *Seven Great Statesmen*, pp. 55–110.

history, philosophy, theology, and law for his materials.[1] It is commonplace to observe that he was thoroughly familiar with the development of those ideas briefly considered in the preceding chapter. An examination of the use which he made of those sources reveals, first, that his premises did not require the conclusion that states have an equal capacity by the law of nations, and second, that Grotius neither formulated a statement of the principle of state equality nor made it an essential element of his system.

THE LAW OF NATURE IN THE SYSTEM OF GROTIUS

The principle of state equality was not a necessary inference from the use which Grotius made of the law of nature. He defined law — *jus* in the broader sense — as " a rule of moral acts obliging to what is right " (*regula actuum moralium obligans ad id quod rectum est*).[2] He divided law into *jus naturale* or natural law, and *jus voluntarium*, i. e., instituted or positive law. Positive law was in turn subdivided into *jus divinum* and *jus humanum* according as it was ordained by God or prescribed by man; and the *jus humanum* included the law of particular states, called *jus civile*, the law of a particular condition, as the commands of a parent, and the law of nations or *jus gentium*.[3] The natural law was defined as

the Dictate of Right Reason, indicating that any act, from its agreement or disagreement with the rational nature has in it a moral turpitude or a moral necessity; and consequently that such act is forbidden or commanded by God, the author of nature.[4]

Its threefold basis was right reason, the sociable character of mankind, and divine will.[5] Its existence was proved *a*

---

[1] Proleg., 42–55. Subdivisions of the Prolegomena are numbered differently in different editions. Citations in the present work follow the numbering in Whewell's edition.

[2] I, 1, 9, 1.   [4] I, 1, 10, 1 (Whewell's transl.). See *Mare liberum*, p. 5.

[3] I, 1, 9–15.   [5] Proleg., 6, 8, 9, 12, 40; I, 2, 1, 3; I, 2, 1, 5.

priori by showing its agreement with the rational and social nature of man and *a posteriori* by showing that all the more civilized nations observed it.[1]

Grotius distinguished the law of nature from positive law in general,[2] and also from the law of nations in particular.[3] The law of nations, *jus gentium*, he defined as the law which regards the relations of several peoples or rulers of peoples, the law which has received its obligatory force from the will of all nations or of many, and which belongs to that society which is established by nations amongst themselves.[4]

Further: as the Laws of each Community regard the Utility of that Community, so also between different Communities, all or most, Laws might be established, and it appears that Laws have been established, which enjoined the Utility, not of special communities, but of that great aggregate System of Communities. And this is what is called the Law of Nations, or International Law; when we distinguish it from Natural Law.[5]

The law of nations in this broader significance was derived from nature, divine command, and custom;[6] its ultimate sanction was the good faith of that greater society to which its rules applied.[7]

It was only on occasion that Grotius appeared to identify the law of nations with the natural law, and then only in respect to certain rules which he held to be the same in both, as where he argued for freedom of the seas from premises grounded mainly in the natural law,[8] or where he said that

---

[1] Proleg., 46; I, 1, 12; I, 2, 1–3; I, 3, 2, 2.

[2] Proleg., 16, 30; I, 1, 9.

[3] Proleg., 17, 37, 40, 53; I, 1, 14; II, 3, 10; II, 8, 1; II, 18, 4; III, 1, 1; III, 1, 5, 5; III, 2, 1–2; III, 3, 6 and 12; III, 4, 15; III, 6, 1–2; III, 18, 1, 1. For a naturalist's opinion of this distinction, see Barbeyrac's Grotius, I, 1, 14, note 3; II, 8, 1, notes 1 and 3; II, 18, 4, note 2; III, 2, 2, note 1; III, 4, 15, note 1; III, 6, 2, 1, note 1; and *infra* p. 44, note 5.

[4] Proleg., 1, 17, 18, 26, 28; I, 1, 14; II, 8, 1; II, 18, 2, 1; III, 3, 12.

[5] Proleg., 17 (Whewell's transl.).

[6] Proleg., 1, 26, 40, 46; II, 16, 31; II, 18, 4, 2; III, 2, 2; III, 19, 11, 1.

[7] III, 25, 1.　　　　[8] See *Mare liberum.*

contracts between sovereigns as such were controlled entirely by the law of nature.[1] It is misleading to say, with reference to these or similar illustrations, that he identified *jus naturale* and *jus gentium;* it would convey a more accurate impression of his method and point of view to say that he derived certain rules almost entirely from reason and the precepts of nature. There is a passage defining *jus gentium* in his first chapter that has given some difficulty. He says:

> Law in a wider sphere is *Jus Gentium*, the Law of Nations, that Law which has received an obligatory force from the will of all nations, or of many.
> I have added "*or of many*," because scarce any Law is found, except Natural Law, (which also is often called *Jus Gentium*,) common to *all* nations. Indeed that is often *Jus Gentium* in one part of the world which is not so in another; as we shall shew when we come to speak of captivity and of *postliminium*.[2]

So far from suggesting an identity between the law of nature and the law of nations, however, this passage was really an attempt to contrast the universality of the ideal law, to which Grotius frequently appealed, with the more limited scope in respect to many of its rules of positive law founded on consent or custom. The naturalists, who succeeded Grotius and who themselves identified the law of nature and the law of nations, found no suggestion of an identity in the passage in question.[3] Their inference, in fact, was quite the contrary. Elsewhere, in passage after passage, Grotius proved his grasp of the distinction between those ideal principles which are ascertained by reason and those positive rules which are grounded on consent. He regretted that

[1] II, 11, 5.
[2] I, 1, 14 (Whewell's transl.).
[3] See Pufendorf, *De jure naturæ et gentium*, II, 3, 23; Barbeyrac's Grotius, I, 1, 14, note 3; Barbeyrac's Pufendorf, II, 3, 23, notes 2 and 3. On the naturalists, see *infra*, pp. 75 ff.

scriptores voces juris naturæ et gentium permiscent, criticised those who had confused the two,[1] and maintained that many things forbidden by natural law were permitted by the law of nations, and, contrariwise, that things permitted by natural law might be forbidden by the law of nations.[2] It is evident that Grotius used nature chiefly as a source from which to derive rules applicable to nations.[3] The plan and purpose of his work did not require an exhaustive treatment of nature's law. Barbeyrac has pointed this out in comparing the work of Grotius and Pufendorf:

As to the subject matter, I have already taken notice, that Grotius pretended not to give a complete system; which might be easily seen, though he himself had not declared it. 'Tis only occasionally that he touches upon even the greatest part of the principal subject matters of natural right. So that, though his views had been more extensive, and less imperfect, than they seem in many things to have been; his plan did not lead him to a full discussion of them; it was enough for him to handle them so far, as might be sufficient to decide the questions, which concerned the principal subject of his book. In a system of the law of nature, an author ought, without dispute, to begin with instructing his reader in the nature of moral entities or beings; in the principles and different qualities of humane actions; and what it is that makes them imputable either as good or evil; in the nature of laws in general; and their different kinds, etc. But we meet with scarce anything in Grotius, relating to all these matters; which compose the first book of my original.[4]

Grotius presented a less comprehensive discussion of natural law than either Suarez before him or Pufendorf who came after. He did not write a philosophical disquisition. His primary purpose was to lay down rules for the international society, that great aggregate system of communities. Had

---

[1] Proleg., 37, 40, 53.

[2] II, 3, 10; II, 18, 4, 3; III, 4, 15, 1.

[3] Its relation to his method is suggested in I, 2, 1–3; II, 18, 1; and III, 1, 5, 5. Cf. Vreeland, *Hugo Grotius*, p. 171.

[4] Barbeyrac's Pufendorf, préf., § 31 (Carew's transl.). Cf. Bonfils, *Manuel*, § 235, p. 140; Pradier-Fodéré, *Traité*, § 166, I, 286.

he referred to practice alone he would have defeated his
purpose as a reformer.   So he recurred to the law of nature
and natural justice, and sought

> to refer the truth of the things which belong to Natural Law to some
> notions, so certain, that no one can deny them, without doing violence
> to his own nature.[1]

It was of the utmost importance that Grotius distinguished the law of nature and the law of nations.   It was
because Pufendorf and the naturalists identified the two
that they were under a logical necessity of concluding that
states have equal rights.[2]   Nor can responsibility for later
blending of the two conceptions into one be attributed to
Grotius, as some have argued.[3]   Whatever confusion there
may have been in his method, Grotius left no doubt in the
minds of his successors as to his opinion on this much controverted question.   When the naturalists asserted that the
law of nature and the law of nations were the same thing
they had no thought of referring to Grotius.   On this point,
they recurred to the opinion of Thomas Hobbes and founded
their system upon reason unadulterated by custom or consent.   Pufendorf expressly condemned the distinction which
Grotius labored so hard to establish.[4]   Barbeyrac denounced
it as *une pure chimère*.[5]   Thomasius' reason for rejecting the
distinction is significant.   It all comes to this, he declared:

---

[1] Proleg., 39 (Whewell's transl.).

[2] *Infra*, pp. 75 ff.

[3] Dunning, *Political Theories from Luther to Montesquieu*, p. 175   Cf. Walker,
History, p. 335.

[4] *De jure naturæ et gentium*, II, 3, 23.

[5] Barbeyrac's Grotius, I, 1, 14, note 3; Barbeyrac's Pufendorf, préf., § 31.
Barbeyrac said: " pour être convaincu, que *Grotius* avoit encore sur plusieurs
choses des idées fausses, ou du moins assez confuses, il suffit de considérer un de
ses principes, qui se répand sur tout son Systême, je veux dire, la supposition d'un
Droit des Gens arbitraire qu'il conçoit fondé sur le consentement tacite des Peuples,
& aiant néanmoins par lui-même force de Loi, autant que le *Droit Naturel*."

Nations are equal among themselves; neither do they recognize a superior among men. Therefore, they cannot be bound by human law.[1]

The same point was stated a little more fully by Burlamaqui, who declared that Grotius' pretended law of nations distinct from the natural law was an idea destitute of all foundation, and who denied the existence of a positive law of nations proved by custom

because, first, all nations are with regard to one another in a natural independence and equality. If, therefore, there is any common law between them, it can proceed only from God their common sovereign.[2]

The naturalists entertained no illusions as to the bearing of the principles of Grotius on the natural equality of states. If it be suggested that there was the germ of naturalistic tendencies in the use which Grotius made of the law of nature, it may be said with equal force that there was also the germ of positivism in his emphasis upon the importance of usage. The translation of the theory of equality into the law of nations depended upon the superstructure which his successors should build upon the foundations that he laid.

It has been suggested that the immutability of the law of nature made equality a necessary inference from its application to separate states.[3] According to Grotius the law of nature was so immutable that it could not be changed by God himself;[4] but by adopting the traditional division of *jus naturale* into that which was characteristic of primitive nature and that which was characteristic of a period of more

---

[1] *Institutionum jurisprudentiæ divinæ*, I, 2, 105. See *infra*, p. 83. To the same effect, Barbeyrac's Pufendorf, II, 3, 23, note 2, *infra*, p. 85, note 2.

[2] *Principes du droit naturel*, II, 6, 8, p. 223. " Car 1° toutes les Nations sont les unes à l'égard des autres dans une indépendance & une égalité naturelle. Si donc il y a entr'elles quelque Loi commune, elle ne peut venir que de Dieu, leur commun Souverain."

[3] Lawrence, *Essays*, pp. 194–195; Olney, in *A. J. I. L.* (1907), I, 418.

[4] I, 1, 10, 5.

complete development, Grotius was able to free himself from most of the restrictions of this hypothetical immutability.[1] It is significant that this very division was used to justify restrictions upon the principle of natural equality, both with respect to individuals and with respect to communities.[2]

There has been a good deal of misunderstanding about the use which Grotius made of the *jus naturale* and *jus gentium* of the Roman Law. It has been suggested that he assumed that they were two names for the same thing, and that he drew heavily from the substance of Roman *jus gentium*, which he assumed to be identical with *jus naturale*, under the mistaken impression that it was intended to be a " law of nations " in the modern significance of that expression.[3] The truth is that Grotius was guilty of neither one of these errors. He had a clearer understanding of the relation between *jus naturale* and *jus gentium* in Roman Law than many of his modern commentators. He was thoroughly familiar, for example, with the difference between them with respect to slavery, a distinction which he embodied in his system.[4] He was careful to point out that they were essentially different; [5] and he was sufficiently explicit to provoke a note from his naturalist translator and editor, Barbeyrac, denying that the Roman Lawyers understood anything more by the *jus gentium* than " what the modern interpreters call the *jus naturale secundarium*." [6] The Roman *jus gentium* was the nearest approximation in posi-

---

[1] II, 8, 1 and 26. See *Mare liberum*, ch. 7, p. 53, where Grotius approves of Vasquez' distinction between primary and secondary laws of nature.

[2] II, 22, 11; III, 7, 1.

[3] Hicks, in *A. J. I. L.* (1908), II, 531–532; Lawrence, *Essays*, pp. 196 ff.; Maine, *Ancient Law*, pp. 102–103; Ritchie, *Natural Rights*, p. 36.

[4] II, 22, 11; III, 7, 1.

[5] Proleg., 53; II, 8, 1 and 26.

[6] Barbeyrac's Grotius, II, 8, 1, note 1. See also Barbeyrac's Pufendorf, II, 3, 23, note 3.

tive law to the ideal principles of the *jus naturale*. It was certain to have a tremendously important influence on Grotius as well as on later writers; but it is a mistake to say that Grotius did not see any difference between the two. It is an even more violent injustice to say that he took the Roman *jus gentium* for a " law of nations " in the modern sense. Unfortunately, he used the same expression to describe both the Roman and the modern conception, sometimes leaving it to the reader to determine from the content the sense in which the term *jus gentium* was used. This was almost certain to result in confusion, but the misunderstanding appears to have been greater among scholars of the last century than among his immediate successors. Grotius tried repeatedly, as he said, to get rid of ambiguity, and to make it clear that the *jus gentium* of the Romans was not the law which pertained to the mutual society of nations among themselves. *Hæc ergo ut discernerentur, laboravimus.*[1]

THE STATE OF NATURE IN THE SYSTEM OF GROTIUS

There was nothing in Grotius' conception of the international society which made the equality of states an essential principle. He advanced little that was new in this respect. Like Suarez he conceived of a society of nations and alleged the necessity of law for that great aggregate system of communities.[2] Unlike the naturalists, who wrote later in the century, he placed no great emphasis upon the idea that international society was analogous to the state of nature. He made comparatively few references to the natural condition of mankind and then quite incidentally in the discussion of other themes. For illustration, he said

---

[1] Proleg., 1, 17, 36, 53; I, 1, 14; II, 8, 1; II, 8, 26; II, 16, 31; II, 18, 2, 1; III, 1, 8, 2; Clark, *Practical Jurisprudence*, p. 362; Taylor, *Int. Pub. Law*, p. 77; Twiss, *Law of Nations*, p. xviii.

[2] Proleg., 17, 23; II, 18, 2; III, 25, 1. Cf. Suarez *Tractatus de legibus*, II, 19, 9, and Wolff's conception of the *civitas maxima, infra*, p. 96.

that civil society was the result of the inability of separate families to protect themselves,[1] that among primitive men in what the poets had sometimes portrayed as the golden age all things were held in common,[2] that a natural condition of mankind existed before political society was formed and judges constituted,[3] that such a condition still prevailed where men lived distributed into families and not into states,[4] and that in the primeval state of nature no men were slaves.[5] The state of nature of which Grotius conceived was one of normally peaceful relationship between men as heads of families and owing no subjection to any higher human authority.[6] However, he made no more than an incidental use of the notion. His appeal was not to men in a state of nature, but to the reason of men in a state of civilization.

Grotius did not develop the argument that men had abandoned the state of nature only in so far as national governments had been formed, while remaining in the natural condition so far as international relations were concerned. This might, perhaps, be implied from one or two passages, but it is characteristic of Grotius that the argument was invoked, if at all, only to provide an answer to particular questions, and when other resources failed. There is a suggestion of the argument in the passages in which he sets forth his theory of punitive war. Consider, for example, the following:

It is to be understood also that kings, and they whose rights are of the nature of royal rights, have the right of requiring punishment, not only for injuries committed against them and their subjects, but for those also which do not peculiarly touch them, but which enormously violate the law of nature and nations in any persons. For the liberty of providing for human society by punishment, which at

---

[1] I, 4, 7, 3.
[2] II, 2, 2; II, 10, 1, 2; *Mare liberum*, p. 23.
[3] II, 20, 8–9.   [5] III, 7, 1.
[4] II, 20, 40, 1 and 4.   [6] I, 4, 7, 3; II, 15, 5; III, 9, 18–19.

first, as we have said, was in the hands of individuals, did, when states and tribunals were instituted, fall to the share of the supreme authorities, not properly as commanding others, but as being themselves subject to none.[1]

The suggestion is misleading, however, for his whole theory of punitive war was irreconcilable, as later writers have pointed out,[2] with the conception of a natural state of equality among nations. There is evidence that Grotius saw the possibility of an analogy between the society of nations and the state of nature. He used something like such an analogy to explain the reason for certain rules of law, as where he compared the pacts of sovereigns with pacts made between men at sea or on a desert island, all of which he said were governed by the natural law;[3] but he never used it in a systematic way to explain the nature of the society of nations.[4] In so far as he developed the idea of a positive law of nations he denied, at least by implication, the idea of an international state of nature.[5] Grotius elaborated upon none of those subtle comparisons by which later writers established the equality of states as a maxim of the law of nations.

The Analogy in the System of Grotius

The analogy between natural persons and the juristic persons of the law of nations was used extensively in the

[1] II, 20, 40 (Whewell's transl.). Cf. Victoria, Rel. VI, *De iure belli*, pp. 172, 185, 187.

[2] Fiore says: " Que dire alors de la théorie de Grotius, qui voulait, en certains cas, légitimer la guerre faite dans le but de punir, *bellum punitivum* ? Admettre un juridiction pénale entre les Etats, ce ne serait pas seulement détruire l'égalité juridique, mais encore porter atteinte aux règles fondamentales du droit de punir, qui ne peut légalement s'exercer en l'absence d'une loi qui puisse être violée, d'un jugement, d'une condamnation et des moyens légaux destinés à en assurer l'exécution." (Antoine's transl.). *Nouveau droit int. pub.*, § 438, I, 380.

[3] II, 11, 5, 3.

[4] See Westlake, *Collected Papers*, p. 48.

[5] See Figgis, *Gerson to Grotius*, p. 285, note 13.

work of Grotius and in a characteristic fashion. As already
pointed out, he made only an occasional use of the analogy
between separate states and men in a state of nature. Of
much more importance was his use of an analogy between
states and men in political society. While he recognized
many defects in such an analogy,[1] he recurred to it frequently to support the rules laid down. He compared the
ruler of a state to the master of a family,[2] clients under the
protection of patrons to international persons protected by
an unequal alliance,[3] and natural persons reduced to slavery
to states reduced by conquest.[4] " And these artificial bodies
have plainly an analogy with natural bodies," he said, in
discussing the termination of sovereignty. *Plane autem
corpora hæc artificialia instar habent corporis naturalis.*[5]

Passages like the above illustrate the use which Grotius
made of the analogy, but they hardly suggest the importance
of his indebtedness to municipal law. His whole treatise
fairly bristled with borrowings. The atmosphere of legal
science in his day was an atmosphere of Roman Law. Grotius had an unfailing supply of principles in the *jus gentium*
of Rome and he used it unsparingly. His classification was
based upon the divisions of municipal law; he borrowed
from municipal law whole categories of rules relating to
property, obligations, and other topics. He borrowed heavily from the jurists, but relatively little, compared to later
publicists, from the theorists. He did not dilate upon the
analogy as a means of explaining the nature of international
relations or of translating the theory of equality into the
law of nations.

[1] I, 3, 7; II, 6, 4; II, 16, 31; *Mare liberum*, p. 47.
[2] I, 3, 16.
[3] I, 3, 21.
[4] II, 21, 7, 2; III, 8, 1–4.
[5] II, 9, 3.

The Idea of Natural Equality in the System
of Grotius

If it is true, as even the naturalists suggested, that the use which Grotius made of the law of nature was inconsistent with the notion of state equality, then it is certainly true that his use of the conception of natural equality required no such conclusion. He was thoroughly familiar with the theory of the natural equality of men:

> By nature, that is, in the primeval state of nature, and without the act of man, no men are slaves, as we have elsewhere said; and in this sense we may assent to what the jurists say, that slavery is against nature. But that slavery should have its origin in human act, that is, in convention or delict, is not repugnant to natural justice, as we have also shewn.[1]

If he had been the pioneer in translating this theory into international law, it would be reasonable to anticipate a statement of it somewhere in his works. However, he nowhere asserted the general equality of states, either expressly or by necessary implication.[2] It was only with regard to cer-

---

[1] III, 7, 1 (Whewell's transl.). See also passages in I, 5, 1; II, 2, 2; II, 10, 1–2. In his address "To the Rulers and to the Free and Independent Nations of Christendom," at the beginning of *Mare liberum* (p. 1), Grotius included a truly Ciceronian statement of the natural basis for the theory of equality among men, although he said nothing expressly of the theory.

[2] It is noteworthy that Pradier-Fodéré, one of the most reliable of nineteenth century authorities on Grotius, does not attribute the idea of state equality to him. He says that Grotius recognized the rights of self-preservation, property, and embassy, but that " les diverses questions concernant ces différents droits ainsi que les devoirs qui correspondent à ces droits, ne sont pas traitées par lui d'une manière distincte; elles se confondent dans l'exposition du vaste sujet de son immortel ouvrage sur le droit de la guerre et de la paix, et se perdent dans l'abondance des matériaux accumulés par son opulente érudition." Pradier-Fodéré cites Vattel as deriving the fundamental rights of states from an application of the theories of the law of nature, the state of nature, and natural equality to the international society. *Traité*, §§ 166–167, I, 286.

Bonfils says: " Dans son immortel ouvrage, Grotius n'a pas traité d'une manière distincte des droits et des devoirs des Etats. Cette matière est comme ensevelie sous les éléments accumulés de sa stupéfiante érudition." *Manuel*, § 235, p. 140.

tain particular interests that Grotius ever attributed to states an equal capacity for rights. There is a notable instance of such an interest in *Mare Liberum*, where he argued that the right to travel and trade with other peoples belonged equally to all nations:

There is not one of you who does not openly proclaim that every man is entitled to manage and dispose of his own property; there is not one of you who does not insist that all citizens have equal and indiscriminate right to use rivers and public places; not one of you who does not defend with all his might the freedom of travel and trade.

If it be thought that the small society which we call a state cannot exist without the application of these principles (and certainly it cannot), why will not those same principles be necessary to uphold the social structure of the whole human race and to maintain the harmony thereof? [1]

Hoc igitur jus ad cunctas gentes æqualiter pertinet.[2] *Mare Liberum* was a chapter in his treatise on the law of prize, and was written somewhat after the fashion of a lawyer's brief to prove that the Dutch had a right to sail to the East Indies and engage in trade there.[3] The argument was based primarily upon natural right.[4] In substance Grotius contended that with respect to the use of the seas that natural equality of right which primitive nature had established had not been and ought not to be restricted. He declared that

all that which has been so constituted by nature that although serving some one person it still suffices for the common use of all other persons, is today and ought in perpetuity to remain in the same condition as when it was first created by nature.[5]

In other words, with respect to this particular interest states might be said to be in a state of nature. This was a clear

---

[1] *Mare liberum*, p. 3 (Magoffin's transl.).
[2] *Ibid.*, p. 8. Cf. Story, The Marianna Flora, 11 Wheaton 1, 42 (1826).
[3] *Ibid.*, p. 7.
[4] *Ibid.*, pp. 5, and *passim*.
[5] *Ibid.*, p. 27 (Magoffin's transl.).

statement of equality of capacity with respect to a certain category of rights, but it was not intended to establish a like equality in respect to all rights. There is no evidence that Grotius intended this or similar statements to have a general significance.

The statements in *Mare Liberum* were much more explicit than anything which appeared in *De Jure Belli ac Pacis*. In the first chapter, where he defined *bellum* and *jus*, Grotius said that anything was unjust which was contrary to the nature of a society of rational creatures, and added:

> But society is either that of equals, as among brothers, citizens, friends, and allies; or it is unequal, by preëminence as Aristotle says, as between parent and children, master and servant, King and subjects, God and men. So justice is either that which prevails among equals, or between governors and the governed in whatever degree. The latter in my opinion may be called the right of superiority (*jus Rectorium*), the former the right of equality (*Æquatorium recte*).[1]

However, Grotius was not using *jus* in a legal sense in this passage at all; and in any event the passage is too vague and ambiguous to have general significance. In the chapter in which Grotius discussed the termination of sovereignty and the division of a state to form several states, he said that when a colony separated from the mother country a new state was created, and he quoted with approval from Thucydides: " They are sent out not to be slaves, but to have equal rights." [2] The quotation referred probably to the rights of the colonists as individuals rather than to rights of the colony as a separate state. It had no legal significance, and so far as Grotius may have intended to apply it to states it carried nothing more than the idea of separateness as opposed to the idea of incorporation in the mother state. In another chapter, he remarked of the right

[1] I, 1, 3, 2. Whewell's rendition of *jus Rectorium* and *Æquatorium recte* as " rectorial rights " and " equatorial rights " respectively is hardly satisfactory.
[2] II, 9, 10.

of persons to defend themselves and their property against attack by subjects of a state with which peace had been concluded:

For peace is concluded, that all the subjects may be in safety: peace is the act of the state for the whole and for the parts. And even if a new cause do arise, it will be lawful, notwithstanding the peace, for the persons attacked to defend themselves and their property. For it is natural, as Cassius says, to repel arms by arms: and therefore we are not readily to believe that this right is abdicated between equals.[1]

It is clear enough, however, that the passage refers to equality among individuals belonging to different states and has no very precise legal significance. There is no evidence that Grotius intended such passages as the above to carry any general import apart from the discussion of particular topics. Barbeyrac, who translated and edited the *De Jure Belli ac Pacis* and the *De Jure Naturæ et Gentium* of Pufendorf with a multitude of notes and cross-references, and who was quite explicit in his own declaration of the principle of state equality,[2] found nothing in any of these passages to warrant a reference to the much less ambiguous statements in Pufendorf. It is incredible that Grotius, who was familiar with the theories of every leading exponent of natural equality among men, and who ransacked all history for authorities in minutiae, could have considered the principle of state equality as of fundamental consequence and have left it with such uncertain support.

There are much less ambiguous passages in the work of Grotius which seem to contradict the idea of state equality. A noteworthy example is found in the second book, where he divided treaties into those establishing that which is conformable to natural law, and those adding something to natural law. The latter were either equal or unequal:

[1] III, 20, 32 (Whewell's transl.).
[2] *Infra*, p. 85.

From the explanation of what are equal conventions, it is easily understood what are unequal. Unusual [unequal] Treaties are either proposed by the superior party, or by the inferior. By the superior, as if he promises assistance without any reciprocal stipulation: by the inferior, when there is an inferiority of claim, are what we have spoken of as Conventions of Command. And these are either without infringement of the sovereignty of the inferior, or such as infringe it.[1]

The treaty between the Romans and the Carthaginians, in which it was provided that Carthage should not make war without the consent of Rome, was cited as an example of an unequal treaty impairing sovereignty. In unequal treaties without impairment of sovereignty the burden imposed on the inferior state might be transitory or permanent. Then followed a long list of examples of permanent burdens, several of which it would be quite impossible to reconcile with later notions of sovereignty. Passages like this one at least suggest that Grotius would have included in the *jus gentium* a great many conventional and customary limitations upon the equality of states. More will be said of inequality among states in the system of Grotius in connection with his conception of sovereignty.

Elsewhere in his treatise Grotius used *æqualitas* or its equivalent in a great variety of meanings, but without any significance for the law of nations. He was thinking of a kind of moral equality when he spoke of equality between belligerents with respect to the justice of a war. He was not thinking of the law of nations at all, but of municipal law in its ethical aspects, in what he said about equality of ownership and equality in contracts.[2]

Sovereignty in the System of Grotius

The principle of state equality was not the result of Grotius' use of the law of nature, the state of nature, natural

[1] II, 15, 7 (Whewell's transl.).
[2] II, 10, 2; III, 1, 2, 2; II, 12, 8-13.

equality, or the analogy. Was it the consequence of his
conception of sovereignty ? This is an important question.
It has been suggested that the principle of equality was the
inevitable outcome of the doctrine of sovereignty as defined
by Grotius and his contemporaries.[1] It is certain that
theories of sovereignty were defended in the sixteenth and
seventeenth centuries which pointed straight to that conclusion. More recently the theory of sovereignty has been
offered frequently as an analytical explanation for the principle that states have equal rights.[2] The definition of sovereignty adopted by Grotius, however, provided neither an
adequate premise for the conclusion of state equality, nor a
satisfactory explanation for such a principle. A comparative study of the classical treatises on international law produced in these two centuries shows that the idea of state
equality did not come into the law of nations through the
doctrine of sovereignty. It came in through the theories of
natural law, natural equality, and the state of nature, that
important trilogy of ideas which had dominated speculation
since the age of antiquity. The doctrine of sovereignty was
offered later as an analytical explanation and justification;
it was never an historical reason for the origin of the principle.

The notion of state power superior to all positive law and
limited only by the laws of God and nature had its inception in the Middle Ages.[3] It received its most adequate
expression before Grotius in the *De la Republique* of Bodin
published in 1576.[4] Bodin defined sovereignty as supreme
power over citizens and subjects unrestrained by laws.[5] The
first and principal function of sovereignty was to give laws
to citizens and subjects without the consent of superior,

---

[1] Hershey, *Essentials*, pp. 58, 148; Taylor, *Int. Pub. Law*, §§ 51, 69, pp. 75, 98.

[2] See *infra*, p. 114.

[3] See Gierke, *Political Theory*, pp. 87-100, and *passim*.

[4] I, 8-10, pp. 89-183. See Nys, *Le droit int.*, II, 235.

[5] I, 8, p. 89. Cf. also the Latin edition, *De republica* (Frankfort, 1622), I, 8, p. 123.

equal, or inferior,[1] a function which vested in that person who, after God, acknowledged no one greater than himself. As for the laws of God and nature, sovereigns and subjects were equally bound by them;[2] but the law of nations could not bind a sovereign any more than his own laws, except in so far as it might be in accord with the laws of God and nature.[3] If certain of the laws of nations were unjust the sovereign might abrogate them, as, for example, in respect to slavery. Suarez presented a similar theory at the beginning of the seventeenth century in his exposition of the ultimate law-making authority.[4]

The treatment of sovereignty in Grotius reflected the influence of Bodin and Suarez in some respects, but it differed widely from the conception of each of them, both in point of view and in details. Grotius denounced all notions of universal authority [5] and recognized the existence of a great society of states.[6] His state was a perfect community of free men, united for the sake of enjoying the advantages of *jus* and for the common welfare.[7] Sovereignty was the essential attribute of the state, the bond that holds the state together, the breath of life that so many thousands breathe:

That Power is called *Sovereign*, whose acts are not subject to the control of another, so that they can be rendered void by the act of any other human will.[8]

Here were included two notions, the positive notion of government, and the negative notion of independence. In most

[1] I, 10, p. 161.
[2] I, 8, pp. 97, 109 ff.
[3] I, 8, p. 118.
[4] *Tractatus de legibus*, III, 9.
[5] II, 22, 13–14; *Mare liberum*, pp. 16, 45, 50, 66.
[6] Proleg., 17; II, 18, 2; III, 25, 1.
[7] I, 1, 14; II, 6, 4. Cf. Twiss, *Law of Nations*, p. 4.
[8] I, 3, 7 (Whewell's transl.); I, 3, 5; II, 9, 3. See Dunning, *Political Theories from Luther to Montesquieu*, pp. 179–186; Merriam, *History of Sovereignty*, pp. 21–24; Walker, *History*, p. 288.

THE EQUALITY OF STATES

58

of his discussion of sovereignty Grotius was concerned with
the former of the two notions. His understanding of the
latter must be constructed chiefly from materials which are
scattered throughout his work. These materials, when collected and coördinated, present an interpretation of sovereignty in its external significance which has been all too
frequently overlooked. They also cast a helpful light upon
the society of states as it was conceived in the Grotian system.

The international society of which Grotius conceived was
not grounded upon an equal capacity for rights among its
members. There was a disposition to recognize quite the
contrary principle. He held that important limitations upon
the exercise of political power were consistent with the enjoyment of international personality and even of perfect
sovereignty. States could be united in a federal bond and
yet remain sovereign.[1] Feudal vassals might be sovereign.[2]
Sovereignty was not infringed by an unequal alliance which
imposed a permanent obligation upon the inferior state to
concede precedence, to have the same friends and enemies,
to refrain from fortifying or posting armies in designated
localities, or from acquiring more than a limited number of
vessels, to abstain from building cities, engaging in trade,
or levying soldiers in certain localities, or to renounce all
former treaties with other states.[3] Even protected or tributary states, analogous to clients in Roman Law, enjoyed
their sovereignty unimpaired; but Grotius admitted that if
such leagues were perpetual, and the superior state was
much the more powerful and had the right of introducing
garrisons, the inferior state was likely to be absorbed by the
superior, or at least to lose a part of its sovereignty.[4] Partly
sovereign states could be the result of treaty or of conquest.[5]

[1] I, 3, 7, 2.   [2] I, 3, 23.   [3] II, 15, 7.
[4] I, 3, 21. On clients in the Roman Law, see Muirhead, *Law of Rome*, p. 8, and
references there cited.
[5] II, 15, 7; III, 19, 10.

Grotius recognized the legitimacy, according to the strict rules of the *jus gentium*, of the practice of enslaving captives in war.[1] The present significance of what he said about slavery lies in the analogy which he drew between slaves and states whose sovereignty had been diminished as a result of conquest. The import of this analogy is suggested by the following passages:

Since the victor can subject individuals to personal servitude, it is not surprising that he should be allowed to reduce a body of men, whether they be a State, or part of a State, to a servitude, either civil or domestic, or mixed. . . .

And hence we may understand what is that mixed government, compounded of mastership and civil rule, of which we have spoken; namely, when servitude is combined with a certain personal liberty. Thus we read of peoples whose arms were taken from them, and who were commanded not to possess any iron except for agriculture; and of others who were compelled to change their language and habits of living. . . .

Even if any victor leave to the conquered people the rights of their state, he may take to himself some things which belonged to the state: for it depends on his own will what limit he chooses to fix to the benefits which he gives.[2]

In his chapter on restraints respecting conquests Grotius recommended that where it was not safe for the conqueror to relinquish all authority over the conquered he should at least leave them as much of their former independence and authority as possible.[3] States whose sovereignty had been thus impaired nevertheless remained international persons as far as they remained sovereign; and in the same measure that they retained sovereignty they were capable of the right of legation,[4] the right to make war,[5] and other rights by the law of nations.

---

[1] III, 8, and 14. He contended that among Christian nations it had become the practice to hold for ransom instead. III, 7, 8-9; III, 21, 25 and 28.

[2] III, 8, 1-4 (Whewell's transl.).

[3] III, 15, 9.   [4] II, 18, 2.   [5] III, 3, 4.

Moreover, when states had come by legitimate course into this partially sovereign status they should remain contented with their condition, for the natural liberty of men or of states was not an inalienable attribute.

Nor again can we say of the liberty, either of individuals, or of cities, or states, (that is, *autonomy* or self-government,) that it is either by natural law, and at all times, an attribute of all, or that in the cases in which it is, it furnishes just ground for war. For when we say that liberty by nature belongs to men or to peoples, we are to understand that, of a natural right preceding all human pacts; and of liberty by negation of slavery, not of liberty in opposition to slavery; so that man is not a slave by nature, but he is not by nature a creature that cannot be a slave. . . . Therefore they who have, by a legitimate course, come into slavery, either personal or civil, ought to be content with their condition; as St. Paul teaches, *Art thou called being a servant? Care not for it.*[1]

So far as his conception of sovereignty was concerned, Grotius was not interested in the elaboration of an abstract theory. He could afford to leave that to political philosophers and others who were in less intimate contact with the practical problems of international relations. His immediate concern was to establish criteria for distinguishing public and formal from private and informal wars. Both custom and humanity justified him in attributing regularity to the wars of rulers possessing less than the widest powers. Instead of conceiving of a society of states having equal capacity for rights, Grotius deferred so far to contemporary practice as to recognize the existence of a society among whose members there were many differences of status, with corresponding differences of capacity.

ILLUSTRATIONS OF THE GROTIAN TRADITION

Enough has been said of the leading principles in the system of Grotius to explain most of those errors into which

---

[1] II, 22, 11 (Whewell's transl.).

later writers have fallen with respect to his supposed contribution to the early development of the principle of state equality. A few illustrations may be given of some of the most common misunderstandings.

It not infrequently happens that the translation of the idea of equality into the law of nations is attributed to Grotius because the real significance of equality as a legal principle is not fully understood. This seems to be the case with Mr. Figgis, who says that the Catholic precursors of Grotius asserted " the complete equality of sovereign states ";

They combined the new recognition of political facts with ancient ideals of unity, and the older conception of law, as an eternal verity. These two elements of thought were both to be found and were necessarily found in the system of politics of that day. Without the one we could not have the conception of States as juristic and equal persons, equal not in power any more than are individuals, but in the fact of being able to direct themselves to conscious ends. Without the other the notion of a unity of these persons, of a bond binding them together, of certain limits of activity they may not overpass, would not have been possible, or would have taken longer to discern.[1]

According to Figgis, this " equality before the Law " of all states was becoming an accomplished fact by the time Grotius wrote:

It is the world of seventeenth and eighteenth century diplomacy which Grotius contemplates, with absolute princes for the most part, territorial sovereignty and the equality of the juristic persons of International Law. This latter doctrine, which we have seen in a more concrete form in the *grand dessein* of Sully, was closely connected with Netherland influences. William the Silent in his apology appealed against Philip II to the fact of his being a *sovereign prince*, as good as he was. The juristic equality of sovereigns was not beginning to be a fact until the close of the sixteenth century.[2]

If Mr. Figgis means the equality before the law of separate states, as contrasted with the idea of universal empire, there

---

[1] *Gerson to Grotius*, pp. 190, 216.   [2] *Ibid.*, pp. 220, 242.

can be no quarrel with his conclusions. If he means equality of capacity for rights the statement is in error, not only with respect to Grotius, but also with respect to the facts of the seventeenth century.

More often the principle is attributed to Grotius because of misinformation with reference to the place occupied by the law of nature, the state of nature, and the idea of natural equality in the Grotian system. Two chapters in Sir Henry Maine's *Ancient Law* have been a most prolific source of misconception in this respect, particularly among English and American students.[1] Maine started from two false premises: first, that *jus naturale* and *jus gentium* in Roman Law were identical;[2] second, that Grotius and the early publicists misconceived the meaning of *jus gentium* in the Roman Law and took it for a law of nations in the modern sense.[3] He said:

Having adopted from the Antonine jurisconsults the position that the Jus Gentium and the Jus Naturæ were identical, Grotius, with his immediate predecessors and his immediate successors, attributed to

---

[1] *Ancient Law*, chs. 3 and 4. In note E, pp. 73–77, Sir Frederick Pollock says: "Maine's third and fourth chapters need more supplemental criticism than any other part of 'Ancient Law.' The mediaeval doctrine of the Law of Nature, and its continuity with the classical Roman doctrine, had been forgotten or misunderstood in England for quite two centuries at the time when these chapters were written; and even many years later there was no obvious way for an English scholar to get back to the right historical lines. . . .

"Maine was not a mediaevalist or a canonist, and shared the general ignorance of English lawyers and scholars of his time."

[2] *Ibid.*, p. 55. Cf. Bryce, *Studies*, p. 584, note 1; Pollock's Note E, p. 75; *supra*, pp. 11, 15.

[3] *Ibid.*, p. 102. In Note H, p. 120, Sir Frederick Pollock says: "That Grotius and his contemporaries misunderstood the classical *ius gentium*, or supposed the modern rules of conduct between sovereign states to be contained in it, I am unable, with great respect for any suggestion of Maine's, to believe. . . . He may or may not have known that in its classical meaning it could, and sometimes did, include, among other rules of conduct sanctioned by general usage, whatever rules are reasonable and customary as between sovereign states. But as a scholar he must have known that *gentes* is not the plural of *civitas* or *populus*, which are the only apt words in classical Latin for a state or nation in its political capacity." Cf. *supra*, p. 46.

the Law of Nature an authority which would never perhaps have been claimed for it, if " Law of Nations " had not in that age been an ambiguous expression. They laid down unreservedly that Natural Law is the code of states, and thus put in operation a process which has continued almost down to our own day, the process of engrafting on the international system rules which are supposed to have been evolved from the unassisted contemplation of the conception of Nature. There is, too, one consequence of immense practical importance to mankind which, though not unknown during the early modern history of Europe, was never clearly or universally acknowledged till the doctrines of the Grotian school had prevailed. If the society of nations is governed by Natural Law, the atoms which compose it must be absolutely equal. Men under the sceptre of Nature are all equal, and accordingly commonwealths are equal if the international state be one of nature. The proposition that independent communities, however different in size and power, are all equal in the view of the law of nations, has largely contributed to the happiness of mankind, though it is constantly threatened by the political tendencies of each successive age. It is a doctrine which probably would never have obtained a secure footing at all if International Law had not been entirely derived from the majestic claims of Nature by the Publicists who wrote after the revival of letters.[1]

What Maine said could have been applied with some qualifications to the teachings of the naturalist school in the last half of the seventeenth century. It was obviously inapplicable to the system of Grotius.

Maine's errors were given somewhat wider circulation through a popular book by Lawrence, entitled *Essays on Some Disputed Questions in Modern International Law.* That part of the fourth essay which dealt with the influence of the theory of natural law upon the system of Grotius was little more than an elaboration of the passage quoted above from *Ancient Law.*[2] Maine's mistaken notions were repeated; and

[1] *Ancient Law*, p. 103.

[2] *Essays*, preface, p. x. Had Lawrence's *Essays* been other than a popular discussion, one would be tempted to quote against him his own words to the effect that " publicists adopt too easily what they find in the works of their predecessors." *Ibid.*, p. 209.

in the elaborating process certain of them, particularly those referring to Grotius' use of the state of nature, received added emphasis. In discussing the system of Grotius, Lawrence said:

We have now to discover how he utilized the theory of Natural Law, and made it the mother of a new and better system of International Law. His method was as follows. Seeing that nations had no longer even in theory a common superior, he argued that they were in a position similar to that of individuals before civil government was established among them. Just as men in such a position were bound by a Law of Nature, so also were states. Natural reason dictated certain rules which were so sacred and immutable that even the Almighty could not alter them. They were part of the very nature and essence of things, and God Himself submitted to be judged by them. These rules bound states as well as individuals, and were the basis of International Law. The practice of all or of most nations could add to them, or go beyond them, but it could not repeal them. They were the immutable part of International Law, whereas the part based upon general consent could vary from time to time. . . .

In elaborating the rules which govern the intercourse of states Grotius was led to adopt into his system a vast amount of pure Roman Law. The later Roman lawyers divided their law into a *Jus Civile* peculiar to Rome, and a *Jus Gentium* common to Rome and other states; and with the single exception of Ulpian they identified the *Jus Gentium* with that *Jus Naturale* which their profession of the Stoic philosophy caused them to believe in. Grotius, seeing this, thought he had discovered in the Roman *Jus Gentium* an international code of antiquity, based upon ideas similar to his own of the applicability of Natural Law to the intercourse of states. . . . When the Roman lawyers became converts to the Stoic philosophy, they regarded their own *Jus Gentium* as a portion of the lost code of Nature, and dignified it for the future by the appellation of *Jus Naturale*. Thus it is not to be wondered at that Grotius imagined their *Jus Gentium* or *Jus Naturale* to be a system of rules for guiding independent states in their mutual·intercourse. . . .

. . . The *Jus Gentium*, regarded as a Natural Code, was applied to the relations of states, because it was believed they stood to one another as men were supposed to stand in a state of nature. One of the most important effects of the change was to extend and intensify the conception of territorial sovereignty, and another was to give effect as a legal doctrine to the principle of the absolute independence and equality of states.

. . . Here again Roman Law gave precision to a theory which had been introduced independently of it. The classical jurists laid down again and again that by nature all men were equal, and one of their great objects in elaborating the *Jus Gentium* was to sweep away all the intricate distinctions between man and man of which the *Jus Civile* was full. Thus Grotius in borrowing from the *Jus Gentium* under the impression that it was meant to be a code of nature applied to states, found ample confirmation of the theory of equality. He made it a cardinal point of his system; and thereby conferred no small benefit upon mankind.[1]

The extracts quoted are replete with misinformation in regard to the relation between *jus naturale* and *jus gentium*, Grotius' understanding of the *jus gentium*, and his use of natural law, natural equality, and the state of nature.

These chapters from Maine and Lawrence have been widely read and not infrequently followed. For illustration, in a useful article by Mr. Hicks on *The Equality of States and The Hague Conferences*, it is asserted that

The doctrine was born with the publication of the great book of Hugo Grotius, " De Jure Belli ac Pacis," in 1625. . . . He adopted the theory, well known to his time, that a law of nature controls the relations of man to man, and applied it to the relations between states. This was Grotius' great accomplishment — to find in the law of nature a new and nonreligious ground for international rights and duties. It was a common conception of the age that there had once existed a time when organized communities were not yet formed and when each individual was at liberty to do whatever he wished. Further, that men in such a condition obeyed certain rules discovered to them by their own reason. These rules were called the laws of nature. People were in a state of nature with reference to each other. Grotius used this law of nature in the following manner: No common superior being left to control the relations of states, the states were free and independent, and they were in a " state of nature "

[1] *Essays*, pp. 194–203.

with respect to each other, just as individuals were before the organization of communities. Thus, states were bound by a law of nature. As to what the law of nature was, recourse was had to Roman Law. Now, the Romans in their judicial system identified the *jus gentium* with the *jus naturale*. That is, when they discovered that there were certain laws common to most of the countries with which they had relations, they came to think of these rules as laws of nature. Grotius followed them in this error, and when he applied the law of nature to states it was really in large part the *jus gentium* which he was using. One of the oft-repeated dogmas of the *jus gentium* was the equality of men. When Grotius applied the system to states, he made an essential part of his legal doctrine the absolute independence and equality of states.[1]

The earliest exposition of state equality is ascribed to Grotius by a third group of writers on the assumption that equality was an inevitable corollary of his conception of sovereignty and independence. This is the position taken by Twiss, who says of the state-system established by the Peace of Westphalia:

> The realization of such a State-System would have been impracticable if Grotius had not previously familiarized the minds of Statesmen with the conception of territorial sovereignty and the rights of independence as incidental to such sovereignty, and further with the doctrine of the equality of States considered as independent political communities.[2]

Taylor declares that

> the Grotian system depends upon a full and unqualified recognition of the doctrine of territorial sovereignty from which flow the corollaries that all states are formally equal, and that territory and jurisdiction are coextensive.[3]

[1] *A. J. I. L.* (1908), II, 531–532. See also *A. S. I. L. Proceedings* (1909), III, 239. Cf. Reeves, in *The University Record* (1917), III, 254. Mr. Hicks is obviously wrong in what he says about the equality of men having been a dogma of the *jus gentium*. Equality was a dogma of the *jus naturale*, and this was the principal reason why the rules of the two could not be identified. See *supra*, pp. 11, 15.

[2] *Law of Nations*, p. xvii.

[3] *Int. Pub. Law*, § 69, p. 98. Also § 51, p. 75. Taylor's citations of *De jure belli ac pacis* in the note on p. 76 have little or nothing to do with the question.

More recently the same opinion has been expressed by Hershey, who says:

the essential principles underlying the Grotian system remain the fundamental principles of International Law. Such are the doctrines of the legal equality and of territorial sovereignty or independence of States.

These fundamental principles, though not clearly stated by Grotius, underlay his system and were fully developed by his successors, more especially by Wolff, Vattel, and G. F. de Martens. They were the inevitable outcome of the acceptance of the dogma of the supreme power or sovereignty of States and princes, as defined by Bodin, Grotius, Hobbes, and other political philosophers during the sixteenth and seventeenth centuries.[1]

If the conclusion stated above with reference to sovereignty in the system of Grotius is sound, then the opinion represented by these writers must be erroneous. Equal protection of the law was a necessary corollary of sovereignty and independence in the Grotian system. Equality of capacity for rights was not an essential corollary; in truth, it was not even a possible corollary.

It is submitted that the opinion represented by Maine, Lawrence, and others must be revised. Publicists have fallen into a careless way of attributing to Grotius theories which he had no part in establishing, except as his appeal to natural law contributed to prepare the way for a later school of writers in which these theories received their complete development. Much more has been read into the work of Grotius than any student of the seventeenth century could have found there. It is certain that for the seventeenth century he was no authority for the proposition that states have equal rights by the law of nations. Men had recourse for that proposition to a group of publicists and moral philosophers who were less concerned with the elaboration of a practical code and more interested in attaining an abstract perfection of ideas.

[1] *Essentials*, p. 58.

CHAPTER III

THE ORIGIN OF THE PRINCIPLE OF STATE EQUALITY

DIVERGENT TENDENCIES AMONG THE SUCCESSORS OF GROTIUS

THE modern law of nations was developed, in its formative period, chiefly by great teachers and publicists. The body of accumulated custom was meager, the evidence of its existence frequently inaccessible. The state of international relations was worse than unsatisfactory to all right-thinking men. So it came about, partly from the want of common usage, partly from the prevalence of certain theories, partly from the desire of the writers to ameliorate existing conditions, and partly, perhaps, from the type of mind which was most frequently devoted to the law of nations, that the primitive stages of the science were influenced largely by those theoretical conceptions which were included in the common heritage of learning from antiquity and the Middle Ages. Development of the theory of the law of nations particularly, and of no inconsiderable part of its substance, was determined by the force of these ideas.

The successors of Grotius were by no means agreed, however, as to the precise application and significance of these theories. Three tendencies appeared among the publicists, represented by the naturalists, the positivists, and the eclectics respectively. The writers are sometimes divided into three schools corresponding to these tendencies.[1] There is no objection to the division, provided it be remembered that

---

[1] On the three schools, see remarks of Despagnet, *Cours*, §§ 31–33, pp. 32–34; Fenwick, in *A. J. I. L.* (1914), VIII, 38; Hély, *Étude*, p. 221; Hershey, *Essentials*, pp. 59–63; Phillipson, in Macdonell and Manson, *Great Jurists*, p. 394.

it is an arbitrary one, and that it does not always offer an adequate explanation for the system of an individual writer. It must be applied, as might be expected, not only to publicists holding views that are widely divergent and hence easily classified, but also to representatives of many shades of opinion between the extremes. As might be expected, also, modern authorities are not always agreed as to the school to which certain of the classical publicists should be accredited.

The divergent tendencies that found expression in these so-called schools had their inception in different conceptions of international society and the law of nations. The philosophical or pure law of nature school held that the law of nations was nothing more than the law of nature applied to separate states in a state of nature; they accordingly denied to the customary, conventional, or positive element any of the attributes of true law apart from the natural law. The positivist or historical school contended that the principles underlying customs and treaties constituted a positive law of nations, distinct from the natural law and of superior practical importance. The eclectics or Grotians, as they are sometimes called, took an intermediate position, retaining Grotius' distinction between the natural and the voluntary law of nations, while treating the two as about equal in importance.

The Influence of Thomas Hobbes

The translation of the theory of natural equality into the law of nations originated with and was first definitely stated by the naturalists, whose inspiration was found in the writings of Thomas Hobbes and whose leader in the seventeenth century was Samuel von Pufendorf. An illuminating chapter might be written on the contributions of Thomas Hobbes to the unreality of international law. His works on legal and political theory, particularly his *Elementa Philosophica de Cive* and *Leviathan*,[1] had an influence upon the subsequent development of the law of nations that is not generally appreciated. Although he wrote no treatise on the law of nations, his influence on its theory was far-reaching and significant. He revived, for the purposes of juridical philosophy, the whole mediaeval theory of natural law, the state of nature, and natural equality. Through his influence these conceptions were handed down in a new and non-scholastic guise to philosophers and jurists of the seventeenth, eighteenth, and nineteenth centuries.

The system of Hobbes was the antithesis of that of Grotius in respect both to its method and its leading principles. Hobbes' method was an undisguised attack upon the processes of the continental jurist. An extreme rationalist, he had a supreme contempt for the erudition with which Grotius sought witnesses for the soundness of his conclusions:

For first, all Truth of Doctrine dependeth either upon *Reason,* or upon *Scripture;* Both which give credit to many, but never receive it from any Writer. Secondly, the matters in question are not of *Fact,* but of *Right,* wherein there is no place for *Witnesses.* There is scarce any of those old Writers, that contradicteth not sometimes both himself, and others; which makes their Testimonies insufficient. Fourthly, such Opinions as are taken onely upon Credit of Antiquity, are not intrinsecally the Judgment of those that cite them, but Words that passe (like gaping) from mouth to mouth. Fiftly, it is many times with a fraudulent Designe that men stick their corrupt Doctrine with the Cloves of other mens Wit. Sixtly, I find not that the Ancients they cite, took it for an Ornament, to doe the like with those that wrote before them. Seventhly, it is an argument of Indigestion; when Greek

---

[1] Hobbes lived 1588–1679. His *Elementa philosophica de cive* was first published in 1642, and again, for wider circulation, in 1647. References are to the Amsterdam edition of 1657, and the English edition in Vol. II of Hobbes' *English Works*, edited by William Molesworth. *Leviathan* first appeared in 1651. Page references are to A. R. Waller's edition in the Cambridge English Classics. There is a brief sketch of Hobbes' life and work by Montmorency, in Macdonell and Manson, *Great Jurists*, pp. 195–219.

and Latin Sentences unchewed come up again, as they use to doe, unchanged. Lastly, though I reverence those men of Ancient time, that either have written Truth perspicuously, or set us in a better way to find it out our selves; yet to the Antiquity it self I think nothing due: For if we will reverence the Age, the Present is the Oldest. Of the Antiquity of the Writer, I am not sure, that generally they to whom such honor is given, were more Ancient when they wrote, than I am that am Writing: But if it bee well considered, the praise of Ancient Authors, proceeds not from the reverence of the Dead, but from the competition, and mutuall envy of the Living.[1]

The contrast in essential principles was no less marked than the contrast in method. All confusion involved in Grotius' definition and use of the law of nature dissolved before the merciless logic of the English philosopher. Where Grotius defined law in terms that left its binding force to be inferred from its character as law, Hobbes anticipated Austin in defining it as the command of a sovereign power.[2] Hobbes divided law into divine and human according to its source, and the divine into natural and positive according to the means whereby God had made his will known to men — natural reason in case of the former, revelation in case of the latter.[3] Natural or moral law was described as " that which God hath declared to all men by his eternal word born with them, to wit, their natural reason." Elsewhere it was defined as precepts or rules

found out by Reason, by which a man is forbidden to do, that, which is destructive of his life, or taketh away the means of preserving the same; and to omit, that, by which he thinketh it may be best preserved.[4]

---

[1] *Leviathan*, Review and Conclusion, pp. 526–527.

[2] *Dominion*, XIV, 1, in *English Works*, II, 183; *Leviathan*, Pt. II, ch. 26, p. 189.

[3] *Dominion*, XIV, 4, in *English Works*, II, 186.

[4] *Leviathan*, Pt. I, ch. 14, p. 86; *Liberty*, II, 1, in *English Works*, II, 16. Cf. Selden's definition: " I cannot fancy to myself what the law of nature means, but the law of God. How should I know I ought not to steal, I ought not to commit adultery, unless some body had told me so ? Surely 'tis because I have been told so. 'Tis not because I think I ought not to do them, nor because you think I ought

Hobbes criticized those who had confounded law and right,
and drew a clear distinction between natural law (*lex naturalis*) and natural right (*jus naturale*). While the former implied restraint, the latter implied liberty, the liberty of every
man to do whatever seemed best for the preservation of his
existence.[1] The equal natural rights of men made the state
of nature in Hobbes' theory a state of war. The natural law,
on the other hand, was a body of rules designed to make life
secure. Its primary precepts were to seek peace and observe
it, to covenant to refrain from the exercise of natural liberty,
and to perform covenants.[2] Its rules were immutable and
eternal,[3] but they were not true law at all except in so far as
they had been delivered in the word of God.[4] Hobbes completely identified the natural law and moral philosophy.[5]

Hobbes' conception of the state of nature is familiar learning. He used the term to describe the condition of mankind
apart from all human institutions, a condition in which there
was no coercive authority, no law but natural law, and in
which a perfect equality of natural rights prevailed.[6] In
such a state of nature every man was endowed with an equal
natural right of self-preservation, which carried with it a
natural right to do everything necessary for self-preserva-

not; if so, our minds might change: Whence then comes the restraint ? From a
higher power, nothing else can bind. I cannot bind myself, for I may untie myself
again; nor an equal cannot bind me, for we may untie one another. It must be a
superior power, even God Almighty. If two of us make a bargain, why should
either of us stand to it ? What need you care what you say, or what need I care
what I say ? Certainly because there is something about me that tells me, *fides
est servanda*, and if we after alter our minds, and make a new bargain, there is *fides
servanda* there too." *Opera omnia*, III, Pt. II, 2041.

[1] *Liberty*, I, 7, in *English Works*, II, 8; *Dominion*, XIV, 3, in *ibid.*, II, 186;
Leviathan, Pt. I, ch. 14, p. 86.
[2] *Liberty*, II and III, in *English Works*, II, 16 ff.; *Leviathan*, Pt. I, chs. 14 and 15,
pp. 86 ff.
[3] *Liberty*, III, 29, in *English Works*, II, 46; *Leviathan*, Pt. I, ch. 15, p. 108.
[4] *Liberty*, III, 33, in *English Works*, II, 49; *Leviathan*, Pt. I, ch. 15, p. 109, and
Pt. II, ch. 26, p. 191.
[5] *Liberty*, III, 30, in *English Works*, II, 47; *Leviathan*, Pt. I, ch. 15, p. 109.
[6] *Ibid.*, Pt. I, ch. 13, pp. 81–86, and *passim*.

tion, and to be supreme judge as to what was necessary to that end.[1] Everyone had a right to everything; profit was the measure of right; natural rights were equivalent to natural mights; and their sanction was force. In short, the state of nature was a state of war.[2]

Aristotle's theory of inequality was rejected, and the idea of natural equality among men was stated with new precision. Hobbes understood by it a natural equality of capacity for natural rights in the state of nature, and for legal rights under the law of nature, in so far as the law of nature could be called true law.[3] The precepts of the law of nature required " that every man be accounted by nature equal to another," that each attribute equal right and power to others, that those things which cannot be divided be used in common in order to preserve equality, and that no man act as arbiter in his own dispute because he could not observe " that same equality commanded by the law of nature, so exactly as a third man would do." [4]

The analogy between the state and the natural body, conspicuous in the work of earlier writers, was at the very foundation of Hobbes' philosophy. He began his *Leviathan* with a detailed description of the state as an artificial man:

For by Art is created that great LEVIATHAN called a COMMON-WEALTH, or STATE, (in latine CIVITAS) which is but an Artificiall Man; though of greater stature and strength than the Naturall, for whose protection and defence it was intended; and in which, the *Soveraignty* is an Artificiall *Soul*, as giving life and motion to the whole body; The *Magistrates*, and other *Officers* of Judicature and Execution, artificiall *Joynts; Reward* and *Punishment* (by which fastned to the seate of the Soveraignty, every joynt and member is moved to performe his duty) are the *Nerves*, that do the same in the Body Naturall; The

[1] *Liberty*, I, 8-10, in *English Works*, II, 9-11.
[2] *Liberty*, I, 12, in *English Works*, II, 11; *Leviathan*, Pt. I, ch. 13, p. 83.
[3] *Liberty*, I, 3 and 10, in *English Works*, II, 6, 9; *Leviathan*, Pt. I, ch. 13, p. 81.
[4] *Liberty*, I, 13-21, in *English Works*, II, 38-42; *Leviathan*, Pt. I, ch. 15, pp. 104-107.

Wealth and *Riches* of all the particular members, are the *Strength;* *Salus Populi* (the *peoples safety*) its *Businesse; Counsellors,* by whom all things needfull for it to know, are suggested unto it, are the *Memory; Equity* and *Lawes,* an artificiall *Reason* and *Will; Concord, Health; Sedition, Sicknesse;* and *Civill war, Death.* Lastly, the *Pacts* and *Covenants,* by which the parts of this Body Politique were at first made, set together, and united, resemble that *Fiat,* or the *Let us make man,* pronounced by God in the Creation.

Anthropomorphism was a dominant note in the system of Hobbes; it was carried to an extreme which Grotius, freely as he used the analogy, would unquestionably have repudiated.[1]

Finally, Hobbes propounded a conception of sovereignty as supreme and unlimited power[2] that was more extreme than anything which had been defended previously. He made the will of the state the source and criterion of all right, thus eliminating all confusion as to the relation of the sovereign to the laws of God, of nature, and of nations. So far as subjects were concerned, the sovereign's judgment was the law of God, the law of nature, and the law of nations. Thus all of Grotius' efforts to hedge in the sovereign by the law of nations were cast aside, while the theoretical perfection of absolutism was attained.

These were the salient features of Hobbes' philosophy which had the most significant influence upon the theory of the law of nations. By substituting the word " states " for the word " men " in what he said about natural law, natural right, the state of nature, and natural equality, it is possible to form a series of postulates strikingly similar to those which dominated thought on international relations for the next two centuries. So far as he considered the law of nations at all, this was precisely what Hobbes suggested. He

---

[1] Cf., for example, remarks of Grotius in *De jure belli ac pacis,* I, 3, 7, and II, 6, 4.

[2] *Dominion,* VI, 18, in *English Works,* II, 88; *Leviathan,* Pt. II, ch. 18, pp. 120–128.

declared that states, once instituted, " do put on the personal proprieties of men," [1] and that with respect to each other they were in a natural condition analogous to that prevailing among men in the state of nature.[2] It followed that the same law

which speaking of the duty of single men we call *natural*, being applied to whole cities and nations, is called the *right of nations*. And the same elements of *natural law and right*, which have hitherto been spoken of, being transferred to *whole cities* and *nations*, may be taken for the elements of the *laws* and *right of nations*.[3]

In other words, the law of nature and the law of nations were the same thing. Thus Hobbes prepared the way for the reception into the law of nations of the theory of natural equality. With him the premises were complete. It remained for another to formulate the obvious conclusion that states are equal by the law and right of nature.

Pufendorf and the Naturalists

The work of Hobbes placed him at once among the foremost political thinkers. His theories became the center of

---

[1] *Dominion*, XIV, 4, in *English Works*, II, 186.

[2] *English Works*, II, preface, p. xv; *Dominion*, XIII, 7, in *English Works*, II, p. 169. Ward says that Hobbes seems to have been the first to think of the state of nature as the foundation of a system of law. *Law of Nations*, I, 5. Figgis thinks that there was much to be said for the idea that the state of international relations was a state of nature in the days of Hobbes. *Gerson to Grotius*, pp. 96, 114. Read what l'abbé de Saint-Pierre said in the preface to his *L'abregé du projet de paix perpetuelle*.

[3] *Dominion*, XIV, 4, in *English Works*, II, 186. See also *Leviathan*, Pt. II, ch. 30, p. 257. The passage quoted from the essay on dominion is the one that is cited as *De cive*, XIV, 4, by all the naturalists from Pufendorf on: " Rursus *naturalis* dividi potest, in naturalem *hominum*, quae sola obtinuit dici *lex natura*, et naturalem *civitatum*, quae dici potest *lex Gentium*, vulgo autem *jus Gentium* appellatur. Praecepta utriusque eadem sunt: sed quia civitates semel institutae induunt proprietates hominum personales, *lex* quam loquentes de hominum singulorum officio, *naturalem* dicimus, applicata totis civitatibus, nationibus, sive gentibus, vocatur *jus Gentium*. Et quae *Legis et juris naturalis* Elementa hactenus tradita sunt, translata ad *civitates et gentes* integras, pro *legum* et *juris Gentium* Elementis sumi possunt."

animated controversy as well as the source of enormous influence throughout western Europe. In 1658, Samuel von Pufendorf spent eight months in a Danish prison, without access to books, meditating on what he had read in Hobbes and Grotius.[1] Several years afterward he published a ponderous volume entitled *De Jure Naturæ et Gentium*,[2] in which he combined many of the theories of Hobbes with a large part of the practical code elaborated by Grotius.[3] Where Grotius had united the inductive and the deductive methods to produce a practical system leavened with a rational idealism, Pufendorf constantly subordinated the actual state of international relations to *a priori* assumptions and unreal conclusions. In an interesting comparison of the work of the two publicists, Barbeyrac has pointed out that where Grotius touched only incidentally upon such topics as natural right, natural equality, and the state of nature, Pufendorf devoted carefully planned chapters to these subjects, that where Grotius used the natural law only to support his conclusions on particular questions, Pufendorf elaborated a complete system of the laws of nature.[4] Where Pufendorf

---

[1] Barbeyrac's Pufendorf, préf., § 30.

[2] Pufendorf lived 1632–1694. His *De jure naturæ et gentium* was first published in 1672. Materials for what follows have been taken from the Amsterdam edition of 1704, Barbeyrac's French translation, and the English translation by Basil Kennett. An abridged edition, entitled *De officiis hominis et civis juxta legem naturalem*, appeared in 1673. See Avril, in Pillet, *Les fondateurs*, pp. 331–383; Franck, *Réformateurs*, pp. 333–343; Phillipson, in Macdonell and Manson, *Great Jurists*, pp. 305–344.

[3] Avril says: "Son maître de philosophie avec lequel il ne reste pas toujours en parfaite communion, ce fut Hobbes. Son maître pour la jurisprudence ne fut autre que Grotius." Pillet, *Les fondateurs*, p. 378. According to Dunning, "Pufendorf's system reveals most distinctly the influence of his two great predecessors, and in general it may be said to be directed toward a conciliation of their conflicting views. Where his philosophy is concerned with the concepts of ethics, he clearly leans to the principles of Grotius; where he takes up more purely political topics, the Hobbesian doctrine assumes the more conspicuous place." *Political Theories from Luther to Montesquieu*, p. 318. Hély says: "Que fait-il ? il mêle aux idées de Grotius quelques opinions de Hobbes, et c'est tout." *Étude*, p. 214.

[4] Barbeyrac's Pufendorf, préf., § 31. See extract from this section, *supra*,

differed from Grotius his opinion was usually traceable to the influence of Hobbes.

An important part of *De Jure Naturæ et Gentium* was devoted to a detailed exposition of the law of nature. Pufendorf rejected Grotius' definition of law, and followed Hobbes in defining it as the injunction or command " by which a sovereign obliges a subject to conform his actions to what he prescribes." [1] His classification of law as either divine or human with reference to its source, and natural or positive with reference to its subject-matter,[2] was also borrowed from Hobbes. Pufendorf rejected Grotius' definition of natural law as only leading around in an inconclusive circle.[3] He defined it himself as that universal and perpetual law which is deliberately ordained by the will of God, is " so exactly congruous with the rational and social nature of man that human kind can not maintain an honest and peaceful society without it," and is capable of being discovered by unperverted human reason.[4]

The state of nature was the starting-point for an important part of Pufendorf's theory. He used the notion in two senses; the first analytical, indicating " such a state as we may conceive man to be placed in by his bare nativity, when abstraction is made of all the rules and institutions, either of human invention, or of the suggestion and revelation of Heaven ";[5] the second historical, as describing an actual

p. 43. It is sometimes said that Pufendorf was to Grotius what the systematizer is to the inventor, what, for illustration, Wolff was to Leibnitz in the domain of international law. See Franck, *Réformateurs*, p. 336; Phillipson, in Macdonell and Manson, *Great Jurists*, p. 315. The comparison seems misleading, however, in view of the fundamental difference between their theories of international relations and the law of nations. See Wildman, *Institutes*, I, 22–29.

[1] I, 2, 6; I, 6, 1–4; I, 6, 14.   [2] I, 6, 18.

[3] II, 3, 4. Barbeyrac thought the difference between their definitions one of words only, and that both traced natural law ultimately to the will of God. See his notes to this section in his translation of Pufendorf.

[4] I, 6, 13 and 18; II, 3, where the definition is developed in great detail.

[5] II, 2, 1.

condition which had prevailed at some time among each of
the various races of men.[1] In either case, he understood by
the state of nature a condition characterized by the absence
of common political organization, a certain community of
goods, and a perfect equality of natural rights.[2] Of equality
in the natural state he said:

And in this respect likewise, the state we are treating of has obtained the name of natural liberty; inasmuch as, antecedent to all
human pact and deed, every man is conceived to be perfectly in his
own power and disposal, and not to be controlled by the pleasure or
authority of any other. On which account, too, every man may be
thus acknowledged equal to every man, since all subjection and all
command are equally banished on both sides.[3]

No man could presume to give sentence in his own controversy " because of that equality which is essential to the state
of nature." [4] Contrary to Hobbes' opinion, Pufendorf held
that the state of nature was normally one of peace, since men
were rational beings from the beginning, and since the dictates of reason guided them before as well as after the formation of political societies.[5] So he could argue that the law
of nature prevailed in the natural state, operating to make
men keep their covenants and observe the rights of others.

Aristotle's dogma of inequality was refuted by Pufendorf,
who asserted the natural equality of men [6] in no uncertain
terms:

Since then human nature agrees equally to all persons, and since no
one can live a sociable life with another, who does not own and respect him as a man; it follows as a command of the law of nature,

[1] I, 1, 7; II, 2, 4; VII, 1, 7; VII, 2, 21.

[2] I, 1, 7 and 16; II, 2; IV, 4, 5; V, 13, 2.

[3] II, 2, 3 (Kennett's transl. somewhat revised).

[4] V, 13, 2. " Nam si vel maxime cupiat, idque vel juratus protestetur, se
pronunciaturum, quod sibi justum fuerit visum: cum tamen alter pari dignatione
suam sententiam æstimare queat, ubi eas contingat discrepare, propter æquali-
tatem, status naturalis comitem, nihil agetur."

[5] II, 2, 9; VII, 6, 2.   [6] III, 2.

that every man should esteem and treat another as one who is naturally his equal, or who is a man as well as he. . . .

. . . For as in well-order'd commonwealths, one subject may exceed another in riches, or in honour, but all are equal sharers in the common liberty; so under this regulation of nature, how much soever a man may surpass his neighbors, as to bodily or intellectual endowments, he is still obliged to pay all natural duties, as readily and as fully as he expects to receive them; nor do those advantages give him the least power or privilege to oppress his fellows. Nor, on the other side, does the bare unkindness of nature, or of fortune, set a man in a worse condition than others, as to the enjoyment of common rights. . . .

And this equality we may call an equality of right; the principle from which it springs is this, that the obligation to a social life equally binds all men, inasmuch as it is the inseparable companion of human nature, considered simply as such.[1]

Hobbes' anthropomorphic description of the state reappeared in Pufendorf;[2] and the notion which it represented had an important influence on the latter's theory of the law of nations. His definition of the state was obviously due to the influence of Hobbes:

It is a compound moral person, whose will, united and tied together by those covenants which before passed among the multitude, is deemed the will of all; to the end, that it may use and apply the strength and riches of private persons towards maintaining the common peace and security.[3]

On the other hand, he took his theory of sovereignty from Grotius.[4] This circumstance seems to have been overlooked by those who have attributed the origin of the principle of state equality to the idea of unlimited sovereignty developed by Bodin and Hobbes. Limitation was entirely compatible with Pufendorf's understanding of sovereignty. His sover-

---

[1] Extracts from III, 2, 1–2 (Kennett's transl.).

[2] VII, 2, 13.

[3] VII, 2, 13 (Kennett's transl.). Cf. Hobbes, *Dominion*, V, 9, in *English Works*, II, 69.

[4] VII, 2–9.

eign was supreme but not absolute; he followed Grotius in recognizing that external sovereignty might be diminished by compact, or as a result of conquest, without being extinguished.[1] He derived the idea that states are equal from other sources.

Thus Pufendorf accepted and developed in greater detail certain of the most important, so far as the law of nations was concerned, of the Hobbesian premises. The principle of state equality was the inevitable conclusion. He defined the state as " a compound moral person," and asserted an absolute parity between the state as an artificial person and the natural man.[2] Thus he was enabled to assimilate the rights and obligations of states to those of natural persons, a point of vast importance to a philosopher who cared more about systematic perfection than about the realities of international relationships. The opinion of Hobbes that the law of nature and the law of nations were the same thing was accepted without qualification:

This opinion we, for our part, readily subscribe to: nor do we conceive that there is any other voluntary or positive law of nations, properly invested with a true and legal force, and obliging as the ordinance of a superior power.[3]

Pufendorf subscribed just as readily to the further opinion of Hobbes that separate states, having no common political superior, stood to each other in the same mutual relation as men in the state of nature.[4]

[1] VIII, 9, 4.

[2] II, 3, 23. Cf. Mackintosh, *Discourse*, p. 44; Twiss, *Law of Nations*, p. 4; Westlake, *Collected Papers*, p. 65.

[3] II, 3, 23 (Kennett's transl.).

[4] II, 2, 1; II, 2, 4; II, 2, 11; VII, 1, 8; VIII, 4, 17–18; VIII, 6, 1; VIII, 10, 2. See Ward, *Law of Nations*, I, 4 ff.; Westlake, *Collected Papers*, p. 11. Of the theory of a state of nature, and its application to international relations, Ward remarks: " This Theory, though often started, and beautifully amplified by the ancient Poets, seems first to have been thought of *as the foundation of a system of Law*, by *Hobbs*, in his famous Book called the Leviathan, in which there is so much

Thus of old, when mankind was divided into distinct families, and now since they are fallen into separate communities, those might have been then, and may now be said to live mutually in a state of nature, neither of whom obey the others, and who do not acknowledge any common master among men. . . . So that commonwealths, and the governors thereof may fairly declare themselves to be in a state of natural liberty, while they are furnished with sufficient strength to secure the exercise of that grand privilege.[1]

Finally, he deduced the conclusion from these premises that states are naturally equal.[2] He could see no virtue in a league to enforce universal peace:

For by such a league or bond, nothing is superadded to the obligation of the law of nature; . . . For we suppose both parties to remain in a natural equality, and consequently not to be held to their covenant by any other tie, than that of reverence towards God Almighty, and fear of such evil as may fall on them, if they break the agreement.[3]

It was evident enough to Pufendorf that states *quæ invicem in statu naturali vivunt* must have equal rights. He rejected as specious the common stock of arguments in favor of precedence, such as antiquity, the extent, riches and power of dominion, the quality of the sovereign power, the magnificence of titles, and the like. Antiquity could not produce a perfect right for " all kingdoms are by their own nature free and independent."[4] Neither could unlimited sovereign power have such an effect, because sovereign princes

must look upon another prince's absolute power, as it relates to them, to be no more than liberty of nature, which in itself gives no man preeminence to another not subject to him.[5]

to admire, and so much to condemn. — It was adopted, and considerably enlarged by *Pufendorf*, and instantly approved of by writers without number."

[1] II, 2, 4 (Kennett's transl. somewhat revised).

[2] II, 2, 4; II, 2, 11; V, 13, 7; VIII, 4, 15–18; VIII, 4, 22; VIII, 6, 10 and 14.

[3] II, 2, 11 (Kennett's transl.). The words quoted applied to natural persons, but Pufendorf held the same doctrine applicable to separate states.

[4] VIII, 4, 17.

[5] VIII, 4, 19 (Kennett's transl.).

Claims to precedence based upon superiority in wealth or power were also rejected:

For where liberty is equal, a disproportion in wealth can make no difference. And therefore, if one prince's territories be six hundred miles in extent, and another's but one hundred, yet the difference in the kingdoms makes none between the sovereigns; for their power is of the same nature in the greater and in the less; and the one may answer the ends of government as well as the other.[1]

Pufendorf suggested that in order to solve the problem of precedence *inter plures æquales*, members might take their places in a common assembly in the order in which they were admitted.[2]

Thus for the first time the principle of state equality was expressly derived from the application of familiar theories of natural law, the state of nature, and natural equality to separate states, and was stated with some approach to precision. The writings of Pufendorf enjoyed an immense success. For nearly a century a majority of the continental writers on the law of nature and of nations acknowledged his leadership. Through the influence of Pufendorf and his successors among the naturalists the natural equality of states became an established principle of international law.

Pufendorf lived to see his theory of the law of nations accepted and proclaimed by a group of distinguished teachers and jurists, among whom no one was more illustrious than the great German jurist and philosopher, Christian Thomasius.[3] According to Thomasius, the law of nations was simply

---

[1] VIII, 4, 18 (Kennett's transl.). " Libertas quippe in æquo posita est, quæ magnitudine opum hautquidquam distinguitur. Pateat igitur unius imperium per sexcenta milliaria, alterius per centum duntaxat. Idem tamen imperium hic in modica sua, quam alter in laxiore ditione obtinet: neque hic minus, quam alter finem civitatum institutarum assequitur."

[2] VIII, 4, 22.

[3] Thomasius lived 1655-1728. His *Institutionum jurisprudentiæ divinæ libri tres, in quibus fundamenta juris naturalis secundum hypotheses illustris Pufendorffii perspicue demonstrantur*, etc., was first published in Latin in 1688, while Thomasius was still professor of natural law at Leipzig. References are to the third Latin

the natural law applied to separate states in a condition of natural equality with reference to one another.[1] He conceived of the *societas inter gentes* as a state of nature,[2] and denied the possibility of a positive law of nations among equals:

> If you will notice, you may answer easily those who, with Grotius, regard *Jus Gentium* as a kind of voluntary and indeed of human law. . . . In brief, this is the answer: nations are equal among themselves; neither do they recognize a superior among men. Therefore, they cannot be bound by human law.[3]

Early in the eighteenth century the *De Jure Naturæ et Gentium* of Pufendorf and the *De Jure Belli ac Pacis* of Grotius were done into French with copious notes and a multitude of cross-references by Jean Barbeyrac.[4] The notes of

edition of 1702. See Franck, *Réformateurs*, pp. 344-354; White, *Seven Great Statesmen*, pp. 113-161.

[1] " Poterit *lex Naturalis* non incommodè *dividi* intuitu societatum humanarum naturalium. Nam alia praecepta ejus dirigunt *societatem communem omnium hominum* viventium inter se in statu naturali, seu ut suprà diximus, in statu æqualitatis, quæ hodiè introductis rebuspublicis dicitur societas Gentium, alia dirigunt officia hominum viventium *in civitate* & societatibus sub civitate comprehensis, puta domesticis.

" *Illud* comuniter appellari solet *Jus Gentium*. Posses adeò *hoc* distinctionis gratia nominare *Jus Naturale strictè dictum*." I, 2, 101-102.

[2] III, 1, 49. " Neque convenienter locutos esse opinamur, qui hanc gentium societatem nomine *universalis Reip. omnium hominum* insigniverunt. Non est Resp. sine imperio, at Societas Gentium imperio caret humano, & sola inter naturales in statu post lapsum *æqualis est*." III, 1, 52.

[3] " Facile autem patet, in controversiâ: *Utrum jus Gentium sit species Juris divini, an humani?* ultimum significatum attendi debere. Quod si observaveris, facilè poteris respondere iis, qui cum Grotio *Jus Gentium speciem juris voluntarii* & quidem *humani* faciunt. Illi enim vel mores Gentium, vel jus pro attributo personae sumtum inculcant.

" *Summa eò redit*: Gentes inter se pares sunt, nec inter homines superiorem agnoscunt. Ergo lege humanâ obligari nequeunt." I, 2, 104-105.

[4] Barbeyrac lived 1674-1744. His translation of Pufendorf appeared in 1706-1708 while he was professor of belles-lettres at the French school of Berlin, and of Grotius in 1719, after he became professor of public law at Groningen. References to the two translations are in each case to editions published at Leyden in 1759. Although he wrote no treatise on the law of nations, the salient features of his system may be constructed from the notes to the above translations.

Barbeyrac were soon rendered into English and appended
to contemporary English editions of the two great classics.
His translations were widely read, and it not infrequently
happened that the reader was influenced full as much by the
editor's notes as by the text itself. Now Barbeyrac was a
thoroughgoing naturalist, as might be inferred from his
frankly expressed preference for Pufendorf.[1] His translations
with the notes undoubtedly did much to discredit temporarily certain of the leading principles of Grotius and to spread
the theories of Hobbes and Pufendorf.

Barbeyrac rejected Grotius' definition of law as " a rule of
moral acts obliging to what is right " because it seemed to
insinuate " that the law obliges by itself, and merely as it is
a law, whereas all laws derive their power of obliging from a
superior who makes them." [2] Accordingly, in true Hobbesian
fashion, he denied all binding force to the law of nature independent of the will of God.[3] He held the common naturalist
doctrines with reference to the state of nature [4] and natural
equality,[5] and assumed that these theories were as applicable
to states as to individuals.[6]

Applying the naturalist philosophy to international relations, Barbeyrac denounced Grotius' distinction between the
law of nations and the law of nature as *une pure chimère*.[7]

[1] Barbeyrac's Pufendorf, préf., § 31.   [2] Barbeyrac's Grotius, I, 1, 9, note 3.

[3] *Ibid.*, I, 1, 10, note 4.

[4] Barbeyrac's Pufendorf, II, 2, notes; IV, 4, 1, note 2; Barbeyrac's Grotius,
II, 2, 2, notes.

[5] Barbeyrac's Pufendorf, III, 2, notes; Barbeyrac's Grotius, Proleg. 8, note 1.

[6] Barbeyrac's Pufendorf, III, 2, 9, note 1; VIII, 4, 1, note 1; Barbeyrac's Grotius, I, 1, 14, note 3; III, 2, 2, note 1. It is significant, as showing the true origin
of the idea of state equality, that Barbeyrac's conception of sovereignty was similar
to that of Grotius and Pufendorf.

[7] Barbeyrac's Grotius, I, 1, 14, note 3. See also Barbeyrac's Pufendorf, préf.,
§ 31, quoted *supra*, p. 44, note 5. Barbeyrac anticipated Wolff in pointing out a
difference in the mode of applying natural law to natural persons and to states.
Barbeyrac's Grotius, I, 1, 14, note 3. He contended that *jus naturale* and *jus
gentium* with the Romans were practically identical. Barbeyrac's Pufendorf, II,
3, 23, note 3; Barbeyrac's Grotius, II, 8, 1, notes 1 and 4.

He argued that custom simply created a presumption that it would be followed unless notice were given to the contrary.[1] Custom could not create true law among equals.[2] Since nations were in a state of nature with reference to one another, they must be in a state of natural equality:

Nations are obliged the more to respect one another as equals because they are always in a state of natural liberty, and consequently in a perfect equality of right toward one another.[3]

The natural equality of states found expression in England later in the century in the *Institutes of Natural Law* of Thomas Rutherforth, a professor of divinity at Cambridge University.[4] The *Institutes* purported to represent the substance of a course of lectures on the *De Jure Belli ac Pacis* of Grotius. However, Rutherforth denied the existence of such a positive law of nations as that of which Grotius had conceived. He justified the classification of international law as positive law only on the ground that an element of consent giving it a positive character could be found in the universal agreement of all nations to recognize the state-

[1] Barbeyrac's Pufendorf, II, 3, 23, note 2; Barbeyrac's Grotius, I, 1, 14, note 3; II, 18, 1, note 1; III, 4, 15, note 1; III, 7, 1, note 2. Thus a sovereign on receiving an embassy might be presumed to submit to established customs unless he expressly declared to the contrary. Similarly, at the outbreak of war a belligerent was presumed to abide by the custom which forbade killing enemies by poison, unless it reserved its liberty and left the other belligerent free to use like means of destruction. The argument was carried to an absurd extreme where he contended, with regard to the custom of enslaving prisoners of war, that the prisoner might declare that he would not be enslaved, thus saving his right and forfeiting his life.

[2] " Mais les Peuples étant tous naturellement égaux les uns aux autres, quand même ils s'accorderoient tous, excepté un seul, à établir certaines Régles, celui-ci, quoiqu' unique, pourroit refuser de s'y soumettre." Barbeyrac's Pufendorf, II, 3, 23, note 2.

[3] " Les Peuples (auxquels on doit aussi appliquer les principes établis dans ce Chapitre) sont d'autant plus obligés à se regarder les uns les autres comme égaux, qu'ils sont toujours dans l'état de la Liberté Naturelle, & par conséquent dans une parfaite égalité de droit les uns par rapport aux autres." Barbeyrac's Pufendorf, III, 2, 9, note 1. The chapter referred to is Pufendorf's chapter on the natural equality of men. See *ibid.*, VIII, 4, 1, note 1.

[4] Rutherforth lived 1712–1771. His *Institutes* was published in 1754–1756.

personality of each.[1] This general agreement of mankind to recognize states as collective moral persons was regarded as the sole foundation for any distinction between the law of nature and the law of nations.   Rutherforth recognized neither usage nor treaties as a source of positive international law.[2] The law of nations was positive only in the manner of applying it.   It was entirely natural in its subject matter:

But the law of nations is positive only in the manner of applying it, and is natural as to its matter: it is the law of nature applied by positive consent, to the artificial persons of civil societies; and, consequently, the dictates of it are only the dictates of right reason, and may be collected by arguing from the nature of things, and from the condition and circumstances of mankind, when they are considered as formed into such societies.[3]

The conclusion that states are naturally equal followed as a matter of course.   Indeed, said Rutherforth, if one understands

what the law of nature is, when it is applied to individual persons in a state of equality, he will seldom be at a loss to judge what it is, when he is to apply it to nations considered as collective persons in a like state of equality.[4]

This process of reasoning, by which the principle of state equality was derived from the application to separate states

---

[1] II, 9, 1.   [2] II, 9,2-4.

[3] II, 9, 5. Cf. the definition of Erskine in his *Principles of the Law of Scotland*. I, 1, 3, also published for the first time in 1754: " The Law of Nations is also the result of reason, and has God for its Author; but it supposes mankind formed into several bodies politic or states; and it comprises all the duties which one state owes to another. These must of necessity be similar to the duties arising between individuals, since both are dictated by reason, so that what is the law of nature when applied to men, considered simply as such, is indeed the law of nations when applied to kingdoms or states." See also, Taylor, *Summary of Roman Law*, p. 53, an abridgment of his *Elements of Civil Law*, first published in 1755; and Blackstone, *Commentaries*, Introd., pp. 39-43.

[4] II, 9, 5. " But since the law of nations is only the law of nature applied to the collective persons of civil societies, and these collective persons are, in respect of one another, in a state of natural equality; if we know what the law of nature would determine in any case between individuals, the law of nations will, in like circumstances, determine in the same manner between civil societies." II, 9, 7.

of the theories of natural law, the state of nature, and natural equality, on an assumed analogy between states and natural persons, was presented in a very lucid statement by Burlamaqui, a celebrated Swiss publicist and teacher, who became one of the most widely influential representatives of the naturalist school in the eighteenth century.[1] His statement may be taken as an excellent summary of the whole case for the naturalists' derivation of the natural equality of states:

Simple human society is of itself and with regard to those who compose it a society of equality and independence. It is subject only to God; no one has a natural and primitive right to command; but each person may dispose of himself and of what he possesses as he thinks proper, under the sole restriction that he keep within the bounds of the natural law and do no wrong to others. . . .

Every society is formed by the concurrence or union of the wills of several persons with a view of acquiring some advantage. Hence it is that societies are considered as bodies and that we give them the name of moral persons, because these bodies are animated in effect by a single will which regulates all their movements. This agrees particularly with the body politic or state. The sovereign is the chief or head, and the subjects the members; all their actions that have any relation to the society are directed by the will of the chief. Wherefore as soon as states are formed they acquire in some manner personal qualities, and we may consequently attribute to them in proportion whatever agrees in particular with men, such as certain actions which are suited to them, certain rights which pertain to them, certain duties which they are bound to fulfil, etc. . . .

This being granted, the establishment of states introduces a kind of society among them, similar to that which exists naturally among men, and the same reasons which induce men to maintain union among themselves ought also to persuade nations or their sovereigns to live on good terms with one another.

It is necessary, therefore, that there should be some law among nations to serve as a rule for mutual intercourse. Now this law can be nothing else but the natural law itself, which is then called the right or law of nations (*droit des gens ou loi des nations*). Natural law, says

---

[1] Burlamaqui lived 1694–1748. His *Principes du droit naturel* was published at Geneva in 1747.

Hobbes very properly, is divided into the natural law of man and the natural law of states, and the latter is what we call the law of nations. Thus the natural law and the law of nations are in reality one and the same thing,[1] and differ only by an external denomination. It should be said, therefore, that the law of nations, properly so called and considered as a law emanating from a superior, is nothing else than the natural law itself applied, not to men regarded simply as such, but to peoples or nations, to states or their chiefs, in the relations they have together and in the interests they have to manage among themselves.

. . . But in order to say something more particular on this subject, let us observe that the natural state of nations with regard to one another is a state of social life and peace. This society is also one of equality and independence, which establishes an equality of right among them, and pledges them to have the same regard and respect for one another. Hence the general principle of the law of nations is nothing more than the general law of sociability, which obliges nations having intercourse with one another to the practice of the same duties as those to which individuals are naturally subject.[2] . . .

When Professor Félice published a new edition of Burlamaqui's works twenty years later, he revised the chapter on equality and added some phrases of his own and others from Vattel, presenting a concise statement of the principle in language very much like that which was to pass from publicist to publicist during the succeeding century:

Natural equality being the basis of all the duties of sociability, we start from this very principle in order to expound them. Hence, this same principle should guide us also in the exposition of the reciprocal duties and rights of nations. Indeed, as men are naturally equal, and as nations are composed only of men, and are considered as being moral persons who enjoy perfect liberty, it follows that they ought to regard one another as naturally equal. The strength or weakness of any one of them does not make any difference in this respect; just as a dwarf is as much a man as a giant, so a small republic is no less a sovereign state than the most powerful kingdom; and, consequently, all the

---

[1] Burlamaqui followed Barbeyrac in assuming that the Roman *jus naturale* and *jus gentium* were the same. *Principes*, p. 226, note 1.

[2] The above extracts are from Pt. II, ch. 6, §§ 1, 4, 5, 7, pp. 218 ff.

rights assumed by the great kingdoms, such as France or Spain, belong also to the republics of Lucca and of San Marino, and all the duties which these republics are obliged to perform are no less obligatory on the kingdoms of France and of Spain.[1]

At the end of the seventeenth century the followers of Pufendorf were the predominant school on the continent of Europe. During the eighteenth century many of their doctrines were taken over by other schools and so passed into the common stock of speculation on the law of nations. This was the case with the principle of state equality and with a good deal of the theory that was associated with it.[2]

THE TENDENCY TOWARD POSITIVISM

The positivists held a different conception of the law of nations, viewing it as preëminently a law of human institution derived from custom, treaties, and the common understanding of nations. While they did not always ignore the law of nature, they usually appealed to it in the guise of reason, or as modified by usage, or as an additional sanction for the positive law of nations. There was relatively little of the abstract and the *a priori* in their treatises.

The positivist tendency was foreshadowed in the work of Gentilis. The first manual of the positive law of nations was the *Juris et Judicii Feciales, sive Juris Inter Gentes*, etc. of Richard Zouche, professor of law at Oxford and judge of the High Court of Admiralty.[3] Zouche recognized the suprem-

[1] Burlamaqui, *Principes du droit de la nature et des gens*, etc., ed. by Félice, new edition by Dupin, IV, p. 434. See *ibid.*, *Sentimens de l'éditeur*, IV, p. x.

[2] Whatever may be the present opinion with reference to the teachings of the naturalists, it hardly seems wise, in view of their important contributions to the modern law of nations, to insist on relegating them to that " limbo of forgotten authors " to which Mr. Abdy consigns Pufendorf, Burlamaqui, Rutherforth, and all their kind. Abdy's Kent, p. 35.

[3] Zouche lived 1590–1660. His manual was first published at Oxford in 1650. References are to parts, sections, and paragraphs, and the page references are to J. L. Brierly's translation in Vol. II of the edition published in the Classics of International Law. Consult also Ompteda, *Litteratur*, pp. 252–265; Phillipson, in

acy of conventional law over the natural. His law between nations comprised both an unwritten law founded on custom and a written law based upon treaties and conventions.[1] It was defined as

the law which is recognized in the community of different princes or peoples who hold sovereign power — that is to say, the law which has been accepted among most nations by customs in harmony with reason, and that upon which single nations agree with one another, and which is observed by nations at peace and by those at war.[2]

Zouche made a systematic use of precedents and examples, including many that were modern. He did not undertake a scientific development of doctrine or indulge in abstract generalizations which could not be applied to actual conditions. So great was his aversion to dogmatic finality that he made it his plan to analyze precedents, state the issues raised, and refrain from adding his own opinion one way or the other.[3]

There was no place in a manual conceived in such a spirit for an elaboration of the natural equality of states. Zouche did remark that peace was of two kinds — the *pax moralis* between superiors and inferiors, as between the head of a family and its members, and the *pax civilis* between equals, as states.[4] He also borrowed from Grotius the dictum of Thucydides that colonists are not sent out to be slaves but to have equal rights.[5] Elsewhere, however, he recognized inequalities of dignity and precedence [6] as well as inequalities of sovereignty or status. Zouche conceived of sovereignty as " universal and supreme power of deciding questions concerning the community between nations both in peace and

---

Macdonell and Manson, *Great Jurists*, pp. 220–247; Scelle, in Pillet, *Les Fondateurs*, pp. 269–330.

[1] I, 1, 1, p. 1.
[2] I, 1, 1 (Brierly's transl.).
[3] To the reader, p. vii.
[4] I, 1, 3, p. 2. See also II, 2, 6, p. 65.
[5] II, 2, 8, p. 66.
[6] I, 4, 1, pp. 12 ff.; I, 4, 2, 2, p. 18; I, 5, 3, p. 29.

in war," [1] but it was not so supreme that it could not be qualified without being destroyed.[2] Thus sovereign states might be in subjection by right of clientship or dependency and yet remain sovereign:

> Free peoples are in subjection by right of *clientship* or dependency, who have bound themselves to loyalty and homage for the sake of protection. . . .
>
> . . . *Clients* differ from *vassals* in this respect, that *vassals* are under the dominion and sovereignty of a supreme lord, whereas princes and peoples who are clients of others, are not under their sovereignty. Thus the jurist Proculus says: " We regard our clients as free, although neither in authority, nor dignity, nor in any of their rights are they our equals." [3]

In brief, Zouche recognized the legal significance of actual inequalities. In sections on the law of status among those at peace and at war, although he limited himself to rudimentary distinctions, he at least suggested that the law of status might constitute an important part of the law of nations.[4] As a positivist Zouche did not dilate upon that equality of natural right which prevails in a state of nature. Searching for the principles that actually determined the conduct of separate states, this disciple of Gentilis and Grotius discovered inequalities of legal capacity which he recognized as having the force of law.

Later in the seventeenth century there appeared in Germany a vigorous protest against the school of natural law. Rachel [5] and Textor [6] denounced the naturalist doctrines.[7]

.[1] I, 1, 2, p. 2.   [2] I, 4, 4, p. 25; I, 7, 2, p. 35.
[3] I, 8, 6, p. 43 (Brierly's transl.); II, 2, 4, p. 64.
[4] II, 2, pp. 61 ff.
[5] Rachel lived 1628–1691. His *De jure naturæ et gentium* was published in 1676. References are to the edition in the Classics of International Law, and page references are to J. P. Bate's translation in Vol. II. See Nys, *Le droit int.*, I, 259.
[6] Textor lived 1637–1701. His *Synopsis juris gentium* was published in 1670. References are to the edition in the Classics of International Law, and page references are to J. P. Bate's translation in Vol. II.
[7] Rachel, I, 3a, 7a; Textor, I, 3a.

Their law of nations was founded upon the law of nature as
modified by custom and by express compact.[1] Thus Rachel,
in the course of his refutation of the naturalists, declared
that even if

one free Nation is not the superior of another, and one can not lay
down Law specially so called for another, yet if they choose to bind
themselves by pacts, they are reciprocally bound just as if by true
Law; so that, should one of them break faith, it by that very fact
makes the other or others its superior so far as that they can compel
it to keep faith.[2]

Rachel accordingly defined the law of nations as

a law developed by the consent or agreement, either expressly or tacitly
given, of many free nations, whereby for the sake of utility they are
mutually bound to one another.[3]

This law of nations was purely arbitrary and might be quite
at variance with the law of nature.[4] Indeed, it might establish as legally just things which would be absolutely condemned in the forum of conscience. Neither Rachel nor
Textor developed the principle of state equality. They apparently regarded separate states as equal so far as the natural law was concerned,[5] but took it for granted that natural
equality could be modified by the positive law of nations
founded on consent.[6]

Bynkershoek [7] in the next century derived the law of nations from reason and usage. Notwithstanding his assertion

[1] See Rachel, *De jure naturæ*, § 20, p. 11; § 33, p. 20; § 58, p. 37; *De jure
gentium*, § 4, p. 158; § 5, p. 159; § 10, p. 163; § 16, p. 170; and Textor, ch. 2,
pp. 8–12.

[2] *De jure gentium*, § 91, p. 208 (Bate's transl.).

[3] *Ibid.*, § 16, p. 170 (Bate's transl.).

[4] *Ibid.*, § 5, p. 159; § 56, p. 190.

[5] Rachel, *De jure naturæ*, § 135, p. 94.

[6] Rachel, *De jure gentium*, §§ 2–3, p. 157. Textor recognized degrees of status
among princes or peoples in what he called " quasi-possession of sovereign power."
See ch. 14, pp. 134–150; ch. 16, pp. 159–166; ch. 20, pp. 216–231.

[7] Bynkershoek lived 1673–1743. His *De foro legatorum* appeared in 1702, *De
dominio maris* in 1721, and *Quæstiones juris publici* in 1737.

that *ratio ipsa Juris Gentium est anima*,[1] he relied mainly upon custom as expressed in treaties or the practice of nations, and thus gave an increased impetus to the positivist tendency. He wrote no general treatise on the law of nations, nor did he develop the principle of state equality.[2]

The leading exponents of the positivist tendency in the eighteenth century were the great German jurists, Moser[3] and Georg Friedrich von Martens.[4] Moser may be regarded as the founder of the modern positivist school. He disclaimed all intention of writing a treatise on the natural or philosophical law of nations, confining himself to the exposition of *ein würckliches Europäisches Völkerrecht* derived from custom and treaties.[5] Moser based equality upon sovereignty as the factor which determines status. He said nothing of natural law, the state of nature, or natural equality. That lack of precision with reference to the notion of sovereignty which had characterized the treatises of Grotius, Zouche, Pufendorf, and many others among the earlier writers was avoided by classifying states into those that were sovereign and those that were semi-sovereign.[6] The benevolent vagueness of a theory of state equality based upon conceptions of international personality, the state of nature, and natural right was cleared away by expressly limiting the application of the principle to fully sovereign states:[7]

[1] *Quæstiones*, I, 2, 10. Read what he says in *Ad lectorum*.

[2] There is some evidence in his work of the influence of naturalist theory, as where he speaks of war as a contest between independent persons: " Ait definitio, eorum, qui suae potestatis sunt. Sive nempe Gentium, sive singulorum hominum, ubi nulla est Civitas: iidem quippe tunc utrique sunt, . . ." *Quæstiones*, I, 1, 2.

[3] Moser lived 1701–1785. His *Versuch des neuesten europäischen Völker-rechts in Friedens- und Kriegs-Zeiten* was published in 1777–1780. References are to parts, books, chapters, and sections.

[4] G. F. von Martens lived 1756–1821. His *Précis du droit des gens* was published in 1788. References are to Charles Vergé's 2d edition.

[5] Vorläuffige Abhandlung, § 1.

[6] I, 1, 1. Moser was apparently the first to make systematic use of the term *semi-sovereign*. See his *Beyträge zu dem neuesten europäischen Völckerrecht in Fridens-Zeiten*, I, 508. Cf. Textor, *supra*, p. 92, note 6.

[7] I, 1, 2.

A state that is independent, that is, one over which no other state or ruler has any authority, is called sovereign. . . .

Independence gives equal rights. As regards the rights resulting from independence all fully sovereign states are equal to one another; on the other hand, semi-sovereign states are unequal to sovereign.[1]

Thus the principle of state equality was stated with new precision and from a new point of view. Moser did not regard states as equal because they were international persons in a state of nature and hence endowed with the same natural rights. He accredited states with an equality of legal capacity when they enjoyed the same status and not otherwise; and he undertook to discover how many kinds of legal status actually existed among international persons. Moser developed, to be sure, only the most rudimentary distinctions with reference to status; but the notion of semi-sovereignty was a contribution which at least suggested the importance of the law of persons in international jurisprudence.

Martens' positivism was not quite so uncompromising. He recognized a natural law of nations which consisted of the law of nature modified and applied to states regarded as persons living in a state of nature.[2] According to the natural law states like individuals enjoyed a perfect equality of natural rights:

Among nations as among individuals there is a perfect equality of natural and absolute rights, that is, apart from diversity of territory, of population, of strength, of religion, of constitution, of the antiquity of the established government, all have the same right to undertake whatever is consistent with the independence of others, and in the unrestricted state no one has a right to coerce others into any positive act whatever in its favor.[3]

---

[1] "Ein Staat heisst souverain, welcher unabhängig ist, das ist, dem kein anderer Staat oder Herr in weltlichen Sachen etwas zu befehlen hat." I, 1, 1, 1.

"Die Unabhängigkeit gibt gleiche Rechte. In Absicht auf die aus der Unabhängigkeit herfliessende Rechte seind alle ganz souveraine Staaten einander gleich; die halbsouveraine hingegen ihnen ungleich." I, 1, 2, 2.

[2] §§ 1 ff., I, 31 ff.   [3] § 125, I, 337.

Martens contended, however, that the natural law had been found insufficient among civilized states, with the result that a positive law of nations founded upon custom and convention had modified that perfect equality of rights established by the law of nature.[1] From this point his position was similar to that of Moser whom he credited with having revived the study of the positive law of nations.[2] Martens' manual was a summary of positive law. He admitted that in actual practice weaker states were frequently unable to exercise that liberty which the natural law attributed to them,[3] and argued for the recognition of at least a few differences of status among international persons.[4]

THE ECLECTICS OR GROTIANS

The difference between the positivists and the eclectics was not always sharply drawn. G. F. von Martens, for illustration, combined an eclectic theory with the substance of positivism. In general, the eclectics adopted a twofold division into the natural or necessary law of nations, which consisted of the law of nature applied to nations, and the voluntary or positive law of nations founded on consent. This in substance was the viewpoint of Leibnitz in the preface of his *Codex Juris Gentium Diplomaticus*.[5] The most illustrious advocate of this point of view was Christian von Wolff,[6] distinguished German jurist and philosopher. Wolff made two significant contributions to the theory of the law

[1] §§ 6 ff., I, 45 ff.   [3] § 119, I, 320.
[2] § 13, I, 68.   [4] §§ 18 ff., I, 91 ff.

[5] Leibnitz lived 1646–1716. His *Codex*, a collection of treaties and state papers preceded by a brief preface in which Leibnitz stated his views on the law of nations, was published in 1693. His *Mantissa codicis juris gentium diplomatici*, a supplement to the *Codex*, appeared in 1700. See Macdonell, in Macdonell and Manson, *Great Jurists*, pp. 283–304.

[6] Wolff lived 1679–1754. His *Jus naturæ* was published 1740–48, and his *Jus gentium* in 1749. The *Institutiones*, an abridgment of the latter work, appeared in 1750. See Olive, in Pillet, *Les fondateurs*, pp. 447–479; Twiss, *Law of Nations, passim;* Westlake, *Collected Papers*, pp. 70–76; Wheaton, *History*, pp. 176–182.

of nations: first, he pointed out that the law of nature could not be applied to separate states in the same way that it applied to natural persons, but must be adapted to the peculiar character of its subjects; second, he based the voluntary law of nations upon the existence of a great commonwealth or *civitas maxima* of which all civilized nations were members.[1] From the point of view of the natural or necessary law of nations states were to be regarded as so many free persons living in a state of nature; from the point of view of the *jus voluntarium* they were members of the *civitas maxima*. Wolff based the equality of states upon the natural or necessary law of nations. His explanation of the principle was practically identical with that of the naturalists:

> All nations are equal by nature. They are regarded as free individual persons living in a state of nature. Wherefore, since all men are naturally equal, all nations are also naturally equal. . . .
>
> Whereas all nations are equal by nature, and men are equal in a moral sense whose rights and obligations are the same, so by nature all nations have the same rights and obligations.[2]

No more lucid statement of the naturalist's explanation of state equality need be desired than that which is to be found in the work of Wolff. So far as this principle was concerned there was no real difference between the theories of the naturalists and of the eclectics. Wolff drew a complete parallel

---

[1] *Jus gentium, præfatio; Institutiones*, §§ 1088, 1090. Wolff distinguished the conventional and the customary from the voluntary law of nations. *Institutiones*, §§ 1091–1092. See Despagnet, *Cours*, § 32, p. 33.

[2] *Jus Gentium*, proleg., §§ 16–17. " C'était répéter l'enseignement des jurisconsultes du temps des Antonins: *Omnes homines natura æquales sunt.*" Nys, *Le droit int.*, II, 235. An equally lucid statement is to be found in Wolff's *Institutiones*, § 1089: " Vi Juris Gentium necessarii gentium omnium eadem est obligatio, eadem sunt jura ac ideo omnes natura æquales, nulli prærogativa aliqua nec præcedentia competit. Nulli jus est in actiones alterius singularum est libertas cujus usus non impediendus a gente alia. Nulla gens alteram lædere, seu jus perfectam ipsius violare debet seu injuriam facere & adversus injuriam intentatam jus defendendi adversus factam jus puniendi competit unicuique. Et præterea singulis quoque gentibus competit jus alias ad certas præstationes sibi obligandi, & per consequens jus perfectum acquirendi auferri nescium ac denique jus belli."

between man and the state, each in a state of nature, and concluded that the same principles in regard to equality applied in each case.[1] Wolff's theories were given wider currency through the work of his brilliant admirer, Emerich de Vattel.[2] Like his great master, Vattel treated the natural law of nations as a separate science consisting of a just and rational application of the law of nature to independent states. This constituted the necessary and immutable law of nations.[3] On other points, however, Vattel's theory represented a retrograde movement in the history of the science. He rejected Wolff's conception of the *civitas maxima*, and founded the voluntary law of nations upon the presumed consent of nations living in the familiar state of natural liberty.[4] His conception of the state was in many respects analogous to that metaphysical notion of state-being which had dominated the thought of the naturalists.[5] Grotius' distinction between the law of nature and the law of nations was criticized by Vattel, who referred to Hobbes as the first to give a distinct though imperfect idea of true international law. It was the glory of Wolff, in his opinion, to have first indicated the real relation between the natural law of men and of nations.[6] Vattel regarded sovereign states as so many free persons living together in a state of nature,[7] and he asserted their perfect equality in the clearest and most precise of language:

---

[1] Cf. *Institutiones*, Pt. I, ch. 3, and Pt. IV, ch. 1, § 1089.

[2] Vattel lived 1714–1767. His *Le droit des gens, ou principes de la loi naturalle, appliqués à la conduite & aux affaires des nations & des souverains* was published in 1758. References are to the edition in the Classics of International Law, and page references are to C. G. Fenwick's translation in Vol. III. See Mallarmé, in Pillet, *Les fondateurs*, pp. 481–601; Phillipson, in Macdonell and Manson, *Great Jurists*, pp. 477–504.

[3] Preface; Introd., §§ 6–9, p. 4.

[4] Preface; Introd., § 21, p. 7. The conventional law was based upon express consent and the customary law upon tacit consent. Introd., §§ 24–25, p. 8.

[5] *Ibid.*, §§ 1–5, p. 3.

[6] Preface.   [7] Introd., §§ 4 ff., pp. 3 ff.

Since men are by nature equal, and their individual rights and obligations the same, as coming equally from nature, Nations, which are composed of men and may be regarded as so many free persons living together in a state of nature, are by nature equal and hold from nature the same obligations and the same rights. Strength or weakness, in this case, counts for nothing. A dwarf is as much a man as a giant is; a small Republic is no less a sovereign State than the most powerful Kingdom.

From this equality it necessarily follows that what is lawful or unlawful for one Nation is equally lawful or unlawful for every other Nation.

A Nation is therefore free to act as it pleases, so far as its acts do not affect the perfect rights of another Nation, and so far as the Nation is under merely *internal* obligations without any *perfect external* obligation. If it abuse its liberty it acts wrongfully; but other Nations cannot complain, since they have no right to dictate to it.

Since Nations are free, independent, and equal, and since each has the right to decide in its conscience what it must do to fulfil its duties, the effect of this is to produce, before the world at least, a perfect equality of rights among Nations in the conduct of their affairs and in the pursuit of their policies. The intrinsic justice of their conduct is another matter which it is not for others to pass upon finally; so that what one may do another may do, and they must be regarded in the society of mankind as having equal rights.[1]

With the above quotation from Vattel, probably more widely quoted than any other statement of the principle, an account of the origin of state equality and of its early development by the publicists may be appropriately concluded. The equality of states was the logical consequence of Pufendorf's application to international relations of the political and legal philosophy of Thomas Hobbes. It was a creation of those publicists who were dominated by the theories of the naturalist school. It was not developed by the early positivists. It was not until the principle had become well established, for all at least who accepted the naturalist the-

[1] Introd., §§ 18–21, p. 7 (Fenwick's transl.). See Pradier-Fodéré, *Traité*, § 167, I, 286.

ories, that the idea of sovereignty was offered as an analytical explanation. Even then the principle could hardly be explained apart from naturalist philosophy. Moser, to be sure, rejected the whole paraphernalia of naturalism; but Martens recurred to naturalist conceptions as his starting-point in expounding a positivist system. So far as equality was concerned there was no essential difference between the theory of the eclectics, represented by Wolff or Vattel, and the view of the naturalists. Thus the equality of states came down to the nineteenth century grounded upon the natural law, the state of nature, natural equality, and the analogy.

CHAPTER IV

THE PRINCIPLE OF STATE EQUALITY IN THE WRITINGS OF THE MODERN PUBLICISTS

THE COMMON STATEMENT OF THE PRINCIPLE

A majority of the publicists writing in the last century have accepted the equality of states as an essential principle of the law of nations.[1] The common statement has not been greatly improved since the days of Burlamaqui, Moser, and Vattel. In truth, there has been a very obvious tendency to repeat hackneyed expositions, which have passed, as Hobbes would say, " like gaping from mouth to mouth." The result has been an unfortunate ambiguity in both thought and expression with reference to the whole subject. Calvo's *Dictionnaire* contains a statement, made up of extracts from various writers, which is perhaps as good a specimen of the common nineteenth century exposition as can be found:

Equality is one of the natural and primitive rights of nations. It is the right by virtue of which every sovereign State may demand that another State shall not assume more extensive rights, in their mutual relations, than it enjoys itself, and shall not free itself from any of the obligations imposed upon all.

The equality of sovereign states is a generally recognized principle of public law. It has a twofold consequence in that it attributes to all States the same rights and imposes upon them reciprocally the same duties.

Natural relations (*rapports*) among States being everywhere the same, and therefore essential, this equality cannot be affected by the casual qualities or attributes of a State, such as antiquity, population, extent of territory, military power, form of the constitution, title of

---

[1] See Huber, *Die Gleichheit der Staaten*, pp. 90, 104, 105; Nys, *Études*, II, 9-14.

its sovereign, state of civilization, respect which it enjoys, etc. No one of these considerations can justify the least difference or the slightest distinction between nations considered as moral persons; from this point of view all participate alike in international law.

Whatever is lawful or unjust for one State is equally so for all others. Quite apart from diversity of territory, form of government, or other characteristic differences, all States have the same right to undertake whatever is consistent with the independence of others; and, strictly speaking, no State has the right to extort from another any positive act in its favor. In brief, by the equality of nations it is to be understood that the rights of each ought to be respected the same as those of every other, without distinction between nations which are powerful and those which occupy only a secondary place in the list of nations. The weaker State has the same right as the stronger State.

The right of equality of States is the necessary consequence of their sovereignty and of their independence. All States enjoy an independent personality; each may assert all rights which are derived from that personality; consequently, their rights are equal.[1]

The Essential Nature of State Equality

What is the essential nature of this equality of rights ? Is it an attribute of the state, a right of the state, or a principle of the law of nations ? The publicists have not agreed on an answer to this question.[2] There are a few writers who treat equality as what Pradier-Fodéré calls *une manière d'être*, i. e., a fundamental quality or attribute of the state as an international person. Vattel regarded states as equal by nature because they were composed of men who were equal by nature, and consequently could be considered as so

[1] I, 286. The rest of the passage is concerned chiefly with rank and ceremonial. Good discussions along traditional lines are to be found in Calvo, *Le droit int.*, §§ 21 ff., I, 356 ff.; Carnazza Amari, *Trattato*, pp. 276 ff.; Chrétien, *Principes*, §§ 160 ff., pp. 162 ff.; Fiore, *Trattato*, §§ 420 ff., I, 289 ff.; Huber, *Die Gleichheit der Staaten;* Kebedgy, in *Z. S. R.* (1900) Neue Folge, XIX, 84–103; Pradier-Fodéré, *Traité,* §§ 442 ff.; II, 1 ff. See also references cited in the following notes.

[2] Huber, *Die Gleichheit der Staaten*, p. 105; Pradier-Fodéré, *Traité* §§ 443–446, II, 5–8; Streit, in *R. D. I. L. C.* (1900) 2e sér., II, 13.

many free persons living in a state of nature.[1] A modern
version of Vattel's idea appears in several of the leading
authorities of the nineteenth century. F. de Martens includes equality among *les qualités internationales* of states,
which he defines as follows:

> By the international qualities of states we mean the inherent qual-
> ities without which they could not figure in the domain of international
> relations and on which their mutual rights are based.[2]

Substantially the same opinion is held by Pomeroy, who
says:

> It seems possible to refer all primary international rights to two
> sources, existing in the essential characteristics or elements of a state.
> These characteristics or elements are (1st), the fact that each state is
> independent and sovereign, a corporate legal person, a free moral
> agent; and (2d), the fact that all states are equal.[3]

As recent a writer as Oppenheim says:

> The equality before International Law of all member-States of the
> Family of Nations is an invariable quality derived from their Inter-
> national Personality. Whatever inequality may exist between States
> as regards their size, population, power, degree of civilisation, wealth,
> and other qualities, they are nevertheless equals as International
> Persons.[4]

The description of equality as an essential characteristic or
invariable quality of the state is due to the influence of
naturalist theories. It is the consequence of conceiving of
the state as a collective person, having attributes analogous to the attributes of the natural persons of which it is
composed.

The naturalist theory of the law of nations also placed a
great deal of emphasis upon the idea of natural rights. Ac-

---

[1] Introd., § 18.   [2] *Traité*, I, 377, 387 (transl. from French ed.).
[3] *Lectures*, p. 82. See also Woolsey, *Int. Law*, p. 35.
[4] *Int. Law*, I, 168. See also Carnazza Amari, *Trattato*, p. 276; Twiss, *Law of
Nations*, pp. 11, 14, 145; Wheaton, *Elements*, pp. 58, 118.

cordingly, many of the modern publicists regard equality as a natural right, or, what amounts to the same thing, as an absolute, primordial, or fundamental right. Pradier-Fodéré objects to the definition of equality as *une manière d'être*, and concludes that it is a true right.[1] Bonfils likewise insists that " this juridical equality is a true right for states." [2] The difference between this view and the one which regards equality as an attribute or characteristic is not of great significance. By natural or primordial rights the publicists mean essential interests. When an interest becomes so essential that the state cannot endure unless it is safeguarded, it is of little moment whether it be called an attribute or a fundamental right.

The tendency among modern publicists is to avoid all difficulty by describing equality as an essential principle of the law of nations. Many writers who retain a naturalist terminology and classification really treat equality as a principle, rather than a natural right or an essential attribute. It is presented as a principle by the ablest of modern publicists, including Bluntschli, Phillimore, Rivier, and others.[3]

The Juridical Significance of State Equality

Whatever the terms with which publicists may attempt to define equality in the law of nations, it is of supreme im-

---

[1] *Traité*, §§ 184, 442, I, 307, II, 5.

[2] *Manuel*, §§ 272, 241, pp. 162, 142. See also Calvo, *Dictionnaire*, I, 286; Despagnet, *Cours*, § 165, p. 217; Field, *Int. Code*, § 16, p. 10; Fiore, *Trattato*, § 361, I, 245; Hershey, *Essentials*, p. 155; Klüber, *Droit des gens*, § 89, p. 132; Nys, *Le droit int.*, II, 235; Piédelièvre, *Précis*, § 267, I, 244.

[3] Bluntschli, *Völkerrecht*, § 81, p. 96; Calvo, *Le droit int.*, § 210, I, 356; Carnazza Amari, *Trattato*, p. 276; Cobbett, *Cases*, I, 50; Chrétien, *Principes*, §§ 163, 176, pp. 165, 177; Halleck, *Int. Law*, p. 97; Heffter, *Völkerrecht*, § 26, p. 47; Holtzendorff, *Handbuch*, § 3, II, 11 ; Huber, *Die Gleichheit der Staaten;* Kebedgy, in *Z. S. R.* (1900) Neue Folge, XIX, 84–103; Kent, *Commentaries*, I, 21; Neumann, *Eléments*, § 8, 28; Nys, *Études*, II, 9; Phillimore, *Commentaries*, I, 216; Rivier, *Principes*, I, 124; Walker, *Manual*, p. 11. Several of the writers cited in note 2 above really treat equality as a principle.

portance that there be a common understanding with reference to its juridical significance, as well as adequate means of expressing that significance so that it can be understood. Unfortunately, there is an extraordinary confusion of thought and of statement on this point in the books. It was suggested at the beginning of the first chapter that equality among persons subject to law may mean either an equality of protection in the enjoyment of rights or an equality of capacity for rights. In systems of municipal law the former principle is usually described as " equality before the law," or as " equal protection of the law," while the latter principle is called simply an equality of rights or of capacity. There seems to be no adequate terminology in the law of nations whereby these two principles may be defined and distinguished. " Equality before the law " is a convenient description of the principle of equal protection, and is commended by its use in this sense in various systems of municipal law.[1] Unhappily, in the law of nations publicists and statesmen have used " equality before the law " and " equality of rights " as though they meant the same thing.[2]

---

[1] See the guaranties of equality in the following constitutions: Argentine, Art. 16; Austria, Fundamental Law Concerning the General Rights of Citizens, Art. 2; Belgium, Art. 6; Brazil, Art. 72, § 2; Bulgaria, Art. 57; Chile, Art. 10, § 1; China, Art. 4; Costa Rica, Art. 25; Cuba, Art. 11; Ecuador, Art. 30; Greece, Art. 3; Guatemala, Art. 16; Haiti, Art. 13; Honduras, Arts. 25, 57; Italy, Art. 24; Luxemburg, Art. 11; Montenegro, Art. 196; Netherlands, Art. 4; Nicaragua, Art. 23; Panama, Art. 16; Paraguay, Art. 26; Persia, Suppl. Fundamental Laws of 1907, Art. 8; Peru, Art. 32; Portugal, Art. 3, § 2; Roumania, Art. 10; Salvador, Arts. 8, 23; Servia, Art. 7; Switzerland, Art. 4; Turkey, Art. 17; Uruguay, Art. 132; Venezuela, Art. 23, § 5, par. 15. For the dates of constitutions cited, and method of citation, see *infra*, p. 192, note 1.

[2] See Barbosa, *La Deux. Confér.*, II, 153, transl. in *The Independent* (1908), LXIV, 79; Bourgeois, *La Confér. Int.* Pt. IV, p. 76, and *La Deux. Confér.*, II, 88, 349; Brown, in *A. J. I. L.* (1915), IX, 326–329; Carvajal, *La Deux. Confér.*, II, 147; Creasy, *Int. Law*, pp. 114–116; Figgis, *Gerson to Grotius*, pp. 190, 216, 220, 242; Hershey, *Essentials*, pp. 59, 155; Hicks, in *A. J. I. L.* (1908), II, 532–534; Kebedgy, in *Z. S. R.* (1900) Neue Folge, XIX, 84–103; Lawrence, *Essays*, pp. 202, 203, 206, 208, 232; Maine, *Int. Law*, p. 55; F. de Martens, *Traité*, I, 380; Scott, *Hague Peace Conferences*, I, 37, 163; de Villa-Urrutia, *La Deux. Confér.*, II, 252.

Both the principles and the means of stating them have been hopelessly confused.

There are some statements of the rule of equality which, if taken literally, imply nothing more than the basic principle of equal protection in the enjoyment of rights. Kent, for example, appears to emphasize equal consideration for rights rather than equality of rights:

Nations are equal in respect to each other, and entitled to claim equal consideration for their rights, whatever may be their relative dimensions or strength, or however greatly they may differ in government, religion, or manners. This perfect equality, and entire independence of all distinct states, is a fundamental principle of public law.[1]

This, however, is not what the publicists mean. When they refer to the equality of states they imply something quite different from equality of protection. The point has been stated clearly by Lorimer, who says:

If all that was meant were that all States are equally entitled to assert such rights as they have, and that they have thus an equal interest in the vindication of law, the assertion would be true of States, as of citizens and individuals. Small States might be more dependent on positive law than great States, but the same may be said of small men as compared with great men. This, however, is not the meaning of the doctrine at all. If we look into the authorities we shall find that what is meant, though of course by no means consistently maintained, is really what is said — viz., that the *rights* of States are equal in themselves, and not merely the *right of asserting* their rights.[2]

The principle of equality is explained by a majority of the publicists as meaning that states have equal rights and obligations. Thus, according to Calvo, equality

has a twofold consequence, in that it attributes to all states the same rights and imposes upon them reciprocally the same duties.[3]

[1] *Commentaries*, I, 21.   [3] *Le droit int.*, § 210, I, 356.
[2] *Institutes*, I, 171.

Taylor defines equality as meaning that " the legal rights of the greatest and smallest states are identical,"[1] while Hershey insists that all independent states have " the same legal rights and obligations."[2] According to Cobbett, equality

really means that all States, whether great or small, have equal rights and duties in matters of international law.[3]

Of course the publicists do not really mean that states have identical legal rights and obligations, for that is manifestly inconceivable. What they really mean, although by no means what they consistently say, is that states have equal natural rights or interests, and that in the protection of these interests the law of nations recognizes an equality of capacity for legal rights among its subjects. The ambiguity results from attempting to explain naturalist conceptions in terms of modern legal science, without a very clear understanding of modern legal science. It would probably have been corrected long since were it not for the chronic tendency of publicists to repeat uncritically their predecessors' definitions.

The meaning of equality as a legal principle is explained by a few of the modern writers in a way that approaches scientific precision. Some define it in terms that suggest equality of rights, and then proceed to explain it as equality of legal capacity. Thus, Heffter refers to equality of rights (*Gleichheit des Rechtes*), but says that equality

means nothing more nor less than that each state may exercise equally with others all rights that are based upon its existence as a state in the international society.[4]

---

[1] *Int. Pub. Law*, § 69, p. 98.   [2] *Essentials*, p. 155.

[3] *Cases*, I, 50. See also Félice's Burlamaqui, *Principes*, IV, 434; Field, *Int. Code*, § 16, p. 10; Halleck, *Int. Law*, p. 97; Klüber, *Droit des gens*, § 89, p. 132; Lawrence, *Int. Law*, § 112, p. 268; F. de Martens, *Traité*, I, 380; Moore, *Digest*, I, 62; Olney, in *A. J. I. L.* (1907), I, 419; Root, in *A. J. I. L.* (1916), X, 213; Wheaton, *History*, p. 636; Woolsey, *Int. Law*, pp. 36, 59.

[4] *Völkerrecht*, §§ 26–27, pp. 47–48. " Mit dem völkerrechtlichen Begriffe eines

Others avoid even this much of ambiguity, explaining the principle, with considerable lucidity of statement, as a matter of legal capacity. According to Pradier-Fodéré, the equality of states should be understood as meaning

that they all have potentially (*virtuellement*) the same rights, that they have an equal power (*pouvoir*) of realizing them, and that they ought to be able to exercise them with the same inviolability.[1]

The clearest and in all respects the most satisfactory discussion of the meaning of equality in the law of nations is to be found in the treatises of Carnazza Amari and Fiore. Carnazza Amari is unequivocal in explaining that states are equal, not in respect to their rights, but in respect to capacity. He says:

This fundamental equality should not be taken to mean that it is necessary for them to develop their existence and realize their rights in the same degree; these rights may differ according to the more or less extensive activity of each state and according to the differences of situation in which the different peoples may find themselves and the varied influence of accompanying circumstances. It is necessary to understand this equality in the sense that all states have potentially the same rights, and enjoy, as Romagnosi has well said, the same inviolability in the exercise and in the realization of their rights. This equality results from the human nature which presents in all states the same characteristics of type; it is a natural fact which has a real existence; it is, therefore, based on human nature; and to violate it is to destroy the very constitution of human kind and of states.

Equality, strictly speaking, is not a right; but it establishes a general limit imposed on states, which have an equal power of realizing the same rights, and which ought to exercise them with the same inviolability when they have become concrete.[2]

vollkommen souveränen Staates sind an und für sich Rechtsungleichheiten unter mehreren derselben unvereinbar. Auch der kleinste Staat in Hinsicht auf politische Bedeutung hat demnach das gleiche Recht mit dem grösseren und mächtigeren in Anspruch zu nehmen. Darin liegt jedoch nichts mehr oder weniger, als dass jeder Staat gleich den anderen alle in der staatlichen Existenz und im völkerrechtlichen Verbande begründeten Rechte ausüben darf."

[1] *Traité*, § 449, II, 11.

[2] " Questa loro uguaglianza fondamentale non deve essere presa nel senso che

Fiore has a very clear and satisfactory statement:

Every state which possesses political personality has the right to
be considered in the international society as the equal of others in
whatever concerns its juridical capacity, the faculty of exercising its
rights, and the extent of international obligations. Whether states
are great or small, weak or strong, a superiority or limitation not
common to all cannot be lawful.

Consequently, we may formulate the following rules:

(a) Whatever is lawful, just, or equitable for one state, should be
equally lawful, just, and equitable for others.

(b) The greater or less extent of territory, number of population,
and power, can never modify the perfect juridical equality of states
in all that concerns the exercise of their rights and the fulfilment of
their duties.[1]

Chrétien, who follows Fiore, expresses the idea clearly and
concisely:

debbano mantenere lo stesso grado di sviluppo di loro esistenza, e di effettuazione
dei loro diritti, i quali possono differire secondo la loro maggiore o minore attività
e secondo la differente posizione in cui possono i popoli trovarsi e la varia in-
fluenza delle circostanze che l'accompagnano, ma nel senso che tutti gli stati hanno
gli stessi diritti in potenza e godono, come bene disse il Romagnosi, della uguale
inviolabilità nell'esercizio e nell'attuazione dei loro diritti. Questa uguaglianza
risulta dalla umana natura che presenta in tutti gli stati i medesimi caratteri tipici,
è un fatto naturale che ha realtà di esistenza; quindi non può essere violata senza
distruggere la costituzione istessa del genere umano e degli stati, e si fonda sulla
natura umana.

L'uguaglianza, rigorosamente parlando, non è un diritto, ma stabilisce un
limite generale imposto agli stati, i quali hanno l'uguale potenza ad effettuare i
medesimi diritti, ma una volta concretati, devono esercitarli con uguale inviolabilità." *Trattato*, p. 277.

1 " Ciascuno Stato ha il diritto di essere considerato nella società internazionale
alla pari degli altri, per quanto attiene alla sua capacità giuridica, alla facoltà di
esercitare i suoi diritti, all'estensione delle sue obbligazioni internazionali. Siano
grandi o piccoli gli Stati, deboli o forti, non potrebbe essere legittima una superiorità
o una limitazione che non fosse commune a tutti.

" Stabiliamo quindi le seguenti regole:

(a) Tutto ciò che è lecito, equo, giusto per uno Stato, deve essere parimente
lecito, equo, giusto per gli altri;

(b) La maggiore o minore estensione del territorio, il numero della popolazione,
la potenza, per nulla possono modificare l'uguaglianza giuridica perfetta degli
Stati, in tutto quello che attiene all'esercizio dei loro diritti e all'adempimento dei
loro doveri." *Trattato*, §§ 420–421, I, 289. See also *Int. Law Cod.*, § 393.

States are equal in the sense that they all have the same juridical capacity, that is to say, that whatever their strength and their wealth may be, they may claim the same rights and are subject to the same obligations. . . .

Its general effect is to attribute to each state, whether it be the principality of Monaco or the Empire of the Czars, *the aptitude to exercise the same rights and to assume the same obligations.*[1]

" It results from this equality," according to Twiss, " that whatever is lawful for one Nation is equally lawful for another, and whatever is unjustifiable in the one is equally unjustifiable in the other ";[2] and the same idea is expressed from another point of view by Wilson, who says that " on the ground of equality, regardless of extent of territory or number of population, each state of the family of nations has a similar status at international law." [3]

THE JUSTIFICATION OF STATE EQUALITY

Why should international persons have an equal capacity for rights ? For this question also publicists have a variety of answers. Their answers cannot be systematically classified; the difference is frequently a matter of emphasis or of point of approach. Perhaps the subject would hardly justify an effort at classification if classification were possible. Nevertheless their answers are of considerable interest, because they shed a good deal of light on the real significance of the principle, and because they constitute in a sense its justification.

---

[1] " Les États sont égaux en ce sens qu'ils ont tous même capacité juridique, c'est-à-dire qu'ils peuvent, quelles que soient d'ailleurs leur force et leur richesse, revendiquer les mêmes droits et sont tenus des mêmes obligations. . . .

" Son effet général est d'attribuer à tout État, quel qu'il soit, principauté de Monaco ou empire des Czars, *l'aptitude à exercer les mêmes droits et à assumer les mêmes obligations.*" *Principes*, §§ 161, 163, pp. 163, 165.

[2] *Law of Nations*, p. 12.

[3] *Handbook*, p. 74. See also Bonfils, *Manuel*, § 272, p. 161; F. de Martens, *Traité*, I, 309; Piédelièvre, *Précis*, § 268, I, 245; Pomeroy, *Lectures*, p. 323; Rivier, *Principes*, I, 123; *Venez. Arbit.* (Counter Case of Great Britain), p. 975.

Many writers of the last century regard equality as a natural right or as a principle which is based upon natural right. Thus Wheaton and Phillimore speak of the " natural equality of states "; Chrétien says that " this juridical equality of states may be called natural "; and Halleck and Taylor declare that sovereign states are " endowed with the same natural rights." [1] Bluntschli rests the principle upon the same foundation:

> Common human nature is the natural bond which binds all peoples to the unity of human kind. Accordingly, each people has a natural right to be respected in its human nature by other peoples, and an obligation to respect this same human nature in them. This is the human equality of peoples before the law (*Rechtsgleichheit*). Throughout all time individual sages have admitted this truth; but it has found recognition for the first time in the modern law of nations, and even today numerous prejudices, religious and racial hatreds, and selfishness stand as obstacles in the way of its general application as a legal maxim (*Rechtssatz*).[2]

There is also a tendency among the publicists to derive the principle of equality from the nature of international society. F. de Martens declares that " the society which unites civilized nations requires that they mutually recognize the equality of their rights." [3] Phillimore lays down two propositions as the basis of international law: (1) states are recognized as free moral persons; (2) each state is a member of a universal community. From the second proposition that each state is a member of a universal community, he says, " seem to be more especially derived the Rights incident to Equality." [4] According to Twiss, independence and equality constitute the basis of the " Natural

[1] See Carnazza Amari, *Trattato*, p. 276; Chrétien, *Principes*, § 161, p. 163; Halleck, *Int. Law*, p. 97; Klüber, *Droit des gens*, §§ 37, 89, pp. 68, 132; Maine, *Ancient Law*, p. 103; Moore, *Digest*, I, 62; Phillimore, *Commentaries*, II, 45; Taylor, *Int. Pub. Law*, § 282, p. 322; Twiss, *Law of Nations*, pp. 145, 179; Wheaton, *Elements*, pp. 118, 295.

[2] *Völkerrecht*, § 2, p. 60.   [3] *Traité*, I, 380.   [4] *Commentaries*, I, 216.

Society of Nations." [1] Calvo makes it a fundamental principle of the international society that

all questions of right arising between nations ought to be settled in a way that will not derogate from that mutual equality in which they are all placed with regard to one another.[2]

Wheaton repeats the eighteenth century dogma that the great society of nations is only " a state of nature." [3] This is the substance of the whole proposition. The notion that equality is derived from the nature of international relationships is simply a modern version of the naturalists' proposition that each state is the equal of every other because it is *une personne morale jouissant de la liberté naturelle*.[4] It is the theory of natural rights regarded from the point of view of international society instead of the point of view of the international person.

A few writers seem to regard equality as a necessary consequence of international personality. They imply that since states are *Rechtspersonen, personnalités morales*, or juristic persons in the law of nations, they must be equal. The notion is rarely pressed to a conclusion as in itself a justification for the principle. It is almost always associated with other ideas.[5]

One of the most common devices for explaining and justifying the equality of states is the analogy between natural

[1] *Law of Nations*, pp. 14, 145.

[2] *Le droit int.*, § 1860, IV, 2.

[3] *Elements*, p. 118.

[4] Klüber, *Droit des gens*, §§ 37, 89, pp. 68, 132. See also Fiore, *Trattato*, § 169, I, 113; Maine, *Ancient Law*, p. 103; Oppenheim, *Int. Law*, I, 20, 168; Pillet, in *R. G. D. I. P.* (1898), V, 71. Huber's more recent analysis of the principle of equality seems to have been influenced largely by what was, in essence, the naturalists' conception of international relationships. *Die Gleichheit der Staaten*, pp. 106–118.

[5] See Bluntschli, *Völkerrecht*, § 81, p. 96; Carnazza Amari, *Trattato*, pp. 269–274, 276 ff.; Klüber, *Droit des gens*, §§ 37, 89, pp. 68, 132; F. de Martens, *Traité*, I, 377, 387; Oppenheim, *Int. Law*, I, 168; Phillimore, *Commentaries*, II, 45; Woolsey, *Int. Law*, p. 35.

persons and states as international persons. The device is an old one and has undergone little change since the seventeenth century. Pradier-Fodéré's use of it, for illustration, is almost Hobbesian in its simplicity:

> The equality which is a right of man is also a right of states, because we know that as soon as states are formed they in some way acquire personal properties, they become moral persons, and we may consequently attribute to them, in proportion, whatever agrees with men in particular, such as certain acts which are suited to them, certain rights which belong to them, and certain duties which they are bound to perform.[1]

Piédelièvre says much the same thing:

> The equality which is a right of man is equally a right of states. Just as all men, having the same essential faculties, have juridical personality and consequently are juridically equal, so states, which are collective personalities, ought to have the same characteristics, deserve individually the same respect, and enjoy the same juridical equality.[2]

Despagnet follows a well-beaten path in asserting that

> This equality is no other than that which reason reveals and conscience commands us to recognize among men, from the point of view of right, in spite of innumerable inequalities of fact, natural or acquired, which exist among them.[3]

The analogy is vindicated in greatest detail in the treatise of Carnazza Amari:

> All men have the same origin, the same type, are physico-spiritual beings, since they are composed of an organic and living body and of a free and immortal soul; they are endowed with the same faculties, since they all have intelligence, free will, and the power to act, faculties which raise them above all other beings. The different human races are not distinguished by any essential differences; in fact, they all reveal the same type, they have the same fundamental characteristics, and they manifest a mysterious harmony which shows that they are all of the same species. This unity of species and of type of human kind is a fact generally recognized by science. Now men, all

---

[1] *Traité*, § 447, II, 8.   [2] *Précis*, § 267, I, 244.   [3] *Cours*, § 167, 218.

having the same fundamental faculties, are all juridical persons and consequently are all juridically equal.

States and nations, resulting from the union of a large number of human beings, have the same characteristics which appear in their members. Now if men are equal by type and in their rights, states, which are collective persons composed of men, are likewise juridically equal beings. Whatever the form of government, the more or less. extensive area, the degree of power, the varied development of knowledge, arts, and riches, the military strength, the more or less favorable climate in which they are located, the fertility or aridity of soil, the difference in the origin of the inhabitants, the different nature of the territory, whether adjacent to the sea or in the interior, states are always juridically equal because they are always collective persons who deserve the same juridical respect. States have the same fundamental rights and their personality ought to be equally respected, whether it concerns the vast empire of Russia or the petty republic of San Marino, civilized France or a barbarous oceanic people; it is thus that the man of great stature and the dwarf, the rich and the poor, are equal before the law which governs the actions of individuals. Thus, international treaties which attribute primitive rights to certain states while denying them to others, which accord to the powerful guaranties of which they despoil the weak, violate equity; for states, whatever may be their differences of form resulting from the same constituent elements of their nature, have the same type and are consequently juridically equal.[1]

---

[1] *Trattato*, p. 276. See also Bluntschli, *Völkerrecht*, § 81, p. 96; Bonfils, *Manuel*, § 235, p. 150; Félice's Burlamaqui, *Principes*, IV, 434; Holtzendorff, *Handbuch*, § 3, II, 11; Kebedgy, in *Z. S. R.* (1900) Neue Folge, XIX, 89, 91, 92; Klüber, *Droit des gens*, § 37, p. 68; F. de Martens, *Traité*, I, 380; Phillimore, *Commentaries*, II, 45; Pollock's Maine, *Ancient Law*, Note H, p. 121; Streit, in *R. D. I. L. C.* (1900) 2ᵉ sér., II, 16. See also Barbosa, *La Deux. Confér.*, II, 150, transl. in *The Independent* (1908), LXIV, 76; Carajal, *La Deux. Confér.*, II, 147; Declaration of Rights of Nations, in *A. J. I. L.* (1916), X, 124; Lansing, in *A. S. J. S. I. D.*, *Proceedings* (1912), pp. 228–243, 232.

Equality was discussed at a meeting of the American Society of International Law in 1909. In the course of the discussion, Mr. John W. Foster said: " I am hardly prepared to say that the equality of states is a legal fiction. I do not think it is a fiction at all; I think it is a reality. Sir, we might compare it, it occurs to me, with the rights of men. In all countries, and especially in democratic or republican countries, all men are entitled to equal rights; but they do not exercise equal influence in the community." *A. S. I. L. Proceedings* (1909), III, 247. Mr. F. W. Aymar relied upon the same analogy: " But for all practical purposes states.

However much they may stress other explanations, a majority of the modern jurists come back eventually to the conception of sovereignty as the fundamental justification for equality. Walker derives his three basic principles of the law of nations, of which equality is the first, from " the fundamental conception of Territorial Sovereignty."[1] Rivier says:

The equality of sovereign states is the necessary consequence of their independence. They are all equally sovereign. They have no power above them. No one of them is placed above the others.[2]

Heffter insists that " it is inconsistent from the point of view of the law of nations to consider fully sovereign states otherwise than as equal in law among themselves ";[3] and Hershey declares that equality is " a necessary consequence of the fundamental right of sovereignty and independence."[4] The statement of Bonfils is a good one:

As far as they are sovereign and independent with respect to each other, states are on a footing of juridical equality among themselves.

are alike; therefore it does not seem to me that this matter is a fiction. Take, for instance, among human beings — we have certain rights which are inherent in us, as human beings. It does not make any difference whether a man is a small man, or whether a person is a large man, whether he is strong or whether he is weak; whether, for instance, he is suffering from disease, or whether he is in perfect physical health, he still has inherent in him certain natural rights; and it seems to me that states, as such, possess certain inherent rights, and it does not make any difference what the size of the state is, as far as the inherent rights of the state are concerned." *Ibid.*, p. 249. The analogy was also emphasized by Mr. A. J. Montague: " The equality of states is as well established as the equality of men; but the nature of this equality is the precise question involved. Men are not equal in character, influence, power, talents and culture; but a legal equality must be accorded every man, or his pursuit of life, liberty and happiness is a futile undertaking. If we do not recognize this legal equality there is no hope for the development of man. So with nations. A legal equality, embracing certain elements of independence and sovereignty as against all comers, must be accorded, or the nation is not a nation, is not a state. It is this recognition of the right of equality or independence which supplies us with the concept of a nation, which enables nations to treat with one another, and out of which international law grows." *Ibid.*, p. 254.

[1] *Manual*, p. 11.
[2] *Principes*, I, 124.
[3] *Völkerrecht*, § 27, p. 48.
[4] *Essentials*, pp. 155–157.

Each may exercise in their plenitude the rights and faculties which result from its existence and from its participation in the international community. The attributes of sovereignty are identical for all.[1]

Kebedgy also emphasizes the importance of sovereignty, of which juridical equality is an essential corollary:

> Sovereignty is the fundamental attribute which the juridical conscience of peoples and the science of international law recognize in the different moral persons forming the society of nations, the persons that we call states; it has as a corollary, of course, the juridical equality and mutual independence of all states. By virtue of their very definition sovereign states do not recognize any one above them; it follows, obviously, that they are all equal and independent by the same right. That is true whatever may be the geographical extent or the material power or the constitutional form of each state, from the petty principality of Monaco, for example, to the vast empire of Russia.[2]

JURIDICAL EQUALITY AND INEQUALITIES OF FACT

States are equal in the law of nations. On this point a majority of the publicists agree. Equality may be presented as an attribute, a right, or a principle; it may be explained as an equality of rights and duties, or more accurately as an equality of legal capacity; it may be justified by appealing to theories of natural right or natural society, the analogy, or sovereignty. However defined, explained, or justified, juridical equality raises a question that has perplexed publicists ever since the theory of natural equality was first opposed to the positivist emphasis upon realities. How may juridical equality be reconciled with patent inequalities of fact ?

[1] *Manuel*, § 272, p. 161.
[2] *Z. S. R.* (1900) Neue Folge, XIX, 84. See also Calvo, *Le droit int.*, § 210, I, 356; Halleck, *Int. Law*, p. 97; Huber, *Die Gleichheit der Staaten*, p. 97; Klüber, *Droit des gens*, § 89, p. 132; Moore, *Digest*, I, 62; Pomeroy, *Lectures*, pp. 264, 313; Streit, in *R. D. I. L. C.* (1900) 2ᵉ sér., II, 14; Taylor, *Int. Pub. Law*, §§ 69, 117, pp. 98, 158; Twiss, *Law of Nations*, p. 11; Walker, *Science*, pp. 112, 115; Wheaton, *Elements*, p. 58; Woolsey, *Int. Law*, pp. 35, 59. See also Barbosa, *La Deux. Confér.*, II, 645, 648; Drago, *ibid.*, II, 249; and Larreta, *ibid.*, II, 15.

All the publicists have to take account of certain obvious facts with reference to which states are quite unequal, such as the number of their inhabitants, the extent of their territory, favorable or unfavorable climate, situation with respect to access to the sea and to trade routes, degree of civilization, form of government, military power, and the like. A majority of the writers dispose of these and similar inequalities by treating them as matters of fact rather than matters of law. The view is that state personality is unaffected by the varied character of the constituent elements of state existence. Inequality is always *l'inégalité effective;* equality is *l'égalité juridique.* Thus Pradier-Fodéré says:

However, among states as among individuals, natural or juridical equality does not necessarily correspond to social or real equality. While each people possesses all rights potentially (*virtuellement*), it does not realize them all equally in the same degree as other peoples. Indeed, all states are naturally and juridically equal from the point of view of absolute right, but all are not equally powerful, influential through their ideas, preponderant on account of their civilization, and formidable because of their material forces. The metaphysicians will discourse in vain on the absolute equality of states from the point of view of natural right; they will always be obliged to recognize in the reality of things an inequality between the Empire of all the Russias, for example, and Portugal, or some Spanish American republic.[1]

A few writers go farther than this and assert that actual inequality among states is not only consistent with juridical equality, but that it is the natural and desirable consequence of the principle of legal equality. This is the position taken by Piédelièvre:

It is unnecessary to hope or to desire that this real inequality disappear, for it is the natural consequence of the personality and liberty of states and to do away with it would be to do away with their independence. It is only the result of the normal progress of nations whose moral power and material wealth are intimately related to the particular aptitudes, the characteristics, and the intelligence of their in-

[1] *Traité,* § 450, II, 11.

habitants, and to the fertility of soil and the geographical location of their territory, so that the inequality of fact which separates them rests on a natural law quite as much as their juridical equality.[1]

Carnazza Amari objects to the expression "inequalities of fact." He insists that what is meant is "inequality of form" (*la disuguaglianza modale*), and that inequality of form is just as rational and juridical as that equality of type of which equal capacity is the natural consequence. He says:

However, this equality of states exists only in their condition, in their fundamental laws, upon which basis concrete inequalities are instituted, which produce different forms without destroying equality of type. In fact, although each people possesses potentially all rights, nevertheless it realizes them only in part. Consequently each state may have concretely rights not existing in others who have not developed equally their capacity, have not exercised it on the same objects, or have not found themselves in like situations. . . .

Equality of type and inequality of form are natural facts; the first is based on the identity of type and the second on the inequality of form which may exist among states. It is, therefore, wrong to speak of equality of right and inequality of fact, because both are rational and juridical; they result from a natural necessity; they exist in fact, and one really meets them in human nature.

Equality of type and inequality of form are in harmony; the one refers to the identical faculty of states to realize concretely the rights which may result from the condition of each and from the different activities which they display, and to the equal inviolability of the rights acquired; the other refers to the different situations in which they find themselves and to the unequal activities of which they give evidence; from the latter the inequality of their concrete rights is derived.[2]

In addition to inequalities of fact or form there are certain actions or practices in international relations, such as the

[1] *Précis*, § 267, I, 244.
[2] *Trattato*, p. 278. See also Fiore, *Int. Law Cod.*, §§ 397–400; Kebedgy, in *Z. S. R.* (1900) Neue Folge, XIX, 89, 92; Streit, in *R. D. I. L. C.* (1900) 2ᵉ sér., II, 16; Walker, *Manual*, pp. 11–13.

hegemony of the great powers, which are admittedly in conflict with the principle of equality as it is usually understood. This raises a point of great difficulty for the publicists, and has influenced several writers to doubt or deny the whole conception of equality in the law of nations. A majority of the writers, however, reconcile practice and principle, and they do it in several ways. Occasionally they recur, as does Nys, to *le rôle de la science*, defending equality against the encroachments of the great powers on premises grounded in reason.[1] The next step is to denounce every violation of equality as *un fait politique* rather than *un fait juridique*. Finally, it is pointed out that the violation of a juridical principle does not destroy it. " If their equality is not always respected in practice that disturbs in no respect the force of the principle," says F. de Martens.[2] Of Bluntschli's rule to the effect that every European state has a right to participate in all deliberations of the great powers when decisions relating to its own affairs are to be made, Streit remarks:

It is true that the rule has been neglected occasionally by the great powers; but these violations do not destroy the principle of international law any more than infractions of the principles of municipal law abolish the latter.[3]

Kebedgy says of the alleged primacy of the great powers:

But these tendencies contrary to right can never establish a right, any more than the abuse of material force can establish a juridical

---

[1] *Études*, II, 45. " En vérité, c'en serait fait du droit international lui-même si de pareils actes pouvaient engendrer de nouvelles notions et de nouvelles règles. Là gît de péril. Le droit international est en grande partie un droit coutumier; c'est dire que les précédents y ont une grand portée et que le fait accompli y est à un haut degré générateur du droit; mais c'est dire aussi que le rôle de la science y est prépondérant. La science doit se garder d'approuver les procédés et les pratiques qu'essaie d'introduire une politique trop habile; elle doit protester quand des théories dépourvues de base rationnelle et de fondement historique prônent l'hégémonie des grandes puissances, montrant en elle une institution destinée à assurer le règne de la liberté et de la justice dans la sphère des relations internationales." See also Huber, *Die Gleichheit der Staaten*.

[2] *Traité*, I, 380.   [3] *R. D. I. L. C.* (1900) 2ᵉ sér., II, 17.

rule, any more than the tendency to break conventional obligations can seriously unsettle the rule with reference to the binding force of treaties. One does not abolish right by denying it. Still less is it well founded to consider its violation as capable of establishing a rule of law. They may tell us to be sure that " quite apart from the equality of the books public life shows us only inequalities." One sees without difficulty the error in this reasoning which intentionally confuses fact with right. From the point of view of right the inequalities of fact necessarily existing among states as among individuals should not be considered. The inequalities, juridically insignificant, which exist from the point of view of social situation, influence, wealth, and force, are not opposed to the existence of the rule of equality for all before the law.[1]

A curious doctrine has been suggested by a few jurists. Although never developed in any detail it seems to imply that while states are equal in law they may be absolutely unable to profit equally from their juridical condition. In other words, they may have equal capacity for rights, but may be unable to exercise the rights for which they have a capacity. Fiore at least suggests the doctrine.[2] F. de Martens says that all states are equal but that " they are not all equally capable of profiting from their rights." [3] The same notion seems to be at the root of Twiss' objection to the term " semi-sovereign." He says:

It is not desirable that this classification of certain States as Semi-Sovereign States should find a place in a system of law which is concerned only with the external relations which States bear to one another as *independent* political communities. The term itself, " Semi-Sovereign," points at once to another system of political law, and suggests rather a subordination of position analogous to that in which the Princes and States of the Germanic Empire stood in former days relatively to the Emperor as their Suzerain or Supreme Lord, than a modification of the manner in which the foreign relations of an *independent* State, as such, are maintained. The international rights of

---

[1] *Z. S. R.* (1900) Neue Folge, XIX, 89.   [2] *Trattato*, § 422, I, 289.

[3] " Cependant ils ne sont pas tous également capables de profiter de leurs droits." *Traité*, I, 381, 309 (Léo's transl.).

the States, which rank in this category, are in *substance* as complete as those of any other independent State, and it is only in the *mode* in which those rights are exercised that a distinction is found to exist.[1]

This distinction between having rights and being able to exercise them was used at the meeting of the Institute of International Law in 1888 to meet the objection that pacific blockade violates equality.[2]   The same doctrine was urged by American delegates at the Second Hague Peace Conference in 1907, in defending the principle of rotation in the composition of a court of arbitral justice.[3]

The difficulty in reconciling juridical equality with inequalities of fact or of form and inequalities of influence has resulted in a tendency to emphasize the theoretical importance of equality as opposed to the practical existence of inequalities.   A few publicists say quite frankly that not only equality, but the whole subject of fundamental rights, must be considered from the point of view of pure theory. Carnazza Amari and Pradier-Fodéré point out that fundamental rights must be proved *a priori*.[4]   The former jurist adds that positive international law

does not exercise any influence on the determination and classification of the rights of states because there is no positive international law which establishes those rights.

The contrast between theory and practice stands out clearly in Scott's discussion of equality of voting strength and in-

---

[1] *Law of Nations*, p. 25.   Cf. Mighell *v.* Sultan of Johore, L. R. ([1894]) 1 Q. B. 149, 153, 162.

[2] The following report of Perels' reply to Geffcken is from the minutes of the Institute: " Quant à l'égalité du droit entre les États, il faut distinguer entre le droit et la possibilité d'exercer un droit.   Le droit d'exercer le blocus existe contre tous les États, bien qu'il ne soit possible que contre les faibles." *A. I. D. I.* (1888), IX, 296.

[3] *La Deux. Confér.*, II, 606, 608, 689; Scott, *Am. Addresses*, pp. 99, 103.   The argument was effectively refuted by the advocates of equality. *La Deux. Confér.*, II, 619, 626.

[4] *Trattato*, pp. 269–274; *Traité*, §§ 181–183, I, 306.

equality of influence in an international conference. He says:

It follows, therefore, that while all States are legally equal, still in this practical world of ours we must not, or at least we can not, ignore the historic fact that nations exercise an influence upon the world's affairs commensurate with their traditions, their industry, their commerce, and their present ability to safeguard their rights. It follows from this that though equal in theory, their influence is often unequal in practice.[1]

Those who are inclined to doubt or deny the principle of equality readily depreciate it as " a theory or alleged principle," *un mot sans portée,* or an " excessive legal theory which is largely a fiction." [2]

It is possible, of course, to take equality of legal capacity for an ideal, while recognizing that in actual practice the ideal can only be imperfectly attained. There is a tendency, reluctantly manifested, to approach the problem from this point of view. Fiore admits that states may be so situated that real equality in some respects can never be attained. After discussing the right of an inland state to have a maritime flag, he concludes:

Although in the abstract all states have equal rights, the enjoyment of some of them, presuming a group of circumstances of fact, may be denied to those to whom the circumstances necessary to the enjoyment and exercise of such rights are completely lacking.[3]

Heffter refers to " positive modifications " of the principle,[4] while Rivier says that "equality is presumed, inequality

[1] *Hague Peace Conferences,* I, 164.

[2] Brown, in *A. J. I. L.* (1915), IX, 326–329; Funck-Brentano et Sorel, *Précis,* pp. 46–47; Olney, in *A. J. I. L.* (1907), I, 419; Scott, *Hague Peace Conferences,* I, 169, 503.

[3] " Quantunque in astratto tutti gli Stati abbiano diritti uguali, il godimento di alcuni di questi, supponendo un complesso di circostanze di fatto, può essere negato a coloro ai quali manchino completamente tali circostanze necessarie al godimento e all'esercizio di tali diritti." *Trattato,* §§ 423–424, I, 290.

[4] " Als Grundprincip für alle souveränen Staaten ergiebt sich Gleichheit des Rechtes, welches daher auch mit seinen positiven Modificationen jenen Special-

should be demonstrated."[1]   Sir Frederick Pollock has stated this view clearly, in a note to his edition of Maine's *Ancient Law:*

The theoretical equality of independent States naturally follows from their recognition as analogous to free persons, who must have full and equal rights in the absence of any definite reason for inequality. This indeed is all that the maxim of men's equality before the law of nature declares or involves according to its classical meaning.[2]

There is a terse expression of the same opinion in Antoine's notes to his translation of Fiore, where he says:

It seems that in order to be quite accurate one should say that each state *ought to have* the right to be the equal of others, quite apart from its importance and its force.   It is a long way between the virtuous desire expressed with reason by the publicists and the reality.[3]

There are not many publicists who admit, in statements as unguarded as those quoted above, that equality in the law of nations is only an ideal.   A good deal of evidence might be collected to illustrate such a tendency, but, in general, writers seem to feel that they are on the defensive.   They distinguish juridical equality from inequalities of fact, form, influence, or policy, with many refinements of reasoning, rather than admit that the true distinction is between the ideal and the actual.

rechten voranzustellen ist." *Völkerrecht*, § 26, p. 47.   Levi says: " All sovereign states, great or small, are equal in the eyes of international law, such equality being subject to modification by compact and usage." *Int. Law*, p. 111.   The usages referred to are those which authorize consular courts, spheres of influence, pacific blockades, and benevolent interventions.

    [1] " L'égalité, principe de droit, n'est point incompatible avec diverses inégalités effectives.   Entre les États comme entre les hommes, il existe en fait et nécessairement des inégalités de situation, d'influence, de force, de richesse.   L'accord exprès ou tacit des nations les admit et les sanctionne.   Ce sont des exceptions, qui doivent s'interpréter de façon limitative, tandis que la règle est d'interprétation extensive.   L'égalité se présume, l'inégalité doit être démontrée." *Principes*, I, 125.

    [2] Note H, p. 121.

    [3] " Il nous semble que pour être complètement exact, ou devrait dire que chaque État *devrait avoir* le droit d'être l'égal des autres, indépendamment de son importance et de sa force.   Il y a loin entre ce désir vertueux exprimé avec raison par les

The Practical Application of State Equality

The practical application of the principle of equality in the positive law of nations has not been much considered. Discussion in the books is usually confined to questions of precedence, ceremonial, and diplomatic etiquette,[1] the essence of which is inequality, albeit, according to most authorities, a social rather than a juridical inequality.

Phillimore and Pomeroy expressly derive from the principle of equality the state's right to protect its citizens at home and abroad, including the question of debts due to citizens from the government of another state, the right to have its government recognized, the right of external marks of honor and respect, and the right to make treaties, to which Pomeroy adds the right of diplomatic and consular representation.[2] Most publicists, however, simply take equality for a general principle underlying all rules of international intercourse, and give little attention to its concrete application in relation to special topics.

The two most important subdivisions of the law of nations in which the application of the principle of state equality has special significance, viz., (1) the law of international ♭persons, and (2) the law of supernational organization, have received scant attention from the publicists. Perhaps, in view of the rudimentary development of the positive law of

publicistes et la réalité." Fiore, *Nouveau droit int. pub.*, § 428, note 1, I, 374. See also § 436, note 1, and § 439, note 2, I, 379, 381. Cf. Funck-Brentano et Sorel, *Précis*, p. 46; Piédelièvre, *Précis*, §§ 282 ff., I, 255 ff.

[1] Bluntschli, *Völkerrecht*, §§ 81–94, pp. 96–101; Bonfils, *Manuel*, §§ 272–278, pp. 161–165; Calvo, *Le Droit int.*, §§ 210–259, I, 356–381; Carnazza Amari, *Traité*, I, 384–406; Chrétien, *Principes*, §§ 165–174, pp. 167–175; Despagnet, *Cours*, §§ 167–171, pp. 218–224; Fiore, *Nouveau droit int. pub.*, §§ 439–451, I, 381–389; Halleck, *Int. Law*, pp. 97–118; Heffter, *Völkerrecht*, § 28, p. 49; Klüber, *Droit des gens,* §§ 89–122, pp. 132–172; F. de Martens, *Traité*, I, 380–387; Oppenheim, *Int. Law*, §§ 117–122, I, 171–177; Piédelièvre, *Précis*, §§ 272–278, I, 248–253; Pomeroy,. *Lectures*, pp. 313–322; Pradier-Fodéré, *Traité*, §§ 442–594, II, 5–117; Rivier, *Principes*, I, 123–131; Ullmann, *Völkerrecht*, § 37, p. 138.

[2] Phillimore, *Commentaries*, II, 1; Pomeroy, *Lectures*, p. 83.

nations in relation to these subjects, they have received as much attention as could be expected; yet one cannot help feeling that adequate consideration of both subjects has been considerably retarded by the influence of naturalist theories.

The law of international persons has been treated in a rudimentary fashion by the writers, with the result that several categories of international persons of qualified status have been recognized.[1] The completely sovereign state has been taken as the normal type, and all qualifications have been admitted grudgingly. The remark of Lawrence that " the classificatory skill of jurists toils far behind the constructive ingenuity of statesmen " deserves to be repeated with a broader application.[2] Nevertheless, the books take account in one way or another of personal unions, confederations, neutralized states, guaranteed states, protectorates, states under suzerainty, partially civilized states, civilized belligerent communities, and civilized insurgent communities. Almost all writers recognize that the principle of equality of capacity can only apply among international persons of the same status.[3] Thus a number of difficulties involved in the application of the principle are avoided, while the foundations are laid for separate consideration of the law of persons.

[1] Bonfils, *Manuel*, §§ 165–194, pp. 91–119; Calvo, *Le droit int.*, §§ 39–77, I, 168–225; Carnazza Amari, *Traité*, I, 259–321; Cobbett, *Cases*, I, 41–68; Despagnet, *Cours*, §§ 75–78, pp. 94–103; Fiore, *Nouveau droit int. pub.*, §§ 332–347, I, 290–304; Fontenay, *Des droits et des devoirs des états entre eux*, pp. 15–27; Halleck, *Int. Law*, pp. 63–72; Hershey, *Essentials*, pp. 99–114; Holtzendorff, *Handbuch*, §§ 24–27, II, 98–117; Liszt, *Völkerrecht*, § 6, pp. 50–60; F. de Martens, *Traité*, I, 311–356; Oppenheim, *Int. Law*, §§ 63–111, I, 107–164; Phillimore, *Commentaries*, I, 94–155; Piédelièvre, *Précis*, §§ 71–114, I, 61–95; Pomeroy, *Lectures*, pp. 45–78; Pradier-Fodéré, *Traité*, §§ 86–123, I, 158–215; Rivier, *Principes*, I, 79–123; Ullmann, *Völkerrecht*, §§ 19–27, pp. 86–118; Wilson, *Handbook*, §§ 6–19, pp. 21–52.

[2] The remark was made with reference to composite states only. *Int. Law*, § 37, p. 59.

[3] See Bonfils, *Manuel*, § 273, p. 162; Cobbett, *Cases*, I, 50; Chrétien, *Principes*, § 175, p. 176; Fiore, *Nouveau droit int. pub.*, §§ 433–435, I, 376–379; Kebedgy, in *Z. S. R.* (1900) Neue Folge, XIX, 88–90; Piédelièvre, *Précis*, §§ 282 ff., I, 255 ff.

It can hardly be said that foundations have been laid so far as the law of supernational organization is concerned; yet a number of jurists have pointed out the importance of the subject, and have suggested the difficulties involved in applying the principle of equality to this subdivision of the positive law of nations as it develops. Huber has discussed the question at some length. He is one of the few writers to appreciate the necessity of distinguishing the law of organization from the rest of international law, and for this his essay deserves a wider reading, whatever one may think of his conclusions. He says:

This equality may be manifested on the one hand in relation to abstract legal principles of a more material and more formal nature, and on the other hand in relation to concrete rules, i. e., in relation to international organizations. Equality is recognized with regard to the first category of legal principles by those who deny it in relation to the second category. The problem centers upon the importance or unimportance of equality within international organizations, in which are comprehended not only such permanent organizations as the unions for law, justice, and administration, but also such occasional or periodical organizations as congresses and conferences, particularly the Peace Conferences.[1]

The relation of equality to the evolution of supernational organization has been principally concerned with three questions: (1) representation, voting, and contributions in

---

[1] *Die Gleichheit der Staaten*, p. 106. " Eine differentielle Behandlung der Staaten ist an sich in allen Beziehungen denkbar, doch ist sie wohl nie in Frage gekommen bei materiellen Rechtsnormen, weil die materielle Norm ein abstraktes Verhältnis zu regeln pflegt, welches ebensowohl zwischen Grossstaaten wie zwischen Kleinstaaten, wie endlich zwischen Staaten von ungleicher politischer Bedeutung vorkommen kann. Anders verhält es sich mit formellen organisatorischen Rechtssätzen, durch welche ein konkretes, gleichzeitig verschiedene Staaten umfassendes Rechtsverhältnis begründet wird. Solange internationale Organisationen, wie es bisher üblich war, den teilnehmenden Staaten angepasst werden, ist eine gleichmässige Berücksichtigung aller ohne weiteres möglich. Anders aber, wenn zunächst für die Organisation feste Grundsätze aufgestellt werden und erst hernach geprüft wird, in welcher Weise den beteiligten Staaten eine Stellung in dieser angewiesen werden könne." *Ibid.*, p. 90.

international congresses, conferences, and unions; (2) the composition of permanent international tribunals; and (3) the position of the great powers in the society of nations. The first question has received relatively little consideration from the publicists. So far as it has been considered it has been generally assumed that complete equality must be the rule. Chrétien says:

> From the idea of equality is to be deduced especially the impossibility of discovering, either in an isolated power, or in the union and alliance of many powers, the germ of any authority whatever relative to others. Conferences or congresses are in principle destitute of all coactive authority relative to the states which have not been called to the assembly or have not taken part; the meeting of all states but one will never have with regard to that one either legislative or judicial power.[1]

The second question has scarcely been considered at all, having come within the domain of practical politics only in recent years.[2]

About the third question there has been a great deal of controversy. It has divided the writers more sharply than any other question arising from the application of the principle of equality to international relations. A majority of the jurists appear to hold the opinion that the hegemony of the great powers is not an impairment of the juridical equality of states. Some hold that the two are entirely compatible, the equality of states being a legal principle, while the hegemony of the great powers is purely political. This appears to be the opinion of Oppenheim, who says:

[1] *Principes*, § 164, p. 166. Huber discusses the question at greater length and reaches a similar conclusion. *Op. cit.*, pp. 106-118. Cf. Bluntschli, *Völkerrecht*, §§ 105-106.

[2] The discussion of plans for permanent international tribunals in the Second Peace Conference at The Hague in 1907 has given the question a degree of practical importance. The question is certain to receive more attention in treatises of the future. See Hicks, in *A. J. I. L.* (1908), II, 530-561; Huber, *Die Gleichheit der Staaten.*

Legal equality must not be confounded with political equality. . . . Politically, States are in no manner equals, as there is a difference between the Great Powers and others. . . .

But, however important the position and the influence of the Great Powers may be, they are by no means derived from a legal basis or rule.[1]

Of the contention that the position of the great powers is legally superior to that of the smaller states, Oppenheim remarks:

This doctrine, which professedly seeks to abolish the universally recognized rule of the equality of States, has no sound basis, and confounds political with legal inequality.[2]

Rivier makes a similar distinction:

Always, by the very nature of things, strong states have exercised a preponderant influence; the political equilibrium was created to oppose the abuse of force. Since 1815, the great powers have ruled Europe. This hegemony, admitted, and useful as long as it is confined within the limits of justice, is *un fait politique* and has to do only with policy. It is in no respect *un principe juridique;* questions of right are not affected by it; it never detracts by itself from the principle of equality. When resolutions are adopted in a congress a great power has no more voice than a small one.[3]

Huber stresses the importance of the fact

that practice and doctrine are in accord, that a legal differentiation of states and a legal hegemony of the great powers do not exist. A number of authors, to be sure, emphasize the extraordinary importance of the great powers that appear in the form of the so-called European Concert, and think that to some extent they are able to perceive therein the germ of a future world organization. For all that, however, there are involved only actual, political differences, which may become legally important in the future, but are not legally important at present.[4]

[1] *Int. Law*, § 116, I, 170.   [2] *Ibid.*, I, 171, note.

[3] *Principes*, I, 125. See also Kebedgy, in *Z. S. R.* (1900) Neue Folge, XIX, 88–90; Walker, *Manual*, pp. 11–13.

[4] *Die Gleichheit der Staaten*, p. 105.

Some writers seem to go even further, and deny, not only the legal nature of the position of the great powers, but also the future possibility of that position becoming the nucleus of a supernational organization. Thus Streit, while professing to take the positivist viewpoint, refutes both the suggestion of Bluntschli and Westlake that the hegemony of the great powers may be an incipient supernational organization and the contention of Holtzendorff that unanimity among the great powers creates a presumption that a general interest exists. He concludes:

International science is somewhat reserved with regard to all proposals for an organization of the society of states. In fact, any such organization seems to be impracticable; it presupposes the territorial stability of all states on the basis of mutual concessions to which it is difficult, not to say impossible, to hope that states will consent; and further, in our opinion, it would be in conflict with the very nature of international society, of which it is characteristic that it is composed of independent and sovereign persons. . . .

It follows from what has been said that the juridical hegemony of the great powers appears neither to indicate nor to be possible as the beginning of an organization of international society.

The superiority, either of all the great powers united or of any one of them, has been at all times a social superiority, which has formed an essential element of the policy of all centuries but which vanishes before the law. It is to be expected that it will always be thus. Juridical equality among states is a principle of the law of nations without which the law of nations could not exist, and consequently it is to the advantage of all states. What individual liberty is for municipal public law, the equality of states is in international law.[1]

Other writers, while opposing just as vigorously the suggestion that the position of the great powers is legally superior to that of other states, admit frankly that it is in conflict with equality and that it represents a tendency which, unless checked, may place important limitations

[1] *R. D. I. L. C.* (1900) 2ᵉ sér., II, 5–25, 22, 24. Cf. Huber, *Die Gleichheit der Staaten*, pp. 89, 90, 106–118.

upon the principle's application. Fiore declares that the pretension of the great powers to control the liberty of smaller states is a violation of equality as that principle is generally understood.[1] In an essay on the European Concert and its relation to international law, Nys contends that the idea of hegemony is in conflict with the principle of equality. He saves the principle by condemning the hegemony of the great powers as an institution of policy:

Within this European Concert, within this European political system, there has been constituted a directing body which includes only the " great powers." In fact, in positive contradiction with the idea of society which involves the notion of equality among the members composing society, the more powerful states of Europe presume to control the destinies of all Europe and to exercise an irresistible influence on the other continents. It is true that the opposition of the United States has defeated the plan outlined by the great powers with reference to America, but it exists for Asia and for Africa. The situation is somewhat novel on the European continent. The hegemony of the great powers is indisputable as a political fact: the whole history of Europe in the nineteenth century bears witness to it. But this hegemony does not and can not constitute a juridical principle.[2]

Nys recognizes the danger that the practice of inequality may impair the principle of equality, and he urges accordingly that the Concert as an institution be condemned:

The pretension can not stand for an instant before the fundamental principles of the law of nations; the diplomatic transactions by which it attempts to support itself do not emanate from the consent of all the members of the society of states, but only from the will of the so-called great powers. . . .

In truth, it may become international law if such transactions can produce new ideas and new rules. There lies the danger. International law is in large part customary law, that is, precedents have a great influence and *le fait accompli* is to an important extent the generator of law; but it is also true that *le rôle de la science* is preponderant. Science ought to guard against the sanctioning of proceedings

[1] *Trattato*, § 429, I, 293; *Int. Law Cod.*, § 396.   [2] *Études*, II, 3.

and practices which try to introduce too subtle a policy; it ought to protest when theories without rational basis or historical foundation extol the hegemony of the great powers as an institution destined to assure the reign of liberty and justice in the sphere of international relations.

The European Concert, taking the term in the sense of government by the great European powers, ought to be rejected and condemned. It is by no means a tribunal; no more does it constitute in any respect the executive power of an international organization in process of development. It is the product of policy, and on the whole it has so far served particularly as an instrument of oppression.[1]

In his general treatise, a later and larger work, Nys repeats the same warning:

The principle of equality has seen the pretensions of the great powers rise up against it, first with regard to Europe and then with regard to the whole world, and the pretensions of the United States with regard to the American continent. These pretensions are unfounded in international law; but they have prevailed on more than one occasion in the domain of facts, and there is a great danger in this because international law is in part customary law, a thing done has an important bearing, and, aided by the dissertations of skillful writers, an erroneous doctrine may grow up and impose itself upon us. It is necessary to combat it: the great powers are neither the tribunal nor the executive power of an international organization; their " concert," their " accord," is a product of policy.[2]

Chrétien is equally explicit in denouncing the activities of the great powers as a violation of the equality of states.

There is a derogation from the principle of equality much more important than that made necessary by political or diplomatic ceremonial; it is the division of European powers into great powers and secondary powers. Included today in the first category are Germany, England, Austria, France, Italy, and Russia. This division, understood as modern international policy understands it, tends to destroy, to the detriment of secondary powers, the fundamental principle of the equality of states. The great powers manifest more and more a tendency to constitute themselves an international tribunal before

[1] *Études*, II, 44–46.   [2] *Le droit int.*, II, 240.

which states of less importance will be henceforth justiciable. They grant permissions or refuse them, ratify acts of sovereignty or annul them, superintend others by virtue of I know not what superior right which they attribute to themselves, setting themselves up as the authorized directors of the international society. They tend, finally, to transform into an authority of right the authority of fact which cannot fail to be the consequence of the superiority of their military forces and of their wealth. It is precisely in doing this that they manifestly violate the principle of the juridical equality of states. We are a long way it is evident from questions of precedence and ceremonial. It is the very liberty of weak states which is threatened; it is the existence of their rights which is attacked. The divergence of views and the latent sources of conflict which, at the present moment [1893], exist between two of the great powers and the other four, will constitute, while they continue, a safeguard and a guaranty for the small states. But on the day when enmities are appeased, when conformity of interests and of views comes to be established, the juridical equality of all states incurs, at least in Europe, a great risk of being no more than a vain word.[1]

Jurists are by no means unanimous on this point however. A large, apparently an increasing, number regard the hegemony of the great powers as the incipient manifestation of supernational institutional development, and they accordingly admit important limitations upon the principle of equality in the law of supernational organization. Representatives of this view may be considered most conveniently with those jurists who doubt or deny the principle of equality.

PUBLICISTS WHO DOUBT OR DENY STATE EQUALITY

From regarding equality as merely an ideal it is a short step to doubting or denying it altogether. The divergence between the opinions of those who accept the principle and the opinions of those who doubt or deny it is not so great as one might assume at first instance. All jurists recognize

[1] *Principes*, § 174, p. 174.

the fundamental principle of equality of protection in the enjoyment of rights. Almost all modern jurists admit some differences of status among international persons. Those who accept the principle of equality regard equal capacity for rights as the normal and the ideal, and inequality as abnormal and something to be discouraged. Those who doubt or deny the principle are more impressed with the extensive prevalence of inequality in the practice of nations, and the unreal and impractical character of equality even as an ideal. Positivist tendencies in the study of the law of nations have brought an increasing number of jurists to the latter opinion.[1]

Funck-Brentano and Sorel distinguish the real from the theoretical law of nations, defining the former as those rules founded on custom and convention which actually determine the conduct of independent states, and the latter as the speculations of writers as to what ought to determine the conduct of independent states. Vattel is described as one of the best known of the theorists, while their own manual is devoted to real or positive law. The notion that international society is a state of nature is emphatically rejected. The principle of state equality is represented as having little practical significance:

All established States are sovereign, but in their mutual relations they do not all possess the same rights of sovereignty. They are equal, therefore, only in theory, particularly as one considers the principle of their sovereignty without taking account of the conditions in which that sovereignty is exercised. All sovereign States are equal as sovereign States: in reality, these identical terms, these words " sovereign State," that we apply to them indiscriminately, designate States of very diverse constitution, sovereignties of a very different nature, and consequently sovereign States perfectly unequal in rights and strength. It is correct to say that when sovereign states enter

[1] A few writers omit equality or treat it under another name. Hall develops much the same idea under the name of independence (*Int. Law*, pp. 17 ff., 47), while Westlake asserts that " the equality of sovereign states is merely their independence under a different name." *Int. Law*, I, 321.

into mutual obligations they employ in the agreement the same abstract right of contracting; but if we examine the very nature of the agreement, the events which have caused it, and the consequences which result from it, we see that this agreement, while resulting from an abstract equality, almost always demonstrates the real inequality of the contracting parties. This inequality is the consequence not only of the disproportion which exists between the extent, wealth, and military power of states; it results also from the political relations which the nations that form states maintain with one another; it results especially from the internal constitution of these nations, from their public and private morals, and from the degree of their intellectual culture. Apart from the application which is made of it the equality of states is a word without significance. This equality exists only as far as it is respected, and states only respect it or enforce respect for it as they understand it. Civil and political equality among the subjects of a single state may become a reality because the laws of the state may be conceived in a way to establish equality and guarantee its practice; but among states there is no public authority (*il n'y a point de lois communes*); equality has no other foundation and no other guaranty than the customs (*mœurs*) of nations; differences in national character, intellectual culture, moral progress, political traditions, productivity, and, finally, of geographical situation destroy all real equality among states. If, in spite of so many causes of diversity, so many sources of contradiction, so many reasons for irregularity, general rules of conduct have been established and considered as equally applicable to all states, these rules acquire a positive importance only as they take account of the conditions in which states are placed in their relations with one another.[1]

The question of equality in its relation to the theory of fundamental rights has been considered by Pillet, who concludes that it is futile, as well as a logical mistake, to treat equality as a fundamental right. Inequality must prevail between civilized and partially civilized states, between sovereign and partially sovereign states, between the guarantors and guaranteed states, between states that are neutralized and states that are not, and, in some respects at

[1] *Précis*, p. 46.

least, between states that are great and states that are small.
The assertion that Russia and Geneva have equal rights,
says Pillet,

has a primary and a very great defect; it is not just. States are not
equal from the point of view of their rights any more than from that
of their wealth and their power.

*Bien éloignée de l'égalité des livres, la vie publique ne nous
montre qu'inégalités,* and that is reason enough why we
should not speak of equality as a fundamental and absolute
right of states.[1]

A briefer study of the theory of independence and equality leads Mr. Philip M. Brown to the conclusion that

" the perfect equality of nations " is very far from being " universally
acknowledged " in the intercourse of states. Statesmen conscious of
their high responsibility cannot honestly face the facts of international
life and say that Great Britain and Liberia are equal. . . .

It would not be just, of course, to infer that a theory or alleged principle is unsound because it may not generally be accepted in practice.
But statesmen are unable to acknowledge the truth of the theory of the
equality of states simply because that theory is in patent antagonism
with the actual facts of international life. From their point of view,
and, it would seem, from the point of view of all reasoning men, it is
unpardonable folly to assume that things which are unequal in almost
every important respect are nevertheless equal to each other.[2]

This opinion has received the support of at least one
statesman and man of affairs. In an address before the
American Society of International Law in 1907, Richard
Olney, formerly United States Secretary of State, said of
the equality of states:

It is a principle which is simple in statement and easy to understand — which *prima facie* seems to be founded in right reason and
calculated to be just and equitable in its working. Yet, while all this

<hr>

[1] *R. G. D. I. P.* (1898), V, 70–71. Pillet's conclusions are combated by Kebedgy, in *Z. S. R.* (1900) Neue Folge, XIX, 84–103.
[2] *A. J. I. L.* (1915), IX, 326–329.

may be theoretically true of the principle of state equality, so much irreconcilable with it has been done within the last hundred years that its continued assertion seems to be an anachronism and a mistake. A crowd of international incidents goes to prove the principle to be one almost more active and better known in its breach than in its observance. . . .

International law will hardly make much progress in the way of scientific development so long as there is doubt as respects one of its basic principles — so long as it continues to lay down a rule, which, however plausible in theory, conflicts with the practice of the most civilized and enlightened states, and, if obeyed, would have inhibited and prevented numerous important international transactions which are universally acknowledged to have been wise in conception and beneficent in operation. It is necessary, therefore, to consider whether there must not be a material modification of the supposed hard and fast rule that every state is the equal of every other and is without a superior entitled to interfere with its absolute freedom of action.[1]

The same point of view was presented by Mr. F. C. Hicks before the American Society of International Law in 1909. Mr. Hicks said:

If the principle is intrinsically incapable of application to an actual state of affairs, it is well to realize the fact at once and begin anew. That the latter is the case may well be argued from two assertions of recent years. First, that the doctrine has ceased to operate for the benefit of those states which most need it; and, second, that if allowed to become operative it would give to minor states undue power in international affairs.

More results have been expected to flow from the fiction than it is capable of producing. Admitting for a moment the legal basis of the fiction, in any given case, practical considerations immediately outweigh any respect for it. The doctrine really exists only in an academic sense and has no inherent virtue or strength. It is invoked only when it happens to fit in with the desires of a state confronted with a problem. At all other times it is ignored except as a reason for ceremonial rules, all of which could be justified on common grounds of courtesy.

[1] *A. J. I. L.* (1907), I, 419–420. Cf. former Secretary Root's address before the same Society, April 27, 1916, printed in *ibid.* (1916), X, 211–221.

It is not a practical doctrine because it connotes conceptions which now require restatement.[1]

The most uncompromising attack on the whole conception of state equality comes from the great Scotch jurist, James Lorimer. Lorimer is sometimes described as a belated naturalist and associated with the school of Pufendorf.[2] It is true that he seeks to establish the law of nations upon the basis of thoroughgoing rationalism, even defining it as the law of nature realized in the relations of separate nations or political communities; but his leading deductions are so diametrically opposed to those of Pufendorf and his school that it seems misleading to associate the two. Lorimer rejects absolutely the notion of state equality. There has been no want of theories, he says, by which men have sought to evade the inevitable problem involved in the classification of states. The theory of universal monarchy and the theory of control by an oligarchy of great powers have both had their champions.

Last, and most baseless of all, we have the prevalent theory of the equality of all powers, a theory which seeks to get rid of the question by denying its existence. Of these three theories it is the last alone which has never been found capable of any practical realization at all; and yet it is the theory which at the present day you will find

---

[1] *A. S. I. L., Proceedings* (1909), III, 241. In the discussion of Mr. Hicks' address, Mr. L. B. Evans said: " It seems to me that we have no clearer instance of legal fiction than this doctrine of the equality of states. I doubt if there has been a single moment since Grotius first promulgated that doctrine when it has actually conformed to the facts in the case. There has never been a time when nations were allowed to act upon the principle that they were equal, that they were possessed of equal rights which they were free to use in accordance with their own conception of what their best interests demanded. . . . It seems to me that if the rules of international law are, as so many writers say, based upon international usage, then it must be said that the doctrine of equality is not now and never has been a part of international law." *Ibid.*, p. 248. Mr. E. C. Stowell said: " I should like to say that I agree with the first speaker in considering the equality of states a fiction and one which has never been very consistently observed." *Ibid.*, p. 252. But compare the remarks of others, quoted *supra*, p. 113, note 1.

[2] See Fenwick in *A. J. I. L.* (1914), VIII, 39; Hershey, in *ibid.* (1912), VI, 34, note 10.

set forth in all the books as that which alone is in accordance with nature, and to which practice must, of course, strive to accommodate itself. Now the equality of all States, the moment they are acknowledged to be States at all, is, if possible, a more transparent fiction than the equality of all individuals who are admitted to be jural persons or jural citizens; because in the case of individuals or citizens there are limits to possible size and power, and consequently to inequality, which do not exist in the case of States. A State may be almost of any size or power, both absolutely and relatively; and unless we are to adopt the theory of absolute centralization and recognize annihilation of nationality as the Nirvâna of international existence, it is of the last importance that the rights of the smaller and weaker States, such as they are, should be carefully preserved. But this will never be effected by placing them in a false position and inducing them to advance claims which they cannot maintain. To assert that, without any superiority in other respects, a State with ten thousand inhabitants is equal to a State with ten million inhabitants, or that a State half the size of an English County is equal to a State that covers half a Continent, is just as false as to assert that a thousand is equal to a million, or that the Canton of Geneva is equal to the Continent of Europe.[1]

Lorimer urges that the law of nations must take account of the relative value of states, and he suggests that the size, quality, and form of the state, and the form of government, are factors which contribute to determine relative value.

A steadily increasing number of writers and jurists reject the principle of equality in so far as its application to supernational organization is concerned. Analytically considered, this should constitute a problem quite distinct from the question of equality of capacity for rights among international persons. The general principle of classification has been stated well enough by Amos, who says:

In every body of Law Systematically arranged, Laws affecting Special Classes of Persons, often called " Laws regulating *Status*,"

---

[1] *Institutes*, I, 170–171. Westlake says that " the equality of states cannot usefully or even intelligibly be presented as a deduction unless the deduction also furnishes a test showing to what states it applies." *Collected Papers*, pp. 86–87.

ought to be distinctly separated from Laws directly relating to the Constitution and Administration of the State, and may usefully be also separated, in order to prevent repetition and to facilitate reference, from the rest of the body of Laws.[1]

Writers on the law of nations, however, generally refuse to make any such separation. Principles and rules applicable to the relations between international persons are assumed to be equally applicable to supernational organization. The reason for this is found in the reluctance of publicists to recognize the existence or even the possibility of supernational institutions. So long as international society is a state of nature, sovereignty unlimited, and states naturally equal, such institutional development is manifestly impossible and law on the subject is nonexistent. This has been the prevailing view of the last century, but there is a significant tendency away from it. The tendency has been much controverted. The controversy has turned chiefly upon the legal position of the great powers.

Even those who defend equality are constrained to admit that something is taking place which threatens to limit the principle's application more definitely than heretofore. Bonfils says:

These powers (the great powers) frequently manifest a tendency to assume, as the Pentarchy from 1815 to 1840, with regard to the other powers, a superior right, a quasi-legislative authority, in taking a position as the directors of the international community.[2]

Chrétien and Nys recognize quite frankly the same tendency.[3]

A great many eminent publicists have gone farther and have recognized, expressly or by implication, the position

---

[1] *Science of Jurisprudence*, p. 235. This distinction is not observed in primitive law. It is characteristic of primitive society that no distinction should be made between legal and political rights.

[2] *Manuel*, § 278, p. 165.

[3] *Supra*, pp. 129–131.

of the great powers as a rudimentary stage in the evolution of ·supernational organization. Thus Bluntschli says:

The so-called pentarchy may be regarded as the beginning of a European organization, but it cannot be regarded as its completion.[1]

Holtzendorff is not wholly unfavorable to the tendency:

It is natural that the smaller states should be less able to resist the collective political action of the great powers. But their voluntary submission to the unanimous counsel of the great powers, through which there is attained at least a strong presumption of the existence of a collective international interest, is more beneficial to their juridical position than that submissiveness to the threats of individual neighboring states of superior power which formerly prevailed.[2]

Brusa thinks that the concert of the great powers has a right to restrain the small states, by coercion if necessary, in order to prevent them from making war.[3] Even Geffcken, while protesting against the opinion represented by Brusa, concedes to the great powers a real superiority in the government of Europe.[4] Antoine insists that

In fact, it is beyond doubt that the great powers exercise an indisputable preponderance and regulate at their pleasure the collective interests of the other states.[5]

Pillet notes the same development:

The chief among them, those that are called the great powers, have in fact monopolized the management of important common interests.

---

[1] " Die sogenannte Pentarchie mag als Anfang einer Organisation Europas, aber sie kann nicht als ihre Vollendung betrachtet werden." *Völkerrecht,* § 103, p. 106.

[2] " Dass sich kleinere Staaten einer politischen Gesammtaction der Grossmächte am wenigsten entziehen können, ist natürlich. Aber ihre (freiwillige) Unterordnung unter einstimmige Rathschläge der Grossmächte, durch welche mindestens eine starke Präsumtion für das Vorhandensein eines internationalen Gesammtinteresses erreicht wird, ist für ihren Rechtsbestand förderlicher, als die ehemalige erzwungene Nachgiebigkeit gegen die Drohungen einzelner übermächtiger Nachbarstaaten." *Handbuch,* § 4, II, 16.

[3] *A. I. D. I.* (1888), IX, 298.   [4] *Ibid.*, p. 293, note 1.

[5] Fiore, *Nouveau droit int. pub.*, § 428, note 1, I, 374.

They are the ones who determine the progress of positive international law, who regulate affairs representing a general interest, and who undertake to avoid the most pressing of the common dangers. Therefore, there is for them an obvious superiority of fact which tends to be transformed into a superiority of right by the increasing respect which their decisions command among interested powers, who, not having been consulted, would have the strict right to refuse to recognize them.[1]

This opinion of the position of the great powers, with its consequent limitation upon the principle of equality, is widely held among British and American writers. Cobbett says that the equality of states is subject to some important qualifications. The first relates to status, the second to the primacy of the great powers:

In the second place, the recognized primacy of the six Great Powers of Europe in relation to matters of European concern, and that of the United States on the continent of America, although primarily political, would seem also to involve an ultimate control over territorial arrangements, and a consequent restriction on the territorial supremacy of other States, which are scarcely in keeping with the theory even of legal equality.[2]

According to Taylor equality has

always been enjoyed *sub modo*, — that is, subject to the irresistible power vested by the conventional or higher law in a committee composed of the representatives of a few of the greater states acting in behalf of the whole. That primacy or overlordship, gradually developed outside of the written treaty law since the Peace of Westphalia, represents the common superior who actually succeeded to the place made vacant by the collapse of the Holy Roman Empire as international director.[3]

In his *Essays*, written more than thirty years ago, Lawrence reached the conclusion that the principle of equality was obsolete:

[1] *R. G. D. I. P.* (1898), V, 71.   [3] *Int. Pub. Law*, § 69, p. 98.
[2] *Cases*, I, 50.

If, then, the principles and rules of the law of nations are really to be deduced from the practice of nations whenever that practice is consistent and uniform, it is time, I think, to give up the doctrine of equality in deference to the stern logic of established facts. For many years Europe has been working round again to the old notion of a common superior, not indeed a Pope or an Emperor, but a Committee, a body of representatives of her leading states. . . .

It seems to me that, in the face of such facts as these, it is impossible to hold any longer the old doctrine of the absolute equality of all independent states before the law. It is dead; and we ought to put in its place the new doctrine that the Great Powers have by modern International Law a primacy among their fellows, which bids fair to develop into a central authority for the settlement of all disputes between the nations of Europe.[1]

In late editions of his *Principles of International Law*, Lawrence takes the slightly more conservative view that the principle is in process of becoming obsolete. After reviewing the manifold activities of the great powers, he says:

We must be cautious in drawing inferences from the facts just recited. Attempts are made to reconcile them with the doctrine of the equality of all sovereign states by pointing out that what they establish is a political inequality, whereas what the old theory asserted was a legal equality. It is a grave question whether the legal and the political aspects of the problem can be parted and kept separate in this way. . . . But in a system of rules depending, like International Law, for their validity on general consent, what is political is legal also, if it is generally accepted and acted on. In the society of nations consent has the force of law, and general consent is shown not only by express agreement, but still more by continuous custom. If, therefore, the authority of the Great Powers has been acknowledged so constantly for the greater part of a century that it has become a part of the public order of Europe, and is accepted and even invoked by the smaller states of Europe, any description of it which refuses to recognize its legality seems inadequate, if not inaccurate.[2]

---

[1] Extracts from pp. 209, 232.

[2] § 114, p. 275. Mr. A. H. Snow asserts that as a matter of fact " the supernational law of the world is made principally through the persuasive hegemony of the group of nations which we call 'the great Powers.' " *A. J. I. L.* (1912), VI, 897.

He finds it difficult, if not impossible, to reconcile current tendencies with an international society founded on equality.

Prediction would be folly. All we can venture to say is that the old order founded on the doctrine of the equality of all independent states seems breaking up before our eyes, as three hundred years ago the mediæval order crumbled beneath the gaze of the men of the Renaissance and the Reformation. . . . May not international society be organizing itself to-day on lines inconsistent with that absolute equality in all things which still seems to some statesmen and publicists almost a sacred dogma? That states must remain equal before the law in such matters as jurisdiction, proprietary rights, and diplomatic privileges is evident. But it seems almost as evident that they cannot remain equal in what we may term political rights and social standing, now that the society of nations has become self-conscious, and is preparing itself for the performance of legislative, administrative, and judicial functions.[1]

The juridical significance of this development in the constitution of international society, and its relation to equality, was pointed out by Mr. Joseph H. Beale in 1904, in an address before the Congress of Arts and Sciences at St. Louis. He said:

The most striking development of the law of nations during the last century has been in the direction of international constitutional law, if I may so call it, rather than of the substantive private law of nations. At the beginning of the period the fundamental doctrine of international law was the equality of all states great or small, and this idea, as one might expect, was fully recognized and insisted on during the first fifty years of the century. There was little development in the law otherwise. Each nation adopted and enforced its own idea of national rights, and was powerless to force its ideas upon other nations. . . .

In the last half of the century, however, there has been an enormous development of combinations, both to affect and to enforce law; and resulting therefrom a development of the substance of the law itself. The associations of civilized nations to suppress the slave trade both

[1] § 116, p. 288. Huber's assertion that Lawrence stands almost alone among the writers in explaining the privileged position of the great powers as a right based upon practice needs to be qualified considerably.

made and enforced a new law. The concert on the Eastern question, the Congress of Paris, the joint action of the Powers in the case of Greece and Crete, and in the settlement of the questions raised by the Russo-Turkish and Japanese wars, the Geneva and Hague conventions, are all proofs of the increasing readiness of the Great Powers to make, declare, and enforce doctrines of law; and they have not hesitated, in case of need, to make their action binding upon weaker states, disregarding, for the good of the world, the technical theory of the equality of all states. While all independent states are still free, they are not now regarded as free to become a nuisance to the world.[1]

Few publicists have stated the significance of the position of the great powers from the point of view of the nineteenth century any better than Westlake, who says that

if each of their proceedings be considered separately, the ratification subsequently conceded to it by the states affected saves it from being a substantial breach of their equality and independence, leaving it open only to the charge of a want of courtesy in manner. It stands as an example of political action, not to be condemned if just. But when such proceedings are habitual they present another character. They then carry the connotation of right which by virtue of human nature accretes to settled custom, and the acquiescence of the smaller powers in them loses the last semblance of independent ratification. We are in presence of the first stages of a process which in the course of ages may lead to organized government among states, as the indispensable condition of their peace, just as organized national government has been the indispensable condition of peace between private individuals. The world in which the largest intercourse of civilized men has been from time to time carried on has not always been distributed into equal and independent states, and we are reminded by what we see that it may not always continue to be so distributed.[2]

---

[1] *H. L. R.* (1905), XVIII, 274–275.

[2] *Int. Law*, I, 322. In the preface to his *Problems of International Practice and Diplomacy*, Sir Thomas Barclay says: " To talk seriously of a League of Peace is not ' mere optimism,' as some short-sighted writers, who dub all progress impractical, have characterized it. Its foundations already exist in the Concert of Europe." In his latest edition of Halleck, Baker appends the following to Halleck's remarks on equality: " Nevertheless, the Great Powers of Europe have obtained such a position of authority that they are able to exercise predominance over other States. This position is now well recognized." Baker's Halleck, *Int. Law*, I, 126.

The hegemony of the great powers was denied, at the beginning of the twentieth century, in the constitution and procedure of the international peace conferences at The Hague. This circumstance has been regarded in many quarters as a triumphal demonstration of equality as a practical principle. Others have concluded from the experience of those conferences that equality must undergo some practical limitations, at least in relation to the development of supernational organization. Thus, Renault, speaking of equality in its relation to the constitution and procedure of the Hague Peace Conferences, has remarked:

> Now the juridical equality of states, taken literally, leads to absurd conclusions. This we must have the courage to say.
>
> I will take an example which I trust will offend no one, even if there should be in this hall persons belonging to the small nations I am about to mention. Can it be admitted that in a question of maritime law the vote of the Grand Duchy of Luxemburg or even of Montenegro should have the same weight as that of Great Britain? Could these small countries, pleading the principle of unanimity, block reforms on which the great maritime powers are agreed? [1]

Hicks concludes from a study of the same question that

> the doctrine of equality was untrue in its origin, was preserved in international law by a verbal consent which is not followed by performance, and was bolstered up by false analogies growing out of a confusion in thought between international and positive law.[2]

Renewed interest in world organization in the twentieth century has brought with it a widespread conviction that the principle of equality, as hitherto understood, is irreconcilable with the development of adequate supernational institutions, and that the principle must be limited in the interest of a better international order. This opinion is

---

[1] *Annales des sciences politiques* (1908), XXIII, 444. Cf. the dictum of Sir Samuel Evans in the case of The Möwe, L. R. [1915] Prob. Div., 1, 12–13; and the case of The Fenix, reported in *A. J. I. L.* (1916), X, 909–915, 910, 912.

[2] *A. J. I. L.* (1908), II, 535. Cf. Huber, *Die Gleichheit der Staaten.*

finding frequent expression in popular writing. The two following illustrations may be taken as somewhat typical.

If nations are not equal in moral, intellectual, or even material influence; if they have not an equal concern in the adjustment of international interests; if they have not an equal voice in the creation, the interpretation, and the enforcement of law; if, in fact, the claim to equality stands squarely in the way of world organization itself; then it is folly to insist on the concept of equality as a basic principle of the law of nations.[1]

If, then, the world is ever to organize itself for the peaceful regulation of international affairs, that organization must provide for the essential inequality of States. If such inequality is not reflected in the pacific machinery, it will make itself felt in war, while the machinery will be left to rust unused.[2]

Whether the opinion that is finding so much popular expression is to be reflected in the publicists is for the future to declare. The event is at present in the hands of those who make the law of nations rather than of those who interpret it.

Suggested Alternative Principles

While the opinion which doubts or denies the principle of equality has gained adherents among the publicists, few have made any serious effort, either to analyze systematically the inequalities which are characteristic of the society of nations, or to discover another principle upon which the law of nations may be assumed to rest. Two problems are

[1] Brown, *International Realities*, pp. 15, 68–72.

[2] Woolf, *International Government*, p. 120. In concluding his recent study of international administration, Mr. Sayre says: " Power to influence the future course of nations springs rather from inherent native capacities than from rights; and if an international organ is to accord truly to the world of facts, the member states which compose it will be given voting power more or less according to their actual world influence. To give to states which are unequal in wealth, in area, in population, in native capabilities, in influence, and in military power, exactly the same voting power in a duly constituted executive organ would be to depart far from justice; and no institution founded on injustice can permanently endure." *Experiments in International Administration*, p. 160.

involved. The first has to do with the capacity of international persons in their ordinary legal relations with one
another, or, to put the matter in another way, with their
capacity for legal rights. The second is concerned with the
capacity of international persons as regards participation
in the privileges and responsibilities of supernational institutional development, in other words, with. their capacity
for political rights. In so far as they have considered these
problems at all, writers have generally regarded them as two
aspects of the same question.

Systematic attempts to discover an alternative principle
have been made by Lorimer and Pillet. The former devotes
some attention to the means of ascertaining the relative
value of states, and concludes that there are four factors
which must be taken into account, viz., the extent or size
of the state or the quantity of materials of which it is composed, the content or quality of the state or of its materials,
the form of the state or the manner in which its materials
are combined, and the government of the state or the manner in which its forces are brought into action.[1] Lorimer's
study is an effort to get at the facts of international life and
to formulate principles in relation to those facts.

Pillet's study, as he himself admits, is purely theoretical.
His theory is founded upon two basic facts: (1) each state
is sovereign, and (2) each state lives in intercourse with
other states. There are accordingly two groups of state
rights, those resulting from internal sovereignty, and those
resulting from international intercourse. Conflicts between
states are always conflicts between sovereignties. Sovereignty is either territorial or personal. Therefore conflicts
between states may be divided into three categories: (1)
conflicts between two external sovereignties, e. g., on the
high seas, in unclaimed territory, or conflicts involving

[1] *Institutes*, I, 182–215.

nationals in a third state; (2) conflicts between two internal sovereignties, e. g., in leased, jointly administered, or disputed territory; (3) conflicts between the external sovereignty of one state and the internal sovereignty of another. The controversies of greatest difficulty fall in the third category, which includes most of the really delicate questions of international relations. For the settlement of these controversies Pillet evolves what he calls, for want of a better name, *la loi du moindre sacrifice*, based upon two propositions: (1) all states are equally interested in the exercise of the functions of sovereignty; (2) the different functions of sovereignty may be classified in an order of importance. His law is formulated in the following terms:

States should be guaranteed in the exercise of their sovereignty in their mutual relations; and, in case of conflict, they are rationally bound to give preference to the public interest which is the more seriously endangered by the dispute.[1]

For the practical application of his law, Pillet suggests briefly how the different attributes of sovereignty may be classified, in the order of their importance, in relation to the different public interests which they represent.[2]

The publicists have given scant attention to the principles underlying the development of supernational institutions, viewed as a separate problem, nor is this to be wondered at in view of the rudimentary character of all development of

---

[1] " Telle est donc, à nos yeux, la loi qui doit servir de fondement à une doctrine rationnelle du droit des gens. S'il fallait lui donner un nom, nous l'appellerions la loi du moindre sacrifice; nous la formulons ainsi: les États doivent se garantir l'exercise de leur souveraineté dans leurs rapports réciproques, et, en cas de conflit, sont rationnellement obligés de donner la préférence à l'intérêt public le plus fort compromis dans le litige. De là aussi la notion du droit primordial de tout État qui est d'obtenir des autres le respect le plus grand possible de sa souveraineté." *R. G. D. I. P.* (1898), V, 244–245.

[2] For the constructive part of Pillet's study, see *ibid.* (1898), V, 236–264, and (1899), VI, 503–532. Cf. Kebedgy's criticism in *Z. S. R.* (1900) Neue Folge, XIX, 84–103.

that kind.[1] Lorimer worked out a detailed scheme of world organization based upon relative value rather than equality,[2] and for this was severely criticized, not to say ridiculed, by his contemporaries. Most of those who doubt or deny equality do no more than to suggest the importance of bringing the principles of the law of nations into closer harmony with the facts of international life.[3]

Summary

There is much that is unsatisfactory about the common exposition of equality which one finds in a majority of the books. Very few publicists distinguish equal protection of the law and equal capacity for rights. Legal and political rights are almost always confounded. The whole subject is confused by intermixing the ideas and the language of naturalist theory with other ideas and expressions borrowed somewhat indiscriminately from modern legal science.

Equality is variously described as an attribute, a right, or a principle. The first is unsatisfactory because it approaches the subject from the wrong angle, predetermines the issue, and confines discussion to pure abstractions. While equality may conceivably be an essential attribute of the theoretically perfect state, the really important consideration is the way in which the law of nations regards

---

[1] The problem is considered in some detail in Huber, *Die Gleichheit der Staaten*. There is, of course, an extensive literature devoted to the idea and to plans of international organization; but this literature has grown up quite apart from treatises on the law of nations. See Meulen, *Der Gedanke der internationalen Organisation*.

[2] *Institutes*, I, 279–287.

[3] In his study of equality and the Hague Conferences, Hicks says: "We have seen that the equality theory is far from perfect, and that the theory of the primacy of the powers is open to very serious objections in that it does not recognize any influence at all as existing in minor powers. Neither of the theories are true to the facts. It seems to us that the true problem is *to find the facts of international life*, and to devise a scheme for the adequate representation of all elements in their true proportions." *A. J. I. L.* (1908), II, 550.

actually existing states. The description of equality as a right is a survival of naturalist theories and is quite inadequate. It leads to the confusion of natural rights or essential interests with legal rights, induces unsound classification, and raises the whole question of fundamental rights. Among a majority of the publicists equality is coming to be regarded as a principle, or foundational rule, which contributes to determine the content of the mass of substantive rules of which the law of nations is composed. This description is adequate, and is free from the objections which may be made to the definition of equality as a right or an attribute.

While some of the more conservative publicists define equality in terms that imply no more than equal protection of the law, or what Lorimer calls an equal interest in the vindication of the law, almost without exception they mean something quite different. Most of them say that they mean an equality of rights, or an equality of rights and obligations. It is unnecessary to add duties or obligations, for duties or obligations are correlative to rights. It is inviting no end of difficulty to speak of equality of rights, as though persons could have identical rights in a world of realities. What is really meant is an equality of capacity for rights, a conception that has been explained most satisfactorily by Carnazza Amari, Fiore, Pradier-Fodéré, and Chrétien.

The traditional justification for the principle of equality was grounded upon natural right, the state of nature, and the analogy. The conceptions of natural right and the international state of nature, while of great historical interest, can hardly justify equality as a principle of true legal significance in a system that is becoming increasingly positive. Even assuming that the state as an aggregate of human beings may be regarded as endowed with the natural rights of human beings, it remains true that natural rights are not legal rights, and that they have no legal significance until they are secured by positive custom or superior authority. There are serious defects in the analogy. If pressed too far it upsets the whole foundation upon which state equality rests. Equality of capacity in municipal law prevails only among persons of the same juristic condition or status, while the tendency in the law of nations, at least in its theory, has been to deny the possibility of status. Witness the cursory and dogmatic way in which most publicists dismiss the whole subject of persons.[1] About the only real similarity between natural and international persons consists in the circumstance that each has legal personality. The *de facto* basis for *de jure* personality is entirely different in the two cases,[2] so different, in truth, that it hardly seems necessary to suggest that a broad analogy introduces an element of unreality into a system of law that is already too much beclouded in nebulous speculation. The suggestion that equality is the necessary consequence of international personality is no justification at all. It is about as significant to say that persons are equal because they are persons as it would be to say that persons are equal because they are equal.

The nearest approach to a scientific explanation for the equality of states is found in the modern tendency to justify the principle as a corollary of sovereignty. From one point of view this is simply offering one abstraction in explanation of another. From another point of view, however, it does suggest a criterion by which the application of the principle may conceivably be determined. Only fully sovereign states are equal, that is to say, only states of a common status have equal capacity. This was Moser's position,[3] and in theory it is sound enough. However, the persistent

[1] *Supra*, p. 124.

[2] The author has discussed this question in somewhat greater detail in *Y. L. J.* (1917), XXVI, 581–591.

[3] *Versuch*, I, 1, 2.

reluctance of publicists either to admit degrees of sovereignty or to look into the *de facto* justification for various claims to sovereignty has greatly retarded any satisfactory solution of the problem. The law of international persons has made no great advance, so far as the books are concerned, since the days of Moser and G. F. von Martens. The net result of regarding equality as an essential corollary of sovereignty has been to shift the question of rights and capacity for rights from one range of speculation to another.

A great deal that is uncertain and unsatisfactory in the books may be traced to the difficulty involved in reconciling juridical equality with *de facto* inequalities. There is something inadequate about saying arbitrarily that all inequalities are matters of fact or form while equality is a matter of law, and yet this is the usual method of approach. A distinction of this sort, if carried too far, will divorce the law from all reality and seriously impair its usefulness. The problem becomes still more acute when *de facto* inequalities are manifested in action, as in the controlling authority asserted by the great powers. Here the publicists fall back on reason, a distinction between law and policy, or a distinction between law and violation of law. Reason, of course, in the last analysis, is only the publicists' opinion as to what the law ought to be. The distinction between law and policy, or legal equality and political inequality, is useful within reasonable limitations, but it may easily be pressed too far by those who seek to interpret a system of law that grows chiefly through custom. The same may be said of the distinction between law and violations of law. A body of law that is largely customary may grow through violations practised uniformly and consistently throughout a considerable period of time. It seems futile to try to get around the difficulty by distinguishing capacity for rights and the capacity to exercise rights. It seems equally futile to separate theory from practice, for unless the theory bears some relation to the practice it becomes superfluous. It is submitted that the most satisfactory approach to the question is that which regards equality of legal capacity as the ideal toward which the practical rules of the law of nations can only approximate. This is the significance of equality of legal capacity in municipal law. Much would be gained for clearness and logical precision if a similar view could be taken in the law of nations. It should be pointed out, however, that, while it has been suggested by a few and implied by others, this point of view has no general acceptance among the publicists.

In so far as the practical application of equality is concerned, publicists have placed the greatest emphasis upon matters of etiquette and ceremonial, matters which are only of secondary importance. The law of international persons has been treated in a somewhat cursory fashion. The law of organization has hardly been treated at all. There are indications, however, that these subjects are to receive more attention in the future. Those who have doubted or denied the equality of states have directed attention to both subjects, while the progress of international events gives them larger importance and a more commanding interest.

CHAPTER V

THE PRINCIPLE OF STATE EQUALITY IN THE DOCUMENTARY SOURCES OF THE PAST CENTURY

THERE has been much less said about the equality of nations outside the treatises of the publicists than one might reasonably expect. This is perhaps due to the nature of the principle, rather than to any lack of interest on the part of judges, arbitrators, statesmen, or diplomats. The principle has been proclaimed occasionally in the formal resolutions of assemblies representing organized propaganda or other interests. It has been discussed in a few opinions by national courts, in a few international arbitrations, and somewhat more frequently in diplomatic papers and the utterances of statesmen. The leading declarations and precedents have been brought together in the following pages. Together with the opinions of the writers, they constitute the authority, so far as printed sources are concerned, for state equality in the modern law of nations.

THE EQUALITY OF STATES IN UNOFFICIAL DECLARATIONS

The Universal Peace Congress at Antwerp in 1894 formulated a statement of three leading principles of international law. The equality of states was the first of the three principles:

Every sovereign state, whether small or great, weak or strong, should be considered as the equal of all others, with a right to the same juridical and natural respect as that which the greatest and strongest of other nations require, both with regard to its individuality and to its privileges in free and organized society.[1]

[1] *R. G. D. I. P.* (1894), I, 458. Cf. the Victory Program of the League to Enforce Peace, adopted as the League's official platform November 23, 1918, in which

The principle has rarely been stated more explicitly, not to say dogmatically, than in the *Declaration of the Rights of Nations* adopted by the American Institute of International Law on January 6, 1916, in order to inform its members with regard to the Institute's point of view and the principles which are to determine its conduct. This Declaration is of particular importance because it expresses opinions which prevail, not only among publicists of Central and South America, but also among the official spokesmen of American republics. There is a whole theory of international law in its preamble, which is in part as follows:

WHEREAS the municipal law of civilized nations recognizes and protects the right to life, the right to liberty, the right to the pursuit of happiness, as added by the Declaration of Independence of the United States of America, the right to legal equality, the right to property, and the right to the enjoyment of the aforesaid rights; and

WHEREAS these fundamental rights, thus universally recognized, create a duty on the part of the peoples of all nations to observe them; and . . .

WHEREAS the nation is a moral or juristic person, the creature of law, and subordinated to law as is the natural person in political society; and

WHEREAS we deem that these fundamental rights can be stated in terms of international law and applied to the relations of the members of the society of nations, one with another, just as they have been applied in the relations of the citizens or subjects of the states forming the Society of Nations; and

WHEREAS these fundamental rights of national jurisprudence, namely, the right to life, the right to liberty, the right to the pursuit of happiness, the right to equality before the law, the right to property, and the right to the observance thereof are, when stated in terms of international law, the right of the nation to exist and to protect and to conserve its existence; the right of independence and the freedom to develop itself without interference or control from other nations; the

it is stipulated that " The representation of the different nations in the organs of the League should be in proportion to the responsibilities and obligations they assume. The rules of international law should not be defeated for lack of unanimity."

right of equality in law and before law; the right to territory within defined boundaries and to exclusive jurisdiction therein; and the right to the observance of these fundamental rights; . . .

In reliance upon these basic principles it is declared, *inter alia*, that

Every nation is in law and before law the equal of every other nation belonging to the society of nations, and all nations have the right to claim and, according to the Declaration of Independence of the United States, " to assume, among the powers of the earth, the separate and equal station to which the laws of nature and of nature's God entitle them." [1]

The official commentary adopted at the same time explains that the right of equality is to be understood in the sense in which it was defined by Sir William Scott in the case of *Le Louis*, and in which it was stated and illustrated by Chief Justice Marshall in the case of *The Antelope* and by Secretary Root in his address before the Third Pan-American Conference at Rio de Janeiro in 1906.[2]

THE EQUALITY OF STATES IN THE DECISIONS OF NATIONAL COURTS

The principle of equality does not admit of exact definition in the decisions of a national court. Its application to a particular set of facts may be judicially determined, but broad definitions are of necessity *obiter dicta*. There are a few cases in which the principle may be said to have been applied to a definite set of facts, although in no case was its

---

[1] The text of the Declaration is printed in *A. J. I. L.* (1916), X, 124; and the text and official commentary in Scott, *The American Institute of International Law: Its Declaration of the Rights and Duties of Nations*, pp. 87–101. See Root, in *A. J. I. L.* (1916), X, 211–221; and Scott, in *ibid.* (1917), XI, 406. The Declaration is criticized by the author in a short essay in *The New Republic* (1916), VI, 91; and by Reeves, in an address on the occasion of the One Hundred and Fourth Convocation of the University of Chicago, August 31, 1917, printed in *The University Record* (1917), III, 249–265, at pp. 260–263.

[2] See *infra*, pp. 159, 161, 178.

application really necessary to the decision of the point at issue. There are a few well known *dicta* by famous judges, in which the principle is stated generally and much after the manner of the classical publicists.

In *The Schooner Exchange* v. *M'Faddon and Others* [1] an American-owned vessel was seized by the French, under the orders and decrees of Napoleon, was converted into a French man-of-war, and in that capacity entered the port of Philadelphia two years later, where it was libelled by its former owners. The libel was dismissed by the district court on the ground that a public armed vessel of a foreign sovereign, in amity with the United States, is not subject to the judicial tribunals of the United States so far as the sovereign's title to the vessel is concerned. This decision was reversed in the circuit court, but affirmed on appeal by the Supreme Court of the United States. In the course of his opinion Chief Justice Marshall said:

The world being composed of distinct sovereignties, possessing equal rights and equal independence, whose mutual benefit is promoted by intercourse with each other, and by an interchange of those good offices which humanity dictates and its wants require, all sovereigns have consented to a relaxation in practice, in cases under certain peculiar circumstances, of that absolute and complete jurisdiction within their respective territories which sovereignty confers. . . .

This perfect equality and absolute independence of sovereigns, and this common interest impelling them to mutual intercourse, and an interchange of good offices with each other, have given rise to a class of cases in which every sovereign is understood to waive the exercise of a part of that complete exclusive territorial jurisdiction, which has been stated to be the attribute of every nation.[2]

It was the decision of the court that a public armed vessel entering the port of a friendly state, under circumstances such as those in controversy, belonged to the class of cases mentioned in Chief Justice Marshall's remarks quoted above.

[1] 7 Cranch, 116 (1812). [2] 7 Cranch, 136, 137 (1812).

The same principle was applied by the Admiralty Division of the British High Court of Justice in 1880, in the case of *The Parlement Belge*.[1] Proceedings *in rem* were instituted against an unarmed mail packet belonging to the Government of Belgium, officered by commissioned officers of the Belgian navy, and running between Ostend and Dover, to secure redress for loss incurred in consequence of a collision. It was held that the vessel came within the rule which extends immunity from jurisdiction to the public vessels of a foreign state. The court recurred to Chief Justice Marshall's opinion in the case of *The Schooner Exchange* v. *M'Faddon and Others*, quoting the passages relating to the equality and independence of sovereigns, and rested the rule of immunity upon that comity among nations which induces every sovereign state to respect the independence and equality of every other sovereign state.[2] In rejecting the contention that immunity was lost because the vessel had been used for trading purposes, the court said:

it has been frequently stated that an independent sovereign cannot be personally sued, although he has carried on a private trading adventure. It has been held that an ambassador cannot be personally sued, although he has traded; and in both cases because such a suit would be inconsistent with the independence and equality of the state which he represents. If the remedy sought by an action in rem against public property is, as we think it is, an indirect mode of exercising the authority of the Court against the owner of the property,

[1] L. R. 5 Prob. Div. 197 (1880).

[2] The passages from Chief Justice Marshall's opinion are quoted on p. 206 of the report. Referring to an argument by the Admiralty advocate in the case of The Prins Frederik (2 Dods. 451, 466, 468) the court said: "The point and force of this argument is that the public property of every state, being destined to public uses, cannot with reason be submitted to the jurisdiction of the Courts of such state, because such jurisdiction, if exercised, must divert the public property from its destined public uses; and that, by international comity, which acknowledges the equality of states, if such immunity, grounded on such reasons, exist in each state with regard to its own public property, the same immunity must be granted by each state to similar property of all other states." P. 210.

then the attempt to exercise such an authority is an attempt inconsistent with the independence and equality of the state which is represented by such owner.[1]

The equality of states has been argued more recently in the *Brazilian Coffee Case.* In order to prevent demoralization of the coffee market by the abnormal crop of 1906, the state of São Paulo, with the approval and support of the government of Brazil, organized a valorization scheme whereby the state took over the surplus crop and placed it under the control of a committee. The United States Department of Justice brought suit against the committee's representative in New York, alleging that the scheme violated the Sherman Anti-Trust Law, and asking to have it declared unlawful, the defendant restrained from withholding the coffee from the market, a preliminary injunction granted, and a receiver appointed with power to sell. On demurrer, the defendant's brief set forth, *inter alia*, that the court had no jurisdiction because the property of a foreign state was involved:

Sovereign states stand on a basis of absolute equality, and all differences between them must be adjusted through the ordinary channels of diplomacy, by the executive departments of the governments. One sovereign will not subject another to the indignity of requiring him to answer for his acts in the courts; and it makes no difference whether the question involved concerns the person or property of the sovereign.[2]

---

[1] P. 220. In Mighell *v.* Sultan of Johore, L. R. [1894] 1 Q. B. 149, the defendant in a suit for breach of promise to marry claimed immunity from jurisdiction as Sultan of Johore, a British protectorate. It was held that a certificate from the foreign or colonial office was conclusive as to the status of such a sovereign and that the court was without jurisdiction. Of the immunity of sovereigns from suit, Lord Esher remarked: " For this purpose all sovereigns are equal. The independent sovereign of the smallest state stands on the same footing as the monarch of the greatest." P. 158. See The Duke of Brunswick *v.* The King of Hanover, 13 L. J. Ch. 107 (1844); De Haber *v.* Queen of Portugal, 20 L. J. Q. B. 488 (1851) ; Vavasseur *v.* Krupp, L. R. 9 Ch. Div. 351 (1878).

[2] Quoted in Stowell and Munro, *International Cases*, I, 161.

The case never came to a decision. Negotiations were opened between the United States and Brazil with the result that the " valorized " coffee was placed on the market and the proceedings discontinued.

The leading cases in which the equality of nations has been discussed have involved the right of visitation and search on the high seas in the suppression of the slave trade. England had almost stopped this traffic during the last years of the Napoleonic wars by exercising the belligerent's right of search. The trade revived, however, with the return of peace, and an effort was made to suppress it by continuing the practice of visit and search in time of peace. A French vessel, *Le Louis*,[1] was overtaken on a slaving voyage by an English vessel, was captured after forcibly resisting search, and was condemned by the Vice Admiralty Court at Sierra Leone for being engaged in the slave trade and for forcibly resisting the search of the king's cruisers. The case was appealed to the High Court of Admiralty in England, where Sir William Scott reversed the decision, laying down the broad principle that the right of visitation and search on the high seas does not exist in time of peace, except in case of piracy, and that the slave trade is not piracy. In denying the right of search in time of peace, Sir William delivered himself of what is no doubt the most famous judicial *dictum*, in regard to the equality of nations, in the recorded decisions of national tribunals:

Upon the first question, whether the right of search exists in time of peace, I have to observe, that two principles of public law are generally recognized as fundamental. One is the perfect equality and entire independence of all distinct states. Relative magnitude creates no distinction of right; relative imbecility, whether permanent or casual, gives no additional right to the more powerful neighbor;[2] and

---

[1] 2 Dodson, 210 (1817). Cf. United States *v.* The Schooner La Jeune Eugenie, U. S. Circuit Court, 2 Mason, 409 (1822).

[2] Cf. Sir William Scott's *dicta* in The Hurtige Hane, 3 C. Rob. 324, 325 (1801);

any advantage seized upon that ground is mere usurpation. This is
the great foundation of public law, which it mainly concerns the
peace of mankind, both in their politic and private capacities, to preserve inviolate. The second is, that all nations being equal, all have
an equal right to the uninterrupted use of the unappropriated parts
of the ocean for their navigation.[1] In places where no local authority
exists, where the subjects of all states meet upon a footing of entire
equality and independence, no one state, or any of its subjects, has
a right to assume or exercise authority over the subjects of another.
I can find no authority that gives the right of interruption to the
navigation of states in amity upon the high seas, excepting that
which the rights of war give to both belligerents against neutrals.[2]

In the United States, an act of Congress of May 15, 1820,
declared the slave trade piracy. The scope of the act was
considered by Chief Justice Marshall five years later in the
case of *The Antelope*.[3] A privateer called *The Columbia*,
sailing under a Venezuelan commission, entered Baltimore
in 1819, clandestinely shipped a crew of thirty or forty men,
proceeded to sea, hoisted the Artegan flag, assumed the
name *The Arraganta*, and sailed for Africa. Her officers
and most of her crew were citizens of the United States. Off
the African coast *The Arraganta* captured an American
vessel, several Portuguese vessels, and a Spanish vessel
called *The Antelope*, and plundered them all of the slaves
which they had on board. A prize crew was placed on *The
Antelope* and the two vessels sailed for Brazil. *The Arraganta*
was wrecked on the Brazilian coast, the captain and most of

The Helena, 4 C. Rob. 3, 6 (1801); and The Madonna Del Burso, 4 C. Rob. 169,
172 (1802).

[1] In the case of The Marianna Flora, 11 Wheaton, 1, 42 (1826), in the Supreme
Court of the United States, Justice Story said: " Upon the ocean, then, in time of
peace, all possess an entire equality. It is the common highway of all, appropriated
to the use of all; and no one can vindicate to himself a superior or exclusive prerogative there."

[2] 2 Dodson, 210, 243 (1817).

[3] 10 Wheaton, 66 (1825). Cf. United States *v*. The Schooner La Jeune Eugenie,
U. S. Circuit Court, 2 Mason, 409 (1822).

the crew being lost or made prisoners. The survivors boarded *The Antelope*, changed her name to *General Rami-rez*, and sailed for Florida. While hovering off the coast of Florida the vessel was taken by a United States revenue cutter and brought in for adjudication, on suspicion that she was either a pirate or engaged in smuggling slaves into the United States. The Spanish and Portuguese Vice Consuls libelled the vessel, each claiming that portion of the slaves conjectured to belong to the subjects of their respective sovereigns. Their claims were opposed by the United States on behalf of the slaves. In a discussion of the general principles involved, preliminary to examining the circumstances of the case, Chief Justice Marshall declared that the legality of the slave trade was well established by the law of nations and that no one nation could make it illegal for others. His observations on the equality of nations have been more widely quoted than those of any other judge except the *dictum* of Sir William Scott quoted above. He said:

In this commerce, thus sanctioned by universal assent, every nation had an equal right to engage. How is this right to be lost ? Each may renounce it for its own people; but can this renunciation affect others?

No principle of general law is more universally acknowledged, than the perfect equality of nations. Russia and Geneva have equal rights. It results from this equality, that no one can rightfully impose a rule on another. Each legislates for itself, but its legislation can operate on itself alone. A right, then, which is vested in all by the consent of all, can be devested only by consent; and this trade, in which all have participated, must remain lawful to those who cannot be induced to relinquish it. As no nation can prescribe a rule for others, none can make a law of nations; and this traffic remains lawful to those whose governments have not forbidden it.

If it is consistent with the law of nations, it cannot in itself be piracy. It can be made so only by statute; and the obligation of the statute cannot transcend the legislative power of the state which may enact it.

If it be neither repugnant to the law of nations, nor piracy, it is almost superfluous to say in this Court, that the right of bringing in for adjudication in time of peace, even where the vessel belongs to a nation which has prohibited the trade, cannot exist. The Courts of no country execute the penal laws of another; and the course of the American government on the subject of visitation and search, would decide any case in which that right had been exercised by an American cruiser, on the vessel of a foreign nation, not violating our municipal laws, against the captors.

It follows, that a foreign vessel engaged in the African slave trade, captured on the high seas in time of peace, by an American cruiser, and brought in for adjudication, would be restored.[1]

After examining the facts of the case before the court it was decided that restitution should be made to the Spanish claimant, but not to the Portuguese claimant because no satisfactory proof of individual proprietary interest had been made.

The equality of states has never been expressly doubted or denied, so far as the author is aware, in any formal judicial utterance in a national court. There are a few *dicta*, however, in which its denial in certain instances is necessarily

---

[1] 10 Wheaton, 66, 122 (1825). In an earlier case involving the seizure of a foreign vessel engaged in the slave trade, United States *v.* The Schooner La Jeune Eugenie, U. S. Circuit Court, 2 Mason, 409, 452 (1822), Justice Story said: "No nation has a right to infringe the law of nations, so as thereby to produce an injury to any other nation. But if it does, this is understood to be an injury, not against all nations, which all are bound or permitted to redress; but which concerns alone the nation injured. The independence of nations guarantees to each the right of guarding its own honour, and the morals and interests of its own subjects. No one has a right to sit in judgment generally upon the actions of another; at least to the extent of compelling its adherence to all the principles of justice and humanity in its domestic concerns. If a nation were to violate as to its own subjects in its domestic regulation the clearest principles of public law, I do not know, that that law has ever held them amenable to the tribunals of other nations for such conduct. It would be inconsistent with the equality and sovereignty of nations, which admit no common superior. No nation has ever yet pretended to be the *custos morum* of the whole world; and though abstractedly a particular regulation may violate the law of nations, it may sometimes, in the case of nations, be a wrong without a remedy." See Pollard *v.* Bell, 8 Term Rep. 434 (1800); The Scotia, 14 Wallace, 170 (1871); United States *v.* One Hundred Barrels of Cement, 27 Fed. Cas. 292, 297–298 (1862).

implied. In several opinions Sir William Scott pointed out that the less civilized states of the Barbary coast and the Levant were not considered subject to the full rigor of the European law of nations. In the case of *The Madonna Del Burso*, referring to the subjects of the Ottoman Empire, he said:

Independent of such engagements [treaties], it is well known that this court is in the habit of showing something of a peculiar indulgence to persons of that part of the world. The inhabitants of those countries are not professors of exactly the same law of nations with ourselves. In consideration of the peculiarities of their situation and character, the court has repeatedly expressed a disposition not to hold them bound to the utmost rigour of the system of public laws on which European states have so long acted in their intercourse with one another.[1]

A much more interesting *dictum* is that of Sir Samuel Evans in the recent case of *The Möwe*. Discussing the binding character of Hague Conventions which had not been ratified by all the belligerents, he said:

Of the belligerents, Montenegro has no navy, and, so far as I know, no mercantile marine — it has a coast line, but only of about thirty miles; and Serbia is a purely inland State, having no seaboard at all. It would scarcely seem desirable that the non-ratification by these Powers should prevent the application of the maritime Conventions; and it may be that the counsellors who have the responsibility of advising the Crown may deem it fit to advise that by proclamation or otherwise this country should declare that it will give effect to the Conventions, whether by the literal terms thereof they are strictly binding or not.[2]

---

[1] 4 C. Rob. 169, 172 (1802). See also The Hurtige Hane, 3 C. Rob. 324, 325 (1801). " Although their notions of justice, to be observed between nations, differ from those which we entertain, we do not, on that account, venture to call in question their public acts." The Helena, 4 C. Rob. 3, 6 (1801).

[2] L. R. [1915] Prob. Div. 1, 13. A similar view was taken by the Imperial Supreme Prize Court in Berlin, in the case of The Fenix, December 17, 1914. See *A.J.I.L.* (1916), X, 909–915, 910, 912.

THE EQUALITY OF STATES IN INTERNATIONAL AWARDS

Express reference to the equality of nations has been almost as uncommon before international tribunals as before the courts of national jurisdiction. Aside from an occasional passing reference in the course of an argument or opinion, it has been considered in only two important international arbitrations, the *Venezuelan Arbitration* before the Hague Tribunal in 1903, and the *North Atlantic Coast Fisheries Arbitration* before the same tribunal in 1910.

The *Venezuelan Arbitration* of 1903 had its origin in a controversy over claims held by citizens of the United States and of several European powers against the Republic of Venezuela. Prolonged diplomatic negotiations having failed to bring an adjustment the governments of Great Britain, Germany, and Italy resorted to joint coercive measures, including a blockade of Venezuelan ports, the seizure of customhouses, and other expedients. As a consequence of these measures Venezuela was constrained to recognize in principle the justice of claims held by subjects of the blockading powers, to pay certain of their claims at once and refer others to a mixed commission, and to assign thirty per cent of the customs receipts at La Guaira and Puerto Cabello as security. Were the subjects of non-blockading powers, having claims against Venezuela, to share equally in the customs receipts assigned as security ? The blockading powers claimed preferential treatment for their subjects. Venezuela and the non-blockading powers contended that all should participate equally. An agreement could not be reached and the point was accordingly referred to arbitration.

In the course of the proceedings at The Hague it was argued for Venezuela and the pacific powers that the principle of equality among nations created a presumption in

favor of equal participation, indeed that preferential treatment for the blockading powers would violate the equality
of sovereign states. This argument may be illustrated from
the Venezuelan Case:

> Such further preferential treatment is objected to because equality
> is equity, and as all nations are equal in the forum of international
> law, they should be accorded equal treatment by this tribunal unless
> some valid and conclusive reason can be adduced for denying them
> such equality.[1]

The same contention was developed further in the Case of
the United States. A closely reasoned passage from the
printed argument of Penfield was based upon the premise
of equality, stated in the following terms:

> While each State is sovereign within its own domain, elsewhere —
> on the high seas and everywhere within the domain of the general
> community — all States are equal, having equal rights and duties of
> respect, of representation, and of justice. Each may demand justice
> for its nationals domiciled in another State, but not to the exclusion
> of the same right of the nationals of other States. The pretension to
> such exclusive right assails the sovereignty of a debtor State. It also
> assails that of other States having claims equally just; and if insisted
> on it would necessarily provoke resentments and lead to inevitable
> conflicts.[2]

The same principle was emphasized in the Case of France:

> What is the general principle applicable in this matter ? . . .
> According to the law of nations, sovereign states are equal among
> themselves, whatever may be the differences of fact which separate
> them. This theoretical equality is often disregarded in fact on account
> of political considerations, but it is proper not to forget that very
> fortunately we stand here on the ground of right. We have what is so
> often asked for in vain — forum et jus.
> Therefore, according to the general principle the different creditor
> states of Venezuela have an equal right to that part of her resources
> which their common debtor has intended to assign to them equally.[3]

---

[1] *Venez. Arbit.*, p. 240. See also M'Veagh's argument for Venezuela, p. 1136.
[2] *Ibid.*, p. 430.   [3] *Ibid.*, pp. 898, 899, 880.

The argument based upon the principle of equality constituted the first point in the Case of Spain:

> The first of these maxims of the law of nations is the existence of a complete and natural equality among the States which constitute the international society of civilized peoples; the second, that the rights of a third party can neither be altered nor curtailed by acts or agreements in which it has had no part. . . .
>
> . . . Can acts of war, such as the events of December to February last, alter this natural, complete, and unchangeable equality, which is one of the keystones of the whole fabric of international law ? Have those acts, perchance, reduced Venezuela internationally to a situation of dependence with regard to the powers which have exercised hostile acts within her territory so far as to create for those powers and their subjects a right of preference over every other State and its subjects in all concerning the Venezuelan Republic ? [1]

The argument from the premise of equality was met very effectively by the blockading powers, however, by pointing out that the application of the principle does not require equality of treatment unless there is equality of position between the contending parties, and that in fact there was not an equality of position among the parties to the present arbitration. Their refutation brings out a point already made in connection with the writings of the publicists, viz., that whatever equality may be called it means an equality of capacity and not of rights. The Counter Case of Great Britain made the distinction very clear:

> The main proposition of law on which the other creditor powers rely is that all nations are entitled to equality of treatment, or, as it is otherwise stated, that " equality is equity." It is perfectly true that all nations, great or small, are to be regarded as on a footing of equality inter se, but this proposition can not possibly be stretched to the extent of meaning that all nations are to have equal rights in all circumstances, or that equality is always equity irrespective of the question whether the parties concerned are in an equal position or not. There is nothing to prevent one nation from agreeing to con-

[1] *Venez. Arbit.*, p. 914.

fer special privileges on another nation, even though that agreement be prejudicial to the interests of a third nation, provided that no vested rights are affected. One nation, for instance, may obtain a preferential tariff from another nation by treaty or by force, but that gives no right in law to any third nation to insist on equal treatment.

It is equally certain that the doctrine of equality can have no application in cases in which the nations concerned are not in a position of equality. A neutral, for instance, cannot claim the privileges of a belligerent. A nation which has nothing to offer in exchange for a concession is not in the same position as a nation which can confer signal advantages in return. A creditor who has taken no steps to enforce the payment of his debt is not in the same position as a creditor who has taken successful proceedings against the debtor.

It is obvious, therefore, for reasons which will hereafter more fully appear, that the maxim has no application to the present case.[1]

Replying to the Spanish argument from the principle of state equality, M. Buenz said:

We cheerfully admit all that, contending at the same time that those principles do not in any way apply to the case at issue.

The blockading powers do not in the least contest the complete and natural equality among the States as States, nor did they ever pretend to have a right to curtail the rights of a third party. On the contrary they added to those rights and improved the status of the third party. But how about the reverse of the medal? Can a third party acquire rights by acts in which it had no part? It was owing to the military operations of the blockading powers that security was promised and her customs pledged to them by Venezuela for their claims. By what title do the other creditor powers demand admission to that right acquired by acts in which they had no part?[2]

The award recognized the soundness of the argument advanced by the blockading powers and granted preferential treatment. It stands as a precedent neither for nor against the equality of states. It is authority for no other proposition than that in a case like the one under consideration

---

[1] *Venez. Arbit.*, p. 975. See also Counter Case of Italy, p. 1028.

[2] *Ibid.*, p. 1190. See also the argument of Sir Robert Finlay, p. 1199.

coercive action may give a privileged position which carries with it the right to preferential treatment.

In the *North Atlantic Coast Fisheries Arbitration* of 1910 the equality of nations was not made an issue in so many words, but it would seem to have been involved in the decision of the first of the seven questions submitted to the tribunal.[1] The treaty of 1818 between the United States and Great Britain conceded to the inhabitants of the United States the liberty to take fish in certain British territorial waters on the North Atlantic coast. After nearly a century of controversy with reference to the scope and meaning of the treaty the two countries agreed in 1909 to have recourse to arbitration.

The very nature of the right defined by the treaty was placed in issue by the first question. Could Great Britain or the colonies enact reasonable regulations for the fisheries without the consent of the United States ? Counsel for the United States denied that such regulations could be applied to the common fisheries,

Unless their appropriateness, necessity, reasonableness, and fairness be determined by the United States and Great Britain by common accord and the United States concurs in their enforcement.[2]

It was argued that the fishing rights constituted an international servitude over the territory of Great Britain, restricting sovereignty, and depriving Great Britain of its independent right of regulation. It was argued further that if sovereignty itself was not limited then Great Britain was at least restricted in the exercise of its sovereignty in the treaty waters.

The tribunal resolved the question into two contentions:

---

[1] *N. A. C. F. Proceedings*, I, 66 ff.; Wilson, *The Hague Arbitration Cases*, pp. 154 ff. The page references to *N. A. C. F. Proceedings*, I, refer to the first part of the volume, and not to the Case of the United States which is paged separately.

[2] *N. A. C. F. Proceedings*, I, 67.

1st. Whether the right of regulating reasonably the liberties conferred by the Treaty of 1818 resides in Great Britain;

2d. And, if such right does so exist, whether such reasonable exercise of the right is permitted to Great Britain without the accord and concurrence of the United States.[1]

Both contentions were decided against the United States. The tribunal denied that the fishing liberty constituted a servitude in derogation of sovereignty because, among other reasons, there was no satisfactory evidence that either British or American statesmen were familiar with the doctrine in 1818; because a servitude predicates an express grant of a sovereign right, whereas the treaty granted a liberty to fish, which was purely an economic right; and because the notion of international servitudes originated among the quasi-sovereignties of the Holy Roman Empire, whereas

in contradistinction to this quasi-sovereignty with its incoherent attributes acquired at various times, by various means, and not impaired in its character by being incomplete in any one respect or by being limited in favour of another territory and its possessor, the modern State, and particularly Great Britain, has never admitted partition of sovereignty, owing to the constitution of a modern State requiring essential sovereignty and independence.[2]

The tribunal regarded the doctrine of international servitudes as being

little suited to the principle of sovereignty which prevails in States under a system of constitutional government such as Great Britain and the United States and to the present international relations of sovereign States.

In the general interest of the community of nations and of the parties to the treaty, it was declared, such a principle could be affirmed " only on the express evidence of an international contract."

---

[1] *N. A. C. F. Proceedings*, I, 74.   [2] *Ibid.*, I, 76.

The contention that reasonable exercise of Great Britain's right of regulation required the accord and concurrence of the United States was also rejected. It was the tribunal's opinion that such a concurrent right would impair the sovereignty and independence of Great Britain.

Finally, to hold that the United States, the grantee of the fishing right, has a voice in the preparation of fishery legislation involves the recognition of a right in that country to participate in the internal legislation of Great Britain and her colonies, and to that extent would reduce these countries to a state of dependence.[1]

Every suggestion of a limitation on the independence or sovereignty of Great Britain was repudiated.

In its award, however, the tribunal recognized the existence of a permanent limitation upon the capacity of Great Britain to regulate its fisheries, a limitation of which Great Britain cannot divest itself by its own act, and one which in a sense affects its capacity in relation to the entire society of nations. The reasons for this limitation were stated as follows:

While therefore unable to concede the claim of the United States as based on the treaty, this Tribunal considers that such claim has been and is to some extent, conceded in the relations now existing between the two Parties. Whatever may have been the situation under the treaty of 1818 standing alone, the exercise of the right of regulation inherent in Great Britain has been, and is, limited by the repeated recognition of the obligations already referred to, by the limitations and liabilities accepted in the special agreement, by the unequivocal position assumed by Great Britain in the presentation of its case before this Tribunal, and by the consequent view of this Tribunal that it would be consistent with all the circumstances, as revealed by this record, as to the duty of Great Britain, that she should submit the reasonableness of any future regulation to such an impartial arbitral test, affording full opportunity therefor, as is hereafter recommended under the authority of Article IV of the special agreement, whenever the reasonableness of any regulation is objected

[1] *N. A. C. F. Proceedings*, I, 84.

to or challenged by the United States in the manner, and within the time hereinafter specified in the said recommendation.[1]

It was decided, therefore, that while the right to regulate without the consent of the United States was inherent in the sovereignty of Great Britain, the exercise of that right must be in good faith and in accord with the treaty; and if the reasonableness of any regulation should be contested by the United States the point must be decided by an impartial authority. The effect of the decision is well summarized in the report of the agent of the United States:

> It is evident, therefore, that as result of the award no regulations limiting the time, manner and implements of fishing can hereafter be imposed upon American fishermen exercising their treaty liberties in Newfoundland and Canadian waters if any objection has been raised to them by the United States, unless their reasonableness, necessity and fairness has been approved by an impartial commission or tribunal. . . .
>
> Although British sovereign rights over the fisheries in British waters are affirmed in the decision, nevertheless the exercise of such rights is effectively limited by the award to the extent above indicated.[2]

As a distinguished Briton is said to have remarked, Great Britain saved her sovereignty but lost the right to exercise it. Stated in terms of equality instead of terms of sovereignty and independence, the somewhat anomalous award on question one amounts to this: it is always to be presumed that a state retains an unrestricted capacity for rights equal to that enjoyed by any other state; but by treaty, usage, special agreement, and formal admission one state may become subject to a permanent limitation upon its capacity to exercise certain rights without becoming subject to an international servitude, in the sense of a limitation on sovereignty.

[1] *N. A. C. F. Proceedings*, I, 84.   [2] *Ibid.*, I, 16.

There is one international case in which the broad general principle of the equality of nations was placed definitely in issue and judicially affirmed as essential to the right decision of the controversy. That case is the recent one of *Salvador* v. *Nicaragua*,[1] decided by the Central American Court of Justice in 1917. As a precedent the case can hardly be said to have international significance; but technically, at least, it is an international case and therefore may be considered here. Salvador filed a complaint with the court against Nicaragua's concession of a naval base to the United States under the terms of the Bryan-Chamorro Treaty. It was contended that the concession constituted a menace to Salvador's national security, violated her rights of co-ownership in the Gulf of Fonseca, and impaired her legitimate hopes for the future as a Central American nation. The Court was petitioned to enjoin Nicaragua from performing its part of the treaty. The Agadir incident was invoked to show that in similar circumstances, when Germany threatened to seize a port for a naval base on the Moroccan coast, Great Britain and France protested that such a base would be a menace to their national security and succeeded in preventing its establishment. Nicaragua denied that there was any parallel between the Agadir incident and the proposed concession in the Gulf of Fonseca. The Court held the concession a menace to Salvador's security, remarking of the Agadir incident:

In the opinion of the Court, the Agadir case is perfectly applicable to the argument maintained by the high party complainant. It matters not that in that case the parties who claimed that their rights were " menaced " were great military Powers. The proposition was there adopted as a fundamental principle of public law that all states are naturally equal and that they are under the same obligations and enjoy the same rights. " The relative magnitude," says Sir William Scott, referring to sovereign states, " creates no distinc-

[1] *A. J. I. L.* (1917), XI, 674–730

tion of right, and any difference that may be claimed in respect to that basis must be considered as a usurpation." [1]

It was further held that Nicaragua was under an obligation to reëstablish and maintain the legal status which had existed prior to the conclusion of the Bryan-Chamorro Treaty; but the Court prudently declined to enjoin Nicaragua from fulfilling the treaty or to grant other relief.

EQUALITY IN THE PROTESTS OF SMALL OR WEAK NATIONS

The equality of nations has been invoked much more frequently in the literature of diplomacy. It has been the theme of protests of the smaller and weaker nations from the apology of William the Silent [2] to the present day. Würtemberg protested formally in 1823 against being excluded from the Congress of Verona:

Whatever confidence may be due by reason of the wisdom and the impartiality of the powers who have inherited the influence which was assumed in Europe by Napoleon, it is nevertheless difficult not to fear for the independence of the smaller states, if ever that protection should be exercised by less devoted or less generous sovereigns. [3]

It was declared that the way in which the great powers were attempting to supervise the common interests of Europe threatened to introduce " more or less alarming principles " into public law, and justified *une réserve expresse les droits inaliénable de tout Etat indépendant.*

When the great powers met in concert in 1869 to adjust the controversy then raging in the near East, Greece refused to participate in the conferences except on terms of equality. The deliberations accordingly proceeded without the assistance of Greece. [4]

---

[1] *A. J. I. L.* (1917), XI, 719.   [2] Figgis, *Gerson to Grotius*, p. 242.
[3] *B. F. S. P.*, X, 895, 896. See Metternich's reply, *ibid.*, p. 898.
[4] *Ibid.*, LIX, 814, 818, 826. Greece might have quoted from the French protest against the suppression of the Republic of Cracow, Paris, December 3,

Again, when the Conference of London was called by the great powers in 1883 to consider the execution of articles 54 and 55 of the Treaty of Berlin with reference to the navigation of the Danube, Roumania asserted its right to participate on the basis of complete equality and justified its claim by citing its interest in the navigation of the Danube, its representation on the Danube commission, the principles of international law, and the express terms of the protocol of the Congress of Aix-la-Chapelle. The Roumanian representative at London declared:

> The participation of Roumania in the work of the Conference *sur le pied de la plus parfaite égalité* with the other powers is indicated by the very nature of things.[1]

The powers declined to admit Roumania on a footing of equality, and Roumania consequently refused to participate at all.[2]

More recently, in the litigation to which reference has already been made, Salvador protested against the Bryan-Chamorro Treaty because

> It must be patent to everyone that the establishment, by a powerful state, of a naval base in the immediate vicinity of the Republic of El Salvador would constitute a serious menace — not merely imaginary, but real and apparent — to the freedom of life and the autonomy of that republic.[3]

More recently still, China has declared, with reference to the Lansing-Ishii agreement, that

> The principle adopted by the Chinese government toward the friendly nations has always been one of justice and equality. . . .
> Hereafter the Chinese Government will still adhere to the principles

---

1846: "Independent Powers who negotiate on a footing of perfect equality, and deliberate on common interests, are never called upon to register decisions and acts adopted without their participation." Hertslet, II, 1075.

[1] Jon Ghica to Granville, London, February 1, 1883, *B. F. S. P.*, LXXIV, 1241.

[2] Same to same, London, February 12, 1883, *ibid.*, p. 1250.

[3] *A. J. I. L.* (1917), XI, 675.

hitherto adopted, and hereby it is again declared that the Chinese Government will not allow itself to be bound by any agreement entered into by other nations.[1]

Throughout Latin America the principle of state equality is regarded as the essential premise of an international Magna Charta. Drago's declaration, in his famous dispatch to the minister of the Argentine Republic at Washington, December 29, 1902, that

Among the fundamental principles of public international law which humanity has consecrated, one of the most precious is that which decrees that all states, whatever be the force at their disposal, are entities in law, perfectly equal one to another, and mutually entitled by virtue thereof to the same consideration and respect,[2]

was received with universal approval in the capitals of Central and South America. Secretary Root's address [3] before the Third Conference of the American Republics at Rio de Janeiro in 1906 evoked a similar enthusiasm. At the Second Hague Peace Conference in 1907 the South American delegates were the most outspoken champions of complete equality.[4] The Declaration of the Rights of Nations,[5] recently issued by the American Institute of International Law, is an accurate epitome of the view that prevails throughout the republics of Central and South America.

EQUALITY IN THE FOREIGN POLICY OF THE UNITED STATES

Throughout its history the United States has professed to stand for the same principle, a position which has been

[1] *New York Times*, November 14, 1917. A press despatch from Paris, dated October 17, 1918, reports that a mass meeting of Jews held at Vienna on October 14, 1918, passed a resolution asking that the Jewish people be admitted into the league of nations with rights equal to those of other nationalities.

[2] *U. S. For. Rel.* (1903), p. 2.

[3] Root, *Latin America and the United States*, p. 6.

[4] *La Deux. Confér.*, I, 333–334, 593; II, 20, 147, 148–155, 158, 180, 182, 618–622, 624–627, 643–650, 838.

[5] *Supra*, p. 154.

frequently affirmed by its official spokesmen. The first formal and official statement of the principle in America is the opening sentence of the Declaration of Independence:

> When in the course of human events, it becomes necessary for one people to dissolve the political bands which have connected them with another, and to assume among the powers of the earth, the separate and equal station to which the Laws of Nature and of Nature's God entitle them, a decent respect for the opinions of mankind requires that they should declare the causes which impel them to the separation.

In the negotiations for peace in 1782, Jay did not consider that independence required any aid or validity from British acts, " provided that nation treated us as she treated other nations, viz., on a footing of equality." [1]

In 1796, the United States minister to England wrote to Secretary Pickering, suggesting that open letters might be obtained from the French and British ministers in order to insure an uninterrupted passage. Secretary Pickering replied:

> If a public minister going to his place of destination must pass through the territories of the belligerent powers, passports for him through a neutral would be expedient; but the ocean being the highway of all nations, it would seem to me to derogate from our equal rights as a sovereign power, to seek protection there under any passport but our own. [2]

---

[1] Jay to Livingston, Paris, November 17, 1782, Wharton, *Revol. Diplom. Corresp. of the U. S.*, VI, 17.

[2] Pickering to King, June 17, 1796, Moore, *Digest*, IV, 559. Referring to the basic principles of foreign policy established during Washington's administration, Johnson says: " The first of these cardinal doctrines was that of impregnable independence, and the equal sovereignty of the United States with any and all other nations of the world. France more than any other had striven to deny and to prevent this, and to make us a mere dependency upon her. But we had wisely and indeed necessitously insisted upon fulfilment of the Declaration of Independence. We were no *quasi*-state, no dwarf or cripple, no mere probationer on sufferance. We were a full-fledged, full-grown nation, possessed of all the functions, powers, and rights of national sovereignty, the peer in legal standing of any other nation in the world; inalienably endowed with full powers, in Jefferson's pithy phrase,

After the United States became strong enough to assert without question its own " equal rights as a sovereign power," the obligation to accord similar rights of equality to other and weaker nations was not infrequently invoked against it by its own statesmen. When President Grant's administration employed the United States navy in support of negotiations for the acquisition of a part of San Domingo, in 1871, Senator Sumner secured the insertion of the following resolutions of protest in the records of Congress:

Resolved, That since the equality of all nations, without regard to population, size, or power, is an axiom of International Law, as the equality of all men is an axiom of our Declaration of Independence, nothing can be done to a small or weak nation that would not be done to a large or powerful nation, or that we would not allow to be done to ourselves; and therefore any treatment of the republic of Hayti by the Navy of the United States inconsistent with this principle is an infraction of international law in one of its great safeguards, and should be disavowed by the Government of the United States.

Resolved, That since certain naval officers of the United States, with large war-vessels, including the monitor called the Dictator and the frigate Severn, with powerful armaments, acting under instructions from the Executive and without the authority of an act of Congress, have entered one or more ports of the republic of Hayti, a friendly nation, and under the menace of open and instant war have coerced and restrained that republic in its sovereignty and independence under International Law; therefore, in justice to the republic of Hayti, also in recognition of its equal rights in the family of nations, and in deference to the fundamental principles of our institutions, these hostile acts should be disavowed by the Government of the United States.[1]

Secretary Bayard gave official expression to the same principle fifteen years later in his report on Pelletier's case:

' to do all acts and things which independent States may of right do.' " *America's Foreign Relations*, I, 201. There is a flavor of vaingloriousness about the statement, but it gives a pretty accurate description of the spirit of American statecraft at the end of the eighteenth century.

[1] March 23, 1871, *Cong. Globe*, 42d Cong., 1st session (1871), Pt. I, p. 235.

By the law of nations, it must be remembered, all sovereign states are to be treated as equals. There is no distinction between strong states and weak; the weak are to have assigned to them the same territorial sanctities as the strong enjoy. There is a good reason for this. Were it not so, weak states would be the objects of rapine, which would not only disgrace civilization, but would destroy the security of the seas, by breeding hordes of marauders and buccaneers, who would find their spoil in communities which have no adequate power of self-defense.[1]

Discussing the question of diplomatic intervention in behalf of disappointed litigants, Secretary Gresham declared in 1893 that " complete reciprocal international equality " existed between the United States and Mexico.[2]

Such casual assertions of the principle, however, were not enough to prevent the growth of the idea, in many parts of South America, that the Monroe Doctrine " implied or carried with it, an assumption of superiority, and of a right to exercise some kind of protectorate over the countries to whose territory that doctrine applies." One of the purposes of Secretary Root's mission to South America in 1906 was " to dispel this unfounded impression." [3] In an address before the Third Conference of The American Republics at Rio de Janeiro on July 31, 1906, he said:

We wish for no victories but those of peace; for no territory except our own; for no sovereignty except sovereignty over ourselves. We deem the independence and equal rights of the smallest and weakest member of the family of nations entitled to as much respect as those of the greatest empire; and we deem the observance of that respect the chief guaranty of the weak against the oppression of the strong. We neither claim nor desire any rights or privileges or powers that we do not freely concede to every American republic. We wish to increase our prosperity, to expand our trade, to grow in wealth, in

[1] Sen. Ex. Doc., 49th Cong., 2d sess. (1886–87), I, No. 64, 14.
[2] Gresham to Ryan, April 26, 1893, Moore, *Digest*, VI, 270.
[3] President Roosevelt's message to Congress, December 3, 1906, House Docs., 59th Cong., 2d sess. (1906–07), I, Pt. I, p. xlviii.

wisdom, and in spirit; but our conception of the true way to accomplish this is not to pull down others and profit by their ruin, but to help all friends to a common prosperity and a common growth, that we may all become greater and stronger together.[1]

Secretary Root's declaration was publicly approved by President Roosevelt in his message to Congress of December 3, 1906. After quoting the passage from Secretary Root's address, printed above, the President continued:

These words appear to have been received with acclaim in every part of South America. They have my hearty approval, as I am sure they will have yours, and I can not be wrong in the conviction that they correctly represent the sentiments of the whole American people.[2]

America's belief in the equality of nations was reaffirmed by former Secretary Root in his welcome to Latin American publicists taking part in the Second Pan-American Scientific Congress at Washington, December 30, 1915. He said:

It is now nearly ten years ago when your people, gentlemen, and the other peoples of South America, were good enough to give serious and respectful consideration to a message that it was my fortune to take from this great and powerful republic of North America to the other American nations. I wish to say to you, gentlemen, and to all my Latin American friends here in this congress, that everything that I said in behalf of the Government of the United States at Rio de Janeiro in 1906 is true now as it was true then. There has been no departure from the standard of feeling and of policy which was declared then in behalf of the American people. On the contrary, there is throughout the people of this country a fuller realization of the duty and the morality and the high policy of that standard.

. . . The great body of the people of these United States love justice, not merely as they demand it for themselves, but in being willing to render it to others. We believe in the independence and the dignity of nations, and while we are great, we estimate our greatness as one of the least of our possessions, and we hold the smallest state, be it upon an island of the Caribbean or anywhere in Central or South Amer-

---

[1] *Latin America and the United States*, p. 10. Cf. " Ethics of the Panama Question," in *Addresses on International Subjects*, p. 175.

[2] *Supra*, p. 178, note 3.

ica, as our equal in dignity, in the right to respect and in the right to
the treatment of an equal. We believe that nobility of spirit, that
high ideals, that capacity for sacrifice are nobler than material wealth.
We know that these can be found in the little state as well as in the
big one. In our respect for you who are small, and for you who are
great, there can be no element of condescension or patronage, for that
would do violence to our own conception of the dignity of independent
sovereignty. We desire no benefits which are not the benefits rendered by honorable equals to each other. We seek no control that we
are unwilling to concede to others, and so long as the spirit of American
freedom shall continue, it will range us side by side with you, great and
small, in the maintenance of the rights of nations, the rights which exist
as against us and as against all the rest of the world.[1]

President Wilson has repeatedly and emphatically asserted
in recent diplomatic utterances that respect for the equality
of nations is to be regarded as a cardinal principle of American foreign policy.[2]

EQUALITY IN THE HAGUE PEACE CONFERENCES

The meeting of the two Peace Conferences at The Hague
in 1899 and 1907 gave rise to some new and perplexing questions with respect to the application of equality as a practical rule.[3] The Conferences themselves were heralded by
many as an affirmation in the domain of practical politics
of the equality of nations.[4] Both in respect to composition
and procedure the first Conference was based upon equality.
The same principle was given greater significance in the
second through the representation of the republics of Central
and South America. Speaking of the participation of the

[1] *Latin America and the United States*, p. 292.   [2] See *infra*, pp. 184–185.
[3] Cf. Hicks, in *A.J.I.L* (1908), II, 530–561, and Huber, *Die Gleichheit der
Staaten*.
[4] In other quarters, on the other hand, they were denounced as conclusive proof
of the impossibility of equality as a practical principle. See *The London Times*,
September 14, 1907, p. 9c; September 21, 1907, p. 9c; October 19, 1907, p. 9c;
October 21, 1907, p. 3f; and October 24, 1907; *The Spectator* (1907), XCIX, 418,
472.

republics of the New World, in the closing session, the first
delegate from the Argentine Republic said:

It signalizes an advantage that is common to us all; it denotes progress and implies an improvement in public law which, because of its
universal nature, requires the "consensus" of all sovereignties without
distinction between states or continents. We may affirm henceforth
that the political equality of states has ceased to be a fiction and that
it abides, established as an obvious reality.[1]

The system of arbitration established by the first Conference has been cited frequently as recognizing the essential equality of states.[2] A very able address by Léon
Bourgeois in support of the convention by which the system
was instituted is often quoted. In the course of that address
he declared:

Gentlemen, what is now the rule among individual men will hereafter obtain among nations. Such international Institutions as these
will be the protection of the weak against the powerful. In the conflicts of brute force, where fighters of flesh and with steel are in line,
we may speak of great Powers and small, of weak and of mighty.
When swords are thrown in the balance, one side may easily outweigh
the other. But in the weighing of rights and ideas disparity ceases,
and the rights of the smallest and weakest Powers count as much in
the scales as those of the mightiest.[3]

At the second Conference an attempt was made to institute two supernational tribunals, a permanent prize court
and a permanent court of arbitral justice. The composition
of the tribunal became one of the most controverted points

[1] *La Deux. Confér.*, I, 593. Huber says that the Second Peace Conference presented " a representation of all civilized states on the basis of a formal equality of
rights for all the associated states." *Die Gleichheit der Staaten*, p. 99.

[2] *La Deux. Confér.*, II, 160, 619, 625, 643. See also Bonfils, *Manuel*, § 278,
p. 165; Huber, *Die Gleichheit der Staaten*, pp. 89, 91. Of the organization
adopted in 1899 for the Permanent Court of Arbitration, Huber says: " Es kann
deshalb gesagt werden, dass die erste Friedenskonferenz dem Grundsatz der Gleichheit der Staaten unverkennbaren Ausdruck gegeben hat."

[3] *La Confér. Int.*, Pt. IV, p. 76 (transl. from Holls, *Peace Conference at The Hague*,
p. 274). See also *La Deux. Confér.*, II, 88.

in each instance, the smaller states demanding perfect equality of representation on the proposed courts, while the great powers were unwilling that permanent tribunals should be constituted on that basis. The controversy provoked more discussion of the principle of equality than had ever taken place before outside the writings of the publicists.

In the case of the prize court, many of the smaller states eventually waived their claim to perfect equality of representation.[1] Others, however, qualified their vote for the project with reservations as to the court's composition. Thus, the Haitian delegation made a formal reservation

as regards article 15, which, for the composition of the Court, has not adopted the principle of absolute equality among all the sovereign Powers called together in that capacity and represented at the Conference.[2]

The Venezuelan delegation protested against the plan because it did not recognize the absolute equality of sovereign states, and abstained from voting. The delegation declared in the first committee that

the Second Peace Conference being a universal assembly, its task was to establish principles which could be universally admitted and to create institutions guaranteeing, in absolute equality, the interests which every state deems essential to its sovereignty.

It would be superfluous, after the prolonged deliberations of the Committee of Examination, to elucidate again a doctrine which may be considered as consecrated by the juridical conscience of the whole world and which, moreover, has been expressly admitted at the time of the calling of the Second Conference, from the moment when it began its labors.[3]

The smaller states were so successful in asserting their claim to equal representation in case of the proposed court of arbitral justice that no convention could be agreed upon.[4]

---

[1] See *La Deux. Confér.*, I, 165–169; II, 11–33, 797, 832, 849.

[2] *Ibid.*, I, 168. The final vote, with abstentions and reservations, is given *loc. cit.*

[3] *Ibid.*, II, 20.   [4] *Ibid.*, I, 332–335; II, 144–160, 177–190, 335, 632, 697.

The delegate from Switzerland was frankly skeptical as to the possibility of constituting such a court, but took the keenest satisfaction in observing that throughout the debates

it had been recognized that the primordial principle of the law of nations, the absolute equality of sovereign states, was perfectly unimpeachable (*parfaitement intangible*).[1]

The Dominican Republic's representative declared that

In spite of material differences of population, territorial extent, wealth, position and political influence in the world, and even of scientific culture, existing among the different states that ought to concur in the formation of this great international tribunal, it is evident that there is no adequate reason for sacrificing, in the scheme of composition, the fundamental principle of the equality of states here where it exists, as it does for private individuals, before the law.[2]

The Brazilian delegate, Barbosa, was the most uncompromising and brilliant exponent of the point of view of the smaller states. His addresses on the subject of equality are classical expositions of the extreme interpretation of that principle.[3] In an impassioned speech before the first committee, he said:

There are, no doubt, between state and state, as between individual and individual, differences of culture, of honesty, of wealth, of physical strength. But is there any difference arising therefrom as to their essential rights? Civil rights are identical for all men. Political rights are the same for all citizens. Lord Kelvin or Mr. John Morley have the same voice in the election of the sovereign Parliament of Great Britain as a workingman mentally famished by the misery of his labors. And yet, is the normal intelligence of said artisan, placed at the lower level by his suffering and toil, to be compared with that of the statesman or of the man of science? Well, then, sover-

---

[1] *La Deux. Confér.*, II, 145. Several of the smaller states denied the necessity and opportuneness of creating a new permanent tribunal. Huber, *Die Gleichheit der Staaten*, p. 93.

[2] *La Deux. Confér.*, II, 147.

[3] *Ibid.*, II, 148–155, 618–622, 624–627, 643–650.

eignty is the prime and elemental right of constituted and independent states. Therefore sovereignty signifies equality. In theory, as in practice, sovereignty is absolute. It knows no grades. The juridical administration of law is a branch of sovereignty. If there must be among States a common organ of justice, all States must have of necessity an equivalent representation.[1]

EQUALITY IN THE DIPLOMATIC PAPERS OF THE WORLD WAR

The world war has brought new professions of faith in the equality of nations. The crushing of small states unfortunately situated in the path of invasion and the idealism which has been born of the world's suffering have aroused a new interest in the safeguarding of little nations. This interest is reflected more and more in the utterances of statesmen. Its common expression is similar to the familiar language of the books.

The American note of March 30, 1915, protesting against the British Order in Council restricting neutral trade with Germany, asserted " the principle of universal equality of sovereignty on the high seas as between belligerents and nations not engaged in war," subject to certain recognized exceptions in case of unneutral service, contraband trade, and blockade.[2] President Wilson asserted the universal application of the principle in his address to the United States Senate of January 22, 1917, outlining the terms upon which the United States would be willing to join the other civilized nations of the earth in guaranteeing the permanence of peace. He said:

Only a peace between equals can last. Only a peace the very principle of which is equality and a common participation in a common benefit. The right state of mind, the right feeling between nations, is as necessary for a lasting peace as is the just settlement of vexed questions of territory or of racial and national allegiance.

[1] *La Deux. Confér.*, II, 150 (Perez' transl.).
[2] *A. J. I. L. Suppl.* (1915), IX, Special Number, 117

The equality of nations upon which peace must be founded if it is to last must be an equality of rights; the guarantees exchanged must neither recognize nor imply a difference between big nations and small, between those that are powerful and those that are weak. Right must be based upon the common strength, not upon the individual strength, of the nations upon whose concert peace will depend. Equality of territory or of resources there of course cannot be; nor any other sort of equality not gained in the ordinary peaceful and legitimate development of the peoples themselves. But no one asks or expects anything more than an equality of rights. Mankind is looking now for freedom for life, not for equipoises of power.[1]

Again, in his inaugural address of March 5, 1917, the President began his declaration of American principles with the assertion

That all nations are equally interested in the peace of the world and in the political stability of free peoples, and equally responsible for their maintenance.

That the essential principle of peace is the actual equality of nations in all matters of right or privilege.[2]

A little later, in his war message to Congress, he declared that the United States would fight

for democracy, for the right of those who submit to authority to have a voice in their own governments, for the rights and liberties of small nations, for a universal dominion of right by such a concert of free peoples as shall bring peace and safety to all nations and make the world itself at last free.[3]

Addressing Congress on December 4, 1917, he reaffirmed his belief in " justice and equality of rights " as essential to permanent foundations of world peace.[4]

[1] *Cong. Record*, 64th Cong., 2d sess. (1917), LIV, Pt. 2, p. 1742.
[2] *Ibid.*, 65th Cong., special sess. (1917), LV, Pt. 1, p. 3.
[3] *Ibid.*, 1st sess. (1917), LV, Pt. 1, p. 104.
[4] *Ibid.*, 2d sess. (1917), LVI, Pt. 1, pp. 21, 23. Addressing an audience of loan workers in New York on September 27, 1918, President Wilson was reported to have formulated the first of five principles, which he enumerated as the practical program of America's peace terms, as follows: " First, the impartial justice meted out must involve no discrimination between those to whom we wish to be

These declarations have had their reaction at other capitals. In the German Government's reply to Pope Benedict's peace note it was insisted that before the outbreak of war

Germany sought within her national frontiers the free development of her spiritual and material possessions, and outside the Imperial territory unhindered competition with nations enjoying equal rights and equal esteem.[1]

The German Government might have cited the Emperor's message of March 21, 1871, to the first Reichstag, in which he declared that

The respect which Germany demands for its own independence will be accorded freely to the independence of all other states and peoples, the weak no less than the powerful.[2]

In outlining to the Reichstag his policies as chancellor on October 5, 1918, Prince Maximilian of Baden was reported to have declared that Germany was willing to join a general league of nations based upon the principle of equal rights for all, both strong and weak.

There is a most explicit affirmation of equality in the statement made by Premier Lloyd George to the British Trade Union Conference on January 5, 1918. Referring to Count Czernin's statement of December 25, 1917, the Prime Minister said:

Does it mean that Belgium, and Serbia, Montenegro and Roumania will be as independent and as free to direct their own destinies as the German or any other nation ? Or does it mean that all manner of interferences and restrictions, political and economic, incompatible with the status and dignity of a free and self-respecting people, are to

just and those to whom we do not wish to be just. It must be a justice that plays no favorites, and knows no standard but the equal rights of the several peoples concerned."

[1] *A. J. I. L. Suppl.* (1917), XI, 219.

[2] Gareis, *Institutionen*, § 24, p. 92.

be imposed ? If this is the intention then there will be one kind of independence for a great nation and an inferior kind of independence for a small nation. We must know what is meant for equality of right among nations, small as well as great, is one of the fundamental issues this country and her Allies are fighting to establish in this war.[1]

SUMMARY

There is little that need be said by way of summary of the formal statements in regard to equality which appear in the documentary literature of the past century. In general, they simply echo the familiar statements of the text-books and treatises. The language of Sir William Scott and Chief Justice Marshall was the language of Burlamaqui, Vattel, and their contemporaries, nor did those distinguished judges add anything to a conception which had already reached a mature development in the writings of the classical publicists. The same conception comes circuitously from the publicists in the American Institute's *Declaration of the Rights of Nations.* The naturalist idea, indeed the very language in which it was expounded, reappears in the protests of smaller nations, before international tribunals, in diplomatic papers, and in the Peace Conferences at The Hague. The application of the principle gives rise to new problems at The Hague, but the principle itself remains unchanged. So in the diplomatic utterances provoked by the recent war the equality of nations is asserted with an understanding and in language, if one be permitted to interpolate " the Laws of Nature and of Nature's God," which would have been understood as readily among statesmen and publicists of the eighteenth century.

---

[1] *British War Aims,* authorized version as published by the British Government, New York, George H. Doran Company, 1918, p. 5. Cf. the statements attributed to the British Secretary of State for Foreign Affairs, Arthur J. Balfour, in regard to equality in a league of nations, in an Associated Press despatch from London, December 7, 1918.

Those who affirm as well as those who deny the principle of equality agree that the practice of nations tends to impose limitations upon it. These limitations, their nature, and significance constitute the subject-matter of succeeding chapters.

CHAPTER VI

INTERNAL LIMITATIONS UPON THE EQUALITY OF STATES

THE NATURE OF INTERNAL LIMITATIONS

IT has been pointed out that equality among members of the society of nations is a matter of capacity. Limitations upon capacity may be either internal or external; internal as they are the result of the state's organic constitution, and external as they are the consequence of relations with other members of international society.

Internal limitations upon equality are imposed by the fundamental organization of the state. Before it can acquire personality in the law of nations the state must have *de facto* existence. This existence requires a considerable population, occupying a definite territory, having a separate political organization or government, and capable of entering into relations, by means of its government, with members of the society of nations. The *de facto* entity thus constituted acquires *de jure* personality through recognition by members of the international community.

As a juristic person in the society of nations the state can express itself only through its government, which is defined and limited in its organic constitution. As Despagnet says:

The relations of the constitutional law of each country to international law are easy enough to understand. We know indeed that by the very necessity of things states can enter into relations among themselves only by means of an agency which is invested, from this point of view, with the powers of the state, and which represents the latter, considered as a moral person, either as it acquires rights or attempts to enforce rights previously acquired, or as it is obliged to respond to its obligations.[1]

[1] *R. G. D. I. P.* (1895), II, 184.

Publicists frequently assert that the law of nations has no concern with the constitution of a state. Phillimore says:

It is a sound general principle, and one to be laid down at the threshold of the science of which we are treating, that International Law has no concern with the form, character, or power of the constitution or government of a State, with the religion of its inhabitants, the extent of its domain, or the importance of its position and influence in the commonwealth of nations.[1]

This must be taken to mean that, so far as the law of nations is concerned, the different peoples are free to set up whatever constitution or government they choose. It cannot be taken to mean that the law of nations is blind to all variations in the constitutions and governments of states, for certain of those variations are the source of important capacities and incapacities with respect to international relations.

In considering the legal capacity of the state as an international person it is important to distinguish capacity for rights and for transactions. A right may be defined as a power in the state of exacting a certain act, forbearance, or benefit, on account of a particular interest, with the aid and assent of the law of nations. A transaction, on the other hand, is an act or manifestation of will on the part of the state, directed to a possible result which is permitted by the law of nations, and the intent and purpose of which is to bring about certain legal consequences. Both of these conceptions are included in the idea of legal capacity. Indeed, the capacity to enter into certain transactions may be quite as important to the state as capacity for rights. If the only agency through which the state can express itself internationally is incapable, under the organic law, of ac-

[1] *Commentaries*, I, 81. See also Pradier-Fodéré *Traité*, § 149, I, 256; Walker, *Manual*, p. 13; Woolsey, *Int. Law*, § 39, p. 39. Cf. Despagnet, in *R. G. D. I. P.* (1895), II, 184–199; Fiore, *Int. Law Cod.*, § 399; Pillet, in *R. G. D. I. P.* (1898), V, 86.

quiring certain rights, entering into certain transactions, or of undertaking other transactions except according to prescribed methods of procedure, then the capacity of the state itself may be said to be organically limited.[1]

Internal limitations upon legal capacity must not be confused with the conception of sovereignty. Since they may be altered or eliminated by amending the constitution, they do not impair sovereignty as that theory is generally understood. However, important as this consideration may be from the point of view of the theory of sovereignty, it has only a potential importance for the law of nations. It is well known that in most states amendments of the fundamental law are made infrequently. Under many constitutions they are made with considerable difficulty. When consummated they effect a mutation in the legal condition or capacity of the state concerned. The law of nations is not presently concerned with potential changes in the legal condition of its subjects. It is concerned immediately with the existing capacities and incapacities of the members of international society.[2] It is obliged to take account of those internal limitations on equality which the people of each state, in order to secure certain desired advantages, have created in perfecting their political organization.

Internal Limitations on the Form of Transactions

The most familiar of internal limitations upon the capacity of international persons are those which affect only the

---

[1] A similar view, in relation to the internal capacity of the state, has been presented by Gray in his comments on the Austinian theory of sovereignty. He says: " The truth is that the ideal or fictitious entity, the State, can manifest itself only through organs, and these organs may be so limited that there are certain acts they cannot perform, and therefore there may be no one sovereign in Austin's sense, with complete powers. Such is the case in the United States of America." *Nature and Sources of the Law*, § 180, p. 76.

[2] The same is true of other than constitutional incapacities. Thus an inland state has no present capacity for certain littoral and maritime rights, although a very small acquisition of territory would give it access to the sea.

form of transactions, i. e., those which require a particular mode of proceeding. Limitations of this kind are exemplified in constitutional provisions with reference to the exercise of the treaty power.[1]   While such limitations do not detract from the completeness of the power, they are nevertheless of great international importance because they determine in large measure the rapidity with which a transaction may be consummated, the secrecy or publicity of the transaction, the extent to which it represents an expression of the popular will on each side, and consequently the good faith with which its provisions are likely to be observed.

The international importance of such limitations has been recognized by statesmen of all times and of widely divergent points of view.   Machiavelli observed that leagues and alliances with republics are more to be trusted than those with princes:

Taking all things together now, I believe that in such cases which involve imminent peril there will be found somewhat more of stabil-

---

[1] The most useful comparative studies of the treaty-making power are Crandall, *Treaties, Their Making and Enforcement;* Meier, *Über den Abschluss von Staatsverträgen;* and Michon, *Les traités internationaux devant les chambres.*

Unless otherwise indicated, constitutions of the different states cited in the notes to the present chapter are the following: Argentine, 1860; Austria, Fundamental Laws of 1867; Austria-Hungary, Austrian Law Concerning Common Affairs, 1867; Belgium, 1831; Bolivia, 1880; Brazil, 1891; Bulgaria, 1879, amended 1893 and 1911; Chile, 1833; China, Amended Provisional Constitution, May 1, 1914; Colombia, 1886; Costa Rica, 1871, with amendments to 1905; Cuba, 1901; Denmark, 1849, revised 1866; Dominican Republic, 1908; Ecuador, 1897; France, Constitutional Laws of 1875; Germany, 1871; Greece, 1864; Guatemala, 1879, amended 1887; Haiti, 1889; Honduras, 1904; Italy, 1848; Japan, 1889; Luxemburg, 1868; Mexico, 1917; Montenegro, 1905; Netherlands, as amended 1887; Nicaragua, 1911; Norway, 1814; Panama, 1904; Paraguay, 1870; Persia, Fundamental Laws of December 30, 1906, and Supplementary Fundamental Laws of October 8, 1907; Peru, 1860; Portugal, 1911; Roumania, 1866, with amendments, of 1879 and 1884; Russia, Fundamental Laws of 1906; Salvador, 1886; Servia 1889, restored in 1903; Spain, 1876; Sweden, 1809; Switzerland 1874; Turkey, 1909; United States, 1789; Uruguay, 1829; Venezuela, 1909.

With a few exceptions, the constitutions indicated above are those which were in force at the outbreak of the World War in 1914. Subdivisions are cited uniformly as articles, sections, and paragraphs, in the order named, without regard to varying practices which prevail in the different countries.

ity in republics than in princes. For even if the republics were inspired by the same feelings and intentions as the princes, yet the fact of their movements being slower will make them take more time in forming resolutions, and therefore they will less promptly break their faith.[1]

There is a striking passage in President Wilson's address to Congress of April 2, 1917, in which the same truth receives explicit recognition:

A steadfast concert for peace can never be maintained except by a partnership of democratic nations. No autocratic government could be trusted to keep faith within it or observe its covenants. It must be a league of honour, a partnership of opinion. Intrigue would eat its vitals away; the plottings of inner circles who could plan what they would and render account to no one would be a corruption seated at its very heart. Only free peoples can hold their purpose and their honour steady to a common end and prefer the interests of mankind to any narrow interest of their own.[2]

The maximum of rapidity, secrecy, and irresponsibility in treaty making has been attained in some states by providing for the definitive conclusion of all treaties by the executive. Such provisions have a peculiar significance in states where the real executive is not hampered by any great degree of responsibility to a representative assembly. Before the Young Turk Revolution treaty making was a prerogative of the Sultan.[3] The situation in Russia before the Revolution was concisely summarized in three short articles of the Fundamental Laws:

The Emperor of all the Russias wields the supreme autocratic power. To obey his authority, not only through fear but for the sake of conscience, is ordered by God himself.

The Emperor has supreme control of all relations of the Russian Empire with foreign powers. He likewise determines the course of the international policy of the Russian Empire.

[1] *Discourses*, I, 59 (Detmold's transl.).
[2] *Cong. Record*, 65th Cong., 1st sess. (1917), LV, Pt. 1, 104.
[3] Const. 1876, Art. 7.

The Emperor declares war and concludes peace, as well as other treaties with foreign countries.[1]

The Emperor of Japan " declares war, makes peace, and concludes treaties." [2] The King of Sweden must ask the opinion of certain of his advisers before concluding treaties:

The King shall have power to conclude treaties and alliances with foreign powers after having, in the manner set forth in the preceding article, consulted the minister of state, the minister of foreign affairs, and one other member of the Council of State summoned for this purpose, or two other members of the Council of State, if the minister of foreign affairs is also minister of state.[3]

The constitutions of certain states require legislative approval before treaties can be concluded, but make an exception of secret articles which, for reasons of state, are left to executive discretion. Under the organic law of Norway the Storthing has power

To have submitted to it the alliances and treaties which the King has entered into with foreign powers on behalf of the state, except secret articles, which shall not, however, conflict with those that are public.[4]

Similarly, the Persian Fundamental Laws of 1906 made an exception of " treaties which for reasons of State and the

[1] Arts. 4, 12, 13 (Dodd's transl.).

[2] Art. 13. See Hornbeck, *Contemporary Politics in the Far East*, Chap. 8.

[3] Art. 12 (Dodd's transl.). The preceding article provides in part as follows: " Ministerial affairs (i.e., all matters which bear upon the relations of the kingdom with foreign powers) shall be prepared, as the King may think proper, by the minister for foreign affairs, whose duty it shall be to present them to the King in the presence of the minister of state and of one other member of the Council of State, or if the minister of foreign affairs is also minister of state, in the presence of two other members of the Council of State summoned for that purpose. . . . After having received and entered upon the minutes the advice of these officers, for which they are responsible, the King shall make his decision in their presence; the minutes of such meetings shall be kept by a person specially designated for this purpose. The King shall inform the Council of State of as much as he may think proper of such decisions, in order that they may also have some knowledge of this department of the government." (Dodd's transl.).

[4] Art. 75, § g (Dodd's transl.).

public advantage, must be kept secret." [1] After the disappearance of the *raison de force majeure* and as soon as the interests and safety of the country required it, such treaties were to be submitted to the legislature with adequate explanations.[2] Other executives conclude less formal agreements without legislative approval.[3] In at least one constitution this authority has been defined with some precision.[4]

In most of the states of Europe treaty-making is regarded as an executive function, but certain categories of treaties require legislative approval. The power is theoretically a prerogative of the Crown in England, but the practice of parliamentary government has made legislative coöperation necessary in certain cases. Anson says:

No one but the King can bind the community by treaty, but can he always do so without the coöperation of Parliament? It would seem to follow from the general principles of our constitution that a treaty which lays a pecuniary burden on the people or which alters the law of the land needs Parliamentary sanction. If it were not so the King, in virtue of this prerogative, might indirectly tax or legislate without consent of Parliament. . . .

Treaties which thus affect the rights of the King's subjects are made subject to the approval of Parliament, and are submitted for its approval before ratification, or ratified under condition.[5]

There is some controversy as to whether a treaty can impair private rights or alienate territory without parliamentary sanction. Constitutional tendencies indicate that these cases will be brought clearly within the category of treaties that cannot be made without legislative coöperation.

English practice has been copied on the Continent, direct legislative participation being substituted for indirect, and

---

[1] Art. 24.   [2] Suppl. Fundam. Laws of 1907, Art. 52.

[3] On this authority in the United States, see Crandall, *Treaties*, §§ 56–61.

[4] Colombia, Art. 120, § 10. Cf. Uruguay, Annex No. 3 (1862).

[5] *Law and Custom of the Constitution*, II, Pt. II, 103, 109. See Anson, *op. cit.*, II, Pt. I, 53, and Pt. II, 102–110; Crandall, *Treaties*, §§ 115–125; Dicey, *Law of the Constitution*, p. 115; Michon, *Les traités*, pp. 309–340.

the whole subject receiving greater constitutional precision. The following provisions of the organic law of Belgium have furnished the prototype for several of the later constitutions:

> The King commands the forces both by land and sea, declares war, makes treaties of peace, of alliance, and of commerce. He shall give information to the two Houses of these acts as soon as the interests and safety of the state permit, adding thereto suitable comments.
>
> Treaties of commerce, and treaties which may burden the state, or bind Belgians individually, shall take effect only after having received the approval of the two Houses.
>
> No cession, exchange, or addition of territory shall take place except by virtue of a law. In no case shall the secret articles of a treaty be destructive of those openly expressed.[1]

Legislative approval is given in the form of a law which provides that the treaty shall have full effect, and which in practice is passed before the exchange of ratifications. Amendments may be offered which are in effect amendments of the treaty. If adopted they require the reopening of negotiations. " Treaties which may burden the state " include only those which impose a direct financial burden. Political treaties of the greatest importance, such as treaties of peace and alliance, do not require legislative approval unless they carry immediate financial obligations, directly affect private rights, or involve territorial adjustments.

Similar limitations upon the exercise of the treaty power are embodied in the constitutional law and practice of most European states.[2] Almost without exception legislative ap-

---

[1] Art. 68 (Dodd's transl.). See Crandall, *Treaties*, § 137; Michon, *Les traités*, pp. 346–373.

[2] Austria, Fundamental Law Concerning the Exercise of Administrative and Executive Power, Art. 6, and the Law Concerning Imperial Representation, § 11, a; Austria-Hungary, § 1, a; Bulgaria, Art. 17; Denmark, Art. 18; France, Constitutional Law on the Relations of the Public Powers, Art. 8; Germany, Art. 11; Greece, Arts. 32, 33; Italy, Art. 5; Luxemburg, Art. 37; Montenegro, Art. 7; Netherlands, Art. 59; Roumania, Art. 93; Servia, Art. 52; Spain, Art. 55. See also China, Art. 25; Turkey, Art. 7. See Crandall, *Treaties*, §§ 126–150; Michon, *Les traités*, pp. 341–432.

proval is required before territory can be ceded, annexed, or exchanged; and the same may be said of treaties involving a direct financial obligation. Treaties of commerce require legislative assent almost everywhere, either by express provision, or as a result of well established practice. In many cases the legislature must approve treaties affecting private rights. The German Constitution of 1871 provided for legislative participation in all treaties whose subject-matter was included within the legislative authority of the Empire:

> So far as treaties with foreign countries relate to matters which, according to Art. 4, are to be regulated by imperial legislation, the consent of the Bundesrat shall be required for their conclusion, and the approval of the Reichstag shall be necessary to render them valid.[1]

The French law differs only in details from that of Belgium, quoted above, and adds treaties of peace to the enumerated categories:

> The President of the Republic shall negotiate and ratify treaties. He shall give information regarding them to the chambers as soon as the interests and safety of the state permit.
>
> Treaties of peace and of commerce, treaties which involve the finances of the state, those relating to the person and property of French citizens in foreign countries, shall be ratified only after having been voted by the two chambers.
>
> No cession, exchange, or annexation of territory shall take place except by virtue of a law.[2]

The significant feature of European constitutions is the extent to which important treaties may be concluded without legislative coöperation. The executive is usually competent to conclude a great many administrative treaties which may be executed within the limits of executive power.

---

[1] Art. 11 (Dodd's transl.). See Crandall, *Treaties*, § 141; Michon, *Les traités*, pp. 407–420.

[2] Constitutional Law on the Relations of the Public Powers, Art. 8 (Dodd's transl.). See Crandall, *Treaties*, §§ 126–136; Michon, *Les traités*, pp. 194–308.

Important political treaties, treaties of alliance, and the like are left exclusively to executive authority.[1] Such transactions are required to be submitted to the legislature as soon as the interests and security of the state permit, but parliaments have been traditionally conservative in demanding information and explanations in such matters.

There is another type of constitutional provision with reference to the exercise of the treaty power which requires the executive to secure the coöperation of one chamber of the legislature in making all treaties. This is the situation in the United States, where the President has power,

by and with the advice and consent of the Senate, to make treaties, provided two-thirds of the Senators present concur.[2]

The President of Cuba is authorized

To conduct all diplomatic negotiations and conclude treaties with foreign nations, provided that these treaties be submitted for approval of the Senate, without which requisite they shall be neither valid nor binding upon the Republic.[3]

There is a similar provision in the organic law of Mexico.[4]

Other executives must have the approval of the full legislative power, including both chambers where the legislature is bicameral, before they can conclude any treaty. This type of limitation exists in Switzerland,[5] in Portugal,[6] and in all the republics of the New World [7] except the United

---

[1] Art. 55 of the Constitution of Spain includes treaties of offensive alliance among those which cannot be ratified until authorized by special law. In Portugal, where the legislature approves all treaties, treaties of alliance are submitted to Congress for examination in a secret session if two-thirds of the members so request. Art. 47, § 7.

[2] Art. 2, § 2. See Butler, *Treaty-Making Power of the United States;* Crandall, *Treaties,* §§ 8–115; Michon, *Les traités,* pp. 446–465; Tucker, *Limitations on the Treaty-Making Power Under the Constitution of the United States.*

[3] Art. 68, § 7 (Rodriguéz' transl.). See also Art. 47, § 6.

[4] Art. 76, I.

[5] Art. 85, § 5. See Crandall, *Treaties,* § 148; Michon, *Les traités,* pp. 435–445.

[6] Art. 26, § 15; Art. 47, § 7. See Crandall, *Treaties,* § 147.

[7] Argentine, Art. 67, § 19; Bolivia, Art. 52, § 14, Art. 54, § 5, Art. 89, § 1; Brazil,

States, Cuba, and Mexico. The Constitution of Brazil may be taken as an example. The President of Brazil is authorized

> To enter into negotiations with other countries, to conclude agreements, conventions, and treaties, always referring such treaties and conventions to the Congress.[1]

The Brazilian Congress has exclusive power " to decide definitely with regard to treaties and conventions with foreign nations." Differences of detail among the several American constitutions are not significant. In addition to the requirement of legislative approval, it is provided in the fundamental law of Uruguay that the executive shall initiate treaties with the advice of the Senate, while in Venezuela the President makes treaties with the consultative vote of the council of state. Legislative approval in Bolivia and Haiti is given in a formal joint session of the two chambers. Colombia makes an exception of international agreements in certain cases, while an amendment to the Uruguayan Constitution stipulates expressly that

> The power given to the General Assembly by clause 7, article 17 of the Constitution, shall be construed as being applicable to all conventions and contracts of whatever nature concluded or entered into by the Executive power with foreign nations.[2]

One other type of internal limitation affecting the procedure of treaty making should be considered. In a few cases the treaty power is divided between central and local

---

Art. 34, § 12, Art. 48, § 16; Chile, Art. 73, § 19; Colombia, Art. 76, § 20, Art. 120, § 10; Costa Rica, Art. 72, § 4, Art. 101, § 9; Dominican Republic, Art. 35, § 17, Art. 53, § 8; Ecuador, Art. 65, § 12, Art. 94, § 6; Guatemala, Art. 54, § 9, Art. 77, § 19; Haiti, Art. 60, § 3, Art. 101; Honduras, Art. 73, § 21, Art. 96, § 25; Nicaragua, Art. 85, § 8, Art. 111, § 10; Panama, Art. 65, §§ 4, 6, Art. 73, § 3; Paraguay, Art. 72, § 18, Art. 102, § 12; Peru, Art. 59, § 16, Art. 94, § 11; Salvador, Art. 68, § 29, Art. 91, §§ 6, 7; Uruguay, Art. 17, § 7, Art. 81, Annex No. 3; Venezuela, Art. 57, § 13, Art. 81, § 5.

[1] Art. 48, § 16 (Dodd's transl.). See also Art. 34, § 12.

[2] Annex No. 3 (Rodriguez' transl.).

governments. It is possible in the United States for a local state government to enter into agreements or compacts with a foreign power, provided the consent of the national Congress can be obtained.[1] The Mexican Constitution of 1857 excepted " coalitions between frontier states for offensive or defensive war against savage Indians " from the general prohibition of all treaties or alliances between states of the federal republic and foreign powers.[2] A more important division of authority is contemplated in the Constitution of Switzerland, which provides:

> By exception the cantons preserve the right of concluding treaties with foreign powers, respecting the administration of public property, and border and police intercourse; but such treaties shall contain nothing contrary to the Confederation or to the rights of other cantons.
>
> Official intercourse between cantons and foreign governments, or their representatives, shall take place through the Federal Council.
>
> Nevertheless, the cantons may correspond directly with the inferior officials and officers of a foreign state, in regard to the subjects enumerated in the preceding article.[3]

Treaties made by the cantons are examined and approved by the Federal Council; if protested by the Federal Council or another canton, they must be approved by the Federal Assembly.[4]

The most important division of this kind is in process of development within the British Empire. While in theory the treaty power of the Empire resides exclusively in the Crown, in practice it is coming to be exercised by the self-governing dominions whenever their interests are chiefly concerned.[5] The British Government withholds ratification

---

[1] Art. 1, § 10. See Crandall, *Treaties*, § 68.

[2] Art. 111, I. This exception has been omitted in the revision of 1917, Art. 117, I.

[3] Arts. 9, 10 (Dodd's transl.).

[4] Art. 85, § 5, Art. 102, § 7.

[5] Despagnet, in *R. G. D. I. P.* (1895), II, 196; Ewart, in *A. J. I. L.* (1913), VII, 268–284; Keith, in *J. C. L.* (1919), 3d series, I, I, 7–16, 13; Keith, *Responsible*

until the dominion parliament has expressed its approval, and its part in the transaction is coming to be a mere matter of form. Canada created a Department of External Affairs in 1909. The words of the statute are significant:

> The Secretary of State, as head of the department, shall have the conduct of all official communications between the Government of Canada and the Government of any other country in connection with the external affairs of Canada, and shall be charged with such other duties as may, from time to time, be assigned to the department by order of the Governor in Council in relation to such external affairs, or to the conduct and management of international or inter-colonial negotiations so far as they may appertain to the Government of Canada.[1]

The first report of the " Under-Secretary of State for External Affairs " shows that the Dominion has already negotiated treaties relating to fisheries, boundaries, and commerce.[2] The self-governing dominions have also been conceded the right to participate independently in important administrative treaties, such as the conventions providing for the Universal Postal Union, the International Institute of Agriculture, and the International Wireless Telegraph Union.[3]

A second category of internal limitations on the form of international transactions relates to the exercise of the war power. The society of nations has learned in bitter experience that "it is a vital international concern where the power of peace and war is lodged in each nation." Before the rise of modern representative governments the war power was usually regarded as an executive function. This

---

Government in the Dominions, pp. 222–236; Todd, *Parliamentary Government in the British Colonies*, pp. 192–218; Tupper, in *J. S. C. L.* (1917) N. s., XVII, 5–18.

[1] 8 & 9 Edw. VII, ch. 13. " Nominally, Canada has no foreign relations, but in reality she regulates them, very largely, as she wishes." Ewart, in *A.J.I.L.* (1913) VII, 269,

[2] Tupper, in *J. S. C. L.* (1917) N. s., XVII, 16.

[3] Myers, in *A. J. I. L.* (1914), VIII, 81–108.

conception of it has survived in a number of constitutions.[1] In some its exercise has been hedged about through the development of parliamentary responsibility; in others there are few or no restrictions on executive decision. Of the situation in England, Anson says:

> The King, acting on the advice of his Ministers, makes war and peace. The House of Commons may refuse supplies for a war, or either House may express its disapproval by resolutions condemnatory of the ministerial policy, or by address to the Crown, or by making the position of the ministry in other ways untenable; but Parliament has no direct means either of bringing about a war or of bringing a war to an end.[2]

The King of Sweden makes war or peace after consulting the Council of State:

> If the King wishes to declare war or to conclude peace he shall convene all the members of the Council of State into extraordinary council, shall lay before them the causes and circumstances to be considered, and shall require their opinions concerning the matter; each of them shall separately enter his opinion in the minutes, under the responsibility referred to in Art. 107. The King may then make and execute such a decision as he considers for the best interests of the country.[3]

Constitutional law and practice in a number of countries require the executive to inform the chambers, so far as the interests and security of the state permit, but in some countries it is not clear that even this much would be required.

Several executives have been deprived of the authority to declare offensive war without the consent of one or both of

---

[1] Austria, Fundamental Law Concerning the Exercise of Administrative and Executive Power, Art. 5; Belgium, Art. 68; China, Art. 22; Denmark, Art. 18; Greece, Art. 32; Italy, Art. 5; Japan, Art. 13; Luxemburg, Art. 37; Montenegro, Art. 7; Netherlands, Art. 58; Persia, Suppl. Fundam. Laws of 1907, Art. 51; Russia, Art. 13; Servia, Art. 52; Spain, Art. 54, § 4; Turkey, Art. 7.

[2] *Law and Custom of the Constitution*, II, Pt. II, 102.

[3] Art. 13 (Dodd's transl.).

the legislative chambers, but have been left free to declare defensive war.[1] This is implied in the organic law of Norway, which forbids the use of the troops and fleet in offensive war without the Storthing's consent, and also in the constitution of Portugal. It was expressly stipulated in the German Constitution of 1871, which provided:

> For a declaration of war in the name of the Empire, the consent of the Bundesrat is required, unless an attack is made upon the federal territory or its coasts.[2]

The executive in Brazil and Colombia may act alone in case of foreign invasion. In Honduras, under the Constitution of 1904, the same rule prevailed when circumstances did not permit the assembling of Congress. Two modern constitutions have associated the upper chamber of the legislature with the executive in the making of offensive war. In Germany, under the Constitution of 1871, the Emperor was obliged to secure the consent of the Bundesrat; in Colombia, the President must be authorized by the Senate.[3]

France, Portugal, and fifteen of the American republics vest the war power in the executive and legislature jointly.[4] Constitutional texts suggest a difference between the rule in France, Argentine, Chile, and several of the smaller republics, where the executive declares war with the consent of the chambers, and a second group, where the legislature declares war on the president's recommendation. There is

---

[1] Brazil, Art. 48, § 8; Colombia, Art. 120, § 11; Germany, Art. 11; Honduras, Art. 96, § 20; Norway, Art. 25; Portugal, Art. 26, § 14.

[2] Art. 11 (Dodd's transl.).

[3] Colombia, Art. 98, § 9; Germany, Art. 11.

[4] France, Constitutional Law on the Relations of the Public Powers, Art. 9; Portugal, Art. 26, § 14; Argentine, Art. 67, § 21, Art. 86, § 18; Bolivia, Art. 54, § 7; Brazil, Art. 34, § 11, Art. 48, §§ 7, 8; Chile, Art. 27, § 2, Art. 73, § 18; Costa Rica, Art. 72, § 6, Art. 101, § 14; Dominican Republic, Art. 53, § 15; Ecuador, Art. 65, § 12, Art. 94, § 11, Art. 110, § 2; Haiti, Art. 58, Art. 60, § 2; Mexico, Art. 73, XII, Art. 89, VIII; Nicaragua, Art. 85, § 18, Art. 111, § 25; Paraguay, Art. 72, § 18, Art. 102, § 16; Peru, Art. 59, § 15; Salvador, Art. 68, § 21, Art. 91, § 6; Uruguay, Art. 17, § 7, Art. 81; Venezuela, Art. 57, § 28, Art. 81, § 2.

no evidence, however, that the difference is anything more than a matter of words. In Bolivia and Haiti the chambers declare war in a formal joint session. In Venezuela a council of state is associated with the President in a consultative capacity.

The declaration of war is a legislative function exclusively in the United States, Switzerland, and several of the smaller republics.[1] The practical difference between constitutions of this type and those which vest the power in the executive and legislature jointly is of no great significance. The executive is everywhere charged with the general conduct of foreign relations. By virtue of this responsibility it is certain to have a large influence on the exercise of the war power.

In a few instances the war power, like the treaty power, is divided between central and local governments. The constituent states of the United States may not engage in war " unless actually invaded, or in such imminent danger as will not admit of delay." [2] A similar exception is embodied in the federal Constitution of Mexico, which provides:

No State shall, without the consent of the Congress: . . .

Make war on its own behalf on any foreign power, except in cases of invasion or of such imminent peril as to admit of no delay. In such event the State shall give notice immediately to the President of the Republic.[3]

The division which exists within the British Empire, although defined with less exactness, is of greater practical importance. The self-governing dominions are not only free, by reason of their constitutional position, to begin a defensive war, but they are also free to participate or not, as they please, in the wars of the Empire. As regards Canada's relation to the war power, Ewart concludes:

[1] United States, Art. 1, § 8; Switzerland, Art. 8, Art. 85, § 6; Cuba, Art. 59, § 12; Guatemala, Art. 54, § 15; Honduras, Art. 73, § 30; Panama, Art. 65, § 7.
[2] Art. I, § 10.   [3] Art. 118 (Branche's transl.).

Canada has asserted her liberty of action with reference to British wars. She has frequently, through her Prime Minister, declared that she will or will not take part in such wars as she may think proper. Both political parties in Canada have agreed that there can be no war-obligation on the part of Canada in the absence of her participation in the diplomacies which involve war.[1]

Restrictions upon the exercise of the treaty and war powers are the most familiar as well as the most important of internal limitations on the form of international transactions. Other limitations appear, however, in a number of constitutions. Foreign troops cannot be brought into the territory of Roumania, Spain, or at least nine of the American republics without the consent of the legislature.[2] Thus, a law is required in Chile

To permit the introduction of foreign troops into the territory of the Republic, and to determine the time of their stay therein.[3]

Similar authority is vested in the Senate in Mexico,[4] and also in Colombia, except that in the latter the President may grant permission during a recess of the Senate, after consulting the council of state.[5] Several American constitutions also require legislative permission before national troops can be sent abroad.[6] The same limitation is sometimes extended to the stationing of foreign warships in territorial waters.[7] In Mexico, the Senate has exclusive power

[1] *A. J. I. L.* (1913), VII, 284. See Keith, in *J. C. L.* (1919), 3d series, I, I, 7–16, 15.

[2] Roumania, Art. 123; Spain, Art. 55, § 3; Argentine, Art. 67, § 25; Bolivia, Art. 52, § 9; Brazil, Art. 34, § 19; Chile, Art. 28, § 7; Ecuador, Art. 65, § 17; Nicaragua, Art. 85, § 20; Paraguay, Art. 72, § 21; Peru, Art. 59, § 14; Uruguay, Art. 17, § 11. In Nicaragua, this power is vested in the executive during a state of war.

[3] Art. 28, § 7 (Dodd's transl.).

[4] Art. 76, III.   [5] Art. 98, § 7, Art. 120, § 12.

[6] Argentine, Art. 67, § 25; Bolivia, Art. 52, § 11; Chile, Art. 28, § 9; Nicaragua, Art. 85, § 20; Paraguay, Art. 72, § 21; Uruguay, Art. 17, § 12. In Nicaragua, this power is vested in the executive during a state of war.

[7] Ecuador, Art. 65, § 17.

To authorize the Executive to allow national troops to go beyond the limits of the Republic, or to permit foreign troops to pass through the national territory, and to consent to the presence of fleets of another nation for more than one month in Mexican waters.[1]

The President of Colombia may permit the stationing of foreign vessels of war within the waters of the nation, after consulting the council of state.[2]

Limitations thus far considered affect only the form of international transactions without going to the substance. Indirectly, however, they affect capacity to enter into these transactions. It can hardly be denied that there are practical inequalities of capacity where states are organically restricted, in undertaking important transactions, to methods of procedure which differ with respect to the time that they require, the degree in which secrecy can be preserved, the possibility of delay or defeat through internal dissension, and the extent to which they are capable of expressing the popular will, to mention only more obvious differences. It may not be practicable or desirable for the law of nations to take account of such inequalities. It may be better for the law to disregard indirect limitations on capacity. However that may be, they exist, and they are bound to influence the law in one way or another, whether treated as of legal significance or regarded merely as matters of fact.

INTERNAL LIMITATIONS ON CAPACITY FOR TRANSACTIONS

There are other internal limitations which go to the very root of an international person's capacity for transactions. They constitute positive restrictions upon that equality of legal capacity which is presumed to exist among the members of international society. Examples may be given of

---

[1] Art. 76, III (Branche's transl.).   [2] Art. 120, § 13.

this type of limitation which affect the state's capacity to make certain treaties, to make war in certain circumstances, and to extradite certain classes of offenders.

Organic incapacities relating to the treaty power may be divided for convenience into two groups; first, those designed to protect the essential bases of state existence; and second, those intended to secure certain interests of a less fundamental character. Limitations of the first group appear more frequently in the fundamental laws, and are created to protect the territory, independence, government, or citizens of the state concerned. In a number of states there is no legal way, short of an organic amendment, by which the national territory can be alienated.[1] A great deal of national sentiment is expressed in the first article of Turkey's Constitution of 1909:

The Ottoman Empire comprises the existing territories and divisions and the privileged provinces. It forms an indivisible whole, and can never allow any part to be detached for any reason whatever.[2]

A similar limitation in Salvador is aimed expressly at the treaty-making power:

None of the constituted powers shall have authority to conclude or approve treaties or conventions by which the form of government herein provided for be in any way altered, or by which the integrity of the territory or the national sovereignty be abridged; this to be understood without prejudice to the provisions of art. 151 of the present Constitution.[3]

---

[1] See Bulgaria, Arts. 1, 2, 141; Cuba, Appendix; Dominican Republic, Art. 3; Luxemburg, Art. 1 (cf. Art. 37); Norway, Art. 1; Roumania, Art. 2; Salvador, Art. 38; Servia, Art. 4; Sweden, Art. 78; Turkey, Art. 1 (cf. Art. 7); Venezuela, Art. 11. The provision in the Cuban Constitution is the consequence of Cuba's peculiar relation to the United States. Although in form an internal limitation, it is in fact an external limitation, and will be considered presently as such.

[2] Art. 1 (transl. from *B. F. S. P.*). Cf. Art. 7 as revised in 1909.

[3] Art. 38 (Rodriguez' transl.). Art. 151 refers to the formation of a Central American union or a great Latin American confederation.

The Venezuelan Constitution provides:

The territory of the nation cannot be alienated, nor leased, ror ceded in any way to a foreign power.[1]

There are a few American constitutions which expressly forbid all international agreements that would impair national sovereignty or independence.[2] An article has already been quoted which prohibits treaties that would alter the form of government. The citizens of the state are sometimes protected by expressly forbidding their extradition, as in Salvador,[3] or by prohibiting all treaties which modify or abridge the constitutional guaranties, as in Mexico.[4] The organic law of Salvador also stipulates that

no treaty or convention which in any way restricts or affects the exercise of the right of insurrection, or violates any constitutional provision, shall ever be ratified.[5]

References above are all to express enactments. Similar limitations are held to be implied in the constitutional law and practice of a number of states.

The attempt has been made in a few constitutions to secure less vital interests by creating similar incapacities. The status of aliens is made the subject of constitutional provisions, beyond the scope of the treaty power, in several countries. It is expressly stipulated that no international agreement shall be made which modifies the title dealing with the status of aliens in the organic law of Salvador.[6] The Venezuelan Government is forbidden to conclude treaties to the detriment of two articles, one imposing responsibilities upon aliens involved in the country's domestic

---

[1] Art 11 (transl. from *B. F. S. P.*).

[2] Cuba, Appendix; Costa Rica, Art. 15; Peru, Art. 2; Salvador, Art. 38. Central American constitutions contain a reservation with reference to the future reconstruction of a Central American union.

[3] Art. 11.　　　　　　　　　　[5] Art. 68, § 29 (Rodriguez' transl.).

[4] Art. 15.　　　　　　　　　　[6] Art. 49.

political controversies, and another denying the right to claim indemnity for property losses caused by any but the lawful authorities.[1] The advantage in being able to assure an asylum to political offenders is secured in Mexico and several Central American republics in similar fashion.[2] The Mexican Constitution provides:

> No treaty shall be authorized for the extradition of political offenders, or of offenders of the common class, who have been slaves in the country where the offense was committed. Nor shall any agreement or treaty be entered into which abridges or modifies the guarantees and rights which this constitution grants to the individual and to the citizen.[3]

Switzerland safeguards economic interests by establishing certain principles with respect to commercial treaties. The Constitution stipulates that import duties shall be as low as possible on raw materials and the necessaries of life, and highest on luxuries. It provides further:

> Unless there are imperative reasons to the contrary, these principles shall be observed also in the conclusion of treaties of commerce with foreign powers.[4]

It is a controverted question in the United States whether and to what extent the treaty power is limited by the authority reserved to the states under the federal system. If the treaty power is possessed by the central government as an attribute of national sovereignty, as some have argued, there is no question of any incapacity of the kind under consideration. On the other hand, if it is in any degree restricted by the residuary powers of the states, there are important limitations on capacity.[5] The controversy can-

---

[1] Arts. 20, 21, 22.

[2] Mexico, Art. 15; Honduras, Art. 16; Nicaragua, Arts. 12, 16; Salvador, Art. 11.

[3] Art. 15 (Branche's transl.).   [4] Art. 29 (Dodd's transl.).

[5] See Anderson, in *A. J. I. L.* (1907), I, 636–670; Bates, *Les traités fédéraux et la législation des états aux États-Unis;* Butler, *Treaty-Making Power of the United*

not be considered here, but its significance in relation to the question of capacity for certain international transactions may be suggested.

An organic inability to enter into treaties goes to the very substance of that legal capacity which is the essence of equality in the law of nations. When such an incapacity is imposed from without it is said to limit independence and sovereignty as well as equality. Pomeroy says:

> The right to enter into treaties at will is certainly one of the most important that belong to states. As all states are equal, they all have the same capacity to contract with other bodies politic. Deprive a nation of any portion of this capacity, and we would reduce it from its position of equality, and at the same time would restrict its complete independence and sovereignty.[1]

When the incapacity is imposed from within independence and sovereignty are not impaired; but the state is certainly reduced from its position of equality, if that conception is to have any practical legal significance.

Only the most rudimentary limitations on the capacity to make war have been developed thus far. In a few states the attempt has been made to discourage arbitrary or unprovoked declarations of war by requiring certain preliminary efforts at a peaceful adjustment, but the restriction is usually defined with benevolent vagueness. The President of Uruguay may declare war, upon previous decision of the General Assembly, " after having exhausted all means to avoid it, without detriment to the national honor and independence." [2] The Brazilian Congress may authorize the government to declare war " when arbitration has failed or cannot take place." [3] Portugal advocates the principle of arbitration in

---

States, I, 4 ff. (presents national sovereignty view); Crandall, *Treaties,* §§ 105–110; Tucker, *Limitations on the Treaty-Making Power Under the Constitution of the United States* (presents states' rights view).

[1] *Lectures,* § 258, p. 323.

[2] Art. 81.   [3] Art. 34, § 11; Art. 48, §§ 7, 8.

its Constitution,[1] while the governments of the Dominican Republic and Venezuela [2] are required to insert a general arbitration clause in all treaties. The most explicit limitation of this kind appears in the Constitution of the Dominican Republic:

> The authorities (" poderes ") instituted under this Constitution shall not declare war until and after having proposed arbitration.
>
> In order to affirm this principle, the following clause shall be inserted in all international Treaties which are concluded by the Republic: " All differences which may arise between the contracting parties shall be submitted to arbitration before appealing to arms." [3]

The extradition of political offenders from certain states is definitely forbidden in the constitution. The same rule is well established practice in other states, but is not a legal incapacity. In certain of the Central American republics there is no legal way of extraditing such an offender, whatever the policy or the particular circumstances may be.[4]

It was suggested above that for reasons of policy the law of nations might conceivably disregard differences in the form of international transactions. The objections to such a policy are evident, although there may be a good deal to be said in its favor. On the other hand, it is difficult to see how the law of nations can disregard differences in capacity for transactions without detracting from its positive significance. Members of the society of nations may be presumed

---

[1] Art. 73. " The Portuguese Republic, without prejudice to its engagements under its Treaties of Alliance, advocates the principle of arbitration as the best method of solving international questions." (Transl. from *B. F. S. P.*).

[2] Art. 138. " In international Treaties the following clause shall be inserted: — ' All differences between the Contracting Parties shall be decided by arbitration without appeal to war.' " (Transl. from *B. F. S. P.*).

[3] Art. 102 (transl. from *B. F. S. P.*). See remarks of Dominican delegate, *La Deux. Confér.*, II, 147. Interesting possibilities in the development of internal limitations are suggested by the idea of autonomous neutralization. See Robinson, in *A. J. I. L.* (1917), XI, 607–616.

[4] Honduras, Art. 16; Nicaragua, Art. 16; Salvador, Art. 11.

to be equal as a general principle; but when it appears that in certain aspects of legal capacity they are organically unequal, it would seem that the law must either take cognizance of the facts or else admit its unreality.

INTERNAL LIMITATIONS ON CAPACITY FOR RIGHTS

What has just been said applies with equal force to internal limitations on capacity for rights. The state, as an international person, may be organically incapable of rights as well as transactions, that is to say, it may be constitutionally without power to conserve certain interests by exacting particular acts, forbearances, services, or benefits. Wherever an incapacity of this sort exists there is a limitation upon that equality which the law of nations presumes among its subjects.

There are internal limitations in several states on that capacity to control the national domain which is presumed among members of the international community. This is true in the case of Panama, although here it is really the consequence of an external limitation which has been formally recognized in the constitution.[1] A better illustration of incapacity for rights of jurisdiction is found in the provisions of several American constitutions declaring the navigation of interior rivers free to all flags.[2]

The law of nations presumes that each of its subjects is capable of regulating the admission of goods and persons from other countries. It has already been pointed out that Switzerland's capacity for levying import duties is limited by the terms of its organic law. In several other states there are important restrictions on the capacity to exclude alien

---

[1] Art. 3. Cf. Costa Rica, Art. 15.

[2] Argentine, Arts. 20, 26; Honduras, Art. 141; Paraguay, Art. 7. Art. 26 of the Constitution of Argentine is as follows: " Navigation on the rivers in the interior of the nation is free to all flags, and subject to no other regulations than those proclaimed by the national authority." (Dodd's transl.).

persons.[1] The provision in the Constitution of Argentine is as follows:

The federal government shall encourage European immigration, and shall not have power to restrict, limit, or obstruct, by taxation of any kind, the entrance into the Argentine territory of foreigners coming to it for the purpose of engaging in the cultivation of the soil, the improvement of industrial business, or the introduction and teaching of arts and sciences.[2]

Bolivia's fundamental law deals with the matter in more general terms:

Every man has the right to enter the territory of the Republic, remain therein, travel through it, leave it, without any other restrictions than those established by international law; . . .[3]

The provisions quoted above may be contrasted with the rule in Venezuela, where the President, with a consultative vote of the Council of State, has power

To prohibit, when he thinks desirable, the immigration of foreigners into national territory, or to expel from it foreigners who have no domicile established in the country.[4]

The recent Mexican Constitution is equally explicit:

the Executive shall have the exclusive right to expel from the Republic forthwith, and without judicial process, any foreigner whose presence he may deem inexpedient.[5]

Again, the law of nations leaves states very large discretion in determining the status of aliens who choose to reside within their boundaries. There must be no manifest denials of justice, no unfair discriminations, no unwarranted confiscations of property, but so long as these general principles

---

[1] Argentine, Art. 25; Bolivia, Art. 4; Ecuador, Art. 37; Paraguay, Art. 6; Spain, Art. 2.

[2] Art. 25 (Dodd's transl.).

[3] Art. 4 (Rodriguez' transl.).

[4] Art. 81, § 7 (transl. from *B. F. S. P.*).

[5] Art. 33 (Branche's transl.).

are observed each state is free to determine the rights of aliens as it pleases. There are a number of states, however, whose capacity for dealing with this question is organically restricted. Reciprocity is stipulated as a general principle in the constitutions of Colombia and Panama.[1] Other constitutions specifically guarantee to aliens the privilege of owning and transferring real property, engaging in business, and other privileges.[2] The organic law of Argentine provides:

> Aliens shall enjoy in the territory of the nation all the civil rights of citizens. They may exercise their trade, business, or profession; own, buy, and transfer real estate; navigate the rivers and coasts; practice freely their religion; make wills, and contract marriage in conformity with the law. They shall not be compelled to become citizens or to pay forced extraordinary taxes.[3]

In Haiti, on the other hand, it is constitutionally impossible for any but Haitians to own real property or acquire it by any means whatever.[4]

The capacity to protect citizens of other states is a matter of grave international concern. Only as it is complete can an international person be assured of freedom from external interference, or demand the fullest protection for its own citizens abroad. Several American republics are curiously limited in this matter, the limitation operating directly in some cases and indirectly in others. The problem of protection is somewhat complicated in a few instances by constitutional provisions which come very near to establishing involuntary naturalization, thus tending to subject aliens to the responsibilities of citizens without free decision.[5] Several

---

[1] Colombia, Art. 11; Panama, Art. 9.

[2] Argentine, Art. 20; Costa Rica, Art. 12; Honduras, Arts. 11, 12, 13; Nicaragua, Art. 13; Paraguay, Art. 33; Peru, Art. 28; Salvador, Art. 47.

[3] Art. 20 (Dodd's transl.).

[4] Art. 6.

[5] See Brazil, Art. 69; Dominican Republic, Art. 7; Guatemala, Art. 5.

American constitutions deny citizens and aliens alike the
right to claim indemnity for damages caused by revolution-
ists.[1] This restriction is aimed at the individual, but in
practice it seems to have an indirect effect upon the state.
The same may be said of another type of provision which
forbids aliens to resort to diplomatic protection.[2] Such a
provision appears in the recent Mexican Constitution:

> Only Mexicans by birth or naturalization and Mexican companies
> have the right to acquire ownership in lands, waters and their appur-
> tenances, or to obtain concessions to develop mines, waters or mineral
> fuels in the Republic of Mexico. The Nation may grant the same
> right to foreigners, provided they agree before the Department of
> Foreign Affairs to be considered Mexicans in respect to such property,
> and accordingly not to invoke the protection of their Governments
> in respect to the same, under penalty, in case of breach, of forfeiture
> to the Nation of property so acquired.[3]

All public contracts in Venezuela must contain a clause,
expressed or implied, by which resort to diplomatic inter-
position is renounced:

> No contract of public interest made by the Federal Government
> or that of the States, by the municipalities, or by any other public
> authority, shall be transferred wholly or in part to a foreign Govern-
> ment; and in all such contracts shall be considered incorporated,
> although it may not be expressed, the following clause: " The dis-
> putes and controversies of whatever nature that may arise in con-
> nection with this contract, and that cannot be settled amicably by
> the Contracting Parties, shall be decided by the competent Tribunals
> of Venezuela, in conformity with its laws, and cannot for any motive
> or any cause become the subject of foreign claims." Companies
> formed to carry out the above-mentioned contracts shall establish
> their legal domicile in the country.[4]

---

[1] Guatemala, Art. 14; Haiti, Art. 185; Honduras, Art. 142; Salvador, Art. 46;
Venezuela, Art. 21. See also Nicaragua, Art. 14.

[2] Guatemala, Art. 23; Honduras, Art. 15; Mexico, Art. 27; Nicaragua, Art. 15.

[3] Art. 27 (Branche's transl.).

[4] Art. 142 (transl. from *B. F. S. P.*).

It is difficult to determine the extent to which provisions like those cited above affect international capacity for rights. Certainly in practice they place a state in an unusual position with respect to other members of the society of nations.

A constitutional division of authority between the central and local governments within a state may create serious incapacities with respect to the protection of aliens. Such a situation exists in the United States where the federal government assumes responsibility for the protection of aliens, but leaves the actual enforcement of that protection to the discretion of the local authorities.[1] The problem may arise under any federal constitution. It is highly developed within the British Empire, where many of the obligations of the Empire are executed by the self-governing dominions. The British North America Act of 1867 provides with respect to Canada:

> The Parliament and government of Canada shall have all powers necessary or proper for performing the obligations of Canada or of any provinces thereof, as part of the British empire, towards foreign countries, arising under treaties between the empire and such foreign countries.[2]

There is a similar division of authority between the British Government and the governments of the other autonomous dominions.

INTERNAL LIMITATIONS ON CAPACITY FOR POLITICAL RIGHTS

Still another type of incapacity, imposed from within, has recently become important and will no doubt grow in importance as the society of nations struggles towards

---

[1] See Borchard, *Diplomatic Protection of Citizens Abroad*, §§ 45, 91, 165, *passim;* Despagnet, in *R. G. D. I. P.* (1895), II, 195.

[2] § 132.

greater perfection of organization. To what extent are the members of international society incapacitated by their fundamental laws from participating in the creation of supernational institutions ?[1] In other words, how far are they organically incapable of what may be called international political rights ?

After the convention for the establishment of an international prize court was drafted, it was discovered that certain states could not submit the judgment of a national final court of appeal to review before an international tribunal. In a *vœu,* included in the Final Protocol of the London Naval Conference, the delegates agreed to call the attention of their respective governments

to the advantage of concluding an arrangement under which such States would have the power, at the time of depositing their ratifications, to add thereto a reservation to the effect that resort to the International Prize Court in respect of decisions of their National Tribunals shall take the form of a direct claim for compensation.[2]

Thirteen states signed an additional protocol at The Hague in 1910, making provision for difficulties of a constitutional nature in the following terms:

The Powers signatory or adhering to the Hague convention of October 18, 1907, relative to the establishment of an international court of prize, which are prevented by difficulties of a constitutional nature from accepting the said convention in its present form, have the right to declare in the instrument of ratification or adherence that in prize cases, whereof their national courts have jurisdiction, recourse to the international court of prize can only be exercised against them in the form of an action in damages for the injury caused by the capture.

In the case of recourse to the international court of prize, in the form of an action for damages, Article 8 of the convention is not applicable; it is not for the court to pass upon the validity or the nullity

---

[1] See the discussion of this question by Wright, in *A. J. I. L.* (1918), XII, 64-95.
[2] *A. J. I. L. Suppl.* (1909), III, 184; Higgins, *The Hague Peace Conferences,* p. 443.

of the capture, nor to reverse or affirm the decision of the national tribunals.

If the capture is considered illegal, the court determines the amount of damages to be allowed, if any, to the claimants.[1]

The United States Senate approved the international prize court convention on condition that the declaration contemplated in the above protocol be included in the instrument of ratification.[2]

The United States has also encountered constitutional difficulties which hamper its participation in certain international administrative arrangements.[3] The significance of limitations of this kind is only beginning to be appreciated. They will undoubtedly become more important in the future as further progress is made towards the creation of supernational authority.

Summary

It has been the purpose of the present chapter to suggest something of the relation which exists between the constitution of the state and the state's legal and political capacity as a member of the community of nations. It seems evident enough that the state's capacity as an international person may be defined and limited in important respects by its organic law. Certain of these limitations prescribe the form of transactions in which the state participates by fixing the procedure of treaty making, war making, and other transactions of less importance. It has been suggested that it may not be practicable, in determining the legal status of the state as an international person, to take account of such procedural limitations. The suggestion should not be permitted to obscure the fact that, indirectly at least, such limitations affect the substance of capacity as well as the

---

[1] Arts. 1, 2; *A. J. I. L. Suppl.* (1911), V, 95.

[2] *Ibid.*, p. 99.

[3] Reinsch, *Public International Unions*, pp. 48, 65, note 1.

particular procedure by which it finds expression. It can not be overlooked that such limitations may be matters of the gravest consequence for the entire international community. Other organic limitations restrict directly the state's capacity for transactions by making it incapable of becoming a party to certain kinds of treaties, declaring war under certain circumstances, or extraditing certain kinds of offenders. Of these three illustrations, it may be noted, constitutional incapacities to participate in certain kinds of treaties are at present of the greatest practical importance. Organic limitations also restrict the state's capacity for legal rights, notably in connection with the control of the national domain, the admission of goods and of persons, the determination of the status of aliens, and the protection of aliens. Finally, organic limitations on capacity for political rights should be distinguished as belonging to a separate category. They have not received a great deal of attention hitherto for the reason that the problem has arisen only in connection with certain of the administrative unions and with the permanent tribunals proposed at the Second Hague Peace Conference; but with the rapidly accelerating demand for a more effective integration of the international community and for the constitution of some recognized supernational authority it is certain that organic limitations on political capacity, as distinguished from legal capacity, will require more attention in the future.

The subject of internal limitations has never received adequate consideration. More often than otherwise it has been dismissed with the dictum that the law of nations has no concern with the constitution of the state. This dictum, it is submitted, requires revaluation. It has been universally approved in the sense that each people must be free to determine its own form of government without external interference; but it certainly cannot be taken to mean that the law of nations is blind to important capacities and incapacities arising out of the organic constitutions of its subjects. Viewing equality in the law of nations as a matter of legal and political capacity, and there is no other way in which it can be viewed without denying the possibility of future development along rational lines, the conclusion is beyond doubt that account must be taken of internal limitations. It is no answer to say that internal limitations may be disregarded because the people in each state have it in their power to amend or eliminate them. As observed at the outset, the law of nations is not presently concerned with potential changes in the legal condition of its subjects; it is concerned with the existing capacities and incapacities of the members of the international community to which its rules apply. If the equality of states is to have practical significance as a legal principle, it will be necessary for the law of nations to take account of those limitations on legal and political capacity which arise in each instance out of the fundamental organization of the state.

CHAPTER VII

EXTERNAL LIMITATIONS UPON THE EQUALITY OF STATES

THE NATURE OF EXTERNAL LIMITATIONS

EXTERNAL limitations upon a state's international capacity are the result of certain relationships which it has with other members of the society of nations. Such limitations are created by general treaties, by certain special treaties creating relationships which obtain general recognition, and by the positive law of nations as proved by common usage. They operate to restrict the legal capacity of the state as an international person, rendering it incapable of acquiring certain international rights or of entering into certain international transactions. External limitations have two important characteristics: (1) the state cannot divest itself of the incapacity by its own act; (2) the state is placed in a position of legal incapacity with respect to the entire community of nations. Wherever limitations of this kind apply only to a single state or to a particular group of states, the state or group affected is in a condition of legal inequality with respect to other members of the society of nations. Inequalities of condition or status have always played an important part in international relations.[1] There are indications that their importance will increase as the international community becomes more closely integrated.

LIMITATIONS INCIDENT TO GEOGRAPHICAL SITUATION

In the first place, it is evident that positive incapacities may be the result of an anomalous or exceptional situation

[1] See *supra*, p. 124, note 1. Huber denies that positive limitations on equality are recognized by international law. *Die Gleichheit der Staaten*, pp. 97 ff.

as regards the physical bases of state existence. Thus, a
state may be so situated geographically as to be incapable
of acquiring certain rights or of entering into certain transactions. The writers have been inclined to dismiss the
problem which this sort of incapacity suggests with the
dictum that states are equal " quite apart from diversity of
territory." The dictum's insufficiency has been recognized,
however, in at least a few instances. Fiore's discussion of
limitations on the equality of an inland state is in point.[1]
The inland state affords an excellent illustration of what is
meant by limitations incident to geographical situation.
The subject has received relatively little attention in the
books, but the practice of nations has necessarily made a
number of important distinctions between the international
capacity of non-maritime states on the one hand and of
states having access to the sea on the other. These distinctions have occasionally found expression in formal convention and in the language of judicial opinion. Article 36 of
the Declaration of London recognized the exceptional status
of an inland state by admitting the applicability of the principle of continuous voyage to conditional contraband " where
the enemy country has no seaboard." During the World
War both German and British courts urged that the failure
of non-maritime belligerents like Servia and Montenegro
to ratify the maritime conventions, submitted by the Second
Hague Conference, should not be permitted to defeat the
operation of those conventions, notwithstanding the express
provision that they should be binding only when ratified by
all the belligerents.[2] It requires no exhaustive marshalling

[1] See *supra*, p. 121; *Int. Law Cod.*, § 398.
[2] See the dictum of Sir Samuel Evans in the case of The Möwe, quoted *supra*,
p. 163. In the case of The Fenix, in the Imperial Supreme Prize Court in Berlin,
December 17, 1914, it was argued that the convention relative to the status of
enemy merchant-ships at the outbreak of hostilities was applicable although it had
not been ratified by non-maritime belligerents. It was said: " Likewise the fact
that Servia and Montenegro did not ratify the convention stands just as little in

of the evidence to show that the inland state is without capacity for a multitude of important maritime rights and transactions. Until the principles of international law have been extensively revised, this type of incapacity must remain a matter of considerable importance in practice as well as in theory.

LIMITATIONS INCIDENT TO THE CHARACTER OF CIVILIZATION

The condition of a state's population, as well as the situation of its territory, may give rise to important limitations on equality. Here again, incapacities arise out of an anomalous or exceptional situation as regards one of the physical bases of state existence. Fundamental differences in the character of civilization have always been the source of important limitations on capacity. A few authorities have implied that such differences do not affect the application of the principle of equality,[1] but this is not the prevailing opinion. Most of the modern publicists recognize that equality can be the rule only among states having common standards of civilization. Fiore has stated the prevailing opinion effectively:

The very necessity of things requires, therefore, that certain states should not be called to enjoy international rights in an integral fashion and with perfect equality. So it is reasonable that the states of Europe should not admit perfect equality of right with Turkey and its dependencies; with the states of Africa, with the exception of Liberia and the English and French colonies; with the states of Asia,

the way of its application in this case, since they are not maritime states, and Art. 6 of the convention must be taken to mean that it shall not apply only if the belligerents, being maritime states, are not parties to it." This argument was approved by the court, which said: " Finally, the circumstance that the belligerent states Servia and Montenegro did not ratify the convention raises no doubt, for the reasons advanced by the claimants, concerning its applicability to the case under review." Transl. in *A. J. I. L.* (1916), X, 910, 912.

[1] See Barbosa, *supra*, p. 183; Carnazza Amari, *supra*, p. 113; Sir William Scott, *supra*, p. 159.

with the exception of Siberia and Hindostan. In fact, certain limitations are made necessary by the exceptional situations in which these countries are placed.

Therefore, we may lay down the following rules:

(a) Full and entire juridical equality ought to be limited to those states among which there have been developed the fundamental juridical ideas essential to the coexistence of states in society.

(b) A state which does not find itself in a position to fulfil its international duties towards other states, either as a result of traditional prejudices, of its internal organization, or its customs and its religious beliefs, can only demand the full enjoyment of international rights in perfect equality on condition that it change its internal organization so as to enable it to fulfil its international duties by giving substantial guaranties on this subject.

(c) As long as such reforms are not carried out within those states, other states which have relations with them ought to observe the stipulations of treaties. As far as international law is unwritten, they ought to observe the rules which, considering the social conditions of the uncivilized state, are compatible with the protection and defense of public rights and private citizens.[1]

Inequalities of legal capacity arising out of differences in civilization are manifested in several important rules of the positive law of nations. Those imposed in the form of extraterritorial jurisdiction, in the application of the right of diplomatic protection of citizens abroad, in the exclusion of aliens, and in the practice of granting asylum in legations and consulates and on public vessels may be considered briefly.

It is fundamentally because of differences in civilization that limitations have been imposed upon the jurisdiction of eastern states over the nationals of western countries residing within their territories.[2] Under treaties, reënforced

---

[1] *Trattato*, §§ 425–427, I, 291; *Int. Law Cod.*, §§ 395, 399. See Bonfils, *Manuel*, § 273, p. 162; Chrétien, *Principes*, § 175, p. 176; Cobbett, *Cases*, I, 45–48; Lorimer, *Institutes*, I, 218; Oppenheim, *Int. Law*, §§ 102–103, I, 154.

[2] See Arminjon, *Étrangers et protégés dans l'Empire ottoman;* Brown, *Foreigners in Turkey;* Calary de Lamazière, *Les capitulations en Bulgarie;* Hall, *Foreign Powers and Jurisdiction of the British Crown;* Heyking, *L'exterritorialité;* Hinckley, *Ameri-*

sometimes by custom,[1] authority over Europeans and Americans in the Near East, the Far East, and many parts of Africa has been vested at different times in consular courts. According to Borchard,

The extraterritorial privileges usually include an exemption from the jurisdiction of the courts of the oriental state; inviolability of the domicil; freedom from arrest by native officials, except when in the act of committing a flagrant crime; if arrested, the right of surrender to the consul for trial and punishment; criminal or civil trial in consular or national courts of the accused or defendant; general jurisdiction of the foreign consul over his nationals, with right to require the assistance of the local authorities; and notification of the consul in case of the arrest of native employees of an American citizen.[2]

The treaty basis for extraterritorial jurisdiction may be illustrated from the treaties in force between the United States and China. Controversies involving subjects of China and citizens of the United States are settled under provisions of the treaties of 1858 and 1880 as follows:

Subjects of China guilty of any criminal act toward citizens of the United States shall be punished by the Chinese authorities according

can Consular Jurisdiction in the Orient; Koo, *Status of Aliens in China;* Lippmann, *Die Konsularjurisdiction im Orient;* Moore, *Digest,* §§ 259–290, II, 593–755; Pélissié du Rausas, *Le régime des capitulations dans l'Empire ottoman;* Piggot, *Exterritoriality;* Rey, *De la protection diplomatique et consulaire dans les échelles du Levant et de Barbarie;* Rioche, *Les juridictions consulaires anglaises dans les pays d'Orient.* See also The Indian Chief, 3 C. Rob. 12, 29 (1800); Papayanni v. The Russian Steam Navigation and Trading Company, 2 Moore P. Cl, N. S., 161 (1863); Dainese v. United States, 15 Ct. Cl. 64, 71 (1879); The Imperial Japanese Government v. The Peninsular and Oriental Steam Navigation Company, 20 A. C. 644, 654 (1895); Secretary of State for Foreign Affairs v. Charlesworth, Pilling and Company, 70 L. J. P. C. 25, 28, 29 (1901); The Derfflinger, No. 1, 1 Br. & Col. P. C. 386, 388 (1915); The Lützow; The Koerber, 1 Br. & Col. P. C. 528 (1915); Casdagli v. Casdagli, 87 L. J. P. 73, 81, 83, 84 (1917), 88 L. J. P. 49 (1918); Foreign Jurisdiction Act (1890), 53 & 54 Vict. c. 37; *M. L. R.* (1919), XVII, 437, 451, 694.

[1] " The so-called extraterritorial rights, resting in their origin upon treaty, have in the course of time, particularly in Turkey, Morocco and other countries, gathered around themselves by custom an accretion of further encroachments upon the local jurisdiction, so as to constitute in some countries a veritable *imperium in imperio.*" Borchard, *Diplomatic Protection of Citizens Abroad,* § 181, p. 431.

[2] *Ibid.,* § 182, p. 433.

to the laws of China; and citizens of the United States, either on shore or in any merchant vessel, who may insult, trouble or wound the persons or injure the property of Chinese, or commit any other improper act in China, shall be punished only by the Consul or other public functionary thereto authorized, according to the laws of the United States. Arrests in order to trial may be made by either the Chinese or the United States authorities.[1]

When controversies arise in the Chinese Empire between citizens of the United States and subjects of His Imperial Majesty, which need to be examined and decided by the public officers of the two nations, it is agreed between the Governments of the United States and China that such cases shall be tried by the proper official of the nationality of the defendant. The properly authorized official of the plaintiff's nationality shall be freely permitted to attend the trial and shall be treated with the courtesy due to his position. He shall be granted all proper facilities for watching the proceedings in the interests of justice. If he so desires, he shall have the right to present, to examine and to cross-examine witnesses. If he is dissatisfied with the proceedings, he shall be permitted to protest against them in detail. The law administered will be the law of the nationality of the officer trying the case.[2]

Controversies between citizens of the United States, or between citizens of the United States and of other foreign countries, may be settled without any participation by Chinese authorities:

All questions in regard to rights, whether of property or person, arising between citizens of the United States in China shall be subject to the jurisdiction and regulated by the authorities of their own Government; and all controversies occurring in China between citizens of the United States and the subjects of any other Government shall be regulated by the treaties existing between the United States and such Governments, respectively, without interference on the part of China.[3]

[1] Treaty of 1858, Art. 11; Malloy, *Treaties*, I, 215.
[2] Treaty of 1880, Art. 4; Malloy, *Treaties*, I, 240.
[3] Treaty of 1858, Art. 27; Malloy, *Treaties*, I, 220. Cf. Treaty with Persia, 1856, Art. 5; Treaty with Siam, 1856, Art. 2; Treaty with Turkey, 1830, Art. 4; Malloy, *Treaties*, II, 1372, 1630, 1319. See Moore, *Extradition*, I, 100, note 5.

The justification for extraterritorial jurisdiction is suggested by Article 15 of the commercial treaty of 1903:

> The Government of China having expressed a strong desire to reform its judicial system and to bring it into accord with that of Western nations, the United States agrees to give every assistance to such reform and will also be prepared to relinquish extra-territorial rights when satisfied that the state of the Chinese laws, the arrangements for their administration, and other considerations warrant it in so doing.[1]

Aside from extraterritorial jurisdiction, there is another limitation upon the capacity of less advanced states which is imposed by international usage in regard to the protection of citizens residing abroad. The general principle upon which the right of protection rests is stated by Borchard as follows:

> The common consent of nations has established a certain standard of conduct by which a state must be guided in its treatment of aliens. In the absence of any central authority capable of enforcing this standard, international law has authorized the state of which the individual is a citizen to vindicate his rights by diplomatic and other methods sanctioned by international law. This right of diplomatic protection constitutes, therefore, a limitation upon the territorial jurisdiction of the country in which the alien is settled or is conducting business.[2]

The theory of state equality would require that this limitation apply to all states equally. In practice, it does not. The application of the right of diplomatic protection increases in rigor in direct proportion to the weakness of local protection afforded by the state of residence. As Borchard says:

> In countries which habitually maintain effective government, the protective function of the national government of a resident alien is usually limited to calling the attention of the local government to the

---

[1] Malloy, *Treaties*, I, 269.
[2] *Diplomatic Protection of Citizens Abroad*, preface, p. v.

performance of its international duty. The right, however, is always
reserved, and in the case of less stable and well-ordered governments
frequently exercised, of taking more effective measures to secure to
their citizens abroad a measure of fair treatment conforming to the
international standard of justice. . . .

The rules of international law in this matter fall with particular
severity upon those countries where law and administration frequently
deviate from and fall below this standard; for the fact that their own
citizens can be compelled to accept such maladministration is not a
criterion for the measure of treatment which the alien can demand,
and international practice seems to have denied these countries the
right to avail themselves of the usual defense that the alien is given
the benefit of the same laws, the same administration, and the same
protection as the national.[1]

This practice imposes positive limitations upon the legal
capacity of all states where the administration of justice
falls below the common standard. Not infrequently it ex-
ceeds the bounds of a reasonable legal limitation. In the
absence of supernational authority each state must determine whether its citizens have received the full measure of
protection. The great powers have abused this responsibility on many occasions, coercing the weaker states of the
world into conceding to resident aliens a more privileged
position than any fair application of international law would
require.

Differences in civilization also create incapacities in certain states in relation to the exclusion of aliens. Entire exclusion of the subjects of a particular state has never been
attempted between states of the white race in the modern
society of nations. Although the admission of Japan to
what has been generally presumed to be a normal status in

---

[1] *Diplomatic Protection of Citizens Abroad*, pp. 27–28. See Mr. Borchard's ad-
mirable treatise for an exhaustive discussion of all aspects of this question, and
particularly pp. 179, 182, 215, 221, 280, 331, 346, 350, 406, 447, 448, 451, 456, 782,
836, 837. Cf. the remarks of the Uruguayan delegate at the Second Hague Conference, *La Deux. Confér.*, II, 270. See Cutting's Case, in Moore, *Digest*, § 201, II,
228–242.

the international community has complicated the question, it would seem that as a general rule each state of full international capacity may demand admission for its nationals into another state on the same terms as are accorded to the nationals of other states of full capacity.[1] It has never been doubted, however, that sufficient dissimilarities in civilization may constitute a legal ground for exclusion. This principle received recognition in the resolutions of the Institute of International Law in 1892.[2] Its significance in relation to equality is suggested in a note on the question of Chinese immigration into the United States in the *Revue Générale de Droit International Public:*

On the one hand, the rule of the equality of states prevents a government from distinguishing between the aliens whom it intends to keep out of its territory: it may not exclude the subjects of one nation and at the same time admit those of another; however, since juridical equality among states assumes the existence of a community of right, the question can arise only among peoples equally civilized.[3]

The practice of granting asylum in legations and consulates and on public vessels,[4] wherever it has survived, constitutes a limitation upon the capacity of the states in which it prevails, and can be justified only on grounds similar to those which explain extraterritorial jurisdiction, inequalities arising out of the protection of citizens abroad, and the exclusion of aliens.

---

[1] Cf. Westlake, *Int. Law*, I, 216.

[2] *A. I. D. I.* (1892), XII, 191, 220. See Musgrove *v.* Chun Teeong Toy (1891), L. R. 16 A. C. 272.

[3] *R. G. D. I. P.* (1894), I, 555.

[4] See Gilbert, in *A. J. I. L.* (1909), III, 562–595; Michaud, *Le droit d'asile en Europe et en Angleterre;* Moore, *Digest*, §§ 291–307, II, 755–883; Moore, in *P. S. Q.* (1892), VII, 1–37, 197–231, 397–418; Robin, in *R. G. D. I. P.* (1908), XV, 461–508; Tobar y Borgoño, *L'asile interne devant le droit international;* *U. S. For. Rel.* (1898), p. 171.

LIMITATIONS INCIDENT TO IMPERFECT UNION

It was pointed out in the preceding chapter that international capacity is sometimes limited by the provisions of a state's organic constitution. In a few instances imperfect unions have been created in which legal capacity has been restricted by division among the several parts of a composite whole. Where such limitations have no other sanction than the state's organic law, they belong to the category of internal limitations; but when they are imposed by a general act of the international community, or of those who are permitted to represent the international community, as by the Peace of Westphalia, the Treaty of Vienna, the Treaty of Paris, or the Treaty of Berlin, they have all the attributes of an external limitation. Imperfect unions are created either by the partial disintegration of what was previously a unified state, or by the confederation of what were previously separate states. In either case the condition is usually transitional, representing a stage in development towards complete disintegration in the first instance and towards complete union in the second. It is important, although transitional, for there has hardly been a time in the history of the international community when this type of state has not had its representative. The course of international events suggests that the state system is still far from that condition of stability which may relegate all such incapacities to the category of historical anomalies.

In the case of a composite international person full legal capacity exists only in the hypothetical union of all partial capacities belonging to the component parts. The composite entity and each of its several parts have only a limited capacity. Since this hypothetical union cannot become a reality while the composite character endures, and since it is only with the entity or with its separate components as such that the law of nations can be concerned, it follows that the society of nations is presented with a group of international persons of which no one has full legal capacity.

The first general act of the modern society of nations wrought the partial disintegration of the Holy Roman Empire into some hundreds of international persons whose legal capacity was limited in the way described above. The Peace of Westphalia [1] formally accorded to the princes and potentates of the Empire a qualified international status. The religious settlement stipulated for an exact and reciprocal equality among them in ecclesiastical affairs, thus assuring their independence from imperial control in this respect.[2] The political settlement divided international capacity between the Empire as a whole and its component states. Article 8 of the Treaty of Osnabrück between the Emperor and Sweden provided as follows:

And in order to provide that henceforth no more differences shall arise in the political status, all and every one of the Electors, Princes, and States of the Roman Empire are so established and confirmed in their former rights, prerogatives, liberties, privileges, the free exercise of territorial right, spiritual as well as temporal, lordships, regal rights and in the possession of all these things by virtue of the present transaction, that they may never in fact be disturbed therein by anyone under any pretext whatever.

[1] On the Peace of Westphalia, see Bernard, *Four Lectures on Diplomacy*, pp. 1–60; Clement, *Mémoires et négociations;* Combes, *Histoire générale de la diplomatie européenne*, I; Hill, *History of Diplomacy*, II, 590–607; Lavisse et Rambaud, *Histoire générale*, V, 579; Le Clerc, *Négociations secrètes;* Mazarin, *Lettres du Cardinal Mazarin;* Pütter, *Geist des westphälischen Friedens;* Urusov, *Résumé historique des principaux traités de paix;* Ward, in *Cambridge Modern History*, IV, 395–433; Wheaton, *History*, p. 67. Good bibliographical notes may be found in the *Cambridge Modern History*, IV, 865; Hill, *History of Diplomacy*, II, 607; Lavisse et Rambaud, *Histoire générale*, V, 584; Vast, *Les grands traités*, I, 7.

The importance of the Peace of Westphalia in the history of the modern law of nations is suggested in Bonfils, *Manuel*, § 87, p. 39; F. de Martens, *Traité*, I, 117; Nys, *Études*, p. 1; Walker, *History*, p. 147; Walker, *Science*, p. 57; Westlake, *Int. Law*, I, 44; Wheaton, *History*, p. 69.

[2] Treaty of Osnabrück, Art. 5; Dumont, VI, I, 473; Koch et Schoell, I, 129.

They shall enjoy without contradiction the right of suffrage in all deliberations concerning the affairs of the Empire, above all where the business in hand shall be to make or to interpret laws, to decide upon a war, to impose a tax, to decree levies and quartering of soldiers, to construct in the name of the public new fortresses within the territories of the states, or to reinforce the garrisons of existing forts, and also where it shall be necessary to make a peace, or alliances, and to treat of other like affairs; none of these or similar things shall be done or decided hereafter without the advice and consent of a free assembly of all the States of the Empire; above all every one of the States of the Empire shall enjoy freely and in perpetuity the right to make alliances among themselves and with foreign countries for the preservation and security of each, provided, nevertheless, that these terms of alliance be not against the Emperor and the Empire, nor against the public peace, nor principally against this transaction, and that they be made without prejudice in any respect to the oath by which each is bound to the Emperor and to the Empire.[1]

The effect of this settlement was to limit the international capacity of the Empire by attributing partial capacities to its component parts. More than three hundred quasi-states were formally inducted into the international community. Neither the Empire nor its states were legally the equals of their neighbors in the society of nations.

It is sometimes said that the principle of equality among nations was established by the Peace of Westphalia. Taylor, for illustration, holds this opinion:

As heretofore explained, the Grotian system depends upon a full and unqualified recognition of the doctrine of territorial sovereignty from which flow the corollaries that all states are formally equal, and that territory and jurisdiction are coextensive. Such was the basis of the settlement embodied in the Peace of Westphalia, so far as the written treaty law was concerned, and upon that basis it has been claimed from that day to this that, before the law of nations, the legal rights of the greatest and smallest states are identical.[2]

---

[1] Dumont, VI, I, 480. See also Treaty of Münster, §§ 64, 65; Vast, *Les grands traités*, I, 34–35; Koch et Schoell, I, 123.

[2] *Int. Pub. Law*, § 69, p. 98. See also Cohen, in *Venez. Arbit.*, p. 1259; Dupuis, *Le principe d'équilibre et le concert européen*, p. 20; Figgis, *Gerson to Grotius*, p. 160;

Equality was established among the component states of the Empire. Equal protection of the law may be said to have received its vindication as an essential international principle. Taylor's statement and all others like it are quite misleading, however, in so far as they imply that the Westphalian settlement established equality of legal capacity among members of the society of nations as a general principle of law. On the contrary, the most important article in each of the two treaties provided expressly for important inequalities of legal capacity in the reconstituted community of nations.

The disintegration of the Ottoman Empire in the nineteenth century suggests certain interesting comparisons with the dismemberment of the Holy Roman Empire in the seventeenth and eighteenth centuries. As outlying Turkish provinces have approached separation from the Empire the European powers have imposed a divided capacity during prolonged periods of transition. Turkey has been permitted to retain certain rights of suzerainty over the detached provinces. The provinces have been accorded an autonomous régime under international guaranty, placed under the effective control of another power, or conceded a qualified international status preliminary to annexation by another power or to complete independence. As a consequence Turkey has never enjoyed full international capacity with respect to its entire dominion, while each of the provinces has been required to pass through a protracted period of partial capacity on the road to complete separation.

Russia secured autonomy for the provinces of Moldavia and Wallachia in 1829.[1] For many years they remained

Lawrence, *Essays*, p. 206; Oppenheim, *Int. Law*, § 44, I, 62; Reeves, in *The University Record* (1917), III, 254; Twiss, *Law of Nations*, p. xvii; Vreeland, *Hugo Grotius*, pp. 241–242; White, *Seven Great Statesmen*, p. 77. Cf. Rachel, *De jure gentium*, § 121; Textor, *Synopsis juris gentium*, ch. 14; Twiss, *Law of Nations*, p. 24.

[1] Treaty of Adrianople, Art. 5; *B. F. S. P.*, XVI, 647, 654.

under Turkish suzerainty and Russian protection. The Treaty of Paris of 1856 placed them under the collective guaranty of the powers;[1] and their independence was recognized, subject to conditions, by the Treaty of Berlin.[2] Servia won virtual independence from Turkey early in the nineteenth century. As a principality under Turkish suzerainty it was placed under the collective guaranty of the powers in 1856,[3] and was recognized as independent, subject to conditions, by the Treaty of Berlin.[4] The same treaty constituted Bulgaria an autonomous and tributary principality under Turkish suzerainty,[5] a condition which continued until Bulgaria's declaration of independence in 1908, and provided administrative autonomy for Eastern Roumelia under the direct political and military authority of the Sultan.[6] The Prince of Bulgaria was recognized as Governor-General of Roumelia in 1886, thus constituting a *de facto* union which became *de jure* with the recognition of Bulgarian independence. The Congress of Berlin handed the provinces of Bosnia and Herzegovina over to Austria-Hungary to be occupied and administered without prejudice to the sovereignty of Turkey.[7] In 1908 the provinces were formally annexed by the dual monarchy. Crete was promised an autonomous régime in 1878,[8] but the promise did not become effective until after the joint intervention of the powers in 1897.[9] Thereafter Crete enjoyed real autonomy, and even

---

[1] Arts. 22–27. See also Convention of 1858, *B. F. S. P.*, XLVIII, 70.

[2] Arts. 43–51.

[3] Treaty of Paris, Arts. 28–29.

[4] Arts. 34–42.   [5] Arts. 1–12.

[6] Arts 13–22. See Bluntschli, in *R. D. I. L. C.* (1881), XIII, 579–582; Serkis, *La Roumélie orientale et la Bulgarie actuelle.*

[7] Art. 25. See also Convention of 1879, *B. F. S. P.*, LXXI, 1132; and Bluntschli, in *R. D. I. L. C.* (1881), XIII, 582–586. The island of Cyprus was assigned by the Sultan in the same year "to be occupied and administered by England." Holland, *European Concert in the Eastern Question*, pp. 354–356.

[8] Treaty of Berlin, Art. 23.

[9] Ion, in *A. J. I. L.* (1910), IV, 277.

a limited international status until its union with Greece in 1912. Egypt secured autonomy and a limited international capacity in 1840, passing later into an anomalous condition under the suzerainty of Turkey and the control of Great Britain, which was terminated in 1914 by the proclamation of a British protectorate.[1] Thus for a century the Near East has presented the society of nations with a disintegrating empire on the one hand and a number of incipient states in various stages of evolution on the other. Neither the empire nor its vassal states have stood in a relation of legal equality to other members of the international community.

The German Confederation, which lasted from 1815 to 1866, is the great historical example of a composite international person formed by the confederation of existing states. The Confederation was created at the Congress of Vienna in 1815,[2] and its organization as an " indissoluble union " was completed by an additional act signed at Vienna May 15, 1820.[3] The additional act of 1820 provided:

> The Germanic Confederation is a union according to international law of the Sovereign Princes and Free Towns of Germany, for the preservation of the independence and inviolability of the States comprised in it, and for maintaining the internal and external security of Germany.
>
> As to its internal relations, this union consists of a community of States independent of each other, with reciprocal and equal rights and obligations stipulated by Treaties. As to its external relations, it constitutes a collective Power, bound together in political unity.[4]

The Confederation had power to make war, contract alliances, and conclude other treaties:

> The Confederation has the right, as a Collective Power, to declare war, to make peace, to contract alliances, and to conclude other

---

[1] See *infra*, p. 238, note 3.
[2] Treaty of Vienna, Arts. 53–64. See Wheaton, *History*, pp. 445 ff.
[3] *B. F. S. P.*, VII, 399–414.
[4] Arts. 1–2; Hertslet, I, 640.

Treaties. According, however, to the object of the Confederation expressed in Article II of the Federal Act, it only exercises this right for its own defence, for the maintenance of the self-existence and external security of Germany, as well as for the independence and inviolability of the individual States of the Confederation.[1]

On the other hand, the component states sent representatives both to one another and to foreign states. They could enter into relations with foreign states so long as they did nothing against the security of any other member or of the Confederation itself. Neither the Confederation as a whole nor its constituent states enjoyed full international capacity. Legally they were not the equals of other members of the international community.

LIMITATIONS INCIDENT TO SUZERAINTY

The disintegration of the Holy Roman Empire and of the Ottoman Empire gave rise to another type of external limitation upon international capacity, incident, in each case, to the suzerainty of the imperial authority over the subject states. The conception of suzerainty had its origin in feudalism, where it was used to describe a well-defined relation between lord and vassal. The great historical example of its application to the relations between separate states was furnished by the Holy Roman Empire, which ended in 1806. The term was revived in the nineteenth century to describe the relation between Turkey and its provinces during the period of their gradual emancipation.

The status of Wallachia and Moldavia was defined in the Treaty of Paris of 1856, as follows:

The Principalities of Wallachia and Moldavia shall continue to enjoy under the Suzerainty of the Porte, and under the Guarantee of the Contracting Powers, the Privileges and Immunities of which they are in possession. No exclusive Protection shall be exercised over them by any of the guaranteeing Powers.

[1] Art. 35; Hertslet, I, 649.

There shall be no separate right of interference in their Internal Affairs.

The Sublime Porte engages to preserve to the said Principalities an Independent and National Administration, as well as full liberty of Worship, of Legislation, of Commerce, and of Navigation.[1]

Provision for the organization of the provinces was made in the Convention of Paris of 1858, which began,

The Principalities of Moldavia and Wallachia, constituted henceforward under the denomination of United Principalities of Moldavia and Wallachia, are placed under the Suzerainty of His Majesty the Sultan.[2]

Recognition of independence, with the termination of suzerainty, was accorded by the Treaty of Berlin in 1878.[3]

Servia received a similar status by the Peace of Paris, the relation of vassal to suzerain being implied in the treaty provisions:

The Principality of Servia shall continue to hold of the Sublime Porte, in conformity with the Imperial Hats which fix and determine its Rights and Immunities, placed henceforward under the Collective Guarantee of the Contracting Powers.

In consequence, the said Principality shall preserve its Independent and National Administration, as well as full Liberty of Worship, of Legislation, of Commerce, and of Navigation.

The right of garrison of the Sublime Porte, as stipulated by anterior regulations, is maintained. No Armed Intervention can take place in Servia without previous agreement between the High Contracting Powers.[4]

Servia's vassalage also was terminated by the Treaty of Berlin.[5]

---

[1] Arts. 22, 23; Hertslet, II, 1260.
[2] Art. 1; *B. F. S. P.*, XLVIII, 70; Hertslet, II, 1332.
[3] Art. 43. See Bluntschli, in *R. D. I. L. C.* (1880), XII, 410–424.
[4] Arts. 28, 29; Hertslet, II, 1262.
[5] Art. 34. See Bluntschli, in *R. D. I. L. C.* (1880), XII, 284–293; Brunswik, *Recueil de documents diplomatiques relatifs à la Serbie.*

The Treaty of Berlin terminated two suzerainties, as indicated above, and created another in the case of Bulgaria:

Bulgaria is constituted an autonomous and tributary Principality
under the suzerainty of His Imperial Majesty the Sultan; it will have
a Christian Government and a national militia.[1]

Bulgaria was to frame its own organic law, and also to elect
its own Prince, subject to confirmation by the Porte and the
assent of the powers. The Ottoman treaties were to remain
in force in the Principality. The payment of a part of the
Ottoman debt and also of an annual tribute were stipulated,
but neither obligation was ever performed. The powers at
first sent only consuls general to Sofia. In 1887 Russia exchanged diplomatic representatives with Bulgaria. Turkey
was represented at Sofia by a High Commissioner, while the
Principality insisted successfully on sending a diplomatic
agent to Constantinople. Bulgaria was represented at the
First Hague Conference, but ranked after Turkey. It was
represented at the Geneva Conference, which Turkey did
not attend, and received alphabetical rank at the Second
Hague Conference, as well as a place in the Permanent Court
of Arbitration and in the scheme of apportioning seats for
the International Prize Court.[2] Bulgarian independence was
declared in 1908.

Egypt,[3] from 1840 to 1914, and Crete,[4] from 1898 to 1912,

[1] Art. 1; Hertslet, IV, 2766. See Andréadès, in R. G. D. I. P. (1908), XV,
585, 586; Balaktschieff, Die rechtliche Stellung des Fürstentums Bulgarien; Bluntschli, in R. D. I. L. C. (1881), XIII, 571–579; Chaunier, La Bulgarie; Karamichaloff, La Principauté de Bulgarie au point de vue du droit international; Lutfi, Die
völkerrechtliche Stellung Bulgariens und Ostrumeliens; Sarüvanoff, La Bulgarie est-
elle un état mi-souverain ?; Scelle, in A. J. I. L. (1911), V, 144–177, 394–413, 680–
704; (1912), VI, 86–106, 659–678.

[2] Ibid. (1911), V, 693–704.

[3] B. F. S. P., XXVIII, 342; A. J. I. L. (1915), IX, 202; Dupuis, Le principe
d'équilibre et le concert européen, Pt. II, chs. 4, 9; Gibbons, New Map of Africa,
chs. 20, 21; Holland, European Concert in the Eastern Question, ch. 4; The Charkieh,
L. R. 4 A. & E. 59 (1873); Abd-ul-Messih v. Farra, L. R. 13 A. C. 431 (1888).

[4] Ion, in A. J. I. L. (1910), IV, 276–284; Streit, in R. G. D. I. P. (1897), IV,
61–104, 446–483; (1900), VII, 5–52, 301–369; (1903), X, 222–282, 345–418.

were recognized as autonomous under the suzerainty of the Sultan. In fact, each enjoyed a very limited international capacity, and in each case the international status was further complicated by the protection of other states. The term " suzerainty " has been little used elsewhere than in connection with the moribund Empire of the Near East. The Convention of Pretoria of 1881 placed the South African Republic under the suzerainty of the Queen of the United Kingdom.[1] The little republic of Andorra still exists under the joint suzerainty of the bishop of Urgel in Spain and France as successor to the Counts of Foix.[2]

The most recent application of suzerainty in international relations was defined in a series of agreements between China and Russia with regard to the status of Outer Mongolia,[3] by virtue of which Mongolia was given a limited international capacity under Russian protection and Chinese suzerainty. An agreement of 1913 between Russia and China provided:

> Russia recognizes that Outer Mongolia is under the suzerainty of China.
> China recognizes the autonomy of Outer Mongolia.[4]

Mongolia's status was further defined in an agreement of 1915 between China, Russia, and Mongolia, as follows:

> Outer Mongolia recognizes China's suzerainty. China and Russia recognize the autonomy of Outer Mongolia forming part of Chinese territory.
> Autonomous Mongolia has no right to conclude international treaties with foreign Powers respecting political and territorial questions. . . .
> China and Russia . . . recognize the exclusive right of the Autonomous Government of Outer Mongolia to attend to all the affairs of

---

[1] *B. F. S. P.*, LXXII, 900.

[2] Westlake, *Int. Law*, I, 25.

[3] *A. J. I. L. Suppl.* (1916), X, 239–258; Williams, in *A. J. I. L.* (1916), X, 798–808.

[4] Arts. 1, 2, in *A. J. I. L. Suppl.* (1916), X, 247.

its internal administration and to conclude with foreign Powers international treaties and agreements respecting all questions of a commercial and industrial nature concerning autonomous Mongolia.[1]

Mongolia was to have complete internal autonomy and its own national army. There was to be no Chinese colonization, and China engaged to send neither civil nor military officials nor troops into Mongolian territory. On the other hand, Mongolia was declared to be a part of the territory of China. China was represented at Urga by a Dignitary who enjoyed the first place of honor on all ceremonial occasions and who might be accompanied by a military escort not to exceed two hundred men. No customs duties could be levied on goods imported by Chinese merchants, and China reserved extraterritorial jurisdiction over its subjects.

The feudal relation of vassal to suzerain has been considerably attenuated in its international application. This may have been due to the peculiar conditions prevailing in the Near East and the Far East, where it has received its only important application in recent times. Whatever the reason, it is true that in most cases its significance as a limitation upon the capacity of vassal states has been concerned chiefly with matters of form.

LIMITATIONS INCIDENT TO PROTECTION

Certain of the most familiar of international incapacities arise out of the relation of protection.[2] This relation has been established in an extraordinary variety of cases between more powerful or more highly civilized states, on the one hand, and small, weak, backward, incipient, or decaying states on the other. It may exist in all degrees, shading off

---

[1] Arts. 2, 3, 5, in *A. J. I. L. Suppl.* (1916), X, 251, 252.

[2] See Engelhardt, in *R. G. I. L. C.* (1892), XXIV, 345–383 (1893), XXV, 230–238, 466–480; Heilborn, *Das völkerrechtliche Protektorat;* Oppenheim, *Int. Law,* §§ 92–94, I, 144; Piédelièvre, *Précis,* § 283, I, 255; Pillet, in *R. G. D. I. P.* (1895), II, 583–608.

imperceptibly from the relationship which imposes only slight limitations on the protected state to the so-called protectorate which has no international capacity at all.[1] It may constitute a stage in the process which leads ultimately to annexation, or, less frequently, in the development which leads to unrestricted international capacity. More infrequently still, it may become a permanent relationship. Whatever its degree or its significance it is generally agreed that it imposes a limitation upon the legal capacity of the protected state.

More often than otherwise protection has been preliminary to annexation. Before annexation has been consummated, however, it has frequently happened that for a long period the society of nations has been presented with a protected state of limited capacity. The Treaty of Vienna constituted the city of Cracow a free, neutral, and independent town under the protection of Austria, Prussia, and Russia.[2] This arrangement continued until 1846, when Cracow was absorbed by Austria.[3] Another part of the settlement of 1815 provided that the Ionian Islands should form " a single, free and Independent State, under the denomination of the United States of the Ionian Islands."[4] The new state was placed under the exclusive protection of Great Britain:

This State shall be placed under the immediate and exclusive Protection of His Majesty the King of the United Kingdom of Great Britain and Ireland, his heirs and successors. The other Contracting Powers do consequently renounce every right or particular pretension which they might have formed in respect to them, and formally guarantee all the dispositions of the present Treaty.[5]

[1] See The King v. The Earl of Crewe, L. R. [1910] 2 K. B. 576.
[2] Art. 6.
[3] Convention between Austria, Prussia, and Russia, in *B. F. S. P.*, XXXV, 1088. See the Austrian Declaration, and British and French protests, in Hertslet, II, 1065, 1068, 1073.
[4] Convention of November 5, 1815, Art. 1, in *B. F. S. P.*, III, 250.
[5] Art. 2, in Hertslet, I, 338. See The Ionian Ships, 2 Spinks, 212 (1855).

In 1863 the Ionian Islands were united to Greece.[1] As a protected state they represented, from 1815 to 1863, the vanishing point of international personality. They were governed by British commissioners, and all relations with other states were conducted by British officials. A separate trading flag and neutrality during British wars were almost the only indications of separate existence.

Protection has also taken the form of guardianship over small or weak states during the period necessary for their development to full capacity. Although the word " protection " has not appeared in the treaties, this has been the practical effect of the responsibilities assumed at different times by the great powers of Europe toward Greece and the Balkan states. Protection appears to be a normal and permanent condition for a petty state like San Marino, which was under the protection of the Pope by formal treaty from the beginning of the seventeenth century, and which has been under " the exclusive protective friendship " of Italy since 1862.[2]

It has often happened, particularly in connection with the states of Africa and the East, that protection as a transitional stage between independence and annexation or its equivalent has been ill-defined and of short duration. Thus in 1906 the Act of Algeciras, framed conjointly by representatives of the Sultan of Morocco, eleven European powers, and the United States, was

based upon the triple principle of the sovereignty and independence of His Majesty the Sultan, the integrity of his domains, and economic liberty without any inequality.[3]

French penetration proceeded apace, however, and five years later a convention between France and Germany recognized

---

[1] Treaty of 1863, in *B. F. S. P.*, LIII, 19; Treaty of 1864, in Hertslet, III, 1589.
[2] Westlake, *Int. Law*, I, 23.
[3] Preamble, in *A. J. I. L. Suppl.* (1907), I, 47.

the end of Moroccan independence and the creation of a French protectorate.[1]

The protectorate treaty of 1912 defined Franco-Moroccan relations as follows:

The French Government shall be represented near his Shereefian Majesty by a resident commissioner general, representative of all the powers of the republic in Morocco, who shall attend to the execution of the present agreement.

The resident commissioner general shall be the sole intermediary of the Sultan near foreign representatives and in the relations which these representatives maintain with the Moroccan Government. In particular, he shall have charge of all matters relating to foreigners in the Shereefian Empire.

He shall have the power to approve and promulgate, in the name of the French Government, all the decrees issued by his Shereefian Majesty.

The diplomatic and consular agents of France shall be charged with the representation and protection of Moroccan subjects and interests abroad.

His Majesty the Sultan pledges himself not to conclude any act of an international nature without the previous approval of the French Republic.[2]

Persia acquired two protectors under the Anglo-Russian accord of 1907,[3] and was well on the way to extinction internationally when the World War began. In 1894 Japan made an alliance with Korea " to strongly establish the independence of Korea." [4] The Treaty of Shimonoseki in 1895 required China to recognize " definitely the full and complete independence and autonomy of Korea." [5] Korean independence was again recognized by Japan and Russia in 1898,[6] and by Japan and Great Britain in 1902.[7] When the

---

[1] Convention of 1911, in *A. J. I. L. Suppl.* (1912), VI, 62.

[2] Arts. 5, 6, in *A. J. I. L. Suppl.* (1912), VI, 207. See Harris, in *A. J. I. L.* (1913), VII, 245–267.

[3] *A. J. I. L. Suppl.* (1907), I, 400.

[4] *Ibid.*, p. 214.

[5] *Ibid.*, p. 378.

[6] *Ibid.*, p. 217.

[7] *Ibid.*, p. 14.

Anglo-Japanese alliance was renewed in 1905, Great Britain recognized Japan's paramount interests in Korea:

> Japan possessing paramount political, military, and economic interests in Korea, Great Britain recognizes the right of Japan to take such measures of guidance, control, and protection in Korea as she may deem proper and necessary to safeguard and advance those interests, provided always that such measures are not contrary to the principle of equal opportunities for the commerce and industry of all nations.[1]

Russia accorded similar recognition to Japan's interests in the Peace of Portsmouth of the same year.[2]   At the outbreak of war with Russia in 1904 Japan had signed a protocol with Korea, which provided:

> For the purpose of maintaining a permanent and solid friendship between Japan and Korea and firmly establishing peace in the Far East, the Imperial Government of Korea shall place full confidence in the Imperial Government of Japan and adopt the advice of the latter in regard to improvements in administration.
>
> The Imperial Government of Japan shall in a spirit of firm friendship ensure the safety and repose of the Imperial House of Korea.
>
> The Imperial Government of Japan definitively guarantees the independence and territorial integrity of the Korean Empire.[3]

This was followed a few months later by another agreement:

> The Korean Government shall engage as financial adviser to the Korean Government a Japanese subject recommended by the Japanese Government, and all matters concerning finance shall be dealt with after his counsel being taken.
>
> The Korean Government shall engage as diplomatic adviser to the Department of Foreign Affairs a foreigner recommended by the Japanese Government, and all important matters concerning foreign relations shall be dealt with after his counsel being taken.
>
> The Korean Government shall previously consult the Japanese Government in concluding treaties and conventions with foreign powers, and in dealing with other important diplomatic affairs, such as the grant of concessions to or contracts with foreigners.[4]

---

[1] *A. J. I. L. Suppl.* (1907), I, 16.   [3] *Ibid.*, p. 217.
[2] *Ibid.*, p. 18.   [4] *Ibid.*, p. 218.

After the conclusion of peace in 1905 Korea was required to yield control and direction of its foreign relations to the Japanese Government.[1] Diplomatic representatives were accredited to the Court of Seoul for some time thereafter; but in 1907 Japan prevented the delegates of Korea from obtaining a hearing at the Second Hague Conference, and in 1910 Korea was formally annexed.[2]

The understanding of 1906 between Great Britain, France, and Italy with respect to Abyssinia apparently brings that country under the joint protection of the three powers. It is agreed that

France, Great Britain, and Italy shall coöperate in maintaining the political and territorial *status quo* in Ethiopia as determined by the state of affairs at present existing, and by the following Agreements: . . .

It is understood that the various Conventions mentioned in this Article do not in any way infringe the sovereign rights of the Emperor of Abyssinia, and in no respect modify the relations between the three Powers and the Ethiopian Empire as stipulated in the present Agreement. . . .

In the event of the *status quo* laid down in Article 1 being disturbed, France, Great Britain, and Italy shall make every effort to preserve the integrity of Ethiopia. In any case, they shall concert together, on the basis of the Agreements enumerated in the above-mentioned Article, . . . [3]

In the agreement of 1912, Russia assumed the protection of the vassal state of Mongolia:

The Imperial Russian Government shall assist Mongolia to maintain the autonomous régime which she has established, as also the right to have her national army, and to admit neither the presence of Chinese troops on her territory nor the colonization of her land by the Chinese.[4]

The possibility that China may pass under the protection of Japan is suggested by recent developments in the Far

[1] *A. J. I. L. Suppl.* (1907), I, 221.   [3] *Ibid.* (1907), I, 226.
[2] *Ibid.* (1910), IV, 280, 282.   [4] *Ibid.* (1916), X, 240. See *supra*, p. 239.

East.[1] This and other applications of the principles of protection await the settlement of pending controversies and the readjustment of the state system.

Protection has received an important application in the New World in the guardianship of the United States over the small republics of the Caribbean and of Central America. The relations of the United States with Cuba are defined in the so-called Platt Amendment, incorporated in an act of the United States Congress, in an appendix to the Cuban Constitution, and in a permanent treaty between the two states. Certain of its most important articles provide as follows:

> The Government of Cuba shall never enter into any treaty or other compact with any foreign power or powers which will impair or tend to impair the independence of Cuba, nor in any manner authorize or permit any foreign power or powers to obtain by colonization or for military or naval purposes, or otherwise, lodgment in or control over any portion of said island.

> The Government of Cuba shall not assume or contract any public debt to pay the interest upon which, and to make reasonable sinking-fund provision for the ultimate discharge of which, the ordinary revenues of the Island of Cuba, after defraying the current expenses of the Government, shall be inadequate.

> The Government of Cuba consents that the United States may exercise the right to intervene for the preservation of Cuban independence, the maintenance of a government adequate for the protection of life, property, and individual liberty, and for discharging the obligations with respect to Cuba imposed by the Treaty of Paris on the United States, now to be assumed and undertaken by the Government of Cuba.

> To enable the United States to maintain the independence of Cuba, and to protect the people thereof, as well as for its own defense, the Government of Cuba will sell or lease to the United States lands necessary for coaling or naval stations, at certain specified points, to be agreed upon with the President of the United States.[2]

[1] *A. J. I. L. Suppl.* (1916), X, 1–18; Hornbeck, *Contemporary Politics in the Far East*, ch. 17; North, in *A. J. I. L.* (1916), X, 222–237.

[2] Treaty of 1903, Arts. 1, 2, 3, 7, in Malloy, *Treaties*, I, 362.

The protection of the United States has also been extended to Panama, under the Treaty of 1903, and to San Domingo and Haiti, under the arrangements for the financial rehabilitation of those republics, and has been contemplated for others of the Central American republics.[1]

LIMITATIONS INCIDENT TO GUARANTY

The relation of guaranty is really a special form of protection. It is created by treaty, and is defined by Piédelièvre as follows:

> Treaties of guaranty are those by which a state binds itself to give aid to another, whenever the other may be injured or threatened in the peaceable enjoyment of its rights. The idea that comes out of the notion of guaranty is therefore an idea of protection and assistance in view of the acquisition or the preservation of certain rights, of assistance against actual or possible threats or injuries, of tutelage exercised over one power by another in order to safeguard its political or international interests.[2]

Where the guaranteed state is incapable of freeing itself from the relationship by its own act and the relationship is recognized by the society of nations generally, there is an inequality of legal capacity of considerable importance. The guarantor acquires a capacity for doing things in behalf of the guaranteed state which states are generally presumed to be capable of doing for themselves. As Piédelièvre says, the relation is one of protection or of tutelage.

Treaties of guaranty have been a common device for assuring the permanence and stability of international arrangements throughout the history of the modern society of nations. The execution of the Peace of Westphalia within the Holy Roman Empire was guaranteed by France and Sweden. The treaties were declared to be a perpetual law and prag-

---

[1] See *infra*, pp. 251, 257, 258, 258, note 1.

[2] *Précis*, § 286, I, 258. See Idman, *Le traité de garantie en droit international;* Milanowitch, *Les traités de garantie au XIXe siècle.*

matic sanction of the Empire,[1] and their enforcement was
assured by the following provision:

That nevertheless the concluded peace shall remain in force and
effect, and that all those who have participated in this transaction
shall be obliged to defend and protect all and every one of the laws or
conditions of this peace against whomsoever it may be, without distinction of religion; and if it happens that any point is violated, the
offended shall first endeavor to turn the offender from his present
course, by submitting the cause to a friendly composition, or to. the
ordinary proceedings of justice; and if the difference cannot be settled
by one or the other of these means in the space of three years, that
each and every one of the parties concerned in this transaction shall
be bound to join the injured party, and to assist with their counsel
and their forces to repel the injury, after the offender shall have given
them to understand that the ways of moderation and of justice avail
nothing; without prejudice in all other respects, however, to the
jurisdiction of each, and of the competent administration of justice,
according to the laws and constitutions of each prince and state, and
that it shall not be permitted to any state of the Empire to pursue
its right by force and by arms.[2]

Koch explains the above provision as follows:

It is clear from this passage that the guaranty in question has for
its object the execution of the treaty in all that concerns the interior
of Germany and the states of the Empire in relation to one another. . . .
The only obligation which that guaranty imposes on the foreign
powers who have participated in the treaty is to concur with their
efforts in the maintenance of the Germanic system and liberty, which
the general interest of Europe has opposed as a barrier to the enterprise of Imperial authority.[3]

The treaties of Westphalia were renewed and confirmed
at Utrecht, the system of guaranties was extended, and
Great Britain became an important factor as guarantor of

[1] Treaty of Osnabrück, Art. 17, in Dumont, VI, I, 488. Cf. Treaty of Münster,
§ 116, in Vast, *Les grands traités*, I, 54.
[2] Treaty of Osnabrück, Art. 17, in Dumont, VI, I, 488. Cf. Treaty of Münster,
§§ 119–120, in Vast, *Les grands traités*, I, 55.
[3] Koch et Schoell, I, 248.

the new political arrangements. The Peace of Utrecht[1] consisted of a series of separate treaties which acquired the significance of a general act through the insertion of clauses of guaranty. Thus in the treaty between France and Prussia it was provided:

The said Most Christian King and the said King of Prussia will consent that the Queen of Great Britain, who has contributed so much through the indefatigable exertions of her Ambassadors Extraordinary and Plenipotentiary, present at the Congress of Utrecht, to the conclusion of peace, and all other Potentates and Princes who wish to enter into like engagements, may give to His Most Christian Majesty and to His Prussian Majesty their promises and obligations of guaranty for the execution and observation of all that is contained in the present treaty.[2]

The treaty between France and Great Britain contained express guaranties of other parts of the general settlement. France's treaty with Portugal was guaranteed in the following terms:

The Treaty of Peace signed today between His Most Christian Majesty and His Portuguese Majesty shall be a part of the present Treaty, as if it were inserted here word for word; Her Majesty the Queen of Great Britain declaring that she has offered her guaranty, which she gives in the most solemn form for the most exact observation and execution of all that is contained in the said treaty.[3]

The system of international guaranties established at Westphalia and Utrecht remained a part of the public order of Europe until the entire state system was overturned following the French Revolution.

In the nineteenth century important settlements of general interest were frequently placed under the collective guaranty of the great powers. The neutralization of Switz-

---

[1] On the Peace of Utrecht, see Gerard, *Peace of Utrecht;* Giraud, *Le traité d'Utrecht;* Weber, *Der Friede von Utrecht.* There is a list of references in Vast, *Les grands traités,* III, 60.

[2] Art. 11, in Vast, *Les grands traités,* III, 126.

[3] Art. 24, in Vast, *Les grands traités,* III, 85.

erland, Belgium, and Luxemburg was secured in this way in each instance.[1]   Greece was constituted an independent state under the guaranty of Great Britain, France, and Russia.   The vassal principalities of Roumania and Servia received the same kind of collective sanction for their separate existence by the Treaty of Paris in 1856.

In the case of Greece a guaranty was contemplated in the Treaty of 1827 between Great Britain, France, and Russia:

The arrangements for reconciliation and Peace which shall be definitively agreed upon between the Contending Parties, shall be guaranteed by those of the Signing Powers who may judge it expedient or possible to contract that obligation.   The operation and the effects of such Guarantee shall become the subject of future stipulation between the High Powers.[2]

The three powers gave their formal guaranty in the Treaty of 1832:

Greece, under the Sovereignty of the Prince Otho of Bavaria, and under the Guarantee of the 3 Courts, shall form a monarchical and independent State, according to the terms of the Protocol signed between the said Courts on the 3d February, 1830, and accepted both by Greece and by the Ottoman Porte.[3]

This guaranty was restated in 1864, when the Ionian Islands were united with Greece:

In consequence, Her Britannic Majesty, His Majesty the Emperor of the French, and His Majesty the Emperor of All the Russias, in their character of signing parties to the Convention of the 7th May, 1832, recognize such Union, and declare that Greece, within the Limits determined by the arrangement concluded at Constantinople between the Courts of Great Britain, France, and Russia, and the Ottoman Porte, on the 21st July, 1832, including the Ionian Islands, shall form a Monarchical, Independent, and Constitutional State, under the

[1] See *infra*, pp. 252–254.

[2] Art. 6, in Hertslet, I, 772.

[3] Art. 4, in Hertslet, II, 895.   See Art. 8 of the Protocol of Feb. 3, 1830, in *ibid.*, II, 841.

Sovereignty of His Majesty King George, and under the Guarantee of the 3 Courts.[1]

In the western world the United States is guarantor of the independence of Panama. Article 1 of the Treaty of 1903 between the two countries provides:

The United States guarantees and will maintain the independence of the Republic of Panama.[2]

Several of the obligations of a guarantor are involved in the responsibilities which the United States has assumed in its treaties with Cuba [3] and Haiti,[4] although, strictly speaking, neither relationship is an international guaranty. In each of the three instances mentioned there are important limitations on international capacity.

More recently the integrity of Norway has been secured by the Treaty of 1907 between that state and four of the great powers. Although the word " guaranty " is not used, this is the effect of the treaty, as its substantive articles indicate:

The Norwegian Government undertake not to cede any portion of the territory of Norway to any power to hold on a title founded either on occupation or on any other ground whatsoever.

The German, French, British, and Russian Governments recognize and undertake to respect the integrity of Norway.

If the integrity of Norway is threatened or impaired by any power whatsoever, the German, French, and Russian Governments undertake, on the receipt of a previous communication to this effect from the Norwegian Government, to afford to that Government their support, by such means as may be deemed the most appropriate, with a view to safeguarding the integrity of Norway.[5]

---

[1] Treaty of 1864, Art. 1, in Hertslet, III, 1591. See Holland, *European Concert in the Eastern Question*, ch. 2; Isambert, *L'indépendance grecque et l'Europe*.

[2] Malloy, *Treaties*, II, 1349.

[3] *Supra*, p. 246.   [4] *Infra*, p. 258.

[5] Treaty of 1907, in *A. J. I. L. Suppl.* (1908), II, 267. Cf. Treaty of 1855, in *B. F. S. P.*, XLV, 33. Cf. Treaty of 1852, with regard to the Danish succession and the integrity of Denmark, in *B. F. S. P.*, XLI, 13.

It may be observed that Norway's status is less restricted than is usually the case where the relation of guaranty is created. In this instance, protection is to be invoked by the guaranteed state, and the treaty may be denounced by any of the parties, including Norway, at the end of ten-year periods.

LIMITATIONS INCIDENT TO NEUTRALIZATION

The collective guaranty of the great powers has been used in three cases in the nineteenth century to sanction a particular status in respect to the guaranteed state, namely, that of perpetual neutralization.[1] In the case of Switzerland, of Belgium, and of Luxemburg neutralization has been so guaranteed, has been generally recognized by other members of the international community, and has limited, in the interest of the neutralized state and of the general European order, the international capacity of each of those countries.

The neutralization of Switzerland dates from the settlement of 1815. A declaration of the eight powers who signed the general act of the Vienna Congress acknowledged that " the general interest demands that the Helvetic States should enjoy the benefit of a perpetual neutrality."[2] This declaration was accepted by the Swiss Confederation[3] and confirmed by the Treaty of Vienna.[4] On November 20, 1815, the five great powers signed an act in which the perpetual neutrality of Switzerland was formally acknowledged and guaranteed in the following terms:

the Powers who signed the declaration of Vienna of the 20th March declare, by this present act, their formal and authentic acknowledg-

---

[1] See Baldassari, *La neutralizzazione;* Descamps, *L'état neutre à titre permanent;* Garner, in *A. J. I. L.* (1915), IX, 72–86; Idman, *Le traité de garantie en droit international;* Milanowitch, *Les traités de garantie au XIXᵉ siècle;* Morand, in *R. G. D. I. P.* (1894), I, 522–537; Piédelièvre, *Précis,* §§ 284–285, I, 256; Wilson, in *The Yale Review* (1915), N. S., IV, 474–486; Winslow, in *A. J. I. L.* (1908), II, 366–386.

[2] Declaration of March 20, 1915, in *B. F. S. P.,* II, 142.

[3] *Ibid.,* p. 147.   [4] Art. 84.

ment of the perpetual neutrality of Switzerland; and they guarantee
to that country the integrity and inviolability of its territory in its
new limits, such as they are fixed, as well by the act of the Congress
of Vienna, as by the Treaty of Paris of this day, and such as they will
be hereafter; . . .

The powers who signed the declaration of the 20th of March
acknowledge, in the most formal manner, by the present act, that
the neutrality and inviolability of Switzerland, and her independence
of all foreign influence, enter into the true interests of the policy of
the whole of Europe.[1]

The Congress of Vienna united Belgium with Holland in
the interest of the European balance of power. Following
the revolt of 1830, the great powers intervened, and, by the
Treaty of London of November 15, 1831,[2] accorded Belgium
an independent and neutralized status under their collective
guaranty:

Belgium . . . shall form an independent and perpetually Neutral
State. It shall be bound to observe such Neutrality towards all other
States. . . .

The Courts of Great Britain, Austria, France, Prussia, and Russia
guarantee to His Majesty the King of the Belgians the execution of
all the preceding Articles.[3]

Holland resisted the arrangement for several years, but
came to terms with Belgium in 1839. In another treaty
the great powers confirmed the agreement and repeated their
guaranty of Belgium's independence and neutralization.[4]

Luxemburg was constituted an independent state in 1815
under the King of Holland and was united with the Germanic
Confederation. After the dissolution of the Confederation

---

[1] *A. J. I. L. Suppl.* (1909), III, 106; *B. F. S. P.*, III, 359. See Aberdeen to
Morier, February 11, 1845, in *B. F. S. P.*, LVII, 833. See Milanowitch, *Les traités
de garantie*, pp. 141–173; Sherman, in *A. J. I. L.* (1918), XII, 241–250, 462–474,
780–795; (1919) XIII, 227–241.

[2] *B. F. S. P.*, XVIII, 645.

[3] Arts. 7, 25, in Hertslet, II, 863, 870.

[4] Treaty of 1839, in *B. F. S. P.*, XXVII, 990, 1000. See Descamps, *La neutralité
de la Belgique;* Milanowitch, *Les traités de garantie*, pp. 173–200.

in 1866 it was placed under the guaranty of the great powers as a permanently neutralized state. The Treaty of London of 1867 provided:

The Grand Duchy of Luxemburg, . . . under the guarantee of the courts of Great Britain, Austria, France, Prussia, and Russia, shall henceforth form a perpetually neutral state.

It shall be bound to observe the same neutrality towards all other states.

The high contracting parties engage to respect the principle of neutrality stipulated by the present article.

That principle is and remains placed under the sanction of the collective guarantee of the powers signing parties to the present treaty, with the exception of Belgium, which is itself a neutral state.

The Grand Duchy of Luxemburg being neutralized, according to the terms of the preceding article, the maintenance or establishment of fortresses upon its territory becomes without necessity as well as without object.

In consequence, it is agreed by common consent that the city of Luxemburg, considered in time past, in a military point of view, as a federal fortress, shall cease to be a fortified city.

His Majesty the King Grand Duke reserves to himself to maintain in that city the number of troops necessary to provide in it for the maintenance of good order.[1]

The above are the most important instances of neutralization, although the principle has had a limited application elsewhere. In 1885 the Congo Free State took advantage of the provisions of the act of the Conference on African affairs to issue a declaration

that in accordance with Article 10 of the General Act of the Conference of Berlin, the Congo Free State declares itself, by these presents, to be perpetually neutral, and that it claims the advantages guaranteed by Chapter III of the same act, at the same time that it assumes the duties which accompany neutrality.[2]

[1] Arts. 2, 3, in *A. J. I. L. Suppl.* (1909), III, 118; *B. F. S. P.*, LVII, 32. See Eyschen, in *R. D. I. L. C.* (1899) 2ᵉ sér., I, 5–42; Milanowitch, *Les traités de garantie*, pp. 275–289.

[2] *A. J. I. L. Suppl.* (1909), III, 26; *B. F. S. P.*, LXXVI, 11, 210. See Reeves, in *A. J. I. L.* (1909), III, 99–118.

Parts of states have been declared neutralized in a few instances, as Savoy by the Treaty of Vienna and the Convention of November 20, 1815,[1] and Corfu and Paxo by the treaties which united the Ionian Islands with Greece.[2] The Black Sea was neutralized from 1856 to 1871, while neutralization in a somewhat different sense was extended to the Straits of Magellan by the Treaty of 1881 between the Argentine Republic and Chile, to the Suez Canal by the Convention of 1888, and to the Panama Canal by treaties between the United States and New Granada, Great Britain, and Panama respectively.[3]

Neutralization imposes certain obvious limitations on legal capacity. War and preparations for war must be restricted to the necessities of defense and must be undertaken with absolute impartiality. In the case of Luxemburg even defensive preparation was interdicted. A cession of territory by a neutralized state would probably require the consent of the guaranteeing powers. Intervention in the affairs of other states, even in the limited number of cases approved by the law of nations, would seem to be inconsistent with neutralization. Neutralized states are also incapacitated for entering into certain kinds of treaties. Thus Belgium could not participate in the guaranty of Luxemburg's neutrality,[4] while Luxemburg, at the Second Hague Conference, abstained from voting on the convention limiting the employment of force for the recovery of contract debts because of its status.[5] Experience has revealed other limitations, some of which are controverted, as incident to the condition of neutralization.

[1] *A. J. I. L. Suppl.* (1909), III, 107. See *infra*, p. 265.
[2] *A. J. I. L. Suppl.* (1909), III, 116.
[3] *Ibid.*, pp. 114, 121, 123, 108, 110, 127, 130.
[4] Treaty of London, 1867, Art. 2.
[5] *La Deux. Confér.*, I, 558.

LIMITATIONS INCIDENT TO SUPERVISION OF FINANCE

The financial control of debtor states [1] is also a special form of protection, sanctioned by international practice, the effect of which is to impose important limitations upon the capacity of the debtor state for an indefinite period, or until a condition of solvency can be restored. Of the practice of nations in this respect, Borchard says:

The European powers have on several occasions intervened to secure the payment of public loans due their subjects. Their action has taken various forms. Sometimes it has been merely the use of good offices and an approval of arrangements for financial control made by national bankers or associations of bondholders with the debtor state, as in the case of Turkey (1881) and Servia (1904); an assumption of limited governmental control, as in the case of the United States in the Dominican Republic (1907); or joint intervention of several powers assuming financial control as in the case of Tunis (1868), of Greece (1897), and of Egypt (1880). This is intervention in the true sense, in that it involves an administrative control over a certain portion of national resources and revenues. It seems to be more proper on the part of a state or states guaranteeing the debt of some weak state placed under their guardianship.[2]

A very detailed scheme of international control was elaborated in case of Greece.[3] The Egyptian Commission of 1880 and the Macedonian Commission of 1906–1909 also gave rise to important incapacities.[4] The Platt Amendment in the treaty between the United States and Cuba includes a form of financial control, the Government of Cuba undertaking to contract no public debts beyond the resources provided by the ordinary revenues.[5]

---

[1] Borchard, *Diplomatic Protection of Citizens Abroad*, §§ 121, 125, pp. 313, 325; Imbert, *Les emprunts d'états étrangers;* Kaufmann, *Das internationale Recht der egyptischen Staatschuld;* Kebedgy, in *J. D. I. P.* (1894), XXI, 59–72, 504–519; and in *R. G. D. I. P.* (1894), I, 261–271; Reinsch, *Public International Unions*, p. 75.

[2] *Diplomatic Protection of Citizens Abroad*, § 121, p. 313.

[3] Martens, *Nouveau recueil général*, 2ᵉ sér., XXV, 475–491.

[4] See the Macedonian Financial *Règlement*, in *A. J. I. L. Suppl.* (1907), I, 209.

[5] *Supra*, p. 246.

Financial protection is defined in detail in the treaty of 1907 between the United States and the Dominican Republic:

And whereas the whole of said plan is conditioned and dependent upon the assistance of the United States in the collection of customs revenues of the Dominican Republic and the application thereof so far as necessary to the interest upon and the amortization and redemption of said bonds, and the Dominican Republic has requested the United States to give and the United States is willing to give such assistance: . . .

That the President of the United States shall appoint a General Receiver of Dominican Customs, who, with such Assistant Receivers and other employees of the Receivership as shall be appointed by the President of the United States in his discretion, shall collect all the customs duties accruing at the several customs houses of the Dominican Republic until the payment or retirement of any and all bonds received by the Dominican Government in accordance with the plan and under the limitations as to terms and amounts hereinbefore recited; . . .

The Dominican Government will provide by law for the payment of all customs duties to the General Receiver and his assistants, and will give to them all needful aid and assistance and full protection to the extent of its powers. The Government of the United States will give to the General Receiver and his assistants such protection as it may find to be requisite for the performance of their duties.

Until the Dominican Republic has paid the whole amount of the bonds of the debt its public debt shall not be increased except by previous agreement between the Dominican Government and the United States. A like agreement shall be necessary to modify the import duties, it being an indispensable condition for the modification of such duties that the Dominican Executive demonstrate and that the President of the United States recognize that, on the basis of exportations and importations to the like amount and the like character during the two years preceding that in which it is desired to make such modification, the total net customs receipts would at such altered rates of duties have been for each of such two years in excess of the sum of $2,000,000 United States gold.

The accounts of the General Receiver shall be rendered monthly to the Contaduria General of the Dominican Republic and to the State Department of the United States and shall be subject to examination and verification by the appropriate officers of the Dominican and the United States Governments.[1]

The recent treaty between the United States and Nicaragua, whereby the United States acquires control of the interoceanic canal route across Nicaraguan territory and a naval base in the Gulf of Fonseca, contemplates a limited financial supervision. The three million dollars gold which the United States pays for the concessions is

to be applied by Nicaragua upon its indebtedness or other public purposes for the advancement of the welfare of Nicaragua in a manner to be determined by the two high contracting parties, all such disbursements to be made by orders drawn by the Minister of Finance of the Republic of Nicaragua and approved by the Secretary of State of the United States or by such person as he may designate.[2]

A very complete scheme of financial protection is outlined in the recent treaty between the United States and Haiti. The treaty contemplates much more than financial rehabilitation, as its more important articles show:

The Government of the United States will, by its good offices, aid the Haitian Government in the proper and efficient development of its agricultural, mineral and commercial resources and in the establishment of the finances of Haiti on a firm and solid basis.

The President of Haiti shall appoint, upon nomination by the President of the United States, a General Receiver and such aids and employees as may be necessary, who shall collect, receive and apply all customs duties on imports and exports accruing at the several custom houses and ports of entry of the Republic of Haiti.

The President of Haiti shall appoint, upon nomination by the President of the United States, a Financial Adviser, who shall be an

---

[1] *A. J. I. L. Suppl.* (1907), I, 231. See Hollander, in *A. J. I. L.* (1907), I, 287–296; and the proclamation of the military occupation of San Domingo by the United States under the above treaty, in *A. J. I. L. Suppl.* (1917), XI, 94. See the unratified loan conventions between the United States and Honduras, and between the United States and Nicaragua, *ibid.* (1911), V, 274, 291. On the relations of the United States with Liberia, see *U. S. For. Rel.* (1910), pp. 694–711; and Falkner, in *A. J. I. L.* (1910), IV, 529–545.

[2] *A. J. I. L. Suppl.* (1916), X, 260.

officer attached to the Ministry of Finance, to give effect to whose proposals and labors the Minister will lend efficient aid. The Financial Adviser shall devise an adequate system of public accounting, aid in increasing the revenues and adjusting them to the expenses, inquire into the validity of the debts of the Republic, enlighten both governments with reference to all eventual debts, recommend improved methods of collecting and applying the revenues, and make such other recommendations to the Minister of Finance as may be deemed necessary for the welfare and prosperity of Haiti.

The Government of the Republic of Haiti will provide by law or appropriate decrees for the payment of all customs duties to the General Receiver, and will extend to the Receivership, and to the Financial Adviser, all needful aid and full protection in the execution of the powers conferred and duties imposed herein; and the United States on its part will extend like aid and protection. . . .

The Republic of Haiti shall not increase its public debt except by previous agreement with the President of the United States, and shall not contract any debt or assume any financial obligation unless the ordinary revenues of the Republic available for that purpose, after defraying the expenses of the government, shall be adequate to pay the interest and provide a sinking fund for the final discharge of such debt.

The Republic of Haiti will not without a previous agreement with the President of the United States, modify the customs duties in a manner to reduce the revenues therefrom; and in order that the revenues of the Republic may be adequate to meet the public debt and the expenses of the government, to preserve tranquillity and to promote material prosperity, the Republic of Haiti will coöperate with the Financial Adviser in his recommendations for improvement in the methods of collecting and disbursing the revenues and for new sources of needed income. . . .

The Government of Haiti agrees not to surrender any of the territory of the Republic of Haiti by sale, lease, or otherwise, or jurisdiction over such territory, to any foreign government or power, nor to enter into any treaty or contract with any foreign power or powers that will impair the independence of Haiti. . . .

The high contracting parties shall have authority to take such steps as may be necessary to insure the complete attainment of any of the objects comprehended in this treaty; and, should the necessity occur, the United States will lend an efficient aid for the preservation of

Haitian independence and the maintenance of a government adequate for the protection of life, property and individual liberty.[1]

The treaty also provides for a native constabulary, to be organized and officered by Americans appointed by the President of Haiti on the nomination of the President of the United States, and for measures of sanitation and public improvement under the direction of American engineers selected in the same way. American officers of the constabulary will be replaced by Haitians as rapidly as the latter become qualified and pass appropriate examinations. Customs receipts are to be applied first to the expenses of the receivership, second to the interest and sinking fund on the public debt, third to the maintenance of the constabulary, and the remainder to the current expenses of the Haitian Government. The General Receiver reports to the Haitian Government and the United States Department of State. The arrangement is for ten years, and for a further period of ten years if, for specific reasons presented by either party, its purpose has not been fully accomplished.

LIMITATIONS INCIDENT TO INTERVENTION

Other limitations upon equality are incident to intervention by one state in the internal affairs of another state.[2] If the relation out of which the right of intervention arises is more than transitory, if it cannot be terminated at the pleasure of the state that is subject to intervention, and if it is recognized by the international community the resulting capacities and incapacities constitute differences of status to which the principle of equality is quite inapplicable. Capacity is expanded on the one hand and restricted on the other, creating inequalities of considerable significance.

---

[1] Arts. 1, 2, 3, 8, 9, 11, 14, in *A. J. I. L. Suppl.* (1916), X, 234–238.

[2] See Floeckher, in *R. G. D. I. P.* (1896), III, 329–333; Hodges, *Doctrine of Intervention;* Kebedgy, *L'intervention en droit international public;* Piédelièvre, *Précis,* §§ 289–312, I, 259–278; Rougier, in *R. G. D. I. P.* (1910), XVII, 468–526.

The legality of intervention in certain circumstances was conceded by many of the classical publicists, particularly among those who wrote before the development of the conception of state equality.[1] The subject has given modern writers a great deal of difficulty, for it is generally agreed that intervention and equality are irreconcilable.[2] There has been a tendency to solve the difficulty by denouncing all intervention as illegal, political, exceptional, or matter of fact as opposed to matter of law. The practice of nations contains few suggestions of a recognized international principle. As Lawrence remarks, " history speaks with a medley of discordant voices." [3]

Notwithstanding the difficulties involved in the subject it must receive some consideration, for interventions on one pretext or another have occurred with great frequency, and in certain instances they clearly have the sanction of the law of nations. For the present purpose they may be divided into three categories: (1) interventions prompted by policy in violation of law; (2) interventions of an exceptional character, justified by equitable considerations, but not recognized by law; (3) interventions justified by law or the peculiar legal relationships existing between certain states. Limitations upon legal capacity arise only out of interventions of the third category.

Intervention to preserve the balance of power [4] is so ill-defined and so consistently abused that it can hardly be

---

[1] Gentilis, *De jure belli*, I, 15; Grotius, *De jure belli ac pacis*, II, 20, 40; Zouche, *Juris et judicii fecialis*, etc., II, 7, 1. Cf. the *Vindiciæ contra tyrannos*, Q. IV.

[2] See Hicks, in *A. J. I. L.* (1908), II, 541; Kebedgy, in *Z. S. R.* (1900) Neue Folge, XIX, 91; Piédelièvre, *Précis*, § 290, I, 260; Pillet, in *R. G. D. I. P.* (1898), V, 87.

[3] *Int. Law*, § 63, p. 125. Hodges says: " European practice in general, to which England is not an exception, has led to numerous interventions on such varied and slight pretexts that it is hard to find, for any long period, a general feeling that intervention is, in principle, contrary to the essence of sovereignty." *Doctrine of Intervention*, p. 148.

[4] See Dupuis, *Le principe d'équilibre et le concert européen*, Pt. I, ch. 6.

included in the third category. It must either be included in another category or justified on other grounds. As already indicated, however, the great political settlements intended to establish a balance of power have frequently contained clauses of guaranty from which interventions of the third category may arise. The legal significance of the international guaranty is here regarded from another point of view. The guaranties of Westphalia gave France and Sweden a right to intervene in the Empire,[1] and subjected the Empire and its states to corresponding incapacities. Similar incapacities were created by the treaties of Utrecht.[2]

Intervention is the corollary of many of the limitations considered elsewhere from another point of view. Thus many interventions are explained by essential differences in civilization. It cannot be doubted that states having extraterritorial rights may intervene if necessary to conserve them. The precedents for intervention on behalf of citizens residing in the less advanced countries of the world are so numerous as to leave no doubt as to the positive principle which justifies them. It is suggested that the so-called interventions in the interests of humanity,[3] wherever they can be justified legally, are really the consequence of differences in civilization, and that wherever this is the situation there exist legal incapacities which can only be removed by the natural processes of orderly progress. Repeated interventions in Turkey,[4] the action taken by the United States in 1898 in relation to Cuba,[5] the intervention of the powers in

---

[1] Treaty of Osnabrück, Art. 17, in Dumont, VI, I, 488; Treaty of Münster, §§ 119-120, in Vast, Les grands traités, I, 55.

[2] France-Great Britain, Arts. 24-25; France-Portugal, Art. 18; France-Prussia, Art. 11; France-Savoy, Arts. 5-7; France-United Provinces, Art. 31; Vast, Les grands traités, III, 85, 118, 126, 133, 156.

[3] Cf. Hodges, Doctrine of Intervention, p. 91; Rougier, in R. G. D. I. P. (1910), XVII, 468-526.

[4] See Holland, European Concert in the Eastern Question.

[5] See Moore, Digest, §§ 908-910, VI, 105-239.

China in 1900,[1] and of the United States in Mexico during the late revolutions [2] afford illustrations.

The protection of one state by another implies intervention if necessary to make protection effective. Intervention is the normal order in connection with the protection of backward or partially civilized states. It is always held in reserve in the protection of more advanced states. The right is expressly stipulated in the treaty between the United States and Cuba, quoted above,[3] and has been exercised by the United States in the performance of its obligations as protecting power.[4]

It has never been seriously doubted that the relation of guaranty implies intervention as a sanction. The European powers have intervened to make effective the collective guaranties undertaken at Vienna, Paris, and Berlin.[5] The guarantors of Greece have been obliged to intervene on more than one occasion.[6] Intervention to enforce a guaranty receives express recognition in the Constitution of Panama, which provides:

The Government of the United States of America shall have the power to intervene in any part of the Republic of Panama to reëstablish public peace and constitutional order, in the event of their being disturbed, if the said Government, by public treaty, assumes the obligation of guaranteeing the independence and sovereignty of this Republic.[7]

The incapacities incident to intervention are also involved in the financial control of debtor states, as appears from the

[1] See Clements, *The Boxer Rebellion*.
[2] See correspondence regarding the American punitive expedition of 1916, in *A. J. I. L. Suppl.* (1916), X, 179–225.
[3] *Supra*, p. 246.   [4] *U. S. For. Rel.* (1906), pp. 454–510.
[5] See the treaties between Great Britain and Prussia, Aug. 9, 1870, and between Great Britain and France, Aug. 11, 1870, in Hertslet, III, 1886, 1889.
[6] See Holland, *European Concert in the Eastern Question*, ch. 2.
[7] Art. 136 (Rodriguez' transl.). See also the Treaty of 1903, in Malloy, *Treaties*, II, 1349.

experience of Egypt, Turkey, and Greece. The United States engages, in the Treaty of 1907 with San Domingo, to " give the General Receiver and his assistants such protection as it may find to be requisite for the performance of their duties." [1] The military occupation of San Domingo has been undertaken recently in the execution of the treaty.[2] Should the necessity occur in Haiti, the United States undertakes to " lend an efficient aid for the preservation of Haitian independence and the maintenance of a government adequate for the protection of life, property, and individual liberty." [3]

LIMITATIONS INCIDENT TO INTERNATIONAL SERVITUDES

The question of servitudes in the law of nations has been the subject of considerable controversy. The authorities were reviewed from divergent points of view in the argument before the Hague Tribunal in the *North Atlantic Coast Fisheries Arbitration* without reaching any very satisfactory conclusions.[4] It is certain that international relationships afford many examples of a restricted condition of jurisdiction which is of the nature of a servitude, whatever it may be called. Distinct from the state's contractual obligations which involve in each case no more than a duty of performance toward the other contracting state, there are incumbrances on the state's jurisdiction, imposed for the benefit or advantage of another state or group of states, and requiring that the state either allow something to be done within its jurisdiction which it would not otherwise be obliged to allow, or that it refrain from doing something which it would other-

---

[1] *Supra*, p. 257.

[2] Proclamation of occupation, in *A. J. I. L. Suppl.* (1917), XI, 94.

[3] *Supra*, p. 259.

[4] See *N. A. C. F. Proceedings*, VIII, 16–31; IX, 306–314, 560–696; XI, 1655–1711, 2123–2130. Cf. The Japanese House Tax Arbitration, in Wilson, *The Hague Arbitration Cases*, pp. 40 ff.; Aix-la-Chapelle-Maastricht Railroad Co. *v.* Thewis and the Royal Dutch Government, in *A. J. I. L.* (1914), VIII, 907–913.

wise be free to do. The state for whose advantage such an incumbrance or limitation exists may assert its right, not only against the state whose jurisdiction is restricted, but also against the entire community of nations.

These incumbrances on jurisdiction are also limitations on legal capacity.[1] In this respect international burdens of the nature of servitudes are essentially different from the servitudes of municipal law. The latter are burdens imposed on ownership and are without any effect on the legal capacity of the owner. The former are burdens on jurisdiction, which is one of the most important elements of international capacity.

The neutralization of northern Savoy in 1815, in support of the neutrality of Switzerland, may be regarded as a servitude of neutrality in the interest of Switzerland. The convention which provided for the neutralization of Switzerland also stipulated:

> The powers acknowledge likewise and guarantee the neutrality of those parts of Savoy, designated by the act of the Congress of Vienna of the 20th May 1815, and by the Treaty of Paris signed this day, the same being entitled to participate in the neutrality of Switzerland, equally as if they belonged to that country.[2]

It is evident that this provision limited Sardinia's international capacity in important respects. The neutralization of the Black Sea by the Treaty of Paris of 1856, as part of the program designed to secure the independence and integrity of the Ottoman Empire, was aimed primarily at Russia. Article 11 provided:

> The Black Sea is neutralized; its waters and its ports, thrown open to the mercantile marine of every nation, are formally and in perpetuity interdicted to the flag of war, either of the powers possessing

---

[1] Cf. Piédelièvre, *Précis*, § 288, I, 259.
[2] Convention of November 20, 1815, in *A. J. I. L. Suppl.* (1909), III, 106; Treaty of Vienna, Art. 92.

its coasts, or of any other power, with the exceptions mentioned in Articles 14 and 19 of the present treaty.[1]

The Russian Government made it perfectly clear that it regarded the stipulation as a restriction on capacity.[2]

Servitudes of a different kind were imposed on the Balkan states by the Treaty of Berlin. They were required to treat the subjects, citizens, and commerce of all the powers on the basis of equality, were forbidden to levy transit duties on goods passing through their territories, and were subjected to other restrictions of less consequence.[3] Limitations upon Roumanian jurisdiction incident to the vesting of extensive powers in the European Commission of the Danube were confirmed and extended. Articles 52 and 53 provided as follows:

In order to increase the guarantees which assure the freedom of navigation on the Danube which is recognized as of European interest, the High Contracting Parties determine that all the fortresses and fortifications existing on the course of the river from the Iron Gates to its mouths shall be razed, and no new ones erected. No vessel of war shall navigate the Danube below the Iron Gates with the exception of vessels of light tonnage in the service of the river police and Customs. The " stationnaires " of the Powers at the mouths of the Danube may, however, ascend the river as far as Galatz.

The European Commission of the Danube on which Roumania shall be represented is maintained in its functions, and shall exercise them henceforth as far as Galatz in complete independence of the territorial authorities. All the Treaties, arrangements, acts, and decisions relating to its rights, privileges, prerogatives, and obligations are confirmed.[4]

---

[1] *A. J. I. L. Suppl.* (1909), III, 114. Articles 14 and 19 made an exception of light coast-guard vessels and of a limited number of light vessels stationed by the powers at the mouth of the Danube to insure the execution of regulations to be adopted with regard to its navigation.

[2] See Gortchakoff to Brunnow, October 19/31, 1870, in *Parliamentary Papers* (1871), LXXII, 1; and same to same, November 8/20, 1870, in *ibid.*, p. 24.

[3] Arts. 5, 8, 11, 12, 27, 29, 30, 35, 37, 39, 44, 48. Note also Arts. 61 and 62 in regard to Turkey.

[4] See Treaty of Paris, 1856, Arts. 16-18; Public Act of November 2, 1865, in

Very important limitations were imposed on Montenegro in connection with the annexation of Antivari and its seaboard:

Montenegro shall have full and complete freedom of navigation on the Boyana. No fortifications shall be constructed on the course of that river except such as may be necessary for the local defence of the stronghold of Scutari, and they shall not extend beyond a distance of 6 kilometers from that town.

Montenegro shall have neither ships of war nor flag of war.

The port of Antivari and all the waters of Montenegro shall remain closed to the ships of war of all nations.

The fortifications situated on Montenegrin territory between the lake and the coast shall be razed, and none shall be rebuilt within this zone.

The administration of the maritime and sanitary police, both at Antivari and along the coast of Montenegro, shall be carried out by Austria-Hungary by means of light coast-guard boats.

Montenegro shall adopt the maritime code in force in Dalmatia. On her side Austria-Hungary undertakes to grant Consular protection to the Montenegrin merchant flag.

Montenegro shall come to an understanding with Austria-Hungary on the right to construct and keep up across the new Montenegrin territory a road and a railway.

Absolute freedom of communication shall be guaranteed on these roads.[1]

Most of these limitations on Montenegro were terminated in 1909, as a result of the readjustments which took place in southeastern Europe in the preceding year.

The Peace Protocol ot 1901 between the powers and China imposed important limitations of a somewhat similar nature on the latter state, such as exclusive control of the legation quarter at Peking by the foreign nations, with the exclusion

Hertslet, *Commercial Treaties*, XII, 884; Protocol of March 28, 1866, in *ibid.*, XII, 919; Regulations of 1911, in *ibid.*, XXVI, 862; Pitisteano, *La question du Danube;* Sayre, *Experiments in International Administration*, pp. 38–47.

[1] Art. 29. Cf. Arts. 52 to 57, in regard to fortifications on the Danube. See Bluntschli, in *R. D. I. L. C.* (1880), XII, 276–284; Brunswik, *Recueil de documents diplomatiques relatifs au Monténégro;* Vaclick, *La souveraineté du Monténégro et le droit des gens moderne de l'Europe.*

of Chinese residents and the right to make the quarter defensible, the razing of forts which might impede free communication between Peking and the sea, the stationing of foreign troops at certain points in China, the control of tariffs, and the undertaking of certain conservancy works by China.[1]

Panama's concession of an interoceanic canal route to the United States carries with it important rights of the nature of servitudes. In addition to granting the United States all the rights which it would have if it were sovereign in the canal zone and auxiliary lands and waters, certain subsidiary rights are conceded in perpetuity or for a long period. Such are the right to use rivers and lakes for navigation, water power, and water supply, the right to acquire property by purchase or eminent domain in the cities of Panama and Colon for works of sanitation, and to collect water and sewerage rates, the right to prescribe sanitary ordinances in the two cities, to make use of their harbors, and, if need be, to maintain public order, and the monopoly of all railroad and canal communication between the Caribbean and the Pacific.[2]

Many other examples of limitations on jurisdiction of the nature of servitudes might be given. Restrictions appurtenant to fishing rights in territorial waters [3] and to leased territories [4] are important applications of similar principles. Perhaps the illustrations given are adequate, however, to indicate the nature of this type of limitation, as well as its importance in relation to the principle of equality.

[1] *A.J.I.L. Suppl.* (1907), I, 388; Clements, *The Boxer Rebellion.*

[2] Treaty of 1903, in Malloy, *Treaties* II, 1349–1357. See also the Treaty of 1914 between the United States and Nicaragua, in *A.J.I.L. Suppl.* (1916), X, 258; and Costa Rica v. Nicaragua, in *A.J.I.L.* (1917), XI, 181, 217.

[3] See the award on question one in the North Atlantic Coast Fisheries Arbitration (1910), in Wilson, *The Hague Arbitration Cases,* pp. 154 ff., discussed *supra,* p. 168. Also Cobbett, *Cases,* I, 160.

[4] See the treaties of 1898 between China and Germany, Russia, France, and Great Britain respectively, in *A.J.I.L. Suppl.* (1910), IV, 285–298.

Limitations Incident to Remedial Processes

Among the most important limitations on the equality of
nations are those which result from the recognition of self-
help as a remedial process in international law.   Individual
vindication of rights and redress of grievances are always
important in the primitive stages of legal development.
They are peculiarly characteristic of the law of nations,
where other remedial processes have had only a rudimentary
development.   The importance of self-help as a legal remedy
has been indicated by leading publicists of all centuries.
Victoria affirmed that *bellum justum est justitiae executio.*[1]
Grotius developed a similar thesis in great detail,[2] while
Zouche defined war as " a lawful contention between different princes or peoples." [3]   Phillimore says:

> The violation of rights *stricti juris* may be redressed by forcible
> means, by the operation of war, which in the community of nations
> answers to the act of the Judicial and Executive Power in the com-
> munity of individuals.[4]

[1] See Rel. VI, *De jure belli*. This conception of the place of self-help in the
Law of Nations seems to have been anticipated as early as 1360 by Legnano, who
explained reprisals as follows: " But when the Empire began gradually to be exhausted, so that now there are some who in fact recognize no superior, and by them
justice is neglected, the need arose for a subsidiary remedy, when the ordinary
remedies fail, but which is on no account to be resorted to when they exist.... But
this extraordinary remedy had its origin in the law of nations. For it is a form of
lawful war. For it is lawful to take arms in defence of one's own body; ... and not
only in defence of one's private and individual body, but also of the mystical body.
For a community is one body, whose parts are the several members of the community; ... and so a community may defend the parts of its own body. It had
its origin, too, in divine law.... From all that has been said, we may infer the
reason of the introduction of this remedy. For its final object is that justice may
obtain its due effect, and its occasion is when there is a failure of remedy, arising
from the neglect of those who govern and rule peoples, and the absence of recognition of superiors in fact, at which time this extraordinary remedy is needed."
Tractatus, ch. 23 (Brierly's transl.).

[2] See *De jure belli ac pacis*, Proleg. 25, 28; and *passim*.

[3] *Juris et judicii fecialis*, etc., I, 6, p. 32.

[4] *Commentaries*, I, 215.

His definition of war is to the same effect:

War is the exercise of the international right of action, to which, from the nature of the thing and the absence of any common superior tribunal, nations are compelled to have recourse, in order to assert and vindicate their rights.[1]

Many of the modern publicists, to be sure, would attach qualifications to Phillimore's definition, but, directly or indirectly, all reach about the same result.

The degree to which the law of nations recognizes self-help as a legal remedy, and even as a source of substantive rights, is well illustrated by the rule as to duress. There is no system of municipal law that makes a general practice of enforcing agreements made under duress. In international law, if duress is applied to the persons of the state's representatives the agreement is not binding, but if to the state itself it is a valid and binding agreement. Grotius' reason is probably as good as any, that without such a rule wars could neither be moderated nor concluded.[2] In the Venezuelan preferential claims case certain of the smaller states argued that force could not be a source of right;[3] but the blockading powers denied the point[4] and were sustained by the award of the tribunal. Of the thirteen conventions framed by the Second Hague Peace Conference, eleven were concerned with war or neutrality. The first American delegate reminded the Conference that they had " done much to regulate war, but very little to prevent it." [5]

---

[1] *Commentaries*, III, 77; Moore, *Digest*, § 1100, VII, 153. See Higgins, *The Hague Peace Conferences*, Introd., p. xi; and cf. Westlake, *Int. Law*, II, 1–5. Moore defines war as " the existence of the legal condition of things in which rights are or may be prosecuted by force."

[2] *De jure belli ac pacis*, III, 19, 11, 1. See the limitations on the rule proposed by the Brazilian delegation at the Second Hague Conference, *La Deux. Confér.*, I, 556. Also a proposition to abolish title by conquest under the public law of America (Moore, *Digest*, § 1156, VII, 315), and Westlake's proposal for limiting reprisals (*L. Q. R.* (1909), XXV, 136).

[3] *Venez. Arbit.*, pp. 867, 1111.   [4] *Ibid.*, pp. 983, 984.

[5] *La Deux. Confér.*, II, 330. Cf. remarks of Renault, *ibid.*, I, 166.

In so far as the law of nations recognizes self-help in any form as a legal procedure for vindicating rights and redressing grievances, it concedes to nations an inequality of legal capacity directly proportioned to the distribution of resources which make for military strength. It is possible to regard the state in its normal peaceful relations as a moral person having, for many purposes, the same legal capacity as every other state, without regard to differences in territory, population, wealth, military strength, and the like; but as soon as the use of these resources in self-help is recognized by the law as a proper remedial process even the fiction of equality becomes a vain and useless thing. Legal capacity can no longer be sharply distinguished from physical capacity. As Léon Bourgeois pertinently observed before the First Hague Conference, " when swords are thrown into the balance, one side may easily outweigh the other." [1]

The impossibility of reconciling self-help with equality has been recognized, particularly in relation to the much controverted questions of pacific blockade and the forcible recovery of contract debts. Pacific blockade was considered by the Institute of International Law in 1888.[2] In opposing its recognition as a legal proceeding, Geffcken said:

Now, all states being equal, it should not be lawful to do anything to a weak state that a strong state would not tolerate. . . .

Finally, it is indisputable that if we review the cases where a so-called pacific blockade has been instituted we will find in every case that it has been used by a powerful state against a weak state.[3] . . . No doubt such a blockade is for a great state a very convenient means of imposing its will on the weak, whereas a war is a grave measure of which one may not anticipate the consequences in advance; but it is an essential principle of the law of nations that states are equal and have equal rights.[4]

---

[1] Quoted *supra*, p. 181.

[2] *A. I. D. I.* (1888), IX, 275, 301. See also Hogan, *Pacific Blockade;* Holland, *Studies*, pp. 130–150; Westlake, in *L. Q. R.* (1909), XXV, 13–23.

[3] See Bulmerincq, in *J. D. I. P.* (1884), XI, 569–583; Cobbett, *Cases*, I, 345–348.

[4] *A. I. D. I.* (1888), IX, 289–293.

Among the advocates of pacific blockade it was argued that the process should be recognized as available to the great powers when acting in concert,[1] and that with respect to the principle of equality it was necessary to distinguish between a right and the possibility of exercising a right. The right of blockade existed for all, but could only be used against the weak.[2]

The more vigorous advocates of equality among the smaller states have not been satisfied with so illusory a distinction. This is brought out clearly in the attempt that has been made to limit the use of self-help as a procedure for obtaining the settlement of claims held by the nationals of one state against another state. Such operations have invariably been carried out against weak states.[3] When Great Britain, Germany, and Italy adopted coercive measures against Venezuela in 1902 [4] there was a unanimous protest throughout Central and South America. In his famous despatch of December 29, 1902, the Minister of Foreign Relations of the Argentine Republic gave particular attention to the forcible collection of public loans. He said:

Among the fundamental principles of public international law which humanity has consecrated, one of the most precious is that which decrees that all states, whatever be the force at their disposal, are entities in law, perfectly equal one to another, and mutually entitled by virtue thereof to the same consideration and respect.

The acknowledgment of the debt, the payment of it in its entirety, can and must be made by the nation without diminution of its inherent rights as a sovereign entity, but the summary and immediate collection at a given moment, by means of force, would occasion nothing less than the ruin of the weakest nations, and the absorption of their governments, together with all the functions inherent in

---

[1] Brusa, *A. I. D. I.* (1888), IX, 298.

[2] Perels, *ibid.*, p. 296. See *supra*, p. 120, note 2.

[3] Borchard, *Diplomatic Protection of Citizens Abroad*, §§ 121, 126, pp. 314, 328; M'Veagh, in *Venez. Arbit.*, p. 1136; Triana, in *La Deux. Confér.*, II, 258.

[4] See *supra*, p. 164.

them, by the mighty of the earth. The principles proclaimed on this continent of America are otherwise.[1]

The forcible collection of contract debts, without distinction between public loans and other contractual obligations, was considered at the Second Hague Conference.[2] A convention was framed, of which the substantive part was as follows:

The Contracting Powers agree not to have recourse to armed force for the recovery of contract debts claimed from the Government of one country by the Government of another country as being due to its nationals.

This undertaking is, however, not applicable when the debtor State refuses or neglects to reply to an offer of arbitration, or, after accepting the offer, renders the settlement of the *Compromis* impossible, or, after the arbitration, fails to submit to the award.[3]

The effect of this convention is to prevent coercion of debtor states unless they refuse to submit to arbitration, or, having submitted to arbitration, refuse to abide by the award. In other words, equality prevails in the absence of bad faith or of an attempt to evade responsibility. Otherwise self-help and inequality become the rule.

This settlement has not been acceptable to those states which have stood most consistently for equality. Brazil, Venezuela, and six small states have never signed the convention. Argentine and ten small states signed with reservations. Only a few of the second rank powers have ratified without reservations.[4] The Argentinian reservation at signature was as follows:

[1] *U. S. For. Rel.* (1903), p. 2. See Drago, in *A. J. I. L.* (1907), I, 692–726; Hershey, in *ibid.*, 26–45; Moulin, *La doctrine de Drago.*

[2] See *La Deux. Confér.*, I, 336–338, 553–561, II, 139–144, 246–253, 258–260, 268–308, 548–553, 916–923; Higgins, *The Hague Peace Conferences*, pp. 184–197.

[3] Art. 1; Higgins, *The Hague Peace Conferences*, p. 180; *A. J. I. L. Suppl.* (1908), II, 81.

[4] Denmark, Haiti, Liberia, Mexico, Netherlands, Norway, Panama, Portugal, and Spain.

1. With regard to debts arising from ordinary contracts between the citizen or subject of a nation and a foreign government, recourse shall not be had to arbitration except in the specific case of denial of justice by the courts of the country which made the contract, the remedies before which courts must first have been exhausted.

2. Public loans, secured by bond issues and constituting the national debt, shall in no case give rise to military aggression or the material occupation of the soil of American nations.[1]

The Bolivian delegate said:

It seems to me, therefore, that the acceptance of the proposition before us will but mean the legitimation by the *Peace* Conference of a certain class of *wars*, or, at least, of interventions resulting from disputes which relate neither to the honor nor vital interests of the creditor States.

In consequence of these forceful reasons, the delegation of Bolivia regrets not to give its entire assent to the proposition under discussion.[2]

Colombia made the following reservation:

It does not agree to the employment of force in any case for the recovery of debts; and neither does it agree to arbitration before recourse to the tribunals of the debtor state.[3]

If it is true that self-help in the form of pacific blockade or forcible recovery of contract debts is inconsistent with equality, and there seems to be no escape from that conclusion, then war is inconsistent with equality *a fortiori*. So long as self-help remains a recognized and important remedial process of the law of nations, it will be necessary to take account of important limitations upon equality of legal capacity. The society of nations may be fortunate, indeed, if it secures unqualified support for the basic principle of equality before the law.

[1] *La Deux. Confér.*, I, 337.
[2] *Ibid.*, II, 142.
[3] *Ibid.*, II, 306.

LIMITATIONS INCIDENT TO SUPERNATIONAL
ORGANIZATION

The creation of true supernational authority, capable of enforcing its decisions on participating states, is obviously a limitation upon the capacity of participating states. As between the states which are members of such an organization this limitation may apply equally and therefore equality of capacity may be unimpaired. Indeed, not only may equality be preserved, but the legal capacity of each may become much more significant through the subordination of individual freedom of action to the common interest and the substitution of orderly procedure for self-help. Where a limited number of states constitute such an organization, however, an inequality of capacity arises between those states and others outside the organization. Attendant advantages may more than compensate for the inequality in relation to other states, but the inequality arises, nevertheless, in a form which the law cannot overlook.

The development of this type of limitation has been almost negligible in the past. It is worthy of mention chiefly because of its possible importance in the future. It has been exemplified in recent times by the creation of the Central American Court of Justice. The Treaty of Washington, December 21, 1907, negotiated under the friendly offices of the United States and Mexico, provided:

The Republics of Central America consider as one of their first duties, in their mutual relations, the maintenance of peace; and they bind themselves to always observe the most complete harmony, and decide every difference or difficulty that may arise amongst them, of whatsoever nature it may be, by means of the Central American Court of Justice, created by the Convention which they have concluded for that purpose on this date.[1]

[1] Art. 1, in *A. J. I. L. Suppl.* (1908), II, 220. See the Protocol of September 17, 1907, in *ibid.* (1907), I, 406. Read the remarks of the Court in Costa Rica *v.* Nicaragua (1916), in *A. J. I. L.* (1917), XI, 181–229, at p. 211. See Anderson, in

The Convention for the establishment of the Court began as follows:

The High Contracting Parties agree by the present Convention to constitute and maintain a permanent tribunal which shall be called the " Central American Court of Justice," to which they bind themselves to submit all controversies or questions which may arise among them, of whatsoever nature and no matter what their origin may be, in case the respective Departments of Foreign Affairs should not have been able to reach an understanding.

This Court shall also take cognizance of the questions which individuals of one Central American country may raise against any of the other contracting Governments, because of the violation of treaties or conventions, and other cases of an international character; no matter whether their own Government supports said claim or not; and provided that the remedies which the laws of the respective country provide against such violation shall have been exhausted or that denial of justice shall have been shown.[1]

The Court was declared to represent the national conscience of Central America. It formulated its rules of procedure, determined its own jurisdiction, executed its orders through the contracting governments or by special commissioners, decreed the preservation of the *status quo* pending a decision, and rendered judgments by default. The contracting governments formally bound themselves to obey and enforce the court's orders, and to lend all the moral support necessary to secure the execution of its judgments. The practical importance of limitations arising out of the creation of an institution like the Central American Court of Justice was suggested by two of the Court's decisions with regard to the Bryan-Chamorro Treaty between Nicaragua and the United States.[2]

A. J. I. L. (1908), II, 144–151; Scott, in *ibid.*, 121–143. The Court was reported closed March 17, 1918. *Ibid.* (1918), XII, 380.

[1] Arts. 1, 2, in A. J. I. L. Suppl. (1908), II, 231.

[2] Costa Rica *v.* Nicaragua (1916), in A. J. I. L. (1917), XI, 181–229; Salvador *v.* Nicaragua (1916), in *ibid.*, 674–730. See note of November 9, 1916, in regard to Nicaragua's protest, in A. J. I. L. Suppl. (1917), XI, 3.

SUMMARY

In contrast with internal limitations upon the equality of states arising out of the state's organic constitution, external limitations upon equality are imposed from without by treaty arrangements securing general recognition and by the usages which are defined in the practice of nations. External limitations are of greater importance, not only because their development is synchronous with the accretion of that common opinion which eventually finds expression in usage and treaties, but also because they are the practical outcome of that vast complexity of relationships which constitutes the *raison d'être* for the law of nations. Their importance has been recognized by the publicists of all centuries, although their true significance has been frequently obscured by those theories which were considered in earlier chapters. The present chapter has been written to indicate the basis upon which the different types of external limitation rest and to suggest the significance of each type in relation to the problem of status among the members of international society.

It has been pointed out, in the first place, that external limitations upon the legal capacity of the state as an international person may be imposed by usage or treaty because of something anomalous or exceptional in the physical bases of state existence. This anomalous condition may consist either in something peculiar about the state's geographical situation, as in case of an inland state, or it may consist in the unusual character of a state's civilization, as in case of those states peculiarly affected by treaty provisions and custom in regard to extraterritorial jurisdiction, the diplomatic protection of citizens abroad, the exclusion of aliens, and the granting of asylum in legations, consulates, or on public vessels. In the second place, external limitations may take the form of an anomalous organization imposed from without and resulting in the division of legal capacity among the several parts of a composite whole. Imperfect unions of this kind have been constituted by the partial disintegration of existing states and by the partial federation of separate states. The condition has always been transitional. Again, external limitations may arise out of an exceptional or anomalous relationship between two or more states. Such limitations were classified as those incident to international suzerainty, international protection, guaranty, neutralization, supervision of finance, and intervention. Wherever these relationships receive general recognition there is a true limitation upon the legal capacity of the subordinate state. External limitations may also arise out of a restricted condition of jurisdiction having many of the characteristics of the servitude of municipal law. Perhaps the most important of all external limitations are those which are necessarily incident to many of the remedial processes recognized by international law, such as pacific blockade, the forcible collection of debts, reprisals, and war. The recognition of self-help as a legitimate remedial process inevitably proportions the legal capacity of states to correspond to the distribution of whatever makes self-help an effective remedy. It tends to obliterate all distinction between legal capacity and physical capacity.

The law of nations will become increasingly scientific and rational as it takes account of limitations on equality of the kind considered in the present chapter. These limitations exist. There is abundant evidence that in one form or another they will become more important in the future. Little advantage can be derived from attempting to subordinate them to theories which tend to deny or distort their true significance.   By frankly recognizing their significance, publicists may contribute substantially to the development of a system of rules which must become a more efficient instrument for the preservation of order and justice in the international community of the future.

CHAPTER VIII

LIMITATIONS UPON THE POLITICAL EQUALITY
OF STATES

INTERNATIONAL CONGRESSES AND CONFERENCES

THE limitations upon equality considered in the two preceding chapters have to do with the legal capacity or status of the state as an international person. The political capacity of the state is something fundamentally different. Legal rights and transactions constitute the principal subject matter of legal capacity, while political capacity is concerned with such matters as representation, voting, and contributions in international conferences and congresses, administrative unions, and arbitral or judicial tribunals. Laws in regard to legal capacity affect the relations between states as individual entities, while laws in regard to political capacity affect their participation in the privileges and responsibilities of collective international activity. A good deal of the confusion in the books on the subject of equality is the consequence of failure to observe this fundamental distinction.

The international congress or conference is the earliest manifestation of a collective international interest and authority. Wherever such a congress or conference is truly international, political equality is assured by recognizing the right of every interested state to participate on an equal footing, by conceding to the delegations of every state an equality of voting strength whenever votes are taken and requiring unanimity for all important decisions, and by limiting the assembly to decisions *ad referendum*, that is to say, by giving it no authority to bind participating states unless they choose to ratify what it does.

The great war congresses have usually been constituted on the basis of equal representation, although occasionally the principle has been arbitrarily denied. The assemblies at Westphalia, Utrecht, and Vienna were called in each instance to settle the terms of peace at the conclusion of a long period of European war. All the interested states sent delegates.[1] Every part of Europe, except England, Poland, Muscovy, and the Ottoman Empire, was represented at Münster and Osnabrück. Great states and small states sent delegates to Utrecht, where a series of separate treaties were negotiated embodying the terms of a general peace. All the European states except Turkey sent envoys to Vienna, but in this case only the delegates of Portugal, Spain, and Sweden, states which had been parties to the alliance against France, were admitted to the deliberations of the five great powers. The three states named did little more than ratify the decisions which the great powers reached, while the envoys of the smaller states were merely permitted to be present at Vienna and make known the wishes of their respective governments.

In the nineteenth century the equal representation of all interested states was recognized in only a few of the conferences called to consider political questions. Belgium, Denmark, the Netherlands, Portugal, Spain, Sweden and Norway, and the United States participated with five of the European great powers and Morocco in the Madrid Conference of 1880.[2] Four years later the same powers, not including Morocco, and with the addition of Russia and Turkey, sent delegates to the Conference on African affairs held at Berlin.[3] Belgium, Spain, and the Netherlands joined

---

[1] The purpose, composition, procedure, and accomplishments of the principal conferences and congresses are conveniently summarized in Satow, *Guide to Diplomatic Practice*, II, chs. 25, 26. For a list of international conferences and congresses, see Baldwin, in *A. J. I. L.* (1907), I, 565–578, 808–829.

[2] *B. F. S.P.*, LXXI, 814.   [3] *Ibid.*, LXXV, 1018, 1178.

with the eight great powers in the Conference of Peking in 1900,[1] and together with the United States, Portugal, Sweden, and Morocco they deliberated with the European Concert at Algeciras in 1906.[2]

On the other hand, the principle of equal representation received repeated recognition in conferences on non-political questions. Fourteen states participated in the Conference of Copenhagen of 1857, called to consider the abolition of the Danish Sound dues.[3] The Conference of Geneva of 1864, for the amelioration of the condition of wounded soldiers in the field, included delegates from fourteen states,[4] and the same number participated at Geneva in 1868 in extending the principles of the Convention of 1864 to maritime warfare.[5] Most of the states of Europe were represented in 1874 at the Brussels Conference on the rules of land warfare.[6] Seventeen delegations from four continents attended the Brussels Conference on the abolition of the slave trade in 1889.[7] Thirty-six states were represented at Geneva in 1906, when the Convention of 1864 was revised.[8] The rule of equal representation has been applied in innumerable conferences and congresses called to agree upon international administrative arrangements of one kind or another. Every one of the American republics has been represented in the International American Conferences. The most far-reaching application of equal representation in a true international assembly occurred at the beginning of the twentieth century in the Peace Conferences at The Hague.

Prior to the Hague Conferences it was not a common practice in international assemblies to reach decisions by voting;

[1] *B. F. S. P.*, XCIV, 686.
[2] Martens, *Nouveau recueil général*, 2ᵉ sér., XXXIV, 3.
[3] *B. F. S. P.*, XLIX, 902.
[4] Martens, *Nouveau recueil général*, XX, 375.
[5] *Ibid.*, p. 400.   [6] *Ibid.*, 2ᵉ sér., IV, 1.
[7] *B. F. S. P.*, LXXXI, 1091; LXXXII, 379.
[8] Martens, *Nouveau recueil général*, 3ᵉ sér., II, 323.

but wherever votes were taken it was almost always understood that there should be equality of voting strength and the requirement of unanimity for important decisions. There was a discussion at the Geneva Conference of 1864, in the first session, as to whether voting should be individual or by delegations. The first French delegate pointed out that

there could be no vote on the articles of the Convention, since the majority could not bind the minority, no matter how small it might be.[1]

At the Geneva Conference of 1868 the decision in regard to voting was recorded as follows:

As to voting, it is understood that, for everything which relates to internal procedure, they will vote as individuals and that, for everything which results in an adoption, or rejection, or simply concerns the taking up of subjects engaging in some manner the attention of the high contracting parties, voting will be by states. It is stipulated, moreover, that a majority will be sufficient to bring a subject up for discussion, but that unanimity will be necessary for definitive adoption.[2]

The rules of the first International American Conference of 1889 provided:

The delegation of each State represented in this Conference shall have only one vote, and the votes shall be given separately by States.[3]

Similar rules have been adopted in later American conferences, in the Geneva Conference of 1906,[4] and in the Peace Conferences at The Hague.

The most important assurance of complete equality in international congresses or conferences is the principle that they have no authority to bind participating states unless

[1] Martens, *Nouveau recueil général*, XX, 380.
[2] *Ibid.*, 403. Cf. procedure at the Congress of Berlin, *B. F. S. P.*, LXIX, 892, 918.
[3] Art. 16, in *Int. Am. Confer.*, I, 58.
[4] Martens, *Nouveau recueil général*, 3ᵉ sér., II, 354.

the participating states choose to ratify their decisions. Such assemblies are sometimes compared to national legislatures; but the comparison is somewhat confusing, for true international assemblies legislate, if they can be said to legislate at all, *ad referendum.* They have no supernational authority whatever. It not infrequently happens that states participate, but fail to ratify what the conference does. At the outbreak of the World War in 1914, more than a third of the states which were represented at the Second Hague Conference in 1907 had failed to ratify any of the conventions which that Conference submitted.[1]

Although political equality in the international conference is secured through equal representation and voting strength, and through the absence of all supernational authority, it cannot be overlooked that the influence of states has never been even approximately equal in such assemblies. Indeed, international conferences have more than once provided the occasion on which small states were coerced into accepting the decisions of their more powerful neighbors. This has been conspicuously true where the questions before the conference were of a political nature. There is evidence enough of substantial inequality even in respect to the non-political conferences. Thus the initiative at Copenhagen in 1857 came from France, Great Britain, and Prussia, while the draft treaty received their preliminary approval before it was submitted to the other states.[2] The special commission appointed to frame the draft convention at Geneva in 1868 consisted of British, German, French, Italian, and Dutch naval officers, while the head of the French delegation occupied the important position of *rapporteur* of the commission.[3]

---

[1] See Pamphlet No. 3, Carnegie Endowment for International Peace, Division of International Law (Washington, 1914). The states were the Argentine Republic, Bulgaria, Chile, Colombia, Dominican Republic, Ecuador, Greece, Italy, Montenegro, Paraguay, Persia, Peru, Servia, Turkey, Uruguay, and Venezuela.

[2] *B. F. S. P.*, XLIX, 902–932.

[3] Martens, *Nouveau recueil général*, XX, 405, 420.

Formal equality is preserved, but actual inequality increases in importance in direct proportion to the magnitude of the interests at stake and of the decisions that are to be made.

Political equality in international congresses and conferences received its most conspicuous application in modern times in the two peace conferences held at The Hague in 1899 and 1907. The importance of political equality and the difficulties involved in its practical application were manifested so strikingly in the constitution and procedure of those assemblies that they are entitled to special consideration at this point.

At the First Hague Conference there were twenty-six states represented, of which twenty were European, two were American, and four Asiatic.[1] Through the efforts of the United States no less than forty-seven states were invited to send delegates to the second Conference, and forty-four were actually represented, of which twenty-one were European (Norway having become a separate state), nineteen were American, and four Asiatic.[2] For the first time in history practically all the independent states of the earth participated in an international conference on the basis of complete equality of representation. The fact was hailed in many quarters as a vindication of political equality. " We may affirm henceforth," declared the first delegate of the Argentine Republic in the closing session, " that the political

---

[1] *La Confér. Int.*, Pt. I, pp. 3–8.

[2] *La Deux. Confér.*, I, 1–14. Speaking before the third International American Conference at Rio de Janeiro, July 31, 1906, Secretary Root said: " Within a few months, for the first time, the recognized possessors of every foot of soil upon the American continents can be and I hope will be represented with the acknowledged rights of equal sovereign states in the great World Congress at The Hague." *Latin America and the United States*, p. 10. See Choate, in *A. S. J. S. I. D. Proceedings* (1910), p. 196; Scott, *Hague Peace Conferences*, I, 95–100.

On the Peace Conferences see Choate, *The Two Hague Conferences;* Hicks, in *A. J. I. L.* (1908), II, 530–561; Higgins, *Hague Peace Conferences;* Holls, *Peace Conference at The Hague;* Huber, *Die Gleichheit der Staaten;* Mérignhac, *La conférence international de la paix;* Scott, *Hague Peace Conferences*.

equality of states has ceased to be a fiction and that it abides established as an obvious reality." [1]

In other quarters the Conference was denounced as a failure and its alleged impotence was attributed to the basic principle of its constitution. One of its most hostile critics, *The London Times*, observed editorially the day after the Conference closed that it

was predestined to fail, because the convocation of such a body at all was based upon a gross violation of the " law of facts." In plain English, the Conference was a sham and has brought forth a progeny of shams, because it was founded on a sham. The only principle upon which all these powers could be induced to send delegates to it was the legal and diplomatic convention that all sovereign States are equal. For certain purposes that convention is useful, but, on the face of it, it is a fiction, and a very absurd fiction at that. Everybody knows that all sovereign States are not equal. The differences between them in population, in territory, in wealth, in armed strength, in their habits of thought, in their conceptions of law and right — in all that goes to make up civilization — are amongst the most obvious and insistent of facts. By pretending to ignore this fundamental and essential truth, the Conference condemned itself to impotence. The simplest common sense is enough to teach us that Powers like Great Britain, France, Germany, Japan, Russia, and the United States will not, and cannot, in any circumstances, allow Haiti, Salvador, Turkey, and Persia to have an equal right with themselves in laying down the law by which their fleets, their armies, their diplomatists, and their jurists are to be guided on matters of the supremest moment. The suggestion that they should submit to such a doctrine is simply fatuous. Such submission would involve the subjugation of the higher civilization by the lower, and would inevitably condemn the more advanced peoples to moral and intellectual retrogression.[2]

It was not so much equality of representation as equality of voting strength that gave rise to difficulties and provoked

[1] *La Deux. Confér.*, I, 593, quoted *supra*, 181. See *ibid.*, II, 20, quoted *supra*, 182; and Huber, *Die Gleichheit der Staaten*.

[2] Oct. 19, 1907, p. 9c. For an especially vitriolic attack on the Conference and equality, read Alfred Stead's letter, in *The London Times*, October 24, 1907, p. 5e.

criticism. The invitation sent out by the Government of the Netherlands to the states invited to send delegates to the first Conference read as follows:

My Government trusts that the . . . Government will associate itself with the great humanitarian work to be entered upon under the auspices of His Majesty, the Emperor of all the Russias, and that it will be disposed to accept this invitation, and to take the necessary steps for the presence of its Representatives at The Hague on the 18th May, next, for the opening of the Conference, at which each Power, whatever may be the number of its Delegates, will have only one vote.[1]

The rules of procedure gave each state one vote in the committees and in plenary sessions.[2] Similar rules were adopted at the second Conference.[3] There was considerable uncertainty as to the effect of a negative vote. Sometimes complete unanimity was held to be essential, while on other occasions a majority was regarded as sufficient to entitle a proposal to be recorded as part of the proceedings. Every state had one vote, however, and all really important decisions required unanimity.

Equality of voting strength and the requirement of unanimity for decisions of consequence were more widely and severely criticized than anything else about the Peace Conferences. Certain sections of the press were particularly vigorous in their attacks on the Conference of 1907. The *Spectator* insisted that the radical defect in its constitution was " the equality of voting-power enjoyed by all the Powers convened, great, minor, and infinitesimally small." [4] *The London Times* attacked the same defect in an editorial entitled " The Danger Point at The Hague," as follows:

Cf. the Victory Program adopted November 23, 1918, as the official platform of the League to Enforce Peace.

[1] Holls, *Peace Conference at The Hague*, p. 34. See the remarks of Asser, in *La Confér. Int.*, Pt. I, p. 202.

[2] *Ibid.*, Pt. I, pp. 18–19.

[3] *La Deux. Confér.*, I, 61–62.   [4] (1907), XCIX, 418, 472.

In the conference which was to settle these questions, subject, of course, to the subsequent ratification of the several Governments represented, there have been assembled upon a footing — which in theory is one of absolute equality — the delegates of the greatest and of the least States upon the globe. The most palpable and material of the realities which decide the true rank and *status* of nations among themselves do not, nominally, affect the authority of their representatives. On military questions the voice of Germany or of France weighs no more than the voice of Belgium. In naval matters Great Britain may be outvoted by Rumania and Salvador, or Japan by China and Persia. Population and wealth, past history and present civilization, are ignored with equal completeness. By a diplomatic fiction, China, Persia, and Turkey are supposed to stand upon the same plane of civilization as the nations of the West, and the most backward and corrupt of South American Republics are imputed the legal attainments and the moral qualities which inspire the judgments and the writings of a Marshall, a Kent, or a Story. In the Conference every Power counts as one, and no Power as more than one. " Sententiae numerantur non ponderantur." The representatives of Countries in which Roman and English law are alike unknown, in which the most rudimentary ideas of evidence and of procedure do not exist, and in which the established Courts habitually violate the first principles of natural justice, are held competent to determine problems which have divided for generations the most accomplished and the most upright of European jurists. That a body so composed could legislate effectively upon the whole of the programme prepared for it, during the few months available for its deliberations, was and is manifestly impossible. That it should so legislate upon any of the more controversial parts of the programme is possible only upon condition that the decision on each subject should be left virtually to the Powers invested with the moral and material authority indispensable to give weight to its recommendations.[1]

The opinion has spread since 1907 that the usefulness of international assemblies like those held at The Hague can not be greatly expanded until some limitations have been imposed on equality in voting and the unanimity rule. Sir

[1] September 14, 1907, p. 9c. See also September 21, 1907, p. 9c; October 19, 1907, p. 9c; October 21, 1907, p. 3f.

Edward Fry, Great Britain's representative at the second Conference, pointed out the defect in his report to the British Foreign Office:

In the next place the machinery of this Conference has proved in a high degree dilatory and confusing, the rights of individual Delegates to take up the time of the Conference, the rights of a majority over a minority in the absence of unanimity, the power of a Chairman to confine the discussions within due limits — these and many other questions demand solution before another meeting of the Conference can prove satisfactory.[1]

Renault, one of the French delegates, has declared that " the juridical equality of states, taken literally, leads to absurd conclusions ":

Can it be admitted that in a question of maritime law the voice of the Grand Duchy of Luxemburg or even of Montenegro should have the same weight as that of Great Britain ? Can these small countries, pleading the principle of unanimity, block reforms on which the great maritime powers are agreed?[2]

It has also been suggested that a plan may have to be devised whereby the weight attributed to the votes of different states will bear some proportion to the real influence which they represent.[3] Westlake has voiced the opinion that in the future all voting had better be avoided.[4]

In another important respect the Hague Conferences illustrate the way in which political equality is preserved in a true international assembly. They are absolutely without supernational authority. Not only is equality assured

[1] Fry to Grey, October 16, 1907, in British Doc. (1908), CXXIV, Misc. No. 1 (Cd. 3857), p. 20.

[2] *Annales des sciences politiques* (1908), XXIII, 444, quoted *supra*, p. 144. See Scott, *Hague Peace Conferences*, I, 37, 163, 169; and the Victory Program adopted November 23, 1918, as the official platform of the League to Enforce Peace.

[3] " In The Hague Conferences it may be needful that some system be devised whereby the vote of Great Britain on naval affairs shall weigh more than that of Switzerland, and that of the United States more than that of Hayti." Wilson, in *L. M. C. I. A.* (1912), XVIII, 117.

[4] *Collected Papers*, p. 536.

in representation, voting, and the unanimity rule, but once the conference has agreed on a convention its agreement is no more than a recommendation to the participating states, which may ratify it or not as they please.[1] As pointed out above, more than a third of the states represented at the Second Hague Conference have never ratified any of the conventions which that Conference submitted.

This lack of supernational authority is after all the most effective safeguard of political equality. There was an unreality about the formal proceedings at The Hague, due to the overwhelming inequality of influence that prevailed among the delegations. The initiative in calling the Conferences came from Russia. The program, organization, and procedure were practically determined by a single government in consultation with a few of the more influential powers. The conventions were framed in most cases by delegates of the great powers, while proposals approved by large majorities were dropped on several occasions because of the opposition of a few of the great powers.[2]

[1] " The international Conference which met at The Hague in 1899 and the second Conference, which met in the same attractive city in 1907, is a diplomatic body. . . . In such an assembly nations are regarded as equal. They send their delegates or representatives. They have an equal vote. Proposals are made and voted upon, but the vote merely implies a recommendation. The completed drafts, called conventions or declarations, are laid before the various governments by the respective delegates, and, if the drafts are found acceptable and are ratified by the governments according to the constitutional methods in force, they thereupon become binding upon the nations which have ratified them, from the time of such ratification. They become universally binding when they have been ratified by the nations participating in the conference. The draft has thus become a national statute, and by the action of the nations it has become an international statute. The conference, therefore, proposes; the national government disposes. If the conference can be called a legislature without a misuse of terms, it is a legislature *ad referendum*." Scott, in *L. M. C. I. A.* (1912), XVIII, 121.

[2] " It is abundantly clear, therefore, that the delegations at The Hague did not and could not possess equal influence in framing the conventions, and that, notwithstanding the principle of legal equality the larger States either forced their views upon the Conference or by their opposition prevented an unacceptable proposition from being accepted." Scott, *Hague Peace Conferences*, I, 165.

The *Autobiography* of the first American delegate at the Hague Conference of

The unreality of equality in the formal proceedings was admitted by delegates from several of the smaller states. The Chinese Minister to Holland presented his government with a memorial on the second Conference, in which he said:

At the Conference there was no possibility of concealing the precise condition of each Power in comparison with another and the mere fact of participating in the Conference implied an admission on the part of the participant that it accepted such a classification. The Great Powers naturally availed themselves of their power to benefit themselves by coercing others on the pretext of law. When they wished to carry some proposal they tried to sway the assembly by an oratorical appeal to each other, and when they wished to defeat a proposal they secretly exercised methods of obstruction to promote disagreement. . . . This shows that a division into great and small Powers is not easily obliterated, and emphasizes the fierce and ever-increasing competition in diplomacy of the present day.

After urging that China perfect itself in the essentials of a great power before another conference was called, he concluded:

If by so doing both our political and legal systems could be brought into order in the next four years, China would be in a position to show that she could hold her own with the other Powers when the invitation to the next Conference reaches her. If she could at the next Conference win a position among the Great Powers, such as that which Japan holds at the present day, what an unspeakable blessing it would be for our country.[1]

Notwithstanding the inevitable inequalities of influence in a conference of nations, a substantial political equality is

1899 contains an interesting account of a conversation with the delegate from Sweden and Norway on the immunity of private property at sea: " Curious things came out during our conversation. Baron de Bildt informed me that, strongly as he favored the measure, and prepared as he was to vote for it, he should have to be very careful in discussing it publicly, since his instructions were to avoid, just as far as possible, any clash between the opinions expressed by the Swedish representatives and those of the great powers. Never before have I so thoroughly realized the difficult position which the lesser powers in Europe hold as regards really serious questions." White, *Autobiography*, II, 296–297.

[1] *The London Times*, February 20, 1908, p. 4b.

preserved wherever all interested states are represented with an equal vote and the requirement of unanimity, and above all wherever such a conference acts *ad referendum* without any supernational authority. The increasing protest against these principles suggests that limitations are likely to be imposed on political equality in such assemblies, or that really important questions will be determined by another type of conference, a type to be considered forthwith.

SUPERNATIONAL CONGRESSES AND CONFERENCES

Parallel to the development of the international congress or conference, in which political equality is preserved as indicated above, there has been evolving within the society of nations another type of institution, which has several of the marks of a rudimentary supernational authority, and which imposes important limitations upon the political equality of states where it does not deny it altogether. This is the concerted action of the great powers.[1]

The concerted action of the great powers has grown up in the last century. Prior to the French Revolution only the vaguest notions of supernational authority had made their appearance in European politics. The existence of an interdependent society of nations with common interests was recognized at Westphalia in 1648. The balance of power[2] was accepted as the basis for common interests. It was to be preserved by means of international guaranties and intervention. The same policy received more explicit definition at Utrecht, and the system of guaranties with intervention as a corollary was developed in greater detail.

---

[1] Dupuis, *Le principe d'équilibre et le concert européen*, pp. 111–513, is by all odds the best account of the European Concert. The following may also be read with profit: Lawrence, *Essays*, pp. 208–233; Nys, *Études*, II, 1–46; Streit, in *R. D. I. L. C.* (1900), 2ᵉ sér., II, 5–25.

[2] On the balance of power, see Donnadieu, *Essai sur la theorie de l'équilibre;* Dupuis, *Le principe d'équilibre et le concert européen;* Kaeber, *Die Idee des europäischen Gleichgewichts.*

The system of guaranties and intervention by the more powerful states provided a very primitive machinery for checking disorder after it had become acute, but it lacked the most rudimentary essentials of an organization capable of anticipating the event and exercising a supervision over the society of nations in the common interest. The idea of coöperative supervision had its first practical application in Europe during the Napoleonic wars. At the first session of the Congress of Châtillon, February 5, 1814, the representatives of the four allied powers declared that they would treat for peace with France " in the name of Europe forming a single whole." [1] On March 10, 1814, the four powers concluded the Treaty of Chaumont, which began:

> The high contracting parties above named solemnly obligate themselves to one another by the present treaty, in case France should refuse to accede to the proposed terms of peace, to devote all the resources of their respective states to the vigorous prosecution of the present war against that power, and to employ them in perfect concert, in order to obtain for themselves and for Europe a general peace, under the protection of which the rights and the liberties of all nations may be established and secured.[2]

The allies also announced their intention of concerting together, after peace had been made with France, with reference to the best means of guaranteeing to themselves and to Europe the continuance of peace. The treaty was to remain in force for a period of twenty years and to be extended thereafter by the powers in concert if circumstances required it.[3] On the rupture of negotiations at Châtillon the allied powers declared in a formal proclamation that the progress of events had made them conscious of the imperative necessity of *la Ligue Européenne.*[4]

[1] Angeberg, I, 105.
[2] *Ibid.*, I, 117; *B. F. S. P.*, I, 121. The treaty was antedated March 1, 1814.
[3] Arts. 5, 16.
[4] *B. F. S. P.*, I, 912. " The significance of the European Coalition during the eight years that followed the signature of the Treaty of Chaumont is, that it rep-

The significance of the allied concert appears in the secret articles of the first Treaty of Paris, May 30, 1814.[1] This treaty outlined the general basis for the pacification of Europe, and provided for a definitive settlement by a congress to be held at Vienna. It was signed by representatives of Portugal, Sweden, and Spain, in addition to France and the four allies; but the first of the secret articles included in each of the treaties between France and the four great powers provided:

The disposition to be made of the territories which His Most Christian Majesty renounces by the 3d article of the public treaty, and the relations from which a system of real and lasting equilibrium in Europe is to result, shall be settled at the congress on the bases determined by the allied powers among themselves, and in accordance with the several dispositions contained in the following articles.

Then followed an outline of the manner in which Europe was to be reconstituted by the four great powers in concert.

When the Congress of Vienna [2] assembled it became evident that the Concert of Europe was limited to the four great powers. All Europe, except Turkey and its dependent principalities, was represented by delegates;[3] but no general meeting of the Congress ever took place. By virtue of the Treaty of Paris, particularly the first of its secret articles, the representatives of Great Britain, Austria, Prussia, and

resented, whatever the motives of the several Allies may have been, an experiment in international government, an attempt to solve the problem of reconciling central and general control by a ' European Confederation ' with the maintenance of the liberties of its constituent states, and thus to establish a juridical system." Phillips, *Confed. of Europe*, p. 9.

[1] Separate treaties containing the same stipulations were concluded on the same day between France and Great Britain, Austria, Portugal, Prussia, Russia, and Sweden. The treaty between France and Spain was signed July 20, 1814. *B.F.S.P.*, I, 151.

[2] Protocols in *B. F. S. P.*, II, 549–773. See also Angeberg, *Le Congrès de Vienne et les traités de 1815;* Debidour, *Histoire diplomatique de l'Europe;* Flassan, *Histoire du Congrès de Vienne;* Klüber, *Acten des Wiener Congresses;* Phillips, *Confederation of Europe;* Pradt, *Du Congrès de Vienne;* Sorel, *L'Europe et la révolution française.*

[3] Altogether 216 *chefs de mission.* Sorel, *ibid.*, VIII, 382.

Russia asserted their right, over the protests of smaller states, to determine the organization and procedure of the Congress and make its decisions.[1] The delegates of the four allied powers and France were constituted a directing committee. Provision was also made for meetings which should include representatives of Portugal, Spain, and Sweden, but it is significant that of sixty-seven protocols only seventeen were signed by delegates of the three countries last mentioned. The great powers rearranged the map of Europe, restored dynasties, confirmed the partition of Poland, united Belgium with Holland, neutralized Switzerland, created the German Confederation, and prescribed rules of international law with respect to the free navigation of rivers, the rank of diplomatic representatives, and the suppression of the slave trade. The spirit in which they went about their work was summarized very well by Palmerston a generation later, in discussing a proposal for a congress of the great powers on the affairs of Italy. He observed that

The Congress of Vienna . . . was assembled under circumstances very different from those which at present exist. The tide of war had swept over the whole surface of Europe from the Rhine to Moscow, and from Moscow back to the Seine; all the smaller States of Europe had been conquered and reconquered, and were considered almost at the arbitrary disposal of the Great Powers whose armies had decided the fate of the war. The statesmen who sat in Congress therefore considered themselves at liberty to parcel out with great freedom the several territories of Europe.

The smaller Sovereigns, Princes, and States, had no representatives in the deciding congress, and no voice in the decisions by which their future destiny was determined. They were all obliged to yield to overruling power, and to submit to decisions which were the result, as the case might be, of justice or of expediency, of generosity or of partiality, of regard to the welfare of nations, or of concession to personal solicitations.[2]

---

[1] Protocol of September 22, 1814, and annex, in *B. F. S. P.*, II, 554, 556.
[2] Palmerston to Marquis of Normandy, October 10, 1848, in *B. F. S. P.*, LI, 672.

It is hardly necessary to remark that the supervision of the society of nations by the concerted action of the great powers, as manifested at Vienna, is absolutely irreconcilable with the notion of political equality. The lesser powers were denied equality of representation; they had no voice in the decisions except as they were required to ratify what the great powers had done; and they had no choice but to accept a settlement which the Concert had agreed upon and which it stood ready to enforce.

On Napoleon's return to France, the Concert was strengthened and the Treaty of Chaumont expressly reaffirmed.[1] Requests from the smaller powers participating in the new campaign that they be admitted to the conference on terms of peace were denied. November 20, 1815, after the second downfall of Napoleon, the four great powers concluded a new treaty of alliance in which the principle of concerted action was again affirmed and the allies were constituted a directing committee for Europe.[2] Article 6 provided:

> To facilitate and to secure the execution of the present Treaty, and to consolidate the connections, which at the present moment so closely unite the four Sovereigns for the happiness of the World, the High Contracting Parties have agreed to renew their Meetings at fixed periods, either under the immediate auspices of the Sovereigns themselves, or by their respective Ministers, for the purpose of consulting upon their common interests, and for the consideration of the measures which at each of those periods shall be considered the most salutary, for the repose and prosperity of Nations, and for the maintenance of the Peace of Europe.

In 1818 the European Directory met at Aix-la-Chapelle to consider the internal condition of France and the question of terminating the military occupation of French territory.[3]

---

[1] *B.F.S.P.* II, 443, 671, 674, 478.

[2] *Ibid.*, III, 248, 273; V, 1216.

[3] Protocols in *B. F. S. P.*, V, 1081, and VI, 11. See Pradt, *L'Europe après le Congrès d'Aix-la-Chapelle.*

The government of France accepted an invitation to join the Concert.[1] Before the Conference assembled a circular was addressed to the other European governments in which it was declared that the meetings were not to have the character of a congress and that no other delegates would be admitted.[2] Nevertheless the Conference heard appeals and received petitions of all kinds from subjects and sovereigns alike, revised the decision made at Vienna with reference to the grades of diplomatic representatives, decided upon the evacuation of French territory by allied troops, and perfected other details of the general settlement. On November 15, 1818, the representatives of the five states agreed to an important set of resolutions explaining the purpose and method of the European Concert of the great powers as follows:

1. That they are firmly resolved never to depart, neither in their mutual relations, nor in those which bind them to other States, from the principle of intimate Union which has hitherto presided over all their common relations and interests — a Union rendered more strong and indissoluble by the bonds of Christian fraternity which the Sovereigns have formed among themselves.

2. That this Union, which is the more real and durable, inasmuch as it depends on no separate interest or temporary combination, can only have for its object the Maintenance of general Peace, founded on a religious respect for the engagements contained in the Treaties, and for the whole of the rights resulting therefrom.

3. That France, associated with other Powers by the restoration of the legitimate Monarchical and Constitutional Power, engages henceforth to concur in the maintenance and consolidation of a System which has given Peace to Europe, and which can alone insure its duration.

4. That if, for the better attaining the above declared object, the Powers which have concurred in the present Act, should judge it necessary to establish particular meetings, either of the Sovereigns themselves, or of their respective Ministers and Plenipotentiaries, there to treat in common of their own interests, in so far as they have

---

[1] *B.F.S.P.*, VI, 16, 17.   [2] *Ibid.*, V, 1216.

reference to the object of their present deliberations, the time and place of these meetings shall, on each occasion, be previously fixed by means of diplomatic communications; and that in the case of these meetings having for their object affairs specially connected with the interests of the other States of Europe, they shall only take place in pursuance of a formal invitation on the part of such of those States as the said affairs may concern, and under the express reservation of their right of direct participation therein, either directly or by their Plenipotentiaries.

5. That the resolutions contained in the present Act shall be made known to all the Courts of Europe, by the annexed Declaration, which shall be considered as sanctioned by the Protocol, and forming part thereof.[1]

Their purpose was further defined in the annexed Declaration:

The intimate Union established among the Monarchs, who are joint parties to this System, by their own principles, no less than by the interests of their people, offers to Europe the most sacred pledge of its future tranquillity.

The object of this Union is as simple as it is great and salutary. It does not tend to any new political combination — to any change in the Relations sanctioned by existing Treaties. Calm and consistent in its proceedings, it has no other object than the maintenance of Peace, and the guarantee of those transactions on which the Peace was founded and consolidated.

The Sovereigns, in forming this august Union, have regarded as its fundamental basis their invariable resolution never to depart, either among themselves, or in their Relations with other States, from the strictest observation of the principles of the Right of Nations; principles, which, in their application to a state of permanent Peace, can alone effectually guarantee the Independence of Each Government, and the stability of the general association.

Faithful to these principles, the Sovereigns will maintain them equally in those meetings at which they may be personally present, or in those which shall take place among their Ministers; whether

---

[1] *B. F. S. P.*, VI, 14; Hertslet, I, 571. The provision in paragraph four for the participation of other states in conferences of the great powers was applied in some cases and disregarded in others. Cf. *B. F. S. P.*, XVIII, 728; and *ibid.*, LXXIV, 1241, 1238.

they be for the purpose of discussing in common their own interests, or whether they shall relate to questions in which other Governments shall formally claim their interference. The same spirit which will direct their councils, and reign in their diplomatic communications, will preside also at these meetings; and the repose of the world will be constantly their motive and their end.[1]

It soon appeared that the great powers were not agreed among themselves with respect to the authority which they had assumed as a supernational directing council for Europe. Revolution broke out in Spain in 1820 and soon spread to Naples. The three powers that had joined in the Holy Alliance in 1815, Austria, Prussia, and Russia, were anxious that the Concert should intervene to suppress revolutionary movements. They regarded such intervention as no more than a proper application of the principles established by the great powers at Paris, Vienna, and Aix-la-Chapelle. In a circular issued at Troppau in 1820, they declared that

The Powers have exercised an undeniable right, in concerting together upon means of safety against those States in which the overthrow of a Government caused by revolution could only be considered as a dangerous example, which could only result in an hostile attitude against constitutional and legitimate Governments. The exercise of

---

[1] *B. F. S. P.*, VI, 18; Hertslet, I, 573. " Under den rein völkerrechtlichen Organisationen begegnen wir einer einzigen, in welcher nicht die absolute Gleichheit der Staaten anerkannt wäre. Es ist dies, sofern man hier von einer rechtlichen Organisation überhaupt sprechen will, die Pentarchie, wie sie besonders durch den Kongress von Aachen gestaltet wurde, beziehungsweise deren Stellung innerhalb der Staatengemeinschaft. Dass damals Tendenzen, zunächst unwidersprochen, sich geltend machten, welche eine Art Vormundschaft der fünf Grossmächte über die übrigen Staaten im Sinne der Heiligen Allianz und der Laibacher Beschlüsse bezweckten, ist gewiss und war auch ganz natürlich, wenn man einerseits das damalige Ruhebedürfnis Europas und anderseits die ohnmächtige Kleinstaaterei ausserhalb der fünf Grossmächte berücksichtigt. Aus dem Wortlaut des Aachener Protokolls lässt sich aber eine eigentliche Organisation nicht ableiten, ebensowenig ein formeller Anspruch der Grossmächte auf Regelung aller internationalen Verhältnisse. Und wenn auch ein solcher gelegentlich erhoben worden ist, so ist dessen allgemeine Anerkennung oder auch nur dessen konstante und tatsächliche Geltendmachung durch die Grossmächte nicht nachweisbar." Huber, *Die Gleichheit der Staaten*, p. 101.

this right became still more urgent, when those who had placed themselves in that position, sought to communicate to neighboring States the misfortune into which they had themselves plunged, and to propagate revolution and confusion around them.

There is in that attitude and that conduct an evident rupture of the pact which guarantees to all the Governments of Europe, besides the inviolability of their territory, the enjoyment of the peaceful relations which exclude all reciprocal infringement of their rights.[1]

Great Britain dissented from this interpretation of the responsibilities assumed by the great powers in concert, and refused to participate in the proceedings at Troppau, Laibach, and Verona.[2] The British Government admitted that individual states might be justified in resorting to intervention, but denied that intervention to prevent the spread of revolutionary propaganda was a legitimate function of the great powers in concert.[3] In 1823 Russia invited the great powers to a conference at St. Petersburg on the affairs of Greece, requesting that their representatives be authorized to communicate decisions directly to Constantinople without reference to their respective governments. Great Britain refused to participate on the proposed basis and the conferences accomplished nothing. The attempt to organize Europe under the established control of the great powers had failed. Thereafter the European Concert claimed the somewhat less ambitious function of preventing, limiting, and liquidating the crises that threatened the established order in the different danger zones of Europe.[4]

Between 1814 and 1823 the " Confederation of Europe " denied the political equality of states. After 1823 the lesser

[1] B. F. S. P., VIII, 1149; Hertslet, I, 658. See also B. F. S. P., VIII, 1147, 1199, 1201.

[2] Papers and correspondence relative to Troppau, Laibach, and Verona, in B. F. S. P., VIII, 1128 ff., and X, 3 ff. See Chateaubriand, Congrès de Vérone.

[3] Castlereagh to British Ministers at Foreign Courts, January 19, 1821, in B. F. S. P., VIII, 1160.

[4] Dupuis, Le principe d'équilibre et le concert européen, pp. 192–198.

powers might claim equality, but wherever their interests came within the purview of the great powers in concert political equality was no more than a fiction. The activities of the European Concert were manifold. It had many failures. It was frequently disrupted through internal dissension; but it also achieved a remarkable record of performance as a rudimentary kind of supernational organism.

The most conspicuous achievements of concerted action among the great powers, as well as some of the most disastrous failures, have been concerned with the problems of the Near East. The entire Concert did not act in the Grecian question, but three of its members, Great Britain, France, and Russia, intervened in the affairs of Greece between 1827 and 1832, destroyed the Turkish fleet, created a new Greek state, defined its boundaries, provided it with a king, and took it under their collective guaranty.[1] On later occasions the same powers confirmed the choice of another king, rendered financial assistance, and made their guaranty effective in other ways. The Concert confirmed the union of the Ionian Islands with Greece in 1863.[2] Four years later it intervened to prevent a war with Turkey over the Cretan question. Greece refused to participate in the conferences *à titre consultatif*, but was constrained to accept the decision reached by the great powers.[3] On several occasions the Concert has refused to let Greece engage in war. Once it has intervened and imposed its own settlement of a boundary dispute, and again it has resorted to pacific blockade to restrain a threatened outbreak of hostilities.[4] In 1897 it

[1] *B. F. S. P.*, XIV, 629; XVII, 3; XVIII, 597; XIX, 2; XXII, 931; XXV, 727; XL, 1204.

[2] *Ibid.*, LIII, 19, 23; LIV, 11, 38.

[3] *Ibid.*, LIX, 584, 813.

[4] *Ibid.*, LXXI, 661; LXXII, 405; LXXVII, 643. Although he explains away practically everything that appears to have been inconsistent with equality in the events of the last century, Huber says: " Immerhin kann nicht bestritten werden, dass in einzelnen Fällen, so bei der Donauschiffahrt und in den kretischen und

vetoed the union of Crete with Greece and instituted an
international control of Greek finances. The various diplomatic papers have referred to a " mandate " and to " medi-
ation "; but the truth is that for nearly a century the great
powers have governed the affairs of Greece in a series of
conferences in which that state has not participated.

Other aspects of the Near Eastern question have occupied
the attention of the European Concert throughout the past
one hundred years. The Concert was temporarily disrupted
over the crisis in Turkey in 1839, but was rehabilitated a
few years later. It was again disrupted, this time with more
disastrous consequences, at the time of the Crimean War.
At the termination of that war the great powers, with Sardinia and Turkey, adjusted the Eastern question at the
Congress of Paris.[1] The treaty determined the status and
provided for the organization of the principalities of the
Danube, defined the status of Servia, neutralized the Black
Sea and confirmed the closing of the Dardanelles and the
Bosphorus, regulated the navigation of the Danube, guaranteed the integrity of the Ottoman Empire, and admitted
Turkey into the public law and concert of Europe. Other
questions of general European interest were also discussed,
including the pacification of Greece, affairs in Italy, and the
revolutionary tendencies of the Belgian press. Finally, the
Declaration of Paris on privateering, blockade, and neutral
trade was prepared and promulgated.

Outrages in the Lebanon district of Syria provoked the
intervention of the Concert in 1860.[2] France undertook to
despatch a force of 6000 men for the work of pacification,
while each of the great powers agreed to maintain an ade-

griechischen Angelegenheiten ein Vorgehen eingeschlagen wurde, welches mit der
Anerkennung der Gleichheit der unmittelbar betroffenen Nichtgrossmächte nicht
wohl vereinbar gewesen; auch sonst begegnet man vereinzelten Kundgebungen der
Grossmächte im Sinne eines Anspruchs auf eine ausschliessliche Regelung von
Verhältnissen dritter Staaten." *Die Gleichheit der Staaten*, p. 100.

[1] *B.F.S.P.*, XLVI, 8, 63.   [2] *Ibid.*, LI, 278, 287.

quate naval force on the Syrian coast. Conferences held at Constantinople approved a *règlement organique* which regulated the administration of the Lebanon thereafter under the supervision of the great powers.

The neutralization of the Black Sea was terminated in 1871.[1] Renewed crises in the Balkans led to a conference of the Concert at Constantinople in 1876, at which a program of administrative reform and readjustment was worked out and communicated to the Porte.[2] Turkey rejected the proposals, was overwhelmed by Russia in a short war, and in 1878 representatives of the great powers assembled at Berlin to revise the terms of peace and effect a general settlement of the Eastern question.[3] None of the small states interested in the settlement were admitted to the Congress of Berlin. Roumania was permitted, after some discussion, to send delegates *à plaider sa cause devant la haute assemblée*.[4] Representatives of Greece and Persia were admitted in a similar capacity at sessions designated for that purpose;[5] but even this barren privilege was not extended to Servia, Montenegro, and the other Balkan populations. At the nineteenth session the president was authorized to communicate unofficially to interested states the decisions reached concerning them. The complete treaty was not to be communicated to them until after it had been ratified.[6] The treaty upon which the great powers finally agreed redrew the map of the Balkans, recognized the independence of Roumania, Servia, and Montenegro, subject to important conditions and limi-

[1] *B. F. S. P.*, LXI, 7, 1193.

[2] *Ibid.*, LXVIII, 1064, 1114. Read the interesting remarks of former President Washburn of Robert College, in *L. M. C. I. A.* (1905), XI, 24.

[3] *B. F. S. P.*, LXIX, 749, 794, 862; Avril, *Négociations relatives au traité de Berlin;* Bluntschli, in *R. D. I. L. C.* (1879), XI, 1-37, 411-430; (1880), XII, 276-294, 410-424; (1881), XIII, 571-586; Choublier, *La question d'Orient depuis le traité de Berlin;* Holland, *European Concert in the Eastern Question.*

[4] *B. F. S. P.*, LXIX, 964, 972, 978.

[5] *Ibid.*, LXIX, 891, 894, 901, 916, 947, 964, 968, 1021, 1031.

[6] *Ibid.*, LXIX, 1075.

tations of the nature of servitudes, and created the autonomous principality of Bulgaria under Ottoman suzerainty.
Eastern Roumelia was accorded an autonomous régime under the military and political authority of the Sultan. Its
governor-general was to be nominated by the Sultan with
the assent of the great powers, and a European commission
was to arrange for its organization. The Porte promised
reforms in Crete, while Bosnia and Herzegovina were handed
over to the administration of Austria-Hungary.

The Treaty of Berlin also contained new provisions with
reference to the navigation of the Danube. A conference of
the great powers and Turkey was held at London in 1883 to
consider the execution of these articles.[1] Notwithstanding
their obvious interest in the forthcoming decisions, the Balkan states were not admitted with a deliberative voice. Their
exclusion was justified on the ground that the Conference
was in a sense a sequel to the Congress of Berlin, in which
the smaller states had not participated; but Count Münster's remarks in the second session were a more accurate
statement of the real reason — if admitted on an equal
footing with the great powers the principle of unanimity
would enable them to veto the Concert's decisions.[2] Bulgaria was required to present its views through the Turkish
ambassador; Servia agreed to participate in a consultative
capacity; while Roumania refused to participate except *sur*

---

[1] *B. F. S. P.*, LXXIV, 20, 1231.

[2] " Le Comte Münster croit devoir s'opposer à l'admission de la Roumanie sur
le même pied que les Grandes Puissances. Le Plénipotentiaire d'Allemagne recon-
naît volontiers le grand intérêt qu'a la Roumanie à la solution heureuse des questions pendantes à la Conférence. Cependant le Gouvernement Allemand serait
d'avis de conserver à celle-ci son caractère Européen en s'abstenant de mettre la
Roumanie au pair des Grandes Puissances. Si, tout en maintenant le principe de
l'unanimité dans la Conférence, on donnait une voix à la Roumanie, on lui créerait
une position qui ne serait nullement désirable, celle de pouvoir à sa volonté imposer
son veto. La Roumanie ne pourrait donc être admise qu'en qualité d'invitée et
non comme maîtresse de maison." Protocol of February 10, 1883, in *B. F. S. P.*,
LXXIV, 1236.

le pied de la plus parfaite égalité. This the great powers refused to concede, so Roumania did not participate at all.[1]

The European Concert has dealt with varied phases of
the Eastern question since the Congress of Berlin. Affairs
in Egypt, Roumelia, Macedonia, and Crete have been considered in its conferences. Sometimes it has been successful,
sometimes not. Its record has been stained by intrigue, dissension, and incapacity for compromising rival jealousies and
ambitions. Its final failure has been the prelude to European war. However, the nearness of these recent events
should not be permitted to obscure the real significance of
concerted action in the Near East as an experiment in supernational control.

In western Europe the Concert of the great powers has
also had a somewhat checkered development. It did not
succeed in preventing crises in Italy, Denmark, and Poland,
nor in liquidating the crises after they became acute.[2] There
is an interesting precedent in connection with the conference on Italian affairs which was proposed in 1859. Sardinia
claimed admission as a directly interested state, but the
powers were unanimous in denying Sardinia's demand. In
a statement to the House of Lords, the British Minister of
Foreign Affairs said:

Your Lordships will recollect that the Russian Government proposed that the five great Powers should alone sit in Congress. This
has been the custom of Europe for a great many years when questions affecting the great public law of Europe have been discussed;
and there appeared to none of us any reason why we should depart
from the usual practice, and make an exception on the present occasion by calling in any other Power to assist us.

The Concert's decision and the reason therefor appeared in
Lord Malmesbury's statement:

---

[1] See *B. F. S. P.*, LXXIV, 1236, 1238, 1241, 1243, 1245, 1250, 1251.

[2] Dupuis, *Le principe d'équilibre et le concert européen*, Pt. II, ch. 6.

All the great Powers resisted that demand, and agreed that it would be very inconvenient to depart from the usual precedents. If Sardinia claimed to sit as a principal in the Congress, because she is interested in Italian affairs and the preservation of the peace of Europe, then the same claim might be made by Switzerland, the smaller German States, or any other country on the confines of Italy who might be in any way affected. It was, therefore, completely determined by all the five Powers, that Sardinia and the other Italian States should be invited to sit in the Congress only after it should have assembled; and that then those States might send delegates to inform the Congress of the wishes of their various Governments.[1]

The crisis caused by the revolt in Belgium in 1830 was liquidated very effectively, although not without disagreement among the great powers as to the best procedure.[2] It was agreed at the Conference of London that Belgium should be independent and permanently neutralized under the collective guaranty of the powers. Boundaries were defined, the public debt divided, Antwerp declared a commercial port, and a stipulation adopted with reference to the free navigation of rivers traversing Belgium and Holland. When Holland rejected the arrangement, Austria, Prussia, and Russia opposed coercion. Coercive measures were adopted by Great Britain and France, however, and in 1839 the original agreement was put into effect under the sanction of all the great powers.

Another grave international crisis arose over Luxemburg in 1867. The difficulty was adjusted by the Concert at the Conference of London by decreeing the permanent neutralization of Luxemburg under the collective guaranty of the powers.[3] At the time of this Conference Italy was added to the council of the great powers.

[1] Parliamentary Debates (1859) 3d series, CLIII, cols. 1836–1837. See Malmesbury to Cowley, March 19, 1859, and Malmesbury to Loftus, March 19, 1859, in B. F. S. P., LVII, 174.

[2] See ibid., XVIII, 645, 723; XIX, 55, 258, 653, 1417, 1420, 1438; XXVII, 990, 1000.

[3] Ibid., LVII, 32; LX, 497.

In 1907, four of the great powers most directly interested joined in a guaranty of the integrity of Norway, and in the following year the same powers were parties to declarations in support of the *status quo* in the territories bordering upon the Baltic and the North Sea.[1]

It has been suggested in the twentieth century that the United States and Japan may be joined with the great powers of Europe to form a World Concert. Such a possibility was demonstrated in the International Naval Conference held at London in 1908 and 1909. The Second Hague Conference had submitted an international prize court convention, which made it desirable to have a clearer understanding with reference to the rules that such a court would apply. Accordingly, the Naval Conference was called by Great Britain to agree upon a code of international maritime law. The head of the British delegation at The Hague had already pointed out that the claim of small states to political equality might lead the greater powers to act by themselves. In his report to the British Foreign Office, Sir Edward Fry said:

> The claim of many of the smaller States to equality as regards not only their independence, but their share in all international institutions, waived by most of them in the case of the Prize Court, but successfully asserted in the case of the proposed new Arbitral Court, is one which may produce great difficulties, and may perhaps drive greater Powers to act in many cases by themselves.[2]

Experience at The Hague and the great importance of the proposed code to the principal naval powers led Great Britain to take the course which Sir Edward Fry had anticipated. The following is from the call of the Conference as issued by the British Government:

[1] *A. J. I. L. Suppl.* (1908), II, 267, 270, 272.
[2] British Doc. (1908), CXXIV, Misc. No. 1 (Cd. 3857), p. 21. See also the French Yellow Book, quoted by Huber, *Die Gleichheit der Staaten*, p. 96.

The rules by which appeals from national prize courts would be decided affect the rights of belligerents in a manner which is far more serious to the principal naval powers than to others, and His Majesty's Government are therefore communicating only with the Governments of Austria-Hungary, France, Germany, Italy, Japan, Russia, Spain, and the United States of America.[1]

As Admiral Stockton, one of the American delegates, has observed:

The experience of the Second Hague Conference showed certain delays and discordances arising from the great number of nationalities assembled. Uruguay could block the proceedings of a Conference where unanimity was required for decision. Besides, many of the countries assembled at The Hague were either manifest shadows or satellites of more powerful states or had no sea frontiers or maritime interests. Hence Great Britain intended to limit her invitation to those powers whose maritime interests were great enough to materially affect the countries concerned.[2]

Although concerted action among the great powers has not developed into an organized supernational authority, it represents a highly significant experiment in supernational control. Considering the absence of a common basis for collective government and the relatively short time in which the experiment has developed, it must be admitted that concerted action is much more remarkable for its achievements than for its failures.[3] It is significant that wherever it has been successful the Concert of the great powers has denied absolutely the political equality of states except among the great powers themselves. Smaller states have been unrepresented in its councils or have been permitted

[1] Malloy, *Treaties*, III, 326. See *The London Times*, September 21, 1907, p. 9c. The Netherlands, as containing the seat of the proposed prize court and the home of the Peace Conferences, was also invited to participate.

[2] *L. M. C. I. A.* (1909), XV, 47. See Stockton, in *A. J. I. L.* (1909), III, 596–618.

[3] See the conclusions of Dupuis, *Le principe d'équilibre et le concert européen*, Pt. II, ch. 11.

to send delegates *à titre consultatif*. They have had no real voice in its decisions and no veto. Under whatever diplomatic fiction the real situation may have been concealed on different occasions, the great powers in concert have exercised a real supernational authority. They have defined boundaries, determined status, and exercised all manner of guardianship over weaker states. They have formulated rules, rendered judgment in controversies, and enforced their decisions.

Publicists have admitted that all this is inconsistent with equality, although many explain it as a matter of fact or policy which does not affect equality in law. Others admit that it violates equality in law and denounce it accordingly, while many of the ablest publicists have regarded concerted action as the incipient manifestation of supernational organization, in which political equality must be limited in the interest of a more stable international order.[1]

This opinion has been voiced by statesmen on many occasions. Speaking of the position of the great powers with reference to Greece and the Cretan question, in a debate in the House of Lords in 1897, Lord Salisbury said:

At least it may be said for them that they are representing a continuity of policy, and that they are maintaining the law of Europe as it has been laid down by the only authority competent to create law for Europe. They have been defied by a State which owes its very existence to the Concert of Europe. Had it not been for the Concert of Europe the Hellenic kingdom would never have been heard of. . . . I feel it is our duty to sustain the federated action of Europe. I think it has suffered by the somewhat absurd name which has been given to it — the Concert of Europe — and the intense importance of the fact has been buried under the bad jokes to which the word has given rise. But the federated action of Europe — if we can maintain it, if we can maintain this Legislature — is our sole hope of escaping from the constant terror and the calamity of war, the con-

---

[1] For the opinions of the writers, see *supra*, pp. 126-131, 138-145.

stant pressure of the burdens of an armed peace which weigh down the spirits and darken the prospects of every nation in this part of the world.[1]

Hanotaux declared in the French Chamber in the same year that the European Concert was *le seul tribunal et la seule autorité devant lesquels tout le monde peut et doit s'incliner.*[2]

It cannot be overlooked that while conferences based on equality have been concerned in the last century chiefly with technical, administrative, or non-political subjects, most of the seriously controverted and political questions have been settled in conferences which deny political equality. Although these institutions are at present in a rudimentary stage the tendency is significant.

INTERNATIONAL ADMINISTRATIVE UNIONS

There is another type of collective international activity which has developed with extraordinary rapidity during the past half century. It is the internationalizing of administration by means of more or less permanent administrative unions. A great many associations of states have been established to watch over and promote international interests which separate states have found themselves incapable of supervising effectively. The development has been somewhat spontaneous. It is still in its infancy. It has already progressed far enough, however, to exhibit important tendencies, of which some are of particular interest from the point of view of political equality.

Administrative unions[3] are usually constituted by an international conference or congress which serves as the constituent assembly and legislature *ad referendum*. Meetings of

---

[1] Parliamentary Debates (1897), 4th series, XLVII, col. 1012.

[2] Quoted by Streit, in *R.D.I.L.C.* (1900), 2ᵉ sér., II, 12. See Lyons to Clarendon, December 20, 1868, in *B.F.S.P.*, LIX, 615.

[3] Conventions, *règlements*, and other documents may be consulted in *Annuaire de la vie internationale*, 1908–09, 1910–11, 2ᵉ sér. For a general survey, see Reinsch,

the conference or congress may occur at regular periods indicated in the convention, or at a time determined in each
case by the preceding conference or congress, or upon special
call by the member states. Many of the unions have a commission, a kind of governing board, which superintends the
work of the bureau and of other agencies of the union, sometimes prepares administrative regulations, and usually exercises some fiscal control over the bureau. Practically all of
the unions have a central office or bureau as their principal
administrative agency. The bureau keeps in touch with the
various national administrations, collects and disseminates
information, and performs the specific administrative duties
entrusted to it by the *règlement.*

Political equality has been abandoned by many of the
most important unions in at least three significant respects,
viz., in representation, voting, and financial support. By
admitting colonies, protectorates, or other possessions to
separate representation, certain unions have accorded to
states with dependencies several times as much representation as other states. Inequality of voting has been
recognized by giving separate votes to dependencies, by apportioning votes in direct proportion to each country's contribution to the union's financial support, and by providing
for majority decisions. Inequality of contribution to the
financial support of the union has become a familiar principle. In a few cases contributions are in proportion to
population, or to the distribution of whatever furnishes the
union's *raison d'être*, as railway mileage or commerce. In a
large number of unions financial support is on a unit basis.
The countries are divided into classes, each class requiring
the contribution of a different number of units. Each country

Public International Unions; Sayre, *Experiments in International Administration;*
Woolf, *International Government*, pp. 153 ff. Huber insists that the development
of international administration has been in general in accord with the equality of
states. See *Die Gleichheit der Staaten*, p. 103.

may decide, on joining the union, the class in which it wishes to be entered.

Eight international administrative unions accord separate representation to dependencies under conditions of varying significance.[1] Some of the most important official unions are among the number, which includes the Universal Postal Union, the International Telegraphic Union, the International Union of Weights and Measures, the International Union for the Publication of Customs Tariffs, the International Institute of Agriculture, the International Wireless Telegraph Union, the International Sanitary Conference, and the International Conference on Expositions. Representatives of dependencies participated in the Conference of Brussels in 1890, at which the Convention concerning the formation of a Union for the Publication of Customs Tariffs was signed; and the Convention provides that

> The States and colonies that have not yet taken part in this convention shall have the privilege of acceding thereto hereafter.[2]

The Convention of 1905 for the creation of an International Institute of Agriculture stipulates explicitly that

> Colonies may, at the request of the nations to which they belong, be admitted to form part of the institute on the same conditions as the independent nations.[3]

The final protocol of the Berlin Conference of 1906, at which the International Wireless Telegraph Union was constituted, contemplated separate representation for dependencies:

> The adherence to the Convention by the Government of a country having colonies, possessions or protectorates shall not carry with it the adherence of its colonies, possessions or protectorates, unless a declaration to that effect is made by such Government. Such colonies,

---

[1] Myers, *Non-Sovereign Representation in Public International Organs;* the same author, in *A. J. I. L.* (1914), VIII, 97.

[2] Art. 14, Malloy, *Treaties*, II, 1998.

[3] Art. 10, *ibid.*, II, 2143.

possessions and protectorates as a whole, or each of them separately, may form the subject of a separate adherence or a separate denunciation within the provisions of Articles 16 and 22 of the Convention.[1]

Inequalities in voting strength are perhaps more significant than multiple representation. They may result, in the first place, from according the right to vote to representatives of dependencies. This is the situation in the Universal Postal Union, the International Telegraphic Union, and the International Union for Weights and Measures, and a similar provision seems to have been contemplated at the International Conference on Expositions.[2] It has been provided for very definitely in the International Wireless Telegraph Union. Article 12 of the Convention of 1906 provides with reference to both diplomatic and administrative conferences:

Such conferences shall be composed of delegates of the Governments of the contracting countries.

In the deliberations each country shall have but one vote.

If a Government adheres to the Convention for its colonies, possessions or protectorates, subsequent conferences may decide that such colonies, possessions or protectorates, or a part thereof, shall be considered as forming a country as regards the application of the preceding paragraph. But the number of votes at the disposal of one Government, including its colonies, possessions or protectorates, shall in no case exceed six.[3]

The same article reappears in the Convention of 1912, with the addition of a list of thirty-four dependencies or groups of dependencies, each of which is to be considered hereafter as forming a single country. Under this arrangement Germany, the United States, France, Great Britain, and Russia each secure five votes for their dependencies; Italy, Holland, and Portugal each secure two; while Belgium, Spain, and

[1] Art. 5, Malloy, *Treaties*, III, 161. This paragraph was embodied in Art. 16 of the revised Convention of 1912.

[2] See *La vie int.*, I, 254–255, 270, 320; and Myers, in *A. J. I. L.* (1914), VIII, 100.

[3] Malloy, *Treaties*, III, 153–154.

Japan each gain one.[1] It may be noted that it was definitely contemplated at Berlin in 1906 that dependencies should exercise their vote at the next conference. Article 1 of the Final Protocol provided:

The High Contracting Parties agree that at the next Conference the number of votes to which each country is entitled shall be decided at the beginning of the deliberations, so that the colonies, possessions or protectorates admitted to the privilege of voting may exercise their right to vote during the entire course of the proceedings of such Conference.[2]

In the second place, several unions base inequality of voting strength upon the principle that privilege ought to be apportioned in the same way as responsibility. The distribution of votes is proportioned according to the contribution which each state makes to the support of the union. Thus the Organic By-Laws of the International Office of Public Hygiene provide:

There is established in Paris an International Office of Public Hygiene under the States which accept participation in its operation. . . .

The Office is placed under the authority and supervision of an International Committee consisting of technical representatives designated by the participating States in the proportion of one representative for each State.

Each State is allowed a number of votes inversely proportioned to the number of the class to which it belongs as regards its participation in the expenses of the Office.[3]

The same principle is recognized in the organization of the International Institute of Agriculture:

There is hereby created a permanent international institute of agriculture, having its seat in Rome.

---

[1] Malloy, *Treaties*, III, 188.   [2] *Ibid.*, III, 160.

[3] *Ibid.*, II, 2216, Arts. 1, 6. An interesting apportionment of voting power was provided in the Articles Concerning the Navigation of the Rhine annexed to the Vienna Congress Treaty of 1815. It was stipulated that in the selection of river inspectors voting power in the Central Commission of Control should be apportioned among the states represented according to " the extent of their respective possessions on the bank." Art. 13, in Hertslet, I, 82.

The international institute of agriculture is to be a government institution, in which each adhering power shall be represented by delegates of its choice.

The institute shall be composed of a general assembly and a permanent committee, the composition and duties of which are defined in the ensuing articles.

The general assembly of the institute shall be composed of the representatives of the adhering governments. Each nation, whatever be the number of its delegates, shall be entitled to a number of votes in the assembly which shall be determined according to the group to which it belongs, and to which reference will be made in article 10. . . .

The executive power of the institute is intrusted to the permanent committee, which, under the direction and control of the general assembly, shall carry out the decisions of the latter and prepare propositions to submit to it.

The permanent committee shall be composed of members designated by the respective governments. Each adhering nation shall be represented in the permanent committee by one member. However, the representation of one nation may be intrusted to a delegate of another adhering nation, provided that the actual number of members shall not be less than fifteen.

The conditions of voting in the permanent committee shall be the same as those indicated in article 3 for the general assemblies.[1]

The distribution of votes and units of assessments is governed by Article 10, as follows:

The nations adhering to the institute shall be classed in five groups, according to the place which each of them thinks it ought to occupy.

The number of votes which each nation shall have and the number of units of assessment shall be established according to the following gradations:

Groups of Nations	Number of votes	Units of Assessment
I	5	16
II	4	8
III	3	4
IV	2	2
V	1	1

[1] Malloy, *Treaties*, II, 2140, Arts. 1, 2, 3, 6, 7. Huber dismisses the International Institute of Agriculture with the remark that " the inequalities that exist in the

Finally, inequality in voting has been established in numerous instances by substituting majority decisions for the unanimity requirement. It is commonly assumed that the traditional notion of political equality is inconsistent with any provision whereby a majority may bind the minority in an international organization. Nevertheless, provision has been made for majority decisions in several international administrative institutions of the first importance. This seems to be the practice in the Congress of the Universal Postal Union.[1] It was expressly stipulated in the International Sanitary Convention of 1903 for the Superior Board of Health of Constantinople. This Board was composed of four Turkish members and one representative from each of the signatory powers, and was empowered to decide on " the measures to be adopted in order to prevent the introduction of epidemic diseases into the Ottoman Empire and their transmission to foreign countries." Article 170 of the Convention provided:

> The decisions of the Superior Board of Health, reached by a majority of the members who compose it, are of an executory character and without appeal.[2]

The European Commission of the Danube is one of the most successful of international commissions and also one of the few which has been invested with real powers of control. This Commission determines administrative questions and fixes tolls by a majority vote. Article 12 of the Regulations fixing the order of procedure in the Commission contains the following provisions:

representation of states in the Institute of Agriculture are irrelevant to the principle of equality, since each state classifies itself and the classification corresponds essentially with the obligation to contribute." *Die Gleichheit der Staaten*, p. 102, note 2.

See Sayre, *Experiments in International Administration*, pp. 158–166.

[1] See *ibid.*, pp. 157, 19–25.

[2] Malloy, *Treaties*, II, 2104.

Decisions are by a majority of votes:

(*a*) When it is a question of form, in particular if it concerns the interior service of the commission, the relations of the commission with its employees, or details of execution of measures decided upon in commission;

(*b*) When it is a question of modifying the tolls of navigation established by virtue of Article 16 of the Treaty of Paris of March 30, 1856.

On important questions [*questions de fond*] for which unanimity is required, decisions made unanimously by the delegates present become final two months after having been communicated to the absent delegates, unless a formal contrary vote is sent by one or several of these delegates before the expiration of the said period of two months.[1]

Article 18 provides that decisions of the same character shall be made by majority vote in the Executive Committee which carries on the work of the Commission between regular sessions. Probably the most striking example of an international institution with real powers of control over

[1] Sayre, *Experiments in International Administration*, Appendix B, p. 185. See also Article 16 of the Treaty of Paris, March 20, 1856, in Hertslet, II, 1258; Demorgny, *La question du Danube;* Pitisteano, *La question du Danube;* Sayre, *op. cit.,* pp. 38–47; Sturdza, *Recueil des documents relatifs à la liberté de navigation du Danube.*

The international commissions which have been created to supervise the navigation of the Rhine have also been authorized to reach decisions by majority vote, but the decisions of these commissions have not been binding until approved by the signatory governments. See Annex XVI of the Vienna Congress Treaty of 1815, Articles Concerning the Navigation of the Rhine, Art. 17, in Hertslet, I, 84; Treaty of March 31, 1831, Art. 94, in Clercq, *Recueil des traités*, IV, 53, and Martens, *Nouveau recueil*, IX, 294; Treaty of October 17, 1868, Art. 46, in Martens, *Nouveau recueil général*, XX, 369; Sayre, *op. cit.,* pp. 131–141, 157.

The principle of majority decisions has also been invoked in other instances which are not strictly relevant to the subject of permanent administrative institutions. In 1881, for example, the Great Powers intervened to establish the boundary between Greece and Turkey. Article 1 of the Treaty provided: " this delimitation will be fixed on the spot by a Commission composed of the Delegates of the Six Powers and of the two parties interested. The Delimitation Commission will pass their Resolutions by a majority of votes, each Power having but one vote." See Hertslet, IV, 3044, 3061, 3069. For another illustration, see the General Act of the Algeciras Conference of 1906, Art. 76, in Martens, *Nouveau recueil général*, 2ᵉ sér., XXXIV, 275.

the member states is the International Sugar Commission which was established by European states in 1902 in order to do away with the abuses incident to the granting of bounties to encourage the production and exportation of sugar. This Commission, composed of delegates from the contracting states, had authority to determine whether bounties were granted in the contracting states, to determine whether non-exporting states had become exporting states and hence subject to certain restrictions contemplated in the Convention, to determine whether bounties were granted in non-contracting states and what special duties on sugar from such states should be imposed in consequence, to authorize an increased surtax in any one of the contracting states on sugar from another contracting state in order to protect the home market, to pass upon requests for admission to the Union from non-contracting states, to nominate a Permanent Bureau, to fix the expenses of the Permanent Bureau and of the Commission itself, and to decide upon the method of apportioning these expenses among the contracting states. In addition to the above, the Commission had important advisory functions. The important powers vested in the Sugar Commission made it all the more significant that its decisions were taken by majority vote.[1] Mr. Sayre concludes a recent discussion of the unanimity requirement in international administration as follows:

[1] See the Convention of March 5, 1902, Art. 7, and also the Final Protocol appended thereto, in Hertslet, *Commercial Treaties*, XXIII, 582, 586. See also the Additional Act of August 28, 1907, in Hertslet, *op. cit.*, XXV, 547; André, in *R. G. D. I. P.* (1912), XIX, 665–689; Politis, in *R. S. L. F.* (1904), II, 1–27; Sayre, *Experiments in International Administration*, pp. 117–131, 189–201. Referring to the International Sugar Commission, Mr. Sayre says: " A striking feature of the Commission is that it is given power to act by a majority vote. The usual diplomatic requirement of unanimity is thus brushed aside in the interest of efficiency; the result adds immeasurably to the power and effectiveness of the Commission. Thus it may come about that an individual state may be compelled to alter or modify a tariff quite against its own sovereign wishes." *Op. cit.*, p. 122.

To make the assertion that the unanimity requirement has, in one way or another, been dispensed with whenever prompt and effective action has seemed imperative, would be too sweeping a statement of the case; for in a number of instances, where the organ is comparatively small, or where single blocking states can be coerced into line through moral or social pressure, the unanimity requirement still remains. Nevertheless, the fact that in those international organizations which have proved most successful the unanimity requirement has in most instances been displaced by the rule of the majority vote, is of sufficient significance to be worthy of serious consideration by those who would give to the League of Nations an executive organ of real efficiency.[1]

As regards the financial support of administrative unions, a few conventions stipulate the rule of equality. The expenses incurred by the International office at Zanzibar, instituted under the Brussels Act of 1890 for the suppression of the slave trade, are divided equally among the powers represented in the office.[2] The same rule applies to the maintenance of the Central American Bureau established under the Convention of 1907.[3] These cases, however, are quite exceptional. The International Bureau of the Union for the Publication of Customs Tariffs is supported by the contracting states in proportion to the amount of their commerce, while the Central Office of International Transports is supported in proportion to railway mileage.[4] Several administrations require contributions in proportion to population, among them the Bureau of Weights and Measures at Paris, the Bureau of the American Republics at Washington, and two bureaus instituted by the Union of American Nations for the Protection of Trade Marks.[5]

---

[1] *Op. cit.*, p. 157. See also pp. 21–25, 29, 33, 46, 53, 122, 135, 150–158.

[2] Malloy, *Treaties*, II, 1985, Art. 76.

[3] *Ibid.*, II, 2413, Art. 8.

[4] *Ibid.*, II, 1997, Art. 9; Martens, *Nouveau recueil général*, 2ᵉ sér., XIX, 327, Art. 1.

[5] Malloy, *Treaties*, II, 1927; *La vie int.*, I, 68, 73; *A. J. I. L. Suppl.* (1917), XI, 17, 18.

The system of contributions that is coming to be more widely adopted than any other for important administrations involves the division of member states into classes and a graded scheme of apportioning units of assessment among the classes. For illustration, the expenses incurred by the International Bureau of Industrial Property at Berne are distributed as follows:

In order to determine the contributive part of each of the countries in this sum total of the expenses, the contracting countries and those which later join the Union shall be divided into six classes, each contributing in proportion to a certain number of units, to wit:

	Units
Class 1	25
Class 2	20
Class 3	15
Class 4	10
Class 5	5
Class 6	3

These coefficients shall be multiplied by the number of countries of each class, and the sum of the products thus obtained will furnish the number of units by which the total expenses are to be divided. The quotient will give the amount of the unit of expense.

Each of the contracting countries shall designate at the time of its accession, the class in which it wishes to be ranked.[1]

The same principle is adopted by the International Telegraphic Union, the Universal Postal Union, the International Union for the Protection of Literary and Artistic

---

[1] Malloy, *Treaties*, III, 374. Huber contends that classification to determine contribution quotas is not inconsistent with equality, but his argument is not very convincing. He says: " The classification of states for the purpose of apportioning contribution quotas and the consequent legal inequalities can not be cited as proof of inequality. For the classification is not into great powers and other states, but is purely objective, resting upon population or other similar criteria. Again, this is an inequality of obligations, not of rights, and only an inequality of rights would be relevant. Finally, the financial element in these international organizations is unimportant so far as being conclusive of a question of principle is concerned." *Die Gleichheit der Staaten*, p. 103.

Works, and the International Wireless Telegraph Union.[1] It applies to the maintenance of the International Institute of Agriculture, the International Office of Public Hygiene, and the International Bureau of the Permanent Court of Arbitration at The Hague.[2]

The tendencies reviewed above, although still in a somewhat rudimentary stage, are significant as indicating the probable course of future development. There are numerous indications that inequality of representation will eventually become the rule rather than the exception. Inequality of representation is most significant where it involves also an inequality of voting strength. Inequality in voting is most important where it prevails in the diplomatic conference or congress, as in the conference of the radiotelegraphy Union, but its importance should not be underestimated in purely administrative bodies like the Institute of Agriculture or the Office of Public Hygiene. It is noted also that in connection with the development of international administration the principle of majority decisions has been substituted for the unanimity rule in several important administrative bodies, and to a limited extent, indeed, in conferences of a diplomatic nature. Inequality in apportioning the burdens of international administration has already become a common practice. Although the functions of international administration are usually technical, in a few instances administrative bodies have been invested with a limited supernational authority. All this seems to indicate that the political equality of states is in process of becoming an obsolete principle so far as the growth of international administration is concerned.

---

[1] *La vie int.*, I, 260, 271; *A. J. I. L. Suppl.* (1913), VII, 121; Malloy, *Treaties*, III, 174.

[2] *Ibid.*, II, 2143, 2218, 2026, 2237.

SUPERNATIONAL JUDICIAL TRIBUNALS

The society of nations has developed thus far only the most primitive types of judicial organization. A certain amount of progress has been made, nevertheless, and the problem has received enough attention to indicate the importance of political equality as a principle which may be involved in the composition, procedure, and authority of such tribunals.

The five Central American republics have had until recently a well organized court, called the Central American Court of Justice, with real supernational authority.[1] No difficulty was experienced in preserving complete political equality so far as the Court's composition was concerned, for the tribunal was instituted by only five small states having in common a strong tradition of confederation. Each republic was permitted to appoint one justice, making a tribunal of five. The Court's procedure and authority, on the other hand, limited the extreme notion of political equality. Decisions were rendered by a majority vote, and the states bound themselves to abide by the Court's decisions.

When it is attempted to organize a court with jurisdiction over a large number of states, differing widely in respect to extent of territory, population, wealth, civilization, military strength, and the like, the problem becomes infinitely more complicated. Something has been made of the fact that the so-called Permanent Court of Arbitration at The Hague, instituted by the Peace Conference of 1899 and perfected at the second Conference in 1907, is based upon the principle of equality.[2] The institution named lacks all of the attributes of a court, however, for it provides nothing more

---

[1] See *supra*, p. 275.

[2] See Bonfils, *Manuel*, § 278, p. 155; Huber, *Die Gleichheit der Staaten*, pp. 89, 91; *La Deux. Confér.* II, 160, 619, 625, 643. Of the organization adopted for the so-called Permanent Court, Huber remarks: "It can therefore be said that the First Peace Conference gave unqualified expression to the principle of the equality of states." *Op. cit.*, p. 91.

than a panel of arbitrators and a procedure which may be resorted to in voluntary arbitration. As Mr. Choate observed at the Second Peace Conference, it is " a court only in name, — a framework for the selection of referees for each particular case." [1]

Statesmen have frequently referred to the Concert of the great powers as a court of appeal for Europe. The opinion is supported by a long record of cases in which the Congress has required small or weak states to accept its decision in controversies in which their interests were involved. Several publicists have held a similar opinion, viewing certain of the activities of the great powers as an indication of a rudimentary development toward supernational judicial authority. While there is a good deal to be said in support of this interpretation, it must be admitted that the development is still very primitive. However it may be interpreted, the Concert is the negation of political equality.

Two attempts were made at the Second Hague Peace Conference in 1907 to prepare the way for the organization of judicial tribunals with real supernational authority. The first of these took shape in the Convention for the establishment of an International Prize Court.[2] The composition of the proposed court was a question of great difficulty. The British delegation first proposed a court to consist of one judge and one deputy judge nominated by each power having a merchant marine of more than 800,000 tons.[3] This

---

[1] *La Deux. Confér.*, II, 311; Scott, *American Addresses*, p. 81.

[2] *La Deux. Confér.*, I, 165–169; II, 11–33, 783, 856, 1071–1106; Brown, in *A. J. I. L.* (1908), II, 476–489; Despagnet, *Cours*, § 683, p. 1161; Gregory, in *A. J. I. L.* (1908), II, 458–475; Higgins, *Hague Peace Conferences*, pp. 407–444; Huber, *Die Gleichheit der Staaten*, pp. 91 ff.; Scott, in *A. J. I. L.* (1911), V, 302–324.

[3] *La Deux. Confér.*, II, 1076. The report of the United States Commissioner of Navigation for 1908 accredits the following powers with a combined steam and sailing tonnage of over 800,000 tons: Great Britain, Germany, United States, France, Norway, Japan, Italy, Russia, the Netherlands, and Sweden. Department of Commerce and Labor, Bureau of Navigation, Report of the Commissioner of Navigation (1908), pp. 71–75. See Barbosa's objections to the British proposals, in *La Deux. Confér.*, II, 797–799.

plan was abandoned in the committee, however, and the scheme of rotation was adopted, whereby every state would appoint one judge and one deputy judge for a six year period, but only the judges appointed by the eight great powers would sit continuously throughout the entire period. Article 15 of the Convention provided:

The Judges appointed by the following Contracting Powers: Germany, the United States of America, Austria-Hungary, France, Great Britain, Italy, Japan, and Russia, are always summoned to sit.

The Judges and Deputy Judges appointed by the other Contracting Powers sit by rota as shown in the Table annexed to the present Convention; their duties may be performed successively by the same person. The same Judge may be appointed by several of the said Powers.[1]

The shorter periods assigned to judges and deputy judges of the lesser powers in the scheme of rotation were presumed to bear some relation to the relative extent of the merchant marine, commerce, and sea power of the states which they represented.[2] This plan made it possible to have a court of fifteen judges, on which all states would have some representation, and which could always be dominated by the eight great powers.[3]

The scheme of rotation was absolutely unacceptable to some of the small states. The first delegate from the Dominican Republic is reported to have said in conversation:

I will not be a party to any convention which does not recognize the same right in my country to a seat in the court as is recognized to Great Britain; not merely a right, but the exercise of that right.[4]

---

[1] The scheme of rotation is given in *La Deux. Confér.*, II, 853–855; Higgins, *Hague Peace Conferences*, p. 430.

[2] See remarks of Lammasch, in *La Deux. Confér.*, II, 836; and of Renault, in the report of the first committee, in *ibid.*, I, 196.

[3] A small court and the preponderance of the great maritime nations were regarded as absolutely essential by the delegates of many of the great powers. See, for example, Sir Edward Fry's declaration, in *ibid.*, II, 817.

[4] Scott, *Hague Peace Conferences*, I, 503. Cf. Admiral Beresford's protest in *The London Times*, December 5, 1911, p. 8a.

A similar attitude was assumed by the Venezuelan delegation.[1] On signing the Convention, no less than ten states made reservations with respect to Article 15.[2]

Perhaps the most significant feature of the debates on the composition of the proposed prize court was the extent to which small state delegates and conspicuous exponents of political equality admitted the principle of classification. A number of delegations from the second rank powers accepted the proposed convention without any reservation, simply making it clear that their course was not to be construed as compromising in any sense the principle of equality on which they intended to insist in the composition of the proposed court of arbitral justice. They took the position that the prize court's jurisdiction would affect only a special category of interests, with respect to which the principle of classification might reasonably be admitted.[3] Barbosa of Brazil, the most vigorous exponent of unqualified political equality present at the Conference, declared explicitly for the principle of classification, while denouncing the plan of rotation reported by the committee as an inequitable application of the principle. He said:

We, for our part, also declare openly for the principle of classification among states, persuaded by the consideration that in the matter of

[1] *La Deux. Confér.*, II, 20, from which an extract is quoted *supra*, p. 182.

[2] Reservations on the final vote are given in *La Deux. Confér.*, I, 168; and reservations at signing in Higgins, *Hague Peace Conferences*, p. 441. The reservation of Haiti is quoted *supra*, p. 182.

[3] *La Deux. Confér.*, I, 166, 167; II, 14, 15, 16, 18, 19, 21, 838. Huber says that, notwithstanding opposition from various quarters, the classification of states according to objective criteria was in general regarded as acceptable in the constitution of a prize court. It was the subjective criteria that were absolutely unacceptable. He says further: " The opposition to the system of rotation, and to the inequality coming to light in its application, was manifested much less in connection with the prize court than with the court of arbitral justice. And in fact the situation was here quite different. As matters stand, the small and the secondary sea powers — leaving the inland states entirely out of account — have enjoyed almost no equality with the great powers in the exercise of prize rights in the existing situation; the retention of exclusively national prize court jurisdiction would offer them

prizes the creation of international jurisdiction affects only the maritime interests of states, whose representation, therefore, should be graduated in proportion to their position on the sea.[1]

If states may be represented on a prize court in proportion to their maritime interests, it is difficult to understand just why they may not be represented on a court of other jurisdiction in proportion to other interests; but this possibility was vigorously combated by the small state delegations at the Second Peace Conference. An attempt was made to agree upon a convention providing for a real judicial tribunal, to be known as the Court of Arbitral Justice.[2] The greatest difficulty was experienced in regard to the proposed court's composition. Several plans were considered, including composition determined by election, by equal representation, by representation in proportion to population, as well as other principles;[3] but the framers of the project eventually adopted rotation as the most practicable way of securing a small tribunal, with some representation for all states, and some recognition of the important diversities among different states. It was proposed that a court of seventeen judges be organized for a period of twelve years. Each state was to appoint a judge; the judges appointed by the eight great powers were to sit for the full period, while those appointed by the other states were to sit in rotation for periods varying from one to ten years, in

no advantage. The creation of an international prize court, however, means an extensive limitation of autonomy to those states which alone actually take prizes, namely, the great powers, and especially those which have a great navy at their disposal." See *Die Gleichheit der Staaten*, pp. 92–95.

[1] *La Deux. Confér.*, II, 12. See his speeches, II, 11–13, 832–836, 849–852.

[2] *Ibid.*, I, 332–335; II, 144–160, 177–190, 309–351, 593–708, 1035–1070; Despagnet, *Cours*, § 739, p. 1358; Higgins, *Hague Peace Conferences*, pp. 498–517; Huber, *Die Gleichheit der Staaten*, pp. 92–94, 107; Scott, in *A. J. I. L.* (1908), II, 772–810; Scott, *American Addresses;* Scott, *An International Court of Justice;* Scott, *The Status of The International Court of Justice.*

[3] *La Deux. Confér.*, II, 1035–1070; Choate, in *ibid.*, II, 689–693; Higgins, *Hague Peace Conferences*, pp. 515–517; Scott, *Hague Peace Conferences*, I, 456–460.

proportion to the population, territorial extent, commerce, and the like of the states which they represented. Mr. Choate, head of the American delegation, has said:

We and Great Britain and Germany and France and Russia all agreed that it should be constituted as the prize court was; that you should take the eight great nations, the greatest in resources, in population, in business, in matters that would come naturally before the consideration of such a court, and that they should each have a judge of the court all the time, and that the other nations, having less occasion for the services and offices of the court, should be graded, according to what we have considered their relative importance, from twelve years, the term for which the eight great nations were to have permanent judges, down to one year.[1]

The scheme of rotation proved to be absolutely unacceptable to the delegates from the smaller states. It was not entirely clear, at least in the earlier discussions, that they objected to the principle of classification *per se*. A delegate from the Argentine Republic suggested that the court's composition might be based on the importance of foreign commerce; a delegate from Venezuela suggested that judges might be apportioned equally among the three continents; while the Chinese delegation favored population as a basis.[2] As the debates progressed, however, the opposition to any plan of proportional representation became uncompromising.

The American delegates attempted to convince the opponents of rotation that by permitting every state to name a judge for the full period equality would be preserved. It was only in the exercise of the right of representation, so the argument ran, that equality would be limited. Thus Mr. Choate said of the plan presented by the committee:

It recognized, and was based upon, the equal sovereignty of the Nations and took account at the same time of the differences that ex-

[1] *A. S. J. S. I. D. Proceedings* (1910), p. 199.
[2] *La Deux. Confér.*, II, 325, 339, 602, 613, 1044. Cf. Choate's reply to the argument for population, *ibid.*, II, 691.

isted between them in population, in territory, in commerce, in language, in systems of law and in other respects, and especially the difference in the interests which the several nations would normally and naturally have at stake in the proceedings before the Court and in the exercise of its jurisdiction. It provided for a Court of seventeen judges to be organized for a period of twelve years and that of the seventeen, eight nations, who will be generally recognized as having the greatest interests at stake in the exercise by the Court of its powers, should each have a judge sitting during the whole period of the organization.

It provided also that each of the other Powers should appoint, in the same way, and at the same time a judge for the same period but who should be called to the exercise of judicial functions in the Court for variously measured periods, according to their population, territorial extent, commerce and probable interest at stake before the Court. These measured periods ranging from ten years down to one.

By this method the absolute and equal sovereignty of each of the forty-five Powers was duly respected and their differences in other respects not lost sight of.[1]

Mr. Scott also emphasized the distinction between the right of representation and the exercise of the right:

Each state — be it large or small, an empire of hundred of millions or a republic of a few hundred thousands — should possess the right to appoint, and should actually appoint, a judge of its own choice for the full period contemplated by the convention, namely twelve years. The exclusion of a single state from the proposed court, or the denial of the right of a single state to appoint, would proclaim the principle of juridical inequality and vitiate in advance a project, however carefully it be drawn and however acceptable it might otherwise be.

It may be admitted, however, that the exercise of the right might be regulated without in any way questioning the existence of the right. If every nation has the right to appoint, and does appoint, a judge, it is no derogation to the principle of sovereignty and equality that the judges so selected may sit at various times and may sit in rotation.[2]

---

[1] *La Deux. Confér.*, II, 689.

[2] *Ibid.*, II, 606. See also *ibid.*, II, 317–320, 606–608; *American Addresses*, pp. 90–96, 99–103; *Hague Peace Conferences*, I, 457. Kamarowsky suggested in *Le tribunal international* (transl. by Westman), published in 1887, that the small states might

This distinction between having a political right and being able to exercise it was refuted effectively by Barbosa. The Brazilian delegate denounced the distinction as *manifestement sophistique:*

Well, then, if the enjoyment of a right may be reduced to one year in twelve, without diminishing its substance, the twelve months of that single year may likewise be still further reduced without impairing the right. If the exercise is reduced to six months, to three months, to one month, it is still only the exercise that is effected. And why not limit it then to weeks? The right will not be prejudiced. Three weeks, one week, even one day of functioning, it is always the exercise that is in question. The immunity of the right would suffer nothing.

Barbosa's argument was summarized in the following passage:

The conditions of exercise only respect the equality of a right when they are *equal* for all those who possess it. On the other hand, inequality in the exercise implies inequality in the right itself, because the value of a right is really measured only by the juridical possibility of exercising it.

And then, to conclude, let us distinguish, as should have been done at the outset, in order to solve the difficulty. There are two distinct rights: the right to nominate and the right to sit. In the right to nominate we will all be equal. But in the right to sit we will be absolutely unequal. Well then! it is this inequality which violates the equality of states.[1]

Led by Barbosa,[2] the delegates of the smaller states were able to defeat any agreement as to the composition of the proposed court. Barbosa declared that it was impossible

waive their right to equal representation on an international court. " En vertu du principe fondamental de l'égalité entre les États, ils auraient tous le droit de désigner un nombre égal de juges. Les petits États pourraient, s'ils le jugeaient à propos, ne pas user de ce droit; cependant leur voix ne serait pas transmissible." *Op. cit.,* p. 499.

[1] *La Deux. Confér.,* II, 626, 619.

[2] *Ibid.,* II, 148–155, 618–622, 624–627, 643–650. See *supra,* p. 183.

for a state to renounce its equality.[1] The delegate from Mexico insisted that the court

ought to be an essentially juridical organism, and in it, in conformity with the fundamental rule of international law — the equality of States — all countries called to the Second Peace Conference, great or small, strong or weak, ought to be represented on the basis of the most absolute, the most perfect equality.[2]

The Danish delegate declared that

the proposal of a rotation which does not recognize the absolute equality of States will not be acceptable to the Government of Denmark.[3]

A member of the Chilean delegation insisted that the proposed court should be constituted on the same principle as the Peace Conference itself:

And the reason for this is most logical. Why, if each State votes in the Conference as a unit in the adoption of all and each of its resolutions, should there be a different representation in the judicial organization charged with putting them into execution ? Why, if each Nation has the importance of a unit in the legislative power which prescribes resolutions and laws, and which is, therefore, the principal and the most fundamental of all the powers, why should not each Nation have an equal representation in the judicial power charged with their application ? [4]

A *Vœu* was incorporated in the Final Act of the Conference, calling the attention of the signatory powers to the advisability of adopting the draft convention and of bringing it into operation as soon as the powers could agree on the court's composition. The adoption of this *Vœu* was made the occasion for a series of formal declarations and reservations with regard to equality. The Brazilian declaration was as follows:

On making this declaration I am instructed, however, by the Brazilian Government to insist, in as precise terms as possible, that it

---

[1] *La Deux. Confér.*, II, 619.   [2] *Ibid.*, II, 650.   [3] *Ibid.*, II, 148.
[4] *Ibid.*, II, 180. Cf. Scott, *American Addresses*, p. 91.

considers as implied in this vote the recognition of the principle of equality among sovereign States, and, therefore, the absolute exclusion — in every future negotiation aiming at the organization of the Court of Arbitration — of both the system of periodicity or rotation in the distribution of judges, and the selection of said judges by foreign electors.[1]

The Chinese delegation voted for the *Vœu*, adding another wish to the effect that

henceforth the sovereign and independent rights and the equality of States, which are the fundamental principles of international arbitral justice, may never be disregarded, as has been done in so lamentable a fashion, and that the new Court anticipated in this wish — in case it should be some day constituted — may have as a basis the same principle of equality which has served in the establishment of the permanent Court of arbitration of 1899.[2]

Fifteen states made reservations in the same spirit as those quoted above, while six states, Belgium, Denmark, Greece, Roumania, Switzerland, and Uruguay, abstained altogether.[3]

In the debates on the prize court and the court of arbitral justice, the political equality of states was considered only in its bearing on the composition of the proposed tribunals. It might have been suggested that the extreme notion of political equality would also be compromised by the provisions in each convention for majority decisions, and by the authority which was contemplated for the tribunals, particularly for the prize court.[4] The controversy centered, however, about the more important matter of representation. Although neither of these projects has been adopted, they represent the most considered as well as the most widely discussed plans for supernational judicial organization thus far presented as within the limits of practi-

[1] *La Deux. Confér.*, II, 148 (Perez' transl.).
[2] *Ibid.*, II, 160.
[3] *Ibid.*, I, 332–335; II, 144–160, 177–190, 335; *supra*, pp. 182–183.
[4] See Japanese declaration, *ibid.*, II, 20.

cable possibility. As such, they contribute to justify the conclusion that the extreme conception of political equality and effective international organization are irreconcilable, and that as the latter develops the former must be limited or abandoned.

<h2 style="text-align:center">SUMMARY</h2>

The fundamental distinction between the legal equality of states in their mutual relations and their political equality in whatever pertains to the development of international organization cannot be emphasized too frequently. In the present chapter this distinction has been taken as the starting point for the consideration of some of the more important precedents for international organization with particular reference to the bearing which they may have upon political equality. The international congress or conference has been presented as the earliest manifestation of a rudimentary organization; and two types have been distinguished, the one truly international, the other more accurately described as supernational. The form of political equality and no inconsiderable part of its substance are preserved in the international congress or conference by means of equality of representation, equality of voting strength and the unanimity rule, and equality in accepting or rejecting the decisions which are taken *ad referendum*. It is significant, however, that political equality in such an assembly becomes less and less substantial as the interests at stake increase in consequence, and that seriously controverted questions have been resolved in a majority of instances by another type of assembly. The supernational congress or conference denies the political equality of states by limiting equal representation to a few of the more powerful states, by eliminating voting, and by making decisions which non-participating states are required to accept. This type of organization has been the subject of repeated protests from the smaller and less powerful states. Its development has been rudimentary at best. Nevertheless it is associated with a long line of important precedents, and it has exhibited tendencies which no study of political equality may disregard. Another tendency, more recent, but quite clearly defined, has made its appearance in connection with the development of international administration. Some of the most important administrative unions have limited the principle of political equality by admitting dependencies to representation, by giving votes to dependencies, distributing votes in proportion to financial contributions and providing for majority decisions, and by apportioning the burdens of financial support according to population, subject-matter, or voluntary classification. International organization for the administration of justice has not developed far enough to give any indication of its probable bearing upon the political equality of states, but the impossibility of reconciling such equality and effective judicial organization has been abundantly demonstrated by the discussions at The Hague with regard to the proposed International Prize Court and the Court of Arbitral Justice. The experience of the past century certainly indicates that as the society of nations is organized more effectively for the protection and the advancement of common interests the traditional notion of political equality will have to be redefined or abandoned.

CHAPTER IX

CONCLUSIONS

THE principle of state equality in international law was a creation of the publicists. It was derived from the application to nations of theories of natural law, the state of nature, and natural equality. An analogy was drawn between nations in international society and men in a state of nature. Thus the natural law became the law of nations, international society was regarded as a state of nature, and nations were presumed to enjoy a perfect equality of natural rights. The conception of state equality was first developed as part of a coherent theory by the naturalists of the seventeenth and eighteenth centuries. Grotius neither discussed the conception nor based his system upon it. It was not established by the Peace of Westphalia. It had its beginning as a naturalist doctrine in the writings of that school of publicists who acknowledged the leadership of Pufendorf and the inspiration of Thomas Hobbes. The early positivists developed no such conception. It was not until the middle of the eighteenth century, in the period of Burlamaqui, Vattel, Wolff, and Moser, that publicists of all schools included the equality of states among their leading principles. Once established by the process of reasoning summarized above, the principle was reënforced by theories of sovereignty. The absolute equality of sovereign states became one of the primary postulates of *le droit des gens théorique*.

The principle of equality has an important legal significance in the modern law of nations. It is the expression of two important legal principles. The first of these may be called the equal protection of the law or equality before the law. States are equal before the law when they are equally protected in the enjoyment of their rights and equally compelled to fulfil their obligations. Equality before the law is not inconsistent with the grouping of states into classes and the attributing to the members of each class of a status which is the measure of capacity for rights. Neither is it inconsistent with inequalities of representation, voting power, and contribution in international organizations. The second principle is usually described as equality of rights and obligations or more often as equality of rights. The description is a heritage from theories of natural law and natural right. What is really meant is an equality of capacity for rights. Equality in this sense is the negation of status. If applied without qualification in international organizations it requires equal representation, voting power, and contribution. Equality before the law is absolutely essential to a stable society of nations. If it is denied the alternatives are universal empire or universal anarchy. Equality of capacity for rights, on the other hand, is not essential to the reign of law. Strictly speaking, it has never been anything more than an ideal in any system of law. Among states, where there is such an utter want of homogeneity in the physical bases for separate existence, there are important limitations upon its utility even as an ideal.

Notwithstanding these limitations, equality of legal capacity has its place as an ideal in the system of international law. It must be recognized that the international legal capacity of the state may be and frequently is restricted by its organic constitution. It must also be recognized that many important limitations upon the legal capacity of certain states are imposed by the positive law of nations. Thorough investigation of these problems from a more rational and more scientific point of view is urgently required. On the other hand, it is vital that the fundamental distinction between equality of legal capacity and equality in international organization be more widely understood and appreciated. At the risk of repetition, this distinction may be explained once more by reference to general legal principles which are more or less familiar to everyone. It is generally assumed that equality of legal capacity among persons subject to law is the ideal toward which a system of private law ought to develop; but it has never been regarded as a necessary corollary that the same principle should be taken for an ideal in perfecting national organization, much less that it should be given practical application in the form of equal participation in government. No civilized state has ever tried to combine universal suffrage, the folk-moot, and the liberum veto. It may be suggested parenthetically that the organization of human beings on such a basis would be less unreal and would give greater promise of success than the organization of nations on the same principle. The problem of international organization should not be confused and complicated by attempting to insist upon the application of the principle of state equality. Conceding that equality of capacity for rights is sound as a legal principle, its proper application is limited to rules of conduct and to the acquiring of rights and the assuming of obligations under those rules. It is inapplicable from its very nature to rules of organization. Insistence upon complete political equality in the constitution and functioning of an international union, tribunal, or concert is simply another way of denying the possibility of effective international organization.

SUPPLEMENTARY CHAPTER

THE EQUALITY OF STATES IN THE PEACE OF PARIS

THE preceding pages were written while the World War was still undetermined. The War has since come to an end and the major terms of a new settlement have been drafted at the Conference of Paris.[1] The new settlement is at present only partially completed. Many of its details, indeed, have been formulated only in prospect; and of the terms already accepted there are some which seem likely to require an early and perhaps a radical revision. It is already evident, however, that much will be finally included which is noteworthy with reference to the equality of states. Although the materials for an exhaustive study are not yet available, it is possible, from the record at hand,[2] to indicate some-

[1] The preliminary Conference of delegates representing the allied and associated powers met at Paris. Its opening session was held on January 18, 1919, and it was formally dissolved on January 21, 1920. It was this Conference which determined the content of treaties of peace with Germany, Austria, Bulgaria, and Hungary and also of several other treaties and conventions intended to supplement the treaties of peace. The German delegation received peace terms at Versailles, the Austrian delegation at St. Germain, and the Bulgarian and Hungarian delegations at Neuilly. The settlement is described throughout the present chapter as the Peace of Paris. At the date of writing, April 20, 1920, the treaties of peace with Bulgaria and with Hungary are available only in unofficial summaries which indicate that their principal provisions are in most respects similar, *mutatis mutandis*, to the treaties with Germany and with Austria. The pending treaty with Turkey is not available in any form.

[2] The following documentary sources are cited in this chapter by the short titles indicated: Rules of the Preliminary Peace Conference at Paris, 1919 (cited Conference Rules), in *A. J. I. L. Suppl.* (1919), XIII, 109; Covenant of the League of Nations (cited League Covenant), English text in *A. J. I. L. Suppl.* (1919), XIII, 128, and in Sen. Doc., No. 49, 66th Cong., 1st sess. (1919); French and English texts in Sen. Doc., No. 85, 66th Cong., 1st sess. (1919); Treaty of Peace with Germany, June 28, 1919 (cited Treaty with Germany), English text in *A. J. I. L. Suppl.* (1919), XIII, 151, and in Sen. Doc., No. 49, 66th Cong., 1st sess. (1919);

thing of the nature and significance of the more noteworthy provisions. An examination of these provisions is justified by the consideration that in important respects the Peace of Paris is the natural sequence of much that was discussed in the preceding chapters and also by the further consideration that this Peace will constitute the point of departure for important international developments in the twentieth century.

Limitations Upon the Legal Capacity of States

It seems evident, in the first place, that the new settlement will make questions of status in the law of nations more important than ever before. Existing states will be subjected to new limitations.[1] A number of new states have

French and English texts in Sen. Doc., No. 85, 66th Cong., 1st sess. (1919); Comments by the German Delegation on the Conditions of Peace, May 29, 1919 (cited German Comments), in *International Conciliation*, No. 143, October, 1919; Reply of the Allied and Associated Powers to the Observations of the German Delegation on the Conditions of Peace, June 16, 1919 (cited Allied Reply), in *International Conciliation*, No. 144, November, 1919; J. R. Clark, *Data on German Peace Treaty* (cited Clark, *Data*), a pamphlet digest prepared for the Senate Committee on Foreign Relations, Washington, 1919; Treaty between the five Principal Allied and Associated Powers and Poland, June 28, 1919 (cited Treaty with Poland), French and English texts in Sen. Doc., No. 82, 66th Cong., 1st sess. (1919); Treaty of Peace with Austria, September 10, 1919 (cited Treaty with Austria), in Sen. Doc., No. 92, 66th Cong., 1st sess. (1919); Treaty between the five Principal Allied and Associated Powers and Roumania, December 9, 1919 (cited Treaty with Roumania), in *Current History* (1920), XI, II, 531; Convention Relating to International Air Navigation, 1919 (cited Air Convention), French and English texts in Sen. Doc., No. 91, 66th Cong., 1st sess. (1919).

[1] It is worth noting that the treaties take account in several instances of internal limitations upon equality. Article 299 of the Treaty with Germany, with reference to the dissolution of contracts between enemies, contains the following clause: "Having regard to the provisions of the constitution and law of the United States of America, of Brazil, and of Japan, neither the present Article, nor Article 300, nor the Annex hereto shall apply to contracts made between nationals of these states and German nationals; nor shall Article 305 apply to the United States of America or its nationals." Article 300, the Annex, and Article 305 contain further provisions with reference to the adjustment of contracts and the competence of the Mixed Arbitral Tribunals which are to be established between Germany and each of the allied and associated powers. See also Allied Reply, p. 75; Treaty with

arisen out of the wreck of former empires, and several of these states are likely to occupy an insecure position in the family of nations for some time to come. Their respective legal capacities as persons in the international community will be conditioned by a variety of limitations.

Some of the new states will be limited because of their geographical situation. Several of them are inland states, while others have only a restricted access to the sea. A great deal of attention was given to this problem at the Conference of Paris, and a variety of provisions for mitigating the incapacities incident to the inland state's position are included in the settlement.[1] Poland, for example, is given an outlet on the Baltic by making the Free City of Danzig a Polish commercial port.[2] Austria is promised free

Austria, Art. 251. The General Conference of the Labor Organization is authorized to submit its proposals in the form of recommendations or draft conventions, but it is further provided as follows: "In the case of a federal State, the power of which to enter into conventions on labor matters is subject to limitations, it shall be in the discretion of that Government to treat a draft convention to which such limitations apply as a recommendation only, and the provisions of this Article with respect to recommendations shall apply in such case." Treaty with Germany, Art. 405; Treaty with Austria, Art. 350. The evolution within the British Empire of what Viscount Grey has recently described as a partnership between free and independent communities finds expression in the separate representation of the British Dominions and India in the Conference itself and also in various institutions of the permanent organization created by the settlement.

[1] In his address to the United States Senate, January 22, 1917, President Wilson said: "So far as practicable, moreover, every great people now struggling towards a full development of its resources and of its powers should be assured a direct outlet to the great highways of the sea. Where this cannot be done by the cession of territory, it can no doubt be done by the neutralization of direct rights of way under the general guarantee which will assure the peace itself. With a right comity of arrangement no nation need be shut away from free access to the open paths of the world's commerce." *Cong. Record*, 64th Cong., 2d sess. (1917), LIV, 1742.

[2] Treaty with Germany, Art. 104. "The town of Danzig has been constituted as a free city, so that the inhabitants are autonomous and do not come under Polish rule, and form no part of the Polish state. Poland has been given certain economic rights in Danzig, and the city itself has been severed from Germany because in no other way was it possible to provide for that ' free and secure access to the sea ' which Germany has promised to concede." Letter transmitting the Allied Reply, in *A. J. I. L.* (1919), XIII, 549. See Allied Reply, pp. 32, 34.

access to the Adriatic.[1] Bulgaria and Hungary will be assured an economic outlet on the Aegean and the Adriatic respectively. Czecho-Slovakia is given the use of free zones in the ports of Hamburg and Stettin,[2] the right to run its own trains over Austrian railways,[3] and the right to have trunk telegraph and telephone lines provided and maintained for the exclusive use of its transit traffic across Austrian territory.[4] Articles providing freedom of transit, freedom of navigation, through transport service, free zones in ports, and free passage for aircraft tend to alleviate the disadvantages of the inland state's position.[5] The right of the inland state to have a maritime flag is expressly stipulated as follows:

The High Contracting Parties agree to recognise the flag flown by the vessels of any Contracting Party having no sea-coast, which are

---

[1] Treaty with Austria, Art. 311. "The clauses relating to ports, waterways, and railways assure to Austria under international guarantees access to the sea by land and water." Letter of the Allied and Associated Powers transmitting the Treaty with Austria, p. 7, in Sen. Doc., No. 121, 66th Cong., 1st sess. (1919).

[2] Treaty with Germany, Arts. 363, 364.

[3] Treaty with Austria, Arts. 322–324.   [4] *Ibid.*, Art. 327.

[5] On freedom of transit, see Treaty with Germany, Arts. 267, 321–326, 378; Treaty with Austria, Arts. 220, 284–289, 326, 330; Treaty with Poland, Arts. 15, 17; Treaty with Roumania, Art. 15. On freedom of navigation and the internationalization of waterways, see Treaty with Germany, Arts. 327, 331–362, 378; Treaty with Austria, Arts. 290–308, 330; Treaty with Poland, Art. 18; Treaty with Roumania, Art. 16. "Arising out of the territorial settlement are the proposals in regard to the international control of rivers. It is clearly in accord with the agreed basis of the peace that inland states should have secure access to the sea along rivers which are navigable to their territory. They [the Allied and Associated Powers] believe that the arrangements they propose are vital to the free life of the inland states." Letter transmitting the Allied Reply, in *A. J. I. L.* (1919), XIII, 550. "Above all, they [the Allied and Associated Powers] have aimed at securing freedom of communications and transit to or from young landlocked states, which, in the absence of definite guarantees, would have regained their political independence only to fall once again under the economic tutelage of Germany." Allied Reply, p. 84. On through transport service, see Treaty with Germany, Arts. 365–369, 378; Treaty with Austria, Arts. 312–316, 330. On free zones in ports, see Treaty with Germany, Arts. 328–330, 378. On free passage for aircraft, see *ibid.*, Arts. 313–320; Treaty with Austria, Arts. 276–283; Air Convention, Art. 2. See Clark, *Data*, pp. 27–30.

registered at some one specified place situated in its territory; such place shall serve as the port of registry of such vessels.[1]

These various provisions and others of similar effect are legally significant, first, because they improve the peculiar legal condition of those inland states which are in a position to take advantage of them, and, secondly, because they concede in effect that the inland state has a peculiar legal condition which is not improved by dogmatic generalizations about equality.

Other new states will be limited in legal capacity because of the character of their civilization. The treaties recognize that degree and character of civilization are essential factors in determining status. Provision is made in Article 22 of the League of Nations Covenant for the tutelage of backward communities by more advanced nations as mandatories on behalf of the League. It is conceded that the character of the mandate must differ according to the stage of development attained by the community, and it is further recognized that

Certain communities formerly belonging to the Turkish Empire have reached a stage of development where their existence as independent nations can be provisionally recognised subject to the rendering of administrative advice and assistance by a Mandatory until such time as they are able to stand alone.

It is because of the peculiar character of the civilization prevailing in the states of middle and southeastern Europe, after long years of racial and religious intermingling and conflict, that those states are expressly limited to certain stipulated principles of government in their treatment of racial, religious, and linguistic minorities.[2]

[1] Treaty with Austria, Art. 225. See also Treaty with Germany, Art. 273.
[2] See Treaty with Germany, Art. 93; Treaty with Austria, Arts. 51, 60, 62–69; Treaty with Poland, Arts. 1–12; Treaty with Roumania, Arts. 1–12; Clemenceau to Paderewski, Paris, June 24, 1919, in *A. J. I. L. Suppl.* (1919), XIII, 416.

The limitations upon legal capacity which are incident to protection, guaranty, neutralization, the supervision of finance, and intervention will continue to be important for old states and new under the terms of the new settlement. Suzerainty finds no place in the treaties concluded to date, but may be revived in the pending Treaty with Turkey.[1] The status of neutralization is terminated for northern Savoy, Belgium, and Luxemburg, but continues in force for Switzerland.[2] The Free City of Danzig is placed under the protection of the League of Nations,[3] and the mandate system contemplates for other communities a kind of protection to be exercised in each instance by the mandatory on behalf of the League.[4] The Constitution of Danzig is guaranteed by the League.[5] Treaty provisions intended to secure the protection of minorities in central and southeastern Europe are declared obligations of international concern and are guaranteed by the League.[6] It is possible that the League's protection or guaranty will be invoked in the settlement of the Adriatic question or in the readjustment now taking place in the Near East. The rehabilitation of the disordered finances of many of the smaller and weaker states is almost certain to require supervision by the stronger powers individually or on behalf of the League.[7] Pending the complete discharge of reparation obligations imposed by the treaties, the central powers are placed under an extraordinary régime of financial supervision administered by a

[1] In the German Comments, p. 13, Danzig is referred to as "a Free State under the suzerainty of Poland." The use of the term is inappropriate, however, and finds no support in the treaty provisions.

[2] Treaty with Germany, Arts. 31, 40, 435; Treaty with Austria, Arts. 83, 84, 375.

[3] Treaty with Germany, Art. 102.   [4] League Covenant, Art. 22.

[5] Treaty with Germany, Art. 103.

[6] Treaty with Austria, Art. 69; Treaty with Poland, Art. 12; Treaty with Roumania, Art. 12. See *supra*, p. 341, note 2.

[7] See agreement between Great Britain and Persia, August 9, 1919, in Sen. Doc., No. 90, 66th Cong., 1st sess. (1919).

powerful Reparation Commission and auxiliary agencies.[1]
The right of intervention is of course a corollary of most of
these relationships. The noteworthy thing about the settlement in this respect, however, is not that protection, guaranty, supervision, and intervention are likely to have frequent application in the future. The significant feature of
the new order is that in many instances at least they may be
undertaken by or on behalf of the League of Nations rather
than by a single state or group of states. If the League
functions with any degree of success, the objection frequently made that such relationships have no legal import
because not generally recognized will lose most of the force
which it may have had in the past. The legal character of
such limitations may hardly be gainsaid if the time ever
comes when they are imposed by an organization which is
authorized to act for international society as a whole.

The Peace of Paris also creates a variety of limitations
upon legal capacity of the nature of servitudes. The best
known, of course, are those imposed upon the central powers,
particularly those which relate to the matter of armament.
The military and naval forces of the central powers are to be
limited as prescribed; their armed forces are to include no
aircraft whatever; conscription is abolished; the manu-
facture of all war materials is to be rigorously supervised
and restricted; the import or export of war materials is prohibited; the construction or acquisition of submarines for
any purpose is forbidden; and important unfortified areas
are created.[2] Most of these limitations have an indefinite

[1] See Treaty with Germany, Part VIII; Treaty with Austria, Part VIII; Clark,
Data, pp. 36–38; German Comments, pp. 14, 60–79, 106–112; Allied Reply, pp. 48–
54; Letter transmitting German Comments, in *A. J. I. L.* (1919), XIII, 542; and
the author's discussion in *M. L. R.* (1920), XVIII, 490–496.
[2] See Treaty with Germany, Part V; Art. 198; Arts. 173–179; Arts. 168, 171;
Art. 170; Art. 191; Arts. 42, 43, 97, 115, 180, 195; Treaty with Austria, Part V;
Art. 144; Arts. 119, 125–128; Arts. 132, 135; Art. 134; Art. 140; Art. 56; Clark,
Data, p. 31; Allied Reply, pp. 39–41.

duration. There are many other limitations which are
equally important from the legal point of view. Mention
may be made of the internationalizing of rivers,[1] the creation of free zones in ports of one state for the benefit of
another state,[2] the cession of the Saar mines,[3] and the cession of the right to construct riparian works on the bank
of a boundary river.[4] Stipulations intended to insure freedom of transit and the equitable treatment of foreign commerce as well as provisions for the protection of racial,
religious, and linguistic minorities are to be imposed upon
most of the states of central and southeastern Europe.[5] The
provisions for the protection of minorities are declared
obligations of international concern and placed under the
guaranty of the League of Nations. They can only be modified with the assent of a majority of the League Council.
Each member of the Council may call attention to any

[1] See *supra*, p. 340, note 5; German Comments, pp. 15, 83; Letter transmitting
German Comments, in *A. J. I. L.* (1919), XIII, 542. See also an Open Letter to the
Allied Nations, signed by prominent Polish citizens, in *New York Times,* November
10, 1919, p. 3.

[2] See Treaty with Germany, Arts. 328–330, 363, 364, 378; Treaty with Austria,
Art. 311. It may be noted in this connection, as illustrating the legal effect of leases
or concessions on the lessor state, that articles abrogating leases held by the central
powers in China describe China as "restored to the full exercise of her sovereign
rights in the above areas." Treaty with Germany, Art. 132: Treaty with Austria,
Art. 116.

[3] Treaty with Germany, Art. 45, and Part III, Sec. IV, Annex, Chap. I.

[4] Treaty with Germany, Art. 358 (described as a servitude in the Treaty);
Treaty with Austria, Art. 306. See other limitations of similar nature, in Treaty
with Germany, Arts. 65, 66, 67, 98.

[5] On freedom of transit and equitable treatment of foreign commerce, see
Treaty with Germany, Arts. 264–281; Treaty with Austria, Arts. 217–233; Treaty
with Poland, Arts. 13–20; Treaty with Roumania, Arts. 13–17; *supra*, p. 340,
note 5, p. 341, note 2. For digest of limitations imposed on Germany's control of
its external and internal commerce, see Clark, *Data,* pp. 25–30. Pending a general
readjustment of international trade and commerce, it was insisted that "Germany
should temporarily be deprived of the right she claims to be treated on a footing of
complete equality with other nations." Allied Reply, p. 60.

On protection of minorities, see *supra*, p. 341, note 2. The stipulations for the
protection of minorities were the subject of vigorous protests from several of the
small states concerned.

threatened infraction of the obligations imposed and the Council may take whatever action it considers proper and effective. Every controversy between a state which is subject to special obligations in regard to the protection of minorities and a state which is represented on the Council, whether involving questions of fact or of law, is to be considered a dispute of an international character which may be referred to the Permanent Court of International Justice for final decision.[1]

Two unique international persons are created by the Treaty with Germany. By the terms of Article 49, Germany renounces the government of the Saar Basin in favor of the League of Nations in the capacity of trustee. The government is entrusted to a Commission appointed by the League Council and invested with all the powers of government within the Saar Basin which have appertained hitherto to the German Empire, Prussia, or Bavaria. It is the Commission's duty "to ensure, by such means and under such conditions as it may deem suitable, the protection abroad of the interests of the inhabitants of the territory of the Saar Basin." This anomalous régime may be made permanent, provided a plebiscite at the end of fifteen years favors that solution in preference to union with either Germany or France, in which case Germany agrees "to make such renunciation of her sovereignty in favour of the League of Nations as the latter shall deem necessary." [2] By Article 100 of the same Treaty, Germany renounces all rights and title over the city of Danzig and a district at the mouth of the Vistula in favor of the United States, the British Empire, France, Italy, and Japan. The five powers undertake

[1] Treaty with Austria, Art. 69; Treaty with Poland, Art. 12; Treaty with Roumania, Art. 12.

[2] Part III, Sec. IV, Annex, pars. 16, 17, 19, 21, 34, 35. See German Comments, pp. 32–36; Allied Reply, pp. 24–26; Letter transmitting the Allied Reply, in *A. J. I. L.* (1919), XIII, 549.

to establish the city and territory as a Free City which will be placed under the protection of the League of Nations. The Constitution of the City will be placed under the League's guaranty. The five powers further undertake to negotiate a treaty between Danzig and Poland which will include the Free City within the Polish customs frontiers, establish a free area within the port, ensure to Poland the free use of port facilities, the control of the transportation system, and the right to develop port facilities and the transportation system, protect persons of Polish origin, speech, or citizenship against discrimination, and provide that "the Polish Government shall undertake the conduct of the foreign relations of the Free City of Danzig as well as the diplomatic protection of citizens of that city when abroad." [1]

It was suggested in an earlier chapter that where a limited number of states set up a supernational organization inequalities of capacity must arise between those states and other states outside the organization. The point is well illustrated in the Paris settlement. In order to ensure peace and promote international coöperation, the treaties provide for a League of Nations with a well defined organization, a carefully outlined plan for the peaceful adjustment of international disputes, a number of important covenants, and sanctions to ensure their observance. All this involves important limitations upon the capacity of each member state. Among member states, of course, these limitations are expected to be more than compensated by the increased security and mutual benefits attained. All states, however, will not be member states. It is by no means assured that each of the forty-five states and self-governing dominions enumerated as original members of the League or as states

[1] Arts. 102–104. See German Comments, pp. 45–46; Allied Reply, pp. 33–34; *supra*, p. 339, note 2; address of President Wilson to United States Senate, July 10, 1919, in *A. J. I. L.* (1919), XIII, 577.

invited to accede will join at the outset.[1] Moreover, the former belligerents, Austria, Bulgaria, Germany, Hungary, the Russian states, and Turkey, and the former neutrals, Abyssinia, Costa Rica, the Dominican Republic, and Mexico, are neither included among the original members nor among the states invited to accede. They may be admitted only by a two-thirds vote of the Assembly in which all members of the League are represented.[2] Meanwhile Article 17 of the Covenant contemplates that substantially the same methods shall be invoked by the League against non-member as against member states in order to compel them to settle their disputes without resorting to war.[3] So long as the League continues and states are divided into members and non-members, the situation will present some interesting and important inequalities of legal capacity among the persons of international law.[4]

In one respect the Paris settlement undertakes to make questions of status much less important. It has been pointed out that the recognition of self-help as a legitimate remedial process in the law of nations makes it necessary, in determining a state's legal capacity, to take account of whatever makes self-help an effective remedy. The treaties of 1919 attempt to amend this situation. In the League of Nations Covenant and supplementary provisions throughout the treaties there is outlined a comprehensive plan for restrict-

[1] None of the treaties have been ratified by the United States at the date of writing.

[2] League Covenant, Art. 1.

[3] "The members of the league and the nonmembers are required, the former by their covenant, the latter by an enforced obligation, to submit all differences between them not capable of being settled by negotiation to arbitration before a tribunal composed as the parties may agree." Taft, in *A. P. S. R.* (1919), XIII, 183.

[4] See German Comments, pp. 17, 25, 91, 117; Letter transmitting German Comments, in *A. J. I. L.* (1919), XIII, 542; Allied Reply, p. 22; Majority Report of Committee on Foreign Relations, United States Senate, September 10, 1919, p. 7, in Sen. Rep., No. 176, 66th Cong., 1st sess. (1919); Root to Hays, March 29, 1919, regarding the League Covenant, in *A. J. I. L.* (1919), XIII, 580, 594.

ing self-help and substituting processes which are legislative, administrative, or judicial in nature. Actual coercion, except in extreme cases, is only to be invoked by or on behalf of the League. This proposed substitution of organized force for self-help, if at all successful, will do more than anything else possibly could do to establish a real distinction between physical or material capacity and legal capacity among states.

Limitations Upon the Political Capacity of States

The outstanding feature of the Peace of Paris, so far as the equality of states is concerned, is its extensive disregard for the traditional conception of political equality.[1] This is strikingly manifested in the organization and procedure of the Peace Conference itself, in the temporary organization created to execute the settlement, and in the permanent organization established to execute the settlement, promote international coöperation, and preserve peace.

As regards the Peace Conference itself, it was hardly to be anticipated that even the appearance of political equality would be preserved except among the five great powers, the United States, the British Empire, France, Italy, and Japan. These powers alone among the great powers emerged from the World War unshaken by external defeat or internal revolution. It was the force at their disposal which determined the outcome of the war.[2] It was the same force which might be expected to dictate the terms of peace. Nor did the event belie expectation. Representatives of the five great powers summoned the Preliminary Peace Conference, which held its first meeting at Paris on January 18, 1919, and deter-

---

[1] For the recognition of internal limitations upon political equality, see *supra*, p. 338, note 1.

[2] See Clemenceau to Paderewski, Paris, June 24, 1919, in *A. J. I. L. Suppl.* (1919), XIII, 416, 418; Finch, in *A. J. I. L.* (1919), XIII, 159, 173.

mined in advance its organization and procedure.[1] For the purposes of representation and participation in the Preliminary Conference, they divided the states into three groups. The first group included the belligerent powers with general interests, namely, the United States, the British Empire, France, Italy, and Japan, whose delegates were entitled to attend all sessions of the Conference and of commissions. The second group included the belligerent powers with special interests, namely, Belgium, Brazil, the British Dominions and India, China, Cuba, Greece, Guatemala, Haiti, the Hedjaz, Honduras, Liberia, Nicaragua, Panama, Poland, Portugal, Roumania, Servia, Siam, and the Czecho-Slovak Republic, whose delegates were entitled to attend sessions at which questions concerning them were discussed. The third group was made up of the powers which had broken off diplomatic relations with enemy states, namely, Bolivia, Ecuador, Peru, and Uruguay, whose delegates also were entitled to attend sessions at which questions concerning them were discussed. It was also provided that neutral states and states in process of formation should be heard, either orally or in writing, on being summoned by the five great powers, at sessions devoted especially to questions in which they were directly concerned and only in so far as those questions were concerned. The apportionment of delegates gave five to each of the five great powers, three each to Belgium, Brazil, and Servia,[2] two each to Australia, Canada, China, Greece, the Hedjaz, India, Poland, Portugal, Roumania, Siam, South Africa, and the Czecho-Slovak Republic, and one each to the remaining states represented at the Conference and to New Zealand.[3]

[1] See Conference Rules, in *A. J. I. L. Suppl.* (1919), XIII, 109; Fenwick, in *A. P. S. R.* (1919), XIII, 199–212; Finch, in *A. J. I. L.* (1919), XIII, 159–186.

[2] Belgium and Servia were at first assigned two delegates each, but the protest which followed the announcement of this decision resulted in the assignment to each of an additional delegate.

[3] Conference Rules, secs. 1, 2. Each delegation was regarded as a unit.

The great powers of course controlled the Conference organization. At the first meeting the permanent President, four Vice-Presidents, and the Secretary General were chosen from among the delegates of the five great powers, and representatives from the same powers were selected to constitute the Secretariat, the Committee on Credentials, and the Drafting Committee. These officers and committees constituted the Bureau of the Conference.[1] At the second plenary session on January 25, 1919, the Bureau submitted draft resolutions providing for commissions to investigate and report on a league of nations, responsibility for the war and the enforcement of penalties, reparation, international labor legislation, and international control of ports, waterways, and railways. The commission on reparation was to consist of not more than three representatives from each of the five great powers and not more than two each from Belgium, Greece, Poland, Roumania, and Servia. The other commissions were to be composed in each instance of two representatives from each of the five great powers and five representatives to be elected by the lesser nations. Small state delegates protested against this allotment of representatives and eventually received additional representation on two of the commissions. In no case, however, were the smaller nations allotted more than a minority of the places on any commission or committee.[2] The commissions sent on missions to Poland and Teschen, the commissions instituted to examine the territorial claims of Roumania, Greece, and Czecho-Slovakia, the Economic Drafting Commission, the Financial Drafting Commission, and the Baltic Commission, among others, were each composed of five representatives designated by the five great powers.

[1] See Conference Rules, secs. 5, 6, 7, 15; Finch, in *A. J. I. L.* (1919), XIII, 167–169.

[2] See *ibid.*, 169–175, 182–184.

At no time, indeed, was the participation of the lesser states in the work of the Conference really significant. The Preliminary Conference held only a few plenary sessions before the German delegates were called in to receive the terms at Versailles, and these plenary sessions were confined to the mere formality of receiving and ratifying reports from the various commissions. The real Conference was made up of representatives from the great powers who alone under the rules were entitled to attend all sessions. Their meetings were as much meetings of the Peace Conference as the plenary sessions and their decisions were not subject to confirmation or review by the larger body. They functioned at first through the so-called Council of Ten made up of two representatives from each of the five powers, later through the Council of Five consisting of one representative of each of the five powers, and finally, when it proved unnecessary to have a Japanese representative present except as the interests of Japan were involved, through the Council of Four composed of the President of the United States and the prime ministers of Great Britain, France, and Italy. All important decisions were made by these inner cabinets of the Conference sitting in secret session.[1]

Political equality has been disregarded quite as completely in the temporary organization established to ensure the execution of the settlement. This organization is one of the striking features of the Peace of Paris. Its typical instrumentality is a commission created to supervise, control, or actually undertake the execution of terms imposed upon

---

[1] For a vivid and very critical account, see Keynes, *Economic Consequences of the Peace*, ch. 3. Cf. accounts of the Congress of Vienna, the Congress of Paris, and the Congress of Berlin by Hazen, Thayer, and Lord, in *Three Peace Congresses of the Nineteenth Century*, pp. 1–69. When the Conference was dissolved on January 21, 1920, a Council of Ambassadors was constituted to supervise routine matters connected with the execution of the settlement, while important issues of international policy were remitted to the decision of the Council of Premiers dominated by the allied great powers of Europe. *Current History* (1920), XI, II, 384.

defeated states.[1] Thus the various military, naval, and air disarmament clauses, for the execution of which a time limit is prescribed, are to be executed under the supervision of Inter-Allied Commissions of Control.[2] Plebiscites in Upper Silesia, East Prussia, Schleswig, and the Klagenfurt area are each to be conducted under the control of an International Commission.[3] New boundaries are to be delimited by Boundary Commissions.[4] The Saar Basin, renounced in favor of the League of Nations as trustee, is to be governed for fifteen years at least by a Governing Commission representing the League.[5] The whole question of reparation in all its ramifications is referred for administration to a powerful Reparation Commission.[6] The allied and associated powers are represented in the occupied territory of Germany by the Inter-Allied Rhineland Commission.[7] Other commissions and tribunals participate in the execution of less im-

---

[1] For fuller discussion of the temporary organization provided in the Treaty with Germany, see the author's article in *M. L. R.* (1920), XVIII, 484–507.

[2] Treaty with Germany, Arts. 203–210; Protocol supplementary to Treaty with Germany, in *A. J. I. L. Suppl.* (1919), XIII, 385; Treaty with Austria, Arts. 149–155. It may be anticipated that similar commissions will be provided in the other treaties.

[3] Treaty with Germany, Art. 88 and Part III, Sec. VIII, Annex; Arts. 94–95; Arts. 96–97; Art. 109; Treaty with Austria, Art. 50. It may be anticipated that similar commissions will be created wherever plebiscites are provided in the other treaties.

[4] Treaty with Germany, Arts. 35, 48, 83, 87, 101, 111; Treaty with Austria, Arts. 29, 36, 48, 55. It may be anticipated that similar commissions will be provided in the other treaties.

[5] Treaty with Germany, Art. 49 and Part III, Sec. IV, Annex, Chap. II.

[6] Treaty with Germany, Part VIII, Sec. I; Treaty with Austria, Part VIII, Sec. I; *M. L. R.* (1920), XVIII, 490–496. The Reparation Commission is created by the Treaty with Germany. The same Commission administers the reparation problem under the Treaty with Austria with a slight modification as regards the representation of small nations and with a special section of consultative or delegated powers only to consider special questions raised by the application of that Treaty. See *infra*, p. 354. It is not unlikely that the same Commission will at least supervise reparation under the other treaties.

[7] Agreement between the United States, Belgium, the British Empire, France, and Germany, with reference to the military occupation of the Rhine, Art. 2, in Sen. Doc. No. 75, 66th Cong., 1st sess. (1919).

portant provisions of the settlement. Mention may be made of the commissions in charge of the repatriation of war prisoners and interned civilians, the identification and care of war graves, the apportionment of social and state insurance reserves, the apportionment of railway rolling stock, the repurchase price of the Saar mines, and the delimitation of free zones in the ports of Hamburg and Stettin.[1] The treaties also provide for Mixed Arbitral Tribunals to decide many of the questions which may arise under clauses dealing with debts, property rights and interests, contracts, prescriptions, judgments, and industrial property.[2]

The salient characteristics of this temporary organization are squarely in conflict with the traditional idea of political equality. In the first place, the régime is dominated at every point by the great powers.[3] The Inter-Allied Commissions of Control are appointed by the great powers. The same powers appoint the International Commissions in control of the plebiscite areas, except that Japan makes no appointment in Upper Silesia or the Klagenfurt, while Norway and Sweden are each invited to appoint one member in Schleswig and the Serb-Croat-Slovene state and Austria are represented in the first and second zones respectively of the Klagenfurt district. Interested states are represented on

[1] Treaty with Germany, Art. 215; Art. 225; Art. 312; Art. 371; Part III, Sec. IV, Annex, Chap. III, par. 36; Art. 364; Treaty with Austria, Art. 161; Art. 171; Art. 275; Arts. 318, 319. It may be anticipated that commissions similar to some of the above will be provided in the other treaties.

[2] Treaty with Germany, Art. 304 and Annex; Treaty with Austria, Art. 256 and Annex. It may be anticipated that similar tribunals will be provided in the other treaties.

[3] Only Great Britain, France, Italy, and Japan of the great powers have been represented on the various commissions to date. The defeat of ratification in the United States Senate has prevented participation by the United States. One of the reservations proposed by the majority party in the Senate would prevent the appointment of representatives by the United States except pursuant to an act of Congress providing for the appointment and defining the appointee's powers and duties. See *Cong. Record*, 66th Cong., 1st sess. (1919), LVIII, 8773, and 2d sess. (1920), LIX, daily number, March 4, 1920, 4147–4149.

the International Boundary Commissions, but three of the
five or five of the seven commissioners, as the case may be,
are appointed in each instance by the great powers. The
great powers control the Governing Commission of the
Saar through their control of the League Council which ap-
points and removes members of the Commission. The
Reparation Commission, as constituted by the Treaty with
Germany, is composed of seven delegates, one appointed by
each of the great powers, one by the Serb-Croat-Slovene
state, and one by Belgium. The working membership, however, is always limited to the delegates of five powers. Those
appointed by the United States, Great Britain, France, and
Italy always participate, while those appointed by the other
three powers participate in turn according to the nature of
the question before the Commission.[1] Under the Treaty
with Austria, the place occupied by the Serb-Croat-Slovene
representative is taken by a delegate appointed for one year
by the representatives of Greece, Poland, Roumania, the
Serb-Croat-Slovene state, and Czecho-Slovakia and chosen
successively from the nationals of each of those states. A
section of the Commission with consultative or delegated
powers only, created to consider special questions raised by
the application of the Austrian Treaty, consists of representatives of four of the great powers and the five states
named above, but it is significant that the great powers
represented are given two votes each.[2] The Inter-Allied
Rhineland Commission is composed of representatives of
the four powers whose armies are in the occupied territory,
namely, the United States, Belgium, the British Empire,
and France.[3] The principal powers also control several of
the less important commissions. In addition to dominating

---

[1] Part VIII, Sec. I, Annex II, par. 2.

[2] *Ibid.*, pars. 2, 3. The great powers will undoubtedly dominate any agencies
created to administer the reparation problem in other states.

[3] Agreement, Art. 2, cited *supra*, p. 352, note 7.

all important institutions of the temporary organization described above, the great powers constitute themselves a directing committee to which are entrusted a host of important functions in connection with the execution of the settlement. The major treaties begin with a distinction set forth in the preamble between the great powers, described as "the Principal Allied and Associated Powers," and the other powers "constituting with the Principal Powers mentioned above the Allied and Associated Powers." [1] Important functions throughout are entrusted either to the Principal Powers or to some institution which they expect to control. So it is that in addition to their control of the Inter-Allied Commissions the Principal Powers as such are in charge of the disarmament of defeated states; [2] in addition to their predominant position on the Boundary Commissions they are recognized in several instances as the supreme authority in control of the delimitation of frontiers; [3] they receive and undertake to dispose of territory renounced by defeated states, [4] as well as other property rights and interests; [5] they undertake to constitute the Free City of Danzig and to negotiate a treaty which will make it for most practical purposes a part of the Polish Republic; [6]

[1] Treaty with Germany; Treaty with Austria. The secondary powers signing these treaties included one African state, Liberia, three Asiatic states, China, the Hedjaz, and Siam, seven European states, Belgium, Greece, Poland, Portugal, Roumania, the Serb-Croat-Slovene state, and Czecho-Slovakia, and eleven Latin American states, Bolivia, Brazil, Cuba, Ecuador, Guatemala, Haiti, Honduras, Nicaragua, Panama, Peru, and Uruguay.

[2] See Treaty with Germany, Arts. 163, 166, 167, 168, 169, 172, 182, 184, 185, 186, 188, 192, 193, 195, 197, 202; Treaty with Austria, Arts. 130, 131, 133, 136, 141, 143, 148.

[3] See Treaty with Germany, Arts. 80, 81, 88, 110; Treaty with Austria, Arts. 29, 59, 89.

[4] See Treaty with Germany, Arts. 99, 110; Treaty with Austria, Art. 91. The great powers will of course undertake most of the mandates over territories renounced by the defeated states.

[5] See Treaty with Germany, Arts. 107, 118, Part VIII, Sec. I, Annex VII, Art. 259; Treaty with Austria, Art. 95, Part VIII, Sec. I, Annex VI, Arts. 210, 300.

[6] See Treaty with Germany, Arts. 100, 102, 104; *supra*, p. 346.

they control the supply of food and raw materials to the defeated states;[1] and they undertake to negotiate treaties with the states of central and southeastern Europe which will ensure the protection of minorities, freedom of transit, and the equitable treatment of foreign commerce.[2]

In the second place, many of the commissions and the Mixed Arbitral Tribunals reach their decisions by majority vote. The need for effective action has resulted in a sweeping modification of the time-honored unanimity rule. Majority decisions are expressly stipulated for the plebiscite Commissions, the Boundary Commissions, the Governing Commission of the Saar, the commissions on the apportionment of insurance reserves, the commission on the repurchase price of the Saar mines, and the Mixed Arbitral Tribunals. The Reparation Commission is bound by the unanimity requirement in deciding six enumerated kinds of questions, but other questions are decided by majority vote. In the special section of this Commission created by the Austrian Treaty majority control is assured to the great powers by giving each of their representatives two votes. In the absence of express provision to the contrary, the chairman of each commission created by the treaties is given a second vote in case of a tie.[3]

In the third place, the institutions of the temporary organization are invested in varying degree with real powers of control. So far from being mere diplomatic bodies, whose decisions are made *ad referendum*, they are real governing institutions within the more or less limited scope of their authority. This is of course conspicuously true in case of a

[1] See Treaty with Germany, Arts. 235, 251; Treaty with Austria, Arts. 181, 200.
[2] See Treaty with Germany, Arts. 86, 93; Treaty with Austria, Arts. 51, 57, 60; Treaty with Poland; Treaty with Roumania; Clemenceau to Paderewski, Paris, June 24, 1919, in *A. J. I. L. Suppl.* (1919), XIII, 416, 417–419. See also Treaty with Germany, Arts. 31, 41, 65, 227; Treaty with Austria, Arts. 83, 380; Treaty with Poland, Art. 21.
[3] Treaty with Germany, Art. 437; Treaty with Austria, Art. 379.

body like the Governing Commission of the Saar Basin. It would seem to be true in some degree at least of such agencies as the Inter-Allied Commissions of Control which represent the governments of the Principal Powers in all that pertains to the disarmament of the defeated states. It is a striking characteristic of other agencies of the temporary régime. The International Commissions in control of plebiscite areas are invested with important powers of government and administration. The International Boundary Commissions are empowered to delimit frontiers on the spot, taking account of local boundaries and economic interests, and it is expressly stipulated that their decisions shall be binding upon the parties concerned. The Reparation Commission is the most powerful of all the instrumentalities established primarily to execute the settlement.[1] It is charged with general supervision and control over an extraordinarily complicated reparation program.[2] The greater number of its functions, of course, are ministerial in nature. It receives all money, goods, and valuable rights which are

---

[1] For an exhaustive analysis of the Commission's functions under the Treaty with Germany, see the author's article in *M. L. R.* (1920), XVIII, 491–496. The Commission is invested with similar functions, *mutatis mutandis*, under the Treaty with Austria.

The German delegation protested vigorously against the powers accorded the Reparation Commission. "The Commission is plainly to have power to administer Germany like the estate of a bankrupt." "It is impossible for any state, especially for a democratic one, to renounce its sovereign rights to the extent demanded." "The Reparation Commission, as is planned at present, would actually be the absolute master of Germany. It would order Germany's economic affairs at home and abroad." "The Commission, which is to have its permanent seat outside Germany, will possess incomparably greater rights in Germany than a German emperor has ever had; under its régime the German people would be for many decades without rights, deprived of all independence and of all initiative in commerce and industry and even in popular education, to a greater extent than ever a nation was in the time of absolutism." German Comments, pp. 14, 66, 108, 110. While the German protest was undoubtedly exaggerated, the allied reply is hardly consistent with the obvious meaning of important treaty provisions. See Allied Reply, p. 50.

[2] "The vast extent and manifold character of the damage caused to the Allied and Associated Powers in consequence of the war has created a reparation problem of extraordinary magnitude and complexity, only to be solved by a continuing body,

required to be paid over or transferred as a part of the reparation program, approves estimates, assesses the value of various kinds of property for credit on the reparation accounts, makes calculations of one sort or another according to principles defined in the treaties, and prescribes the details of a great variety of transactions. In its most important functions, however, the Commission is by no means restricted to ministerial administration. The determination of the total reparation obligation which the defeated states will be expected to assume in each instance may be described more appropriately as a judicial function. The power to hear and decide claims in regard to the physical restoration of invaded areas is of a similar nature. Other important powers are administrative in the sense in which that term is understood in Europe and in which it has more recently come to be understood in America. They involve wide discretion in matters of the greatest moment, including the construction and delivery of merchant shipping, deliveries of coal and other products, the acquisition and surrender of interests in public utilities and concessions abroad, investigations of the resources of defeated states, and the securing and discharging of enormous reparation obligations. The Commission's decisions, made in accordance with the powers conferred upon it, go into effect at once without further ratification or approval. As regards Germany, at least, they are sanctioned by an express provision for the use of military force.[1] The Inter-Allied Rhineland Commission is invested with authority to issue ordinances having the force of law, both for the occupying military

limited in personnel and invested with broad powers to deal with the problem in relation to the general economic situation. The Allied and Associated Powers, recognizing this situation, themselves delegate power and authority to a Reparation Commission." Allied Reply, p. 49.

[1] If the Commission finds at any time that Germany refuses to observe its reparation obligations, parts of the Rhine territory which have been evacuated by forces of the allied and associated powers will be immediately reoccupied. Art. 430.

authorities and the German civil authorities, "so far as may be necessary for securing the maintenance, safety, and requirements of the allied and associated forces," and also to declare a state of siege in all or part of the occupied territory whenever it is deemed necessary.[1] Reference thus far has been made only to the formally constituted commissions. It should also be observed that wherever the great powers have constituted themselves an informal council or committee to execute the settlement there is real power of control coupled with sanctions of the most effective sort.

The temporary régime created to ensure the execution of the Peace of Paris is an experiment in international organization of unusual interest and significance. It is significant as regards the political equality of states chiefly because of its extensive departures from principles which have been considered essential to political equality. A theory which has been thought to require equality of representation, unanimity, and decisions *ad referendum* may hardly be said to have figured largely in a régime in which effective representation is generally limited to the great powers, in which decisions are frequently taken by majority vote, and in which the various agencies are invested with real authority over matters of important international concern.

Probably the most significant feature of the Peace of Paris, so far as the political equality of states is concerned, is its departure from the traditional applications of the principle in the provisions for a permanent organization. This organization consists of the League of Nations and auxiliary institutions. The original membership is planned to include twenty-seven states, four self-governing dominions, and India, all signatories of the Treaty with Germany, and as many of the enumerated non-signatory states as accede without reservation. The former belligerents, Aus-

---

[1] Agreement, Arts. 3, 5, 13, cited *supra*, p. 352, note 7.

tria, Bulgaria, Germany, Hungary, the Russian states, and Turkey, and the former neutrals, Abyssinia, Costa Rica, the Dominican Republic, and Mexico, are included in neither group; but provision is made for the subsequent admission of any state, dominion, or colony which shall give effective guaranties of its intention to observe international obligations and shall accept regulations prescribed by the League in regard to armament.[1] The League's principal instrumentalities are an Assembly, a Council, and a permanent Secretariat. The Assembly is a large body consisting of representatives of all the members.[2] The Council, on the other hand, is a small body made up at the outset of representatives of the five great powers and of four other powers selected by the Assembly.[3] The Secretariat includes a Secretary-General, appointed by the Council with the approval of a majority of the Assembly, and the necessary secretaries and staff.[4] There is also a permanent Labor Organization consisting of a General Conference and an International Labor Office controlled by a Governing body.[5] Each member sends four delegates to the General Conference, two representing the Government, one the employers, and one the workers.[6] The Governing Body in control of the

[1] League Covenant, Art. 1; Annex. The Covenant of the League has been incorporated in each of the peace treaties concluded to date as Part I, Arts. 1–26. The League organization was formally launched at a meeting of the Council at Paris on January 16, 1920. *Current History* (1920), XI, II, 200, 400.

[2] League Covenant, Art. 3. The defeat of ratification in the United States Senate has prevented the representation of the United States on any of the League institutions organized to date. One of the reservations proposed by the majority party in the Senate would prevent the appointment of representatives by the United States except pursuant to an act of Congress providing for the appointment and defining the appointee's powers and duties. See *supra*, p. 353, note 3.

[3] League Covenant, Art. 4. Until the appointment of representatives by the four other powers first selected by the Assembly, Belgium, Brazil, Greece, and Spain are to be represented on the Council.

[4] *Ibid.*, Art 6

[5] Treaty with Germany, Art. 388. The articles providing for the permanent Labor Organization have also been incorporated in each of the peace treaties concluded to date.   [6] *Ibid.*, Art. 389.

Labor Office is composed of twenty-four persons, of whom twelve are selected to represent Governments, six are elected by delegates to the General Conference representing employers, and six by delegates representing workers. Of the twelve selected to represent Governments, eight are nominated by the members which are of the chief industrial importance and four by members selected for the purpose by the Government delegates of the other states at the Conference. Any question as to which are the member states of chief industrial importance is to be decided by the Council of the League.[1] The Labor Office is in charge of a Director who is appointed by the Governing Body and assisted by a staff of his own selection.[2] The League will have no judicial institutions at the outset, but plans for a Permanent Court of International Justice are to be formulated by the Council and submitted to the members for adoption.[3] Of administrative institutions, in addition to those already mentioned, there will be a great variety. One permanent commission will be created to advise the Council in regard to the limitation of armaments and another to receive and examine the reports of mandatories and to advise the Council on matters relating to the observance of mandates.[4] The European Commission of the Danube and the Rhine Central Commission are continued with important changes of representation, and provision is made for several new international commissions to take charge of the administration of other rivers.[5] All the river commissions include representatives of non-riparian states. The proposed Convention relating to International Air Navigation provides for an International Commission for Air Navigation composed of one representative of Great Britain and one of each of the

[1] Treaty with Germany, Art. 393.   [3] League Covenant, Art. 14.
[2] *Ibid.*, Arts. 394, 395.   [4] *Ibid.*, Arts. 9, 22.
[5] Treaty with Germany, Arts. 340, 341, 342, 346, 347, 354, 355; Treaty with Austria, Arts. 301, 302.

British Dominions and of India, two representatives of
each of the other four great powers, and one representative
of each of the other contracting states.[1] Existing international bureaus, so far as the consent of the parties to the
general treaties by which they are established can be obtained, and all international bureaus and commissions
established in the future are to be placed under the direction
of the League.[2]

The covenants of the League of Nations are perhaps of
greater importance than its organization. In Article 10 the
member states "undertake to respect and preserve as against
external aggression the territorial integrity and existing
political independence of all members of the League." In
Article 12 they "agree that if there should arise between
them any dispute likely to lead to a rupture, they will submit the matter either to arbitration or to inquiry by the
Council, and they agree in no case to resort to war until
three months after the award by the arbitrators or the report
by the Council." Measures for fulfilling the obligation imposed by Article 10 are to be recommended by the Council
in each case. More detailed provision is made for the execution of Article 12. The controversies to be settled by arbitration are defined as those which the members "recognize
to be suitable for submission to arbitration and which cannot be satisfactorily settled by diplomacy." This definition
is expressly made to include controversies in regard to the
interpretation of treaties, questions of international law,
questions of material fact, and questions involving the
extent and nature of reparation. The parties to the dispute
may either agree upon a court of arbitration or it may be
stipulated in any convention existing between them. It is
agreed that arbitral awards will be carried out in good faith
and that no state will resort to war against a member which

[1] Art. 35.   [2] League Covenant, Art. 24.

complies with the award. If a member fails to comply, the Council will propose measures for making the award effective.[1] All serious controversies which are not submitted to arbitration must be submitted to an inquiry by the Council. Either party may accomplish this by giving notice to the Secretary-General, whereupon the parties must communicate statements of their case with all relevant facts and papers to the Secretary-General and the Council will attempt to settle the dispute. Failing a settlement, the Council will publish a report of the case with recommendations.[2] If this report is approved by all members of the Council, other than representatives of parties to the controversy, it is agreed that no member shall go to war with the member which complies with the recommendations. Otherwise complete liberty of action is reserved. The Council may refer any dispute to the Assembly, and is obliged to do so if either party requests it within fourteen days after submission.[3]

Sanctions are provided to ensure the observance of the covenants. Resort to war in disregard of the covenants is to be regarded as *ipso facto* an act of war against all other members; and the members undertake to sever trade and financial relations, prohibit all intercourse between their nationals and nationals of the covenant-breaking state, and prevent all financial, commercial, or personal intercourse between nationals of the covenant-breaking state and the

[1] League Covenant, Art. 13.

[2] If the dispute is claimed by one party and is found by the Council to arise out of a matter which by international law is solely within the domestic jurisdiction of that party, the Council will report accordingly and will make no recommendations. *Ibid.*, Art. 15.

[3] In attempting to settle disputes thus referred, the Assembly will be controlled by the same provisions which apply to the Council, except that its report and recommendations, failing a settlement, will become effective if concurred in by the delegates of all members represented on the Council and by a majority of the delegates of other members, exclusive in each case of delegates representing parties to the dispute. *Ibid.*, Art. 15.

nationals of any other state, whether a member of the League or not. The use of joint forces to protect the covenants of the League is also contemplated, although not expressly made obligatory, and free passage is promised for such forces. The members agree to a fair apportionment of the burdens incident to all coercive measures. Covenant-breaking states may be expelled from the League by a unanimous vote of the Council, disregarding, of course, any vote cast by a representative of the expelled state.[1] Moreover, the above sanctions may be applied to states which are not members of the League. In the event of a dispute between a member and a non-member, or between non-members, the parties may be invited to accept the obligations of membership for the purpose of such dispute upon conditions prescribed by the Council. If a state refuses the invitation and resorts to war against a member, all the sanctions outlined above are to be invoked against the aggressor. If both parties to a dispute refuse such an invitation, the Council may take such measures and make such recommendations as will prevent hostilities and bring about a settlement of the controversy.[2]

Covenants and sanctions are made more efficacious by an agreement upon certain new principles. In the first place, it is agreed that any war or threat of war, whether immediately affecting members or not, is to be regarded as a matter of concern to the whole League; and it is declared to be the friendly right of each member to bring to the attention of the Assembly or the Council any circumstance whatever affecting international relations which threatens to disturb

[1] League Covenant, Art. 16. "Armed force is in the background of this program, but it *is* in the background, and if the moral force of the world will not suffice, the physical force of the world shall. But that is the last resort, because this is intended as a constitution of peace, not as a league of war." Address of President Wilson on presenting the draft of the Covenant to the third plenary session, February 14, 1919, in *A. J. I. L.* (1919), XIII, 570, 573.

[2] League Covenant, Art. 17.

international peace.[1] The second principle is publicity for international transactions in order that public opinion may have an opportunity to operate. More or less of publicity will always accompany the settlement of controversies by arbitration. In case of controversies referred to the Council for inquiry, the publication of everything submitted may be ordered forthwith. If the dispute is settled the terms and appropriate explanations are to be made public, and if it is not settled the report and recommendations are made public. Moreover, any member represented on the Council may publish a statement of the facts and of its own conclusions.[2] All treaties or international engagements entered into hereafter by any member of the League are to be registered with the Secretariat and published by it as soon as possible. They are to become binding only when registered.[3] The third principle establishes a right to have decisive individual action by any state delayed until public opinion has had an opportunity to find expression in measures which may prevent war. The principle is formulated in the covenant of Article 12 that members will in no case resort to war until three months after an award by arbitrators or a report by the Council.

It is a conservative prediction that if the League of Nations functions with any degree of success the traditional conception of political equality among states will become obsolete. The League denies the political equality of states at the outset in the provision which is made for the admission of members. The first group of original members includes twenty-seven states, four self-governing dominions, and India, and the second group includes thirteen states which are invited to accede. It has already been pointed out that a number of states are included in neither group. Although the League's pacific machinery is intended to have the

---

[1] League Covenant, Art. 11.   [2] *Ibid.*, Art. 15.   [3] *Ibid.*, Art. 18.

most important effects upon non-member states, such states may be admitted to membership only by a two-thirds vote of the Assembly after giving guaranties and after accepting regulations in regard to armament.[1] There are also important inequalities of representation in the League and in its various instrumentalities. The list of original members includes the British Empire, four British self-governing dominions, and India. Article 1 provides that "any fully self-governing State, Dominion or Colony" may be admitted to membership by the Assembly. The representation of dominions or colonies is calculated to give the great colonial powers a larger representation in League institutions than is accorded to other states. The effect is manifest in such an institution as the Assembly where all *members* have equal representation. Representation on the Council, which is in all respects the League's most important instrumentality, is limited to the five great powers and to four other powers designated by the Assembly.[2] Additional members may be given representation by the Council with the Assembly's approval, but in view of international experience it is safe to predict that effective control will always be retained by the more powerful states. It is stipulated, following the precedent established at Aix-la-Chapelle, that any member not represented on the Council shall be in-

[1] See *supra*, pp. 346, 347. "The whole agreement is at present necessarily tentative. It cannot really be a League of Peace in operation for a number of years to come. It is now and in the immediate future must be rather an alliance of approximately one-half of the active world against or for the control of the other half." Root to Hays, regarding the League Covenant, in *A. J. I. L.* (1919), XIII, 580, 594.

[2] "This covenant of the league of nations is an alliance and not a league, as is amply shown by the provisions of the treaty with Germany which vests all essential power in five great nations. Those same nations, the principal allied and associated powers, also dominate the league through the council." Majority Report from the Committee on Foreign Relations of the United States Senate, September 10, 1919, p. 7. "It is regrettable that there are no technical authorities or impartial tribunals to offset the select committee controlled by the Great Powers, which may submit the whole civilized world to its control at the expense of the independence and equality of rights of the smaller states." German Comments, p. 17.

vited to send a delegate when matters specially affecting the interests of that member are under consideration. An apportionment of representation favorable to the more powerful states appears in other League institutions. Thus, of the twelve Government delegates on the Governing Body of the International Labor Office, it has been pointed out that eight are nominated by the member states which are of the chief industrial importance and that it is left to the Council of the League to decide which member states belong in this category. The more powerful states also receive most of the non-riparian representation on the international river commissions. As a provisional measure, it is said, Great Britain, France, and Italy, with Roumania, are the only states to be represented on the European Commission of the Danube. The same non-riparian states will be represented on the new International Commission in control of the Danube above the point where the competence of the European Commission ceases. Great Britain and Italy each have two representatives on the Rhine Central Commission; Great Britain, France, Italy, and Belgium each have a representative on the Elbe Commission, and Great Britain, France, Denmark, and Sweden each have a representative on the Oder Commission.[1] The proposed International Commission for

[1] The central powers protested against the apportionment of representation on the commissions. "The German river system, with all its rivers and canals, is to be administered by international commissions, in which Germany in no case is to have a majority." German Comments, pp. 83, 15. The reasons for non-riparian representation were set forth in the Allied Reply. "Delegates from non-riparian states are included in the River Commissions as well as representatives of the riparian states, in the first place as representing the general interest in free circulation on the rivers regarded as transit routes; and, secondly, so that within the River Commissions themselves they may act as a check on the strongest riparian state abusing her preponderating influence to the detriment of the others." Allied Reply, p. 85. "The provision for the presence of representatives of important non-riparian states on the commissions is security that the commissions will consider the interests of all." Letter transmitting the Allied Reply, in *A. J. I. L.* (1919), XIII, 550. See also Letter transmitting the Treaty with Austria, p. 42.

"The objectionable feature of the Commissions lies in their membership. In

Air Navigation includes one representative of Great Britain and one of each of the British Dominions and of India, two representatives of each of the other four great powers, and one representative of each of the other contracting states.

Inequalities in voting power and majority decisions are no less significant than inequalities of representation. Inequality of representation usually involves inequality of voting power. The Covenant of the League provides that each member shall have one vote in the Assembly. This means that an empire with colonial representation wields several times the voting power of a state without multiple representation.[1] Voting power in such institutions as the

each case the voting is so weighted as to place Germany in a clear minority. On the Elbe Commission Germany has four votes out of ten; on the Oder Commission three out of nine; on the Rhine Commission four out of nineteen; on the Danube Commission, which is not yet definitely constituted, she will be apparently in a small minority. On the government of all these rivers France and Great Britain are represented; and on the Elbe for some undiscoverable reason there are also representatives of Italy and Belgium. Thus the great waterways of Germany are handed over to foreign bodies with the widest powers; and much of the local and domestic business of Hamburg, Magdeburg, Dresden, Stettin, Frankfurt, Breslau, and Ulm will be subject to a foreign jurisdiction. It is almost as though the powers of Continental Europe were to be placed in a majority on the Thames Conservancy or the port of London." Keynes, *Economic Consequences of the Peace*, p. 110.

[1] This feature of the Covenant has been vigorously assailed in the United States Senate. "Great Britain now has under the name of the British Empire one vote in the council of the league. She has four additional votes in the assembly of the league for her self-governing dominions and colonies, which are most properly members of the league and signatories to the treaty. She also has the vote of India, which is neither a self-governing dominion nor a colony but merely a part of the Empire and which apparently was simply put in as a signatory and member of the league by the peace conference because Great Britain desired it. Great Britain also will control the votes of the Kingdom of Hedjaz and of Persia. With these last two of course we have nothing to do. But if Great Britain has six votes in the league assembly no reason has occurred to the committee and no argument had been made to show why the United States should not have an equal number. If other countries like the present arrangement, that is not our affair; but the committee failed to see why the United States should have but one vote in the assembly of the league when the British Empire has six." Majority Report of the Committee on Foreign Relations, p. 4. The Senate has of course debated the question at great length. For example, see *Cong. Record*, 66th Cong., 1st sess. (1919), LVIII, 5971–5983, 6326–6331, 6439–6445, 7355–7373, 7431–7439, 7488–7504, 7548–7559, and 2d sess. (1920),

League Council, the Governing Body of the Labor Office, and the river commissions is of course restricted to the states which are represented. In the proposed Commission for Air Navigation an apportionment of votes is adopted which assures control to the great powers. For the purpose of voting, Great Britain, the British Dominions, and India count as one state, but each of the five great powers is given "the least whole number of votes which, when multiplied by five, will give a product exceeding by at least one vote the total number of votes of all the other contracting States." The other contracting states have one vote each.[1] In a number of instances majority decisions have been substituted for the unanimity requirement. Article 5 lays down the rule that "except where otherwise expressly provided . . . decisions at any meeting of the Assembly or of the Council shall require the agreement of all the Members of the League represented at the meeting." It is otherwise expressly provided for a limited number of decisions of considerable consequence. The same Article provides that all matters of procedure may be decided by majority vote in the Assembly and in the Council. The Assembly approves the nomination of additional members to be represented on

LIX, daily numbers, March 8, 1920, 4306–4314, March 9, 1920, 4357–4370. The point is covered by one of the proposed reservations, recently amended to read as follows: "Until part 1, being the covenant of the League of Nations, shall be so amended as to provide that the United States shall be entitled to cast a number of votes equal to that which any member of the league and its self-governing dominions, colonies, or parts of empire, in the aggregate shall be entitled to cast, the United States assumes no obligation to be bound, except in cases where Congress has previously given its consent, by any election, decision, report, or finding of the council or assembly in which any member of the league and its self-governing dominions, colonies, or parts of empire, in the aggregate have cast more than one vote. The United States assumes no obligation to be bound by any decision, report, or finding of the council or assembly arising out of any dispute between the United States and any member of the league if such member, or any self-governing dominion, colony, empire, or part of empire united with it politically has voted." *Ibid.*, 4370. Cf. Viscount Grey's Letter to The London Times, printed in *Current History* (1920), XI, II, 399.

[1] Air Convention, Art. 35.

the Council and the appointment of the Secretary-General by a majority vote. It admits new members to the League by two-thirds majority. Its report on disputes referred to it by the Council may operate to prevent war if concurred in by the delegates of members represented on the Council and by a majority of the other delegates, exclusive in each case of representatives of parties to the dispute.[1] In the Council a number of important matters connected with the execution of the settlement may be decided by majority vote. The Council acts by majority, for example, in all matters pertaining to the Saar Basin, in extending the period during which certain articles in regard to the treatment of nationals of the allied and associated powers are to remain in force, in ordering any investigation in Germany or Austria while the treaties remain in force, in assenting to the modification of treaty stipulations for the protection of minorities, in approving the proposed treaties for assistance to France as engagements consistent with the League Covenant, and in deciding that the treaties last mentioned may be safely terminated.[2] In contrast with the Assembly and the Council, the General Conference of the Labor Organization, except where otherwise expressly provided, decides all questions "by a simple majority of the votes cast by the Delegates present." In excluding delegates, deciding to meet elsewhere than at the seat of the League, including items in its agenda over the objection of a member's Government, adopting recommendations or draft conventions, and initiating amendments to the labor clauses of the treaties, the

[1] See League Covenant, Arts. 4, 6, 1, 15.

[2] See Treaty with Germany, Part III, Sec. IV, Annex, Chap. III, par. 40; Art. 280; Art. 213; Treaty with Austria, Art. 232; Art. 159; Art. 69; Treaty with Poland, Art. 12; Treaty with Roumania, Art. 12; Treaty between the United States and France, Art. 3, and Treaty between Great Britain and France, Art. 3, in Sen. Doc., No. 63, 66th Cong., 1st sess. (1919). It may be anticipated that the Council will be authorized to act by majority in deciding a limited number of questions involved in the execution of the other treaties.

Conference's decisions are made by two-thirds vote of the delegates present.[1] There are no decisions for which the unanimity requirement is stipulated. As regards the river commissions, it has already been pointed out that the European Commission of the Danube decides administrative questions and fixes tolls by majority vote.[2] It is expressly provided that the new Commission in control of the upper Danube shall take its decisions by majority.[3] Similar stipulations will no doubt be incorporated in the new agreements which are to define the powers of the other commissions.[4] The proposed Commission for Air Navigation may admit states which participated in the recent war and which are not members of the League to adhere to the Air Convention after January 1, 1923, by a three-fourths vote. It may amend the technical annexes by three-fourths vote, propose amendments to the Convention by two-thirds vote, and decide disputes in regard to the technical regulations by simple majority. The point is not covered by an express provision, but it would seem that where the necessary majority has not been indicated a simple majority vote would be enough.[5]

Inequalities of representation and voting strength are peculiarly significant in institutions which have real power over matters of international concern. It is noteworthy that League institutions have a little real power. Their functions may be said in general to be concerned with two problems: their immediate business is to ensure the execution of the new settlement; their ultimate function is to

[1] Treaty with Germany, Arts. 403, 389, 391, 402, 405, 422. Although the point is not covered by express provision, it seems probable that the Governing Body of the Labor Office will act by majority vote in the absence of provision to the contrary. See *ibid.*, Art. 412.

[2] See *supra*, pp. 316–317.

[3] Treaty with Austria, Art. 303.

[4] Treaty with Germany, Arts. 343, 344, 348, 354.

[5] Air Convention, Art. 35.

promote international coöperation and preserve peace. Certain League institutions have been equipped for the execution of the settlement with important special powers. The League itself becomes trustee for the Saar Basin, undertakes to protect Danzig and guarantee its constitution, and exercises an ill-defined supervision over the mandatories to which former colonies and territories of the central powers are entrusted.[1] Further responsibilities may be assumed under treaties still pending. The Council of the League makes several appointments to positions in the temporary régime, including three members of the Saar Boundary Commission, the Governing Commission of the Saar, one of the three experts on the price of the Saar mines, the High Commissioner of Danzig, the president of the Mixed Arbitral Tribunal in each instance in which the parties fail to agree on a candidate, and a number of special arbitrators.[2] Several important decisions in connection with the execution of the treaties are left to the League. The League decides, for example, on the effect to be given the plebiscite in Eupen and Malmédy; it decides on the permanent disposition to be made of the Saar Basin after the plebiscite; it decides disputes in regard to the revival of treaties; and it must approve any general conventions relating to the international régime of transit, waterways, ports, or railways.[3] The Council of the League fixes the conditions, methods, and date of voting in the Saar plebiscite; it settles the arrangements in regard to amounts of coal, duration of contracts, and prices

[1] Treaty with Germany, Arts. 49, 102, 103; League Covenant, Art. 22.

[2] Treaty with Germany, Art. 48; Part III, Sec. IV, Annex, Chap. II, pars. 16, 17, 18, Chap. III, par. 36; Arts. 103, 304; Treaty with Austria, Arts. 256, 309, 310, 320, 321, 327.

[3] Treaty with Germany, Art. 34; Part III, Sec. IV, Annex, Chap. III, par. 35; Arts. 289, 338, 379; Treaty with Austria, Arts. 241, 299, 331. After the Polish mandate has been in effect for twenty-five years the League will decide on the disposition to be made of Eastern Galicia. *Current History* (1919), XI, I, 400. Other decisions may be entrusted to the League as the settlement is completed.

in the event that the Saar mines are eventually restored to
Germany and France acquires in consequence the stipulated
right to purchase coal for industrial and domestic needs; it
may assent to the alienation of Austrian independence; it
may extend the period of certain treaty obligations; it must
decide finally the conditions of transfer of social and state
insurance reserves unless these conditions are settled by
special conventions between the parties; it may order any
investigations of the central powers which it considers necessary; it must approve the proposed treaties between the
United States and France and between Great Britain and
France for assistance to the latter in case of unprovoked
aggression by Germany and it is to decide when these treaties
may be safely terminated; and it may take measures to ensure the observance of treaty provisions for the protection of
minorities and may also assent to the modification of such
provisions.[1] Finally, the League through one or more of its
institutions is entrusted with the execution of several important transactions relating to the settlement. After the
plebiscite in the Saar and the League's decision as to the
future of the region, the Council will make all necessary
provisions for the establishment of the permanent régime.[2]
If Germany and Poland fail to agree, the terms of conventions between them relative to railroad, telegraphic, and
telephonic facilities will be settled by the Council.[3] After
Germany has been admitted to the League, the armament
establishment fixed in the Treaty may be modified by the
Council.[4] The League will provide a river commission for
the Niemen on request from any riparian state.[5] Several of

[1] Treaty with Germany, Part III, Sec. IV, Annex, Chap. III, pars. 34, 37; Arts.
80, 280, 378, 312, 213; Treaty with Austria, Arts. 88, 232, 330, 275, 159, 69; Treaty
between United States and France, Art. 3, and between Great Britain and France,
Art. 3; Treaty with Poland, Art. 12; Treaty with Roumania, Art. 12.
[2] Treaty with Germany, Part III, Sec. IV, Annex, Chap. III, par. 39.
[3] *Ibid.*, Art. 98.
[4] *Ibid.*, Art. 164.   [5] *Ibid.*, Art. 342.

the articles relating to commerce and transport may be revised by the Council after a few years from the date at which
ratification brings them into effect.[1]

In so far as League institutions are equipped to ensure
permanent peace, their most important powers, with a few
exceptions, are of an advisory or ministerial character. The
Assembly has almost no power at all. In presenting the
draft of the Covenant to the third plenary session, President
Wilson remarked that the Assembly had been given "unlimited rights of discussion." [2] It may discuss "any matter
within the sphere of action of the League or affecting the
peace of the world," but it has few powers of any real importance. Probably the most important are the power to
admit new members to the League by two-thirds vote, to
select the states which are to be represented on the Council
with the five great powers, and to settle disputes referred to
it by the Council.[3] The powers of the Council are defined in
the same generous terms and with somewhat greater effect.
The Council is the League's most powerful institution. The
most important of its functions are advisory; for example,
the duty to formulate and submit plans for a permanent
court, to formulate plans for the reduction of armaments, to
endeavor to settle disputes referred to it for inquiry and,
failing a settlement, to make a report with recommendations,
to advise as to the means of fulfilling the obligation imposed
by Article 10, and to recommend the forces to be contributed
by members in order to protect the covenants of the League.[4]
In a few instances it has real power to control. It is authorized, for illustration, to change the seat of the League
at any time, to define the authority of mandatories in the
absence of previous agreement among League members, to

---

[1] Treaty with Germany, Art. 378; Treaty with Austria, Art. 330.
[2] *A. J. I. L.* (1919), XIII, 572.
[3] League Covenant, Arts. 1, 3, 4, 15.
[4] *Ibid.*, Arts. 14, 8, 15, 10, 16.

prescribe the conditions and modifications under which the covenant may be applied to disputes in which states outside the League are parties, and to expel a covenant-breaking state from the League.[1] It may increase its own membership with the approval of the Assembly.[2] In the event of war or threat of war, it may join the Assembly in taking "any action that may be deemed wise and effectual to safeguard the peace of nations."[3] The most important functions of the Labor Organization are advisory or ministerial in character.[4] The river commissions will exercise an extensive administrative control over the navigation of rivers,[5] and if the proposed Commission for Air Navigation is established it will probably enjoy a somewhat less extensive administrative control over the navigation of the air.[6]

The expenses of the League Secretariat are apportioned among member states according to the familiar unit and

---

[1] League Covenant, Arts. 7, 22, 17, 16.　　　[2] *Ibid.*, Art. 4.

[3] *Ibid.*, Art. 11. This clause is of course much less significant than it appears to be because neither the Council nor the Assembly has power to do anything more in such an event than to recommend and advise.

[4] Treaty with Germany, Arts. 400 ff. The General Conference of the Labor Organization discusses labor questions of international importance and submits proposals to the member states in the form of recommendations or of draft conventions. It also initiates amendments to the labor clauses of the treaties. The Governing Body of the Labor Office prescribes the form and content of annual reports of members, prepares the agenda for meetings of the Conference, controls the preliminary procedure when controversies arise in regard to the observance of labor conventions, and exercises a general supervision over the administration of the Labor Office. The principal business of the Labor Office is to collect and distribute information.

[5] Treaty with Germany, Arts. 346, 354, 348, 343, 344; Treaty with Austria, Arts. 301, 303. See Sayre, *Experiments in International Administration*, pp. 38–47, 131–141.

[6] The Commission is authorized to determine its own procedure (Art. 35), to exercise a variety of ministerial or administrative functions (Arts. 9, 15, 17, 28, 29, 35, Annex H, 3), to settle disputes relating to the technical regulations (Art. 38), to fix regulations for the issuance of certificates and licenses (Art. 13, Annex B, Annex E), to regulate the methods of employing wireless on aircraft of a prescribed capacity engaged in public transport and extend the obligation to carry wireless to other classes of aircraft (Art. 14), to amend the technical annexes, and to initiate modifications of the Convention (Art. 35).

voluntary classification system in force for the International Bureau of the Universal Postal Union.[1] Included among these expenses are the sums paid out by the Secretary-General for the support of the Labor Organization.[2] The proposed Commission for Air Navigation will be supported by the contracting states in proportion to the number of votes at their disposal.[3]

Whatever its immediate future may be, the League of Nations must be regarded as a remarkable attempt to provide the international community with a permanent organization. The precedents which it establishes are noteworthy. Inequalities resulting from the exclusion of certain states may be explained as temporary incidents which will disappear when the world is eventually restored to a normal peace basis. On the other hand, inequalities in the apportionment of representation, voting strength, and contributions are intended to be permanent. They indicate a deeply rooted conviction that the world cannot be organized on the basis of political equality as political equality has been traditionally understood. It is especially noteworthy that the institutions which have been constituted with the least regard for traditional conceptions of equality are the institutions which have been invested with the greatest powers both in connection with the execution of the settlement and with the plan for securing peace.

SUMMARY

It is impossible at this date to say how much of the settlement consummated at Paris will prove relatively permanent and how much will be amended in the readjustments which

---

[1] League Covenant, Art. 6. The scheme for determining contributions in support of the Postal Union Bureau divides the member states into seven classes. States in the first class contribute twenty-five times as much as states in the seventh class. See Hertslet, *Commercial Treaties*, XXV, 492.

[2] Treaty with Germany, Art. 399.   [3] Air Convention, Art. 35.

appear to be imminent. Perhaps it is not important to know.
The terms are not significant because of their content so
much as they are for the principles applied and the tendencies manifested. These principles and tendencies are not
likely to be much amended. In general, as regards limitations
upon the legal capacity of states, the Peace of Paris presents
a logical application of familiar principles. Certain types of
limitation are more conspicuous than others. The problem
of the inland state receives more attention than ever before.
Financial supervision is uniquely illustrated in the reparation program. Stipulations for disarmament, the international control of waterways, and the protection of minorities
afford interesting examples of limitations of the nature of
servitudes. A few international persons of limited capacity
are created. The legal nature of these and other limitations
is definitively established in so far as they are now sanctioned by the collective approval of the League of Nations.
If the League functions with any degree of success, an important step will have been taken in the direction of substituting orderly processes for self-help and the most serious
limitation upon the legal equality of states will have been
substantially mitigated.

The outstanding feature of the Peace of Paris is its tendency to limit the political equality of states. This is quite in
accord with earlier precedents but is more strikingly manifested in the new settlement than ever before. Attention
has been directed to limitations upon political equality in
the Peace Conference itself, in the temporary régime created
to ensure the execution of the settlement, and in the permanent organization established to execute the settlement
and preserve peace. In the Conference itself small states
were invited to participate and meetings were actually
held; but only the five great powers were permitted to be
represented at all sessions and these powers dominated the

Conference organization and settled the peace terms. In the temporary régime representation was limited to a few states and for most practical purposes to the five great powers; the principle of majority decisions was extensively substituted for the unanimity requirement; and the commissions were invested in varying degree with real powers of control. Similar limitations are even more significant in the League organization which is intended to be permanent. Inequalities of representation and voting strength, majority decisions in a few noteworthy instances, and a limited amount of real authority over matters of international concern are features of the permanent organization which cannot be reconciled with traditional notions of political equality. If this most recent adventure in international organization is an indication of the probable course of future development, as there is reason to believe, the traditional idea of political equality will have to be regarded as an obsolete conception in theory as well as in fact.

BIBLIOGRAPHY

BIBLIOGRAPHY

TREATIES, CONVENTIONS, PROTOCOLS, STATE PAPERS, ARBITRATION PROCEEDINGS, CONSTITUTIONS AND OTHER DOCUMENTS

Albin, Pierre, *Les grands traités politiques; recueil des principaux textes diplomatiques depuis 1815 jusqu'à nos jours, avec des commentaires et des notes*, Paris, 1911.

Annuaire de la vie internationale, 1908–09, 1910–11, 2ᵉ sér., Brussels, 1909–12. 2 vols. (Cited *La vie int.*)

Berlin, Treaty of, 1878, A.J.I.L. Suppl. (1908), II, 401–424.

British and Foreign State Papers, 1812 and later years, London, 1841 et seq. 107 vols. to 1915. (Cited *B.F.S.P.*)

Bulgaria, Constitution of 1879, as amended in 1893 and 1911, *B.F.S.P.*, CVII, 615.

China, Amended Provisional Constitution, promulgated May 1, 1914, Peking, 1914.

Clercq, A. J. H. de, and Clercq, J. de, *Recueil des traités de la France publié sous les auspices du Ministère des affaires étrangères*, Paris, 1864 et seq. 20 vols.

Dodd, W. F., *Modern Constitutions*, Chicago, 1909. 2 vols.

Dominican Republic, Constitution of 1908, *B.F.S.P.*, CI, 975.

Dumont, Jean, *Corps universel diplomatique du droit des gens; etc.*, Amsterdam, 1726–31. 8 vols. (Cited Dumont.)

Foreign Relations of the United States, Washington, 1870 et seq. (Cited *U. S. For. Rel.*)

Garden, Guillaume de, *Histoire générale des traités de paix et autres transactions principales entre toutes les puissances de l'Europe depuis la paix de Westphalie*, Paris, 1848–87. 15 vols.

Greece, Constitution of 1864, *B.F.S.P.*, LVI, 572.

Hertslet, Edward, *Hertslet's China Treaties*, 3d ed., London, 1908. 2 vols.

Hertslet, Edward, *The Map of Africa by Treaty*, 3d ed., London, 1909. 3 vols.

Hertslet, Edward, *The Map of Europe by Treaty*, London, 1875–91. 4 vols. (Cited Hertslet.)

Hertslet, Lewis, *A Complete Collection of the Treaties and Conventions, and Reciprocal Regulations, at Present Subsisting between Great Britain and Foreign Powers, and of the Laws, Decrees, and Orders in Council, Concerning the Same; so far as They Relate to Commerce and Navigation; etc.*, compiled and edited by Lewis Hertslet and others, London, 1840–1913. 26 vols. (Cited Hertslet, *Commercial Treaties*.)

382   BIBLIOGRAPHY

Howell, T. B., *A Complete Collection of State Trials*, etc., London, 1816–28. 34 vols.

International American Conference, 1889, Washington, 1890. 4 vols. (Cited *Int. Am. Confer.*)

Koch, C. G., et Schoell, F., *Histoire abrégée des traités de paix, entre les puissances de l'Europe, depuis la paix de Westphalie*, Paris, 1817–18. 15 vols. (Cited Koch et Schoell.)

Luxemburg, Constitution of 1868, B.F.S.P., LVIII, 249.

Martens, G. F. von, *Recueil des principaux traités*, etc., ed. by G. F. von Martens and others, Göttingen and Leipzig, 1817 *et seq.* (Cited Martens, *Recueil;* Martens, *Nouveau recueil;* Martens, *Nouveau recueil général.*) This series, with changing titles and editors, is the principal repository of treaties and other international documents from 1761 to date.

Mexico, Constitution of 1917, transl. by H. N. Branch, Supplement to *Annals of the American Academy of Political and Social Science*, May, 1917, Philadelphia, 1917.

Montenegro, Constitution of 1905, B.F.S.P., XCVIII, 419.

Moore, J. B., *A Digest of International Law*, Washington, 1906. 8 vols.

Moore, J. B., *History and Digest of the International Arbitrations to Which the United States Has Been a Party*, Washington, 1898. 6 vols.

Nicaragua, Constitution of 1911, B.F.S.P., CVII, 1038.

North Atlantic Coast Fisheries Arbitration, Proceedings Before the Permanent Court of Arbitration at The Hague, 1910, Sen. Doc. No. 870, 61st Cong., 3d sess., Washington, 1912–13. 12 vols. (Cited *N.A.C.F. Proceedings.*)

Pan-American Scientific Congress, Proceedings of the Second, 1915–16, Sec. VI, International Law, Public Law, and Jurisprudence, Washington, 1917.

Persia, Constitutional Laws of 1906–1907, B.F.S.P., CI, 527.

Portugal, Constitution of 1911, B.F.S.P., CV, 766.

Ribier, Gabriel de, *Répertoire*, etc., Paris, 1895–99. 2 vols. A continuation of Tétot, *Répertoire*, etc.

Rodriguez, J. I., *American Constitutions*, Washington, 1906–07. 2 vols.

Roumania, Constitution of 1866, with amendments of 1879 and 1884, B.F.S.P. LVII, 263; LXXI, 1176; LXXV, 1105.

Rousset de Missy, Jean, *Recueil historique d'actes, négociations, mémoires et traitez depuis la paix d'Utrecht jusqu'à présent*, The Hague, 1728–55. 21 vols.

Servia, Constitution of 1889, B.F.S.P., LXXXI, 508.

Strupp, Karl, *Urkunden zur Geschichte des Völkerrechts*, Gotha, 1911–12. 3 vols.

Sturdza, D. A., *Recueil des documents relatifs à la liberté de navigation du Danube*, Berlin, 1904.

Tétot, *Répertoire des traités de paix, de commerce, d'alliance, etc., conventions et autres actes conclus entre toutes les puissances du globe, principalement depuis la paix de Westphalie jusqu'à nos jours*, Paris, 1866–70. 2 vols.

The Hague, The First International Peace Conference at: *La Conférence Internationale de la Paix, 1899*, The Hague, 1899. (Cited *La Confér. Int.*)

The Hague, The Second International Peace Conference at: *La Deuxième Conférence Internationale de la Paix, 1907*, The Hague, 1907. 3 vols. (Cited *La Deux. Confér.*)

Treaties, Conventions, International Acts, Protocols and Agreements Between the United States of America and Other Powers, 1776–1909, compiled by W. M. Malloy, Washington, 1910. With a supplement compiled by Garfield Charles, Washington, 1913. 3 vols. (Cited Malloy, *Treaties.*)

Turkey, Constitution of 1909, B.F.S.P., CII, 819.

Vast, Henri, *Les grands traités du règne de Louis XIV*, Paris, 1893–99. 3 vols. (Cited Vast.)

Venezuela, Constitution of 1909, B.F.S.P., CV, 886.

Venezuelan Arbitration Before The Hague Tribunal, 1903, Sen. Doc. No. 119, 58th Cong., 3d sess., Washington, 1905. (Cited *Venez. Arbit.*)

CASES CITED

Abd-ul-Messih *v.* Farra, (1888) Great Britain, the Judicial Committee of the Privy Council, reported in Law Reports, 1888, 13 Appeal Cases 431.

Aix-la-Chapelle-Maastricht Railroad Company *v.* Thewis and the Royal Dutch Government, (1914) Germany, the Supreme Court of Cologne, VII Civil Division, reported in *A.J.I.L.* (1914), VIII, 907–913.

Brazilian Coffee Case, United States *v.* Sielcken, (1912) United States, the United States District Court for the southern district of New York. Extracts and comment in *A.J.I.L.* (1912), VI, 702–706; Stowell and Munro, *International Cases*, I, 159.

Casdagli *v.* Casdagli, (1917) Great Britain, the Probate, Divorce and Admiralty Division of the High Court of Justice and the Court of Appeal, reported in 87 Law Journal Reports, new series, Probate, Divorce and Admiralty Division 73; (1918) Great Britain, the House of Lords, reported in 88 Law Journal Reports, new series, Probate, Divorce and Admiralty Division 49.

Costa Rica *v.* Nicaragua, (1916) Central America, the Central American Court of Justice, reported in *A.J.I.L.* (1917), XI, 181–229.

Dainese *v.* United States, (1879) United States, the United States Court of Claims, reported in 15 Court of Claims Reports 64.

De Haber *v.* Queen of Portugal, (1851) Great Britain, the Court of Queen's Bench, reported in 20 Law Journal Reports, new series, Common Law 488.

Imperial Japanese Government *v.* Peninsular & Oriental Steam Navigation Company, (1895) Great Britain, the Judicial Committee of the Privy Council, reported in Law Reports, 1895, 20 Appeal Cases 644.

Le Louis, (1817) Great Britain, the High Court of Admiralty, reported in 2 Dodson's Admiralty Reports 210.

Mighell *v.* Sultan of Johore, (1893) Great Britain, the Court of Appeal, reported in Law Reports, 1894, 1 Queen's Bench Division 149.

Musgrove *v.* Chun Teeong Toy, (1891) Great Britain, the Judicial Committee of the Privy Council, reported in Law Reports, 1891, 16 Appeal Cases 272.

Papayanni *v.* The Russian Steam Navigation and Trading Company, (1863) Great Britain, the Judicial Committee of the Privy Council, reported in 2 Moore's Privy Council Cases, new series, 161.

Pollard *v.* Bell, (1800) Great Britain, the Court of King's Bench, reported in 8 Term Reports 434.

Prins Frederik, (1820) Great Britain, the High Court of Admiralty, reported in 2 Dodson's Admiralty Reports 451.

Salvador *v.* Nicaragua, (1917) Central America, the Central American Court of Justice, reported in *A.J.I.L.* (1917), XI, 674–730.

Secretary of State for Foreign Affairs *v.* Charlesworth, Pilling and Company, (1901) Great Britain, the Judicial Committee of the Privy Council, reported in 70 Law Journal Reports, new series, Privy Council Cases 25.

The Antelope, (1825) United States, the Supreme Court of the United States, reported in 10 Wheaton's Reports 66.

The Charkieh, (1873) Great Britain, the High Court of Admiralty, reported in Law Reports, 1872-75, 4 Admiralty and Ecclesiastical Reports 59.

The Derfflinger, No. 1, (1915) Great Britain, the British Prize Court for Egypt, reported in 1 British and Colonial Prize Cases 386.

The Duke of Brunswick *v.* The King of Hanover, (1844) Great Britain, the Court of Chancery, reported in 13 Law Journal Reports, new series, Chancery 107.

The Fenix, (1914) Germany, the Imperial Supreme Prize Court in Berlin, reported in *A.J.I.L.* (1916), X, 909–915.

The Helena, (1801) Great Britain, the High Court of Admiralty, reported in 4 C. Robinson's Admiralty Reports 3.

The Hurtige Hane, (1801) Great Britain, the High Court of Admiralty, reported in 3 C. Robinson's Admiralty Reports 324.

The Indian Chief, (1800) Great Britain, the High Court of Admiralty, reported in 3 C. Robinson's Admiralty Reports 12.

The Ionian Ships, (1855) Great Britain, the Admiralty Prize Court, reported in 2 Spink's Ecclesiastical and Admiralty Reports 212.

The King *v.* The Earl of Crewe, (1910) Great Britain, the Court of Appeal, reported in Law Reports, 1910, 2 King's Bench Division 576.

The Lützow: The Koerber, (1915) Great Britain, the British Prize Court for Egypt, reported in 1 British and Colonial Prize Cases 528.

The Madonna Del Burso, (1802) Great Britain, the High Court of Admiralty, reported in 4 C. Robinson's Admiralty Reports 169.

The Marianna Flora, (1826) United States, the Supreme Court of the United States, reported in 11 Wheaton's Reports 1.

The Möwe, (1914) Great Britain, the Probate, Divorce and Admiralty Division of the High Court of Justice, reported in Law Reports, 1915, Probate Division 1.

The Parlement Belge, (1880) Great Britain, the Court of Appeal, reported in Law Reports, 1879–80, 5 Probate Division 197.

The Schooner Exchange *v.* M'Faddon and Others, (1812) United States, the Supreme Court of the United States, reported in 7 Cranch's Reports 116.

The Scotia, (1871) United States, the Supreme Court of the United States, reported in 14 Wallace's Reports 170.

United States *v.* One Hundred Barrels of Cement, (1862) United States, the United States District Court, reported in 27 Federal Cases 292.

United States *v.* The Schooner La Jeune Eugenie, (1822) United States, the United States Circuit Court, reported in 2 Mason's Reports 409.

Vavasseur *v.* Krupp, (1878) Great Britain, the Chancery Division of the High Court of Justice, reported in Law Reports, 1878, 9 Chancery Division 351.

PERIODICALS

American Journal of International Law, New York, 1907 *et seq.* 12 vols. to 1919. (Cited *A.J.I.L.*)

American Journal of International Law, Supplement, New York, 1907 *et seq.* 12 vols. to 1919. (Cited *A.J.I.L. Suppl.*)

American Political Science Association, Proceedings, Lancaster, Pa., and Baltimore, 1904–13. 10 vols. (Cited *A.P.S.A. Proceedings.*)

American Political Science Review, Baltimore, 1906 *et seq.* 12 vols. to 1919. (Cited *A.P.S.R.*)

American Society for the Judicial Settlement of International Disputes, Proceedings, Baltimore, 1910 *et seq.* 5 vols. to 1916. (Cited *A.S.J.S.I.D. Proceedings.*)

American Society of International Law, Proceedings, New York, 1908 *et seq.* 11 vols. to 1918. (Cited *A.S.I.L. Proceedings.*)

Annales des sciences politiques, Paris, 1886 *et seq.* Title changes. 36 vols. to 1917.

Annals of the American Academy of Political and Social Science, Philadelphia, 1890 *et seq.* 78 vols. to 1919.

Annuaire de l'Institut de Droit International, Paris, Brussels, Berlin, 1877 *et seq.* 26 vols. to 1914. (Cited *A.I.D.I.*)

Archives diplomatiques, Paris, 1861 *et seq.* 190 vols. to 1913. (Cited *Arch. dipl.*)

Columbia Law Review, New York, 1901 *et seq.* 18 vols. to 1919. (Cited *C.L.R.*)

Harvard Law Review, Cambridge, Mass., 1887 *et seq.* 31 vols. to 1919. (Cited *H.L.R.*)

International Law Notes, London, 1916 *et seq.* 3 vols. to 1919.

Journal du droit international privé, Paris, 1874 *et seq.* 43 vols. to 1917. (Cited *J.D.I.P.*)

Journal of the Society of Comparative Legislation, London, 1896 *et seq.* Beginning 1918, *Journal of Comparative Legislation and International Law.* 20 vols. to 1919. (Cited *J.S.C.L.*)

Lake Mohonk Conference on International Arbitration, annual reports since 1895. (Cited *L.M.C.I.A.*)

Law Quarterly Review, London, 1885 *et seq.* 31 vols. to 1916. (Cited *L.Q.R.*)

Michigan Law Review, Ann Arbor, Mich., 1902 *et seq.* 16 vols. to 1919. (Cited *M.L.R.*)

Political Science Quarterly, New York, 1886 *et seq.*   33 vols. to 1919.   (Cited
    P.S.Q.)
Questions diplomatiques et coloniales: revue de politique extérieure, Paris,
    1897 *et seq.*   36 vols. to 1914.
Revue de droit international et de législation comparée, Brussels, 1869 *et seq.*
    45 vols. to 1914.   (Cited *R.D.I.L.C.*)
Revue de science et de législation financières, Paris, 1903 *et seq.*   14 vols. to
    1917.   (Cited *R.S.L.F.*)
Revue générale de droit international public, Paris, 1894 *et seq.*   23 vols. to
    1917.   (Cited *R.G.D.I.P.*)
Yale Law Journal, New Haven, Conn., 1891 *et seq.*   27 vols. to 1919.   (Cited
    Y.L.J.)
Zeitschrift für schweizerisches Recht, Basel, 1882 *et seq.*   34 vols. to 1916.
    (Cited *Z.S.R.*)
Zeitschrift für Völkerrecht und Bundesstaatsrecht, Breslau, 1906 *et seq.*   9 vols.
    to 1915.   (Cited *Z.V.B.*)

ANCIENT AND MEDIAEVAL SOURCES

Accursius, *Institutionum· iuris civilis . . . cum Accursiana interpretatione*,
    etc., Lyons, 1542.
Aeneas Sylvius, *De ortu et authoritate Imperii Romani*, etc., Goldast, *Mo-
    narchia*, II, 1558–1566.
Alcuin, *Interrogationes et responsiones in Genesin*, Migne, *Patrologia*, C, cols.
    515–566.
Aristotle, *Nicomachean Ethics*, transl. by J. E. C. Welldon, London, 1892.
Aristotle, *Politics*, transl. by Benjamin Jowett, Oxford, 1885.   2 vols.
Aristotle, *Rhetoric*, transl. by Theodore Buckley, London, 1853.
Azo, *Summa Azonis*, Lyons, 1583.
Barham, Francis, *The Political Works of Marcus Tullius Cicero*, London,
    1842.   2 vols.
Beaumanoir, Philippe de, *Coutumes de Beauvaisis*, ed. by A. Salmon, Paris,
    1899–1900.   2 vols.
Brachylogos totius iuris civilis, sive corpus legum, etc., Lyons, 1557.
Bracton and Azo, *Select Passages from the Works of Bracton and Azo*, ed.
    by F. W. Maitland, publications of the Selden Society, VIII, London,
    1895.
Britton, ed. and transl. by F. M. Nichols, Oxford, 1865.   2 vols.
Buchanan, George, *De jure regni apud Scotos*, in *Opera omnia*, I, Leyden,
    1725.
Cicero, *De legibus*, in *Scripta quae manserunt omnia*, ed. by C. F. W. Mueller,
    Pt. IV, II, 380–450, Leipzig, 1878.
Cicero, *De legibus*, transl. by Francis Barham, in *The Treatises of Marcus
    Tullius Cicero*, ed. by C. D. Yonge, pp. 389–483, London, 1853.
Cicero, *De republica*, in *Scripta quae manserunt omnia*, ed. by C. F. W.
    Mueller, Pt. IV, II, 271–379, Leipzig, 1878.
Cicero, *De republica*, transl. by G. G. Hardingham, London, 1884.

Cicero, *Scripta quae manserunt omnia*, ed. by C. F. W. Mueller, Leipzig, 1878–98. 4 pts. in 10 vols.

Cope, E. M., *An Introduction to Aristotle's Rhetoric*, London and Cambridge, 1867.

Corpus Juris Civilis, ed. by Krueger, Mommsen, Schoell, and Kroll, Berlin, 1904–08. 3 vols.

Corpus Juris Civilis, books I to XV of the *Digest*, transl. by C. H. Monro, Cambridge, 1904–09. 2 vols.

Corpus Juris Civilis, Institutes, transl. by J. B. Moyle, 5th ed., Oxford, 1913.

Gaius, *Institutes*, transl. by Edward Poste, 4th ed. by E. A. Whittuck, Oxford, 1904.

Gasquy, Armand, *Cicéron jurisconsulte, avec une table des principaux passages relatifs au droit contenus dans les œuvres de Cicéron*, Paris, 1887.

Gaudenzi, Augosto, *Bibliotheca iuridica medii ævi*, ed. by Augosto Gaudenzi, Bologna, 1888.

Goldast, Melchior, *Monarchiæ S. Romani Imperii*, Frankfort, 1668. 3 vols. (Cited *Monarchia*.)

Gratian, *Decretum*, Migne, *Patrologia*, CLXXXVII.

Homeyer, C. G., *Des Sachsenspiegels erster Theil, oder das Sächsische Landrecht*, ed. by C. G. Homeyer, Berlin, 1861.

Irnerius, *De æquitate*, in *Questiones de iuris subtilitatibus*, ed. by Hermann Fitting, pp. 88–92.

Irnerius, *Questiones de iuris subtilitatibus*, ed. by Hermann Fitting, Berlin, 1894.

John of Salisbury, *Polycraticus*, Migne, *Patrologia*, CXCIX, cols. 385–822.

John of Salisbury, *Polycraticus*, ed. by C. C. I. Webb, Oxford, 1909. 2 vols.

Jonas of Orleans, *De institutione laicali*, Migne, *Patrologia*, CVI, cols. 122–278.

Kniep, Ferdinand, *Gai institutionum commentarius primus*, Jena, 1911.

Lactantius, *Divinarum institutionum*, Migne, *Patrologia*, VI, cols. 110–822.

Lactantius, *Works*, transl. by William Fletcher, Edinburgh, 1871. 2 vols.

Legnano, Giovanni da, *Tractatus de bello, de represaliis et de duello*, ed. by T. E. Holland, with transl. by J. L. Brierly, Classics of International Law, Washington, 1917.

Lodge, Thomas, *The Workes of Lucius Annæus Seneca*, London, 1620.

Machiavelli, *The Historical, Political, and Diplomatic Writings of Niccolo Machiavelli*, transl. by C. E. Detmold, Boston, 1882. 4 vols.

Marsilius of Padua, *Defensor pacis*, Goldast, *Monarchia*, II, 154–312.

Migne, J. P., *Patrologiæ cursus completus. Series prima, secunda*, Paris, 1844–64. 221 vols. (Cited *Patrologia*.)

Monro, C. H., *The Digest of Justinian* (transl. of books I to XV), Cambridge, 1904–09. 2 vols.

Morell, Thomas, *The Epistles of Lucius Annaeus Seneca*, London, 1786. 2 vols.

Moyle, J. B., *The Institutes of Justinian translated into English*, 5th ed., Oxford, 1913.

Poste, Edward, *Gai institutiones, or Institutes of Roman Law by Gaius*, 4th ed. by E. A. Whittuck, Oxford, 1904.

Rickaby, Joseph, *Aquinas Ethicus: or the Moral Teachings of St. Thomas* (a transl. of the principal portions of the second part of *Summa theologica*), London, 1896. 2 vols.

Rogerius, *Summa codicis*, Gaudenzi, *Bibliotheca iuridica medii ævi*, I, 7–174.

Rufinus, *Summa decretorum*, ed. by Heinrich Singer, Paderborn, 1902.

St. Ambrose, *De Joseph patriarcha*, Migne, *Patrologia*, XIV, cols. 641–672.

St. Augustine, *De civitate Dei*, Migne, *Patrologia*, XLI, cols. 13–804.

St. Augustine, *De civitate Dei*, transl. by John Healey, The Temple Classics, London, 1903. 3 vols.

St. Gregory the Great, *Moralium libri*, Migne, *Patrologia*, LXXV, cols. 509–1162; LXXVI, cols. 9–782.

St. Gregory the Great, *Regulæ pastoralis liber*, Migne, *Patrologia*, LXXVII, cols. 13–128.

St. Isidore, *Etymologiarum*, Migne, *Patrologia*, LXXXII, cols. 73–728.

St. Salvian, *De gubernatione Dei*, Migne, *Patrologia*, LIII, cols. 25–158.

St. Thomas Aquinas, *De regimine principum ad regem Cypri*, in *Opera*, XIX, 524–619.

St. Thomas Aquinas, *Opera*, Venice, 1745–60. 28 vols.

St. Thomas Aquinas, *Summa theologica*, Paris, 1856–61. 9 vols.

St. Thomas Aquinas, *Summa theologica*, principal portions of the second part, transl. by Joseph Rickaby, London, 1896. 2 vols.

Seneca, *Ad Lucilium epistularum moralium*, ed. by Otto Hense, Leipzig, 1914.

Seneca, *Ad Lucilium epistulae morales*, with an English transl. by R. M. Gummere, London, 1917. Vol. I, Letters I to LXV.

Seneca, *De beneficiis*, ed. by Carolus Hosius, Leipzig, 1914.

Stephan of Tournai, *Summa decretorum*, ed. by J. F. von Schulte, Giessen, 1891.

Stephanus Junius Brutus, *Vindiciæ contra tyrannos*, Edinburgh, 1579.

William of Ockham, *Dialogus*, Goldast, *Monarchia*, II, 392–957.

Wyclif, *De civili dominio*, ed. by R. L. Poole, Johann Loserth, and F. D. Mathew, London, 1884–1904. 4 vols.

GENERAL WORKS [1]

Alcorta, Amancio, *Cours de droit international public*, French ed., Paris, 1887.

Alvarez, Alejandro, *Le droit international américain*, Paris, 1910.

Amos, Sheldon, *A Systematic View of the Science of Jurisprudence*, London, 1872.

Angeberg, Comte de, *Le Congrès de Vienne et les traités de 1815*, Paris, 1864. 2 vols.

Anson, W. R., *The Law and Custom of the Constitution*, 3d ed., Oxford, 1897–1908. 3 vols.

Arminjon, Pierre, *Étrangers et protégés dans l'Empire ottoman*, Paris, 1903.

Arnold, E. V., *Roman Stoicism*, Cambridge, 1911.

Austin, John, *Lectures on Jurisprudence*, 5th ed. by Robert Campbell, London, 1885. 2 vols. paged continuously.

---

[1] Most of these works are cited by the author's name or by a short title.

Avril, Adolphe, *Négociations relatives au traité de Berlin et aux arrangements qui ont suivi*, 1875–86, Paris, 1886.

Ayala, Balthazar, *De jure et officiis bellicis et disciplina militari libri III*, ed. by John Westlake, with transl. by J. P. Bate, Classics of International Law, Washington, 1912. 2 vols.

Balaktschieff, *Die rechtliche Stellung des Fürstentums Bulgarien*, Würtzburg, 1893.

Baldassarri, Aldo, *La neutralizzazione*, Rome, 1912.

Barbeyrac, Jean, *An Historical and Critical Account of the Science of Morality* (preface to Barbeyrac's Pufendorf), transl. by Carew, in 5th ed. of Kennett's transl. of Pufendorf, London, 1749.

Barclay, Thomas, *Problems of International Practice and Diplomacy*, London and Boston, 1907.

Bates, L. T., *Les traités fédéraux et la législation des états aux États-Unis*, Paris, 1915.

Bernard, Mountagne, *Four Lectures on Subjects Connected With Diplomacy*, London, 1868.

Blackstone, William, *Commentaries on the Laws of England*, Oxford, 1765–69. 4 vols.

Bluntschli, J. K., *Das moderne Völkerrecht der civilisirten Staaten als Rechtsbuch dargestellt*, Nördlingen, 1878.

Bluntschli, J. K., *Gesammelte kleine Schriften*, Nördlingen, 1879–81. 2 vols.

Bluntschli, J. K., *Le droit international codifié*, transl. by C. Lardy, 3d ed., Paris, 1881.

Bodin, Jean, *The Six Bookes of a Commonweale*, transl. by Richard Knolles, London, 1606.

Bodin, Jean, *Les six livres de la republique*, Paris, 1577.

Bonfils, Henry, *Manuel de droit international public*, 6th ed. by Paul Fauchille, Paris, 1912.

Bonnuci, Alessandro, *La legge comune nel pensiero greco*, Perugia, 1903.

Borchard, E. M., *The Diplomatic Protection of Citizens Abroad*, New York, 1915.

Borner, Wilhelm, *Das Weltstaatsprojekt des Abbé de Saint-Pierre*, Berlin and Leipzig, 1913.

Bourgeois, Léon, *Pour la société des nations*, Paris, 1910.

Brini, Guiseppe, *Ius naturale*, Bologna, 1889.

Brown, P. M., *Foreigners in Turkey: Their Juridical Status*, Princeton, 1914.

Brown, P. M., *International Realities*, New York, 1917.

Brunswik, Benoit, *Le traité de Berlin, annoté et commenté*, Paris, 1878.

Brunswik, Benoit, *Recueil de documents diplomatiques relatifs au Monténégro*, Constantinople, 1876.

Brunswik, Benoit, *Recueil de documents diplomatiques relatifs à la Serbie*, Constantinople, 1876.

Bryce, James, *Studies in History and Jurisprudence*, New York, 1901.

Buckland, W. W., *The Roman Law of Slavery: the Condition of the Slave in Private Law from Augustus to Justinian*, Cambridge, 1908.

Burigny, J. L. de, *The Life of the Truly Eminent and Learned Hugo Grotius*, transl. into English, London, 1754.

Burigny, J. L. de, *Vie de Grotius*, Amsterdam, 1754. 2 vols.

Burlamaqui, J. J., *Principes du droit de la nature et des gens*, ed. by Félice (1766–69), new ed. by Dupin, Paris, 1820–21. 5 vols.

Burlamaqui, J. J., *Principes du droit naturel*, Geneva, 1747.

Burlamaqui, J. J., *The Principles of Natural Law*, transl. by Nugent, London, 1748.

Butler, Charles, *The Life of Hugo Grotius*, London, 1826.

Butler, C. H., *The Treaty Making Power of the United States*, New York, 1902. 2 vols.

Bynkershoek, Cornelis van, *A Treatise on the Law of War* (the first book of *Quæstiones juris publici*), transl. by P. S. Du Ponceau, Philadelphia, 1810.

Bynkershoek, Cornelis van, *Quæstionum juris publici libri duo*, Leyden, 1737.

Calary de Lamazière, R., *Les capitulations en Bulgarie*, Paris, 1905.

Calvo, Carlos, *Dictionnaire de droit international public et privé*, Berlin and Paris, 1885. 2 vols.

Calvo, Carlos, *Le droit international théorique et pratique*, 4th ed., Paris, 1887–96. 6 vols.

Cambridge Modern History, Cambridge, 1902–12. 13 vols.

Carlyle, R. W., and Carlyle, A. J., *A History of Mediæval Political Theory in the West*, Edinburgh and London, 1903–15. 3 vols.

Carnazza-Amari, Giuseppe, *Traité de droit international public*, transl. by Montanari-Revest, Paris, 1880–82. 2 vols.

Carnazza-Amari, Giuseppe, *Trattato sul diritto internazionale pubblico di pace*, 2d ed., Milan, 1875.

Caumont, Aldrick, *Étude sur la vie et les travaux de Grotius; ou, Le droit naturel et le droit international*, Paris, 1862.

Chateaubriand, Vicomte de, *Congrès de Vérone*, Leipzig, 1838. 2 vols.

Chaunier, Auguste, *La Bulgarie. Étude d'histoire diplomatique et de droit international*, Paris, 1909.

Choate, J. H., *The Two Hague Conferences*, Princeton, 1913.

Choublier, Max, *La question d'Orient depuis le traité de Berlin*, 2d ed., Paris, 1899.

Chrétien, Alfred, *Principes de droit international public*, Paris, 1893.

Clark, E. C., *Practical Jurisprudence*, Cambridge, 1883.

Clément, Nicolas, *Mémoires et négociations secrètes de la cour de France, touchant la paix de Munster*, Amsterdam, 1710. 4 vols.

Clements, P. H., *The Boxer Rebellion*, Columbia University Studies in History, Economics and Public Law, LXVI, No. 3, New York, 1915.

Cobbett, Pitt, *Cases and Opinions on International Law*, 3d ed., London, 1909–13. 2 vols.

Combes, François, *Histoire générale de la diplomatie européenne*, Paris, 1854–56. 2 vols.

Crandall, S. B., *Treaties, Their Making and Enforcement*, 2d ed., Washington, 1916.

Creasy, E. S., *First Platform of International Law*, London, 1876.

Crucé, Émeric, *The New Cyneas of Émeric Crucé*, ed. and transl. by T. W. Balch, Philadelphia, 1909.

Cuq, Édouard, *Les institutions juridiques des Romains envisagées dans leurs rapports avec l'état social et avec les progrès de la jurisprudence*, Paris, 1891–02. 2 vols.

Debidour, Antonin, *Histoire diplomatique de l'Europe depuis l'ouverture du Congrès de Vienne jusqu'à la fermeture du Congrès de Berlin (1814–78)*, Paris, 1891. 2 vols.

Demorgny, G., *La question du Danube*, Paris, 1911.

Descamps, E. E. F., *La neutralité de la Belgique au point de vue historique, diplomatique, juridique et politique*, Brussels and Paris, 1902.

Descamps, Emmanuel, *L'état neutre à titre permanent; étude de droit international comparé*, Brussels and Paris, 1912.

Despagnet, Frantz, *Cours de droit international public*, 4th ed. by Ch. de Boeck, Paris, 1910.

Dicey, A. V., *Law of the Constitution*, 8th ed., London, 1915.

Donnadieu, Léonce, *Essai sur la théorie de l'équilibre*, Paris, 1900.

Dunning, W. A., *A History of Political Theories, Ancient and Mediaeval*, New York, 1902.

Dunning, W. A., *A History of Political Theories From Luther to Montesquieu*, New York, 1905.

Duplessix, E., *La loi des nations; projet d'institution d'une autorité internationale, législative, administrative et judiciaire, projet de code de droit international public*, Paris, 1906.

Duplessix, E., *L'organisation internationale*, Paris, 1909.

Dupuis, Charles, *Le principe d'équilibre et le concert européen*, Paris, 1909.

Ehrlich, Eugen, *Die Rechtsfähigkeit*, Berlin, 1909.

Erskine, John, *Principles of the Law of Scotland*, Edinburgh, 1754. 2 vols. in 1.

Field, D. D., *Draft Outlines of an International Code*, 2d ed., New York, 1876.

Figgis, J. N., *Studies of Political Thought From Gerson to Grotius, 1414–1625*, 2d ed., Cambridge, 1916.

Fiore, Pasquale, *International Law Codified and Its Legal Sanction*, transl. from 5th Italian ed. with an introduction by E. M. Borchard, New York, 1918.

Fiore, Pasquale, *Nouveau droit international public*, 2d ed., transl. by Ch. Antoine, Paris, 1885–86. 3 vols.

Fiore, Pasquale, *Trattato di diritto internazionale pubblico*, 4th ed., Turin, 1904–16. 3 vols.

Flassan, G. de R. de, *Histoire du Congrès de Vienne*, Paris, 1829. 3 vols.

Fontenay, J., *Des droits et des devoirs des états entre eux*, Leipzig, 1887.

Franck, Adolphe, *Réformateurs et publicistes de l'Europe; dix-septième siècle*, Paris, 1881.

Frisch, Hans von, *Das Fremdenrecht; die staatsrechtliche Stellung der Fremden*, Berlin, 1910.

Funck-Brentano, Theophile, et Sorel, Albert, *Précis du droit des gens*, Paris, 1877.

Gareis, Karl, *Institutionen des Völkerrechts*, 2d ed., Giessen, 1901.

Gentilis, Albericus, *De iure belli libri tres*, ed. by T. E. Holland, Oxford, 1877.

Gentilis, Albericus, *De legationibus libri tres*, Hanover, 1594.

Gentilis, Albericus, *Hispanicæ advocationis*, Amsterdam, 1661.

Georgevitch, Vladan, *Les Albanais et les grandes puissances*, transl. by Alexis Kara-Georgovitch, Paris, 1913.

Gerard, J. W., *The Peace of Utrecht*, New York and London, 1885.

Gierke, Otto, *Political Theories of the Middle Age*, transl. by F. W. Maitland, Cambridge, 1913.

Giraud, Charles, *Le traité d'Utrecht*, Paris, 1847.

Grotius, Hugo, *De jure belli ac pacis libri tres*, reproduction of edition of 1646, Classics of International Law, Washington, 1913.

Grotius, Hugo, *De jure belli ac pacis libri tres*, accompanied by an abridged transl. by William Whewell, Cambridge, 1853. 3 vols.

Grotius, Hugo, *Le droit de la guerre et de la paix*, transl. by Jean Barbeyrac, Leyden, 1759. 2 vols. paged continuously.

Grotius, Hugo, *Le droit de la guerre et de la paix*, transl. by Paul Pradier-Fodéré, Paris, 1867. 3 vols.

Grotius, Hugo, *The Rights of War and Peace, in Three Books*, transl. into English, London, 1738.

Grotius, Hugo, *The Freedom of the Seas*, ed. by J. B. Scott, with transl. by R. V. D. Magoffin, New York, 1916.

Hall, W. E., *A Treatise on International Law*, 6th ed. by J. B. Atlay, Oxford, 1909.

Hall, W. E., *A Treatise on the Foreign Powers and Jurisdiction of the British Crown*, Oxford, 1894.

Hallam, Henry, *Introduction to the Literature of Europe in the Fifteenth, Sixteenth, and Seventeenth Centuries*, New York, 1859. 2 vols.

Halleck, H. W., *International Law*, New York, 1861.

Halleck, H. W., *International Law*, 4th ed. by G. S. Baker, London, 1908. 2 vols.

Heffter, A. W., *Das Europäische Völkerrecht der Gegenwart*, 3d ed., Berlin, 1855.

Heffter, A. W., *Le droit international de l'Europe*, transl. by Jules Bergson, 4th ed. by F. H. Geffcken, Berlin and Paris, 1883.

Heilborn, Paul, *Das völkerrechtliche Protektorat*, Berlin, 1891.

Hély, Victor, *Étude sur le droit de la guerre de Grotius*, Paris, 1875.

Hershey, A. S., *The Essentials of International Public Law*, New York, 1912.

Heyking, Alphonse de, *L'exterritorialité*, Berlin, 1889.

Higgins, A. P., *The Hague Peace Conferences*, Cambridge, 1909.

Hill, D. J., *A History of Diplomacy in the International Development of Europe*, New York, 1905-14. 3 vols.

Hill, D. J., *World Organization as Affected by the Nature of the Modern State*, New York, 1911.

Hinckley, F. E., *American Consular Jurisdiction in the Orient*, Washington, 1906.

Hobbes, Thomas, *Elementa philosophica de cive*, Amsterdam, 1657.

Hobbes, Thomas, *Leviathan*, London, 1651.

Hobbes, Thomas, *Leviathan*, ed. by A. R. Waller, Cambridge, 1904.

Hobbes, Thomas, *The Elements of Law, Natural and Politic*, ed. by Ferdinand Tönnies, London, 1889.

Hobbes, Thomas, *The English Works of Thomas Hobbes of Malmesbury*, ed. by Sir William Molesworth, London, 1839–45. 11 vols.
Hodges, H. G., *The Doctrine of Intervention*, Princeton, 1915.
Hogan, A. E., *Pacific Blockade*, Oxford, 1908.
Holland, T. E., *The European Concert in the Eastern Question*, Oxford, 1885.
Holland, T. E., *Studies in International Law*, Oxford, 1898.
Holland, T. E., *The Elements of Jurisprudence*, 12th ed., Oxford, 1916.
Holls, F. W., *The Peace Conference at The Hague, and Its Bearing on International Law and Policy*, New York, 1900.
Holtzendorff, Franz, *Handbuch des Völkerrechts*, Berlin, 1885–89. 4 vols.
Hornbeck, S. K., *Contemporary Politics in the Far East*, New York, 1916.
Hosack, John, *On the Rise and Growth of the Law of Nations*, London, 1882.
Huber, Max, *Die Gleichheit der Staaten*, a pamphlet reprinted from pp. 88–118 of *Juristische Festgabe des Auslandes zu Josef Kohlers 60 Geburtstag*, Stuttgart, 1910.
Hunter, W. A., *A Systematic and Historical Exposition of Roman Law in the Order of a Code*, transl. by J. A. Cross, 3d ed., London, 1897.
Idman, K., *Le traité de garantie en droit international*, Helsingfors, 1913.
Imbert, H. M., *Les emprunts d'états étrangers*, Paris, 1905.
Isambert, Gaston, *L'indépendance grecque et l'Europe*, Paris, 1900.
Johnson, W. F., *America's Foreign Relations*, New York, 1916. 2 vols.
Jones, C. L., *Caribbean Interests of the United States*, New York, 1916.
Kaeber, Ernst, *Die Idee des europäischen Gleichgewichts in der publizistischen Literatur vom 16. bis zur Mitte des 18. Jahrhunderts*, Berlin, 1907.
Kaltenborn, Karl von, *Die Vorläufer des Hugo Grotius auf dem Gebiete des Ius Naturae et Gentium sowie der Politik im Reformationszeitalter*, Leipzig, 1848.
Kamarowsky, L. A., *Le tribunal international*, transl. by Serge de Westman, Paris, 1887.
Kant, Immanuel, *Eternal Peace, and Other International Essays*, transl. by W. Hastie, Boston, 1914.
Kant, Immanuel, *Sämmtliche Werke*, Leipzig, 1867–68. 8 vols.
Karamichaloff, La *Principauté de Bulgarie au point de vue du droit international*, Lausanne, 1897.
Karlowa, Otto, *Römische Rechtsgeschichte*, Leipzig, 1885–1901. 2 vols.
Kaufmann, Wilhelm, *Das internationale Recht der egyptischen Staatsschuld*, Berlin, 1891.
Kebedgy, M. S., *L'intervention en droit international public*, Paris, 1890.
Keith, A. B., *Responsible Government in the Dominions*, London, 1909.
Kent, James, *Commentaries on American Law*, 12th ed. by O. W. Holmes, Jr., Boston, 1873. 4 vols.
Kent, James, *Commentary on International Law*, ed. by J. T. Abdy, 2d ed., Cambridge, 1877.
Klüber, J. L., *Acten des Wiener Congresses, in den jahren 1814 und 1815*, Erlangen, 1815–19. 8 vols.
Klüber, J. L., *Droit des gens moderne de l'Europe*, 2d ed. by M. A. Ott, Paris, 1874.

394 BIBLIOGRAPHY

Koo, V. K. W., *The Status of Aliens in China*, Columbia University Studies in History, Economics and Public Law, I, No. 2, New York, 1912.

Korkunov, N. M., *General Theory of Law*, transl. by W. G. Hastings, Boston, 1909.

Laferrière, L. F. J., *L'influence du stoicisme sur la doctrine des jurisconsultes romains*, in *Mémoires de l'academie des sciences moral et politiques de l'Institut Impérial de France* (1860), X, 579–685.

Lamberty, G. de, *Mémoires pour servir a l'histoire du XVIII siècle*, The Hague, 1724–40. 14 vols.

Lasson, Adolf, *Prinzip und Zukunft des Völkerrechts*, Berlin, 1871.

Lavisse, Ernest, et Rambaud, Alfred, *Histoire générale du IVᵉ siècle à nos jours*, Paris, 1893–1901. 12 vols.

Lawrence, T. J., *Essays on Some Disputed Questions in Modern International Law*, 2d ed., Cambridge, 1885.

Lawrence, T. J., *The Principles of International Law*, 5th ed., New York, 1913.

Le Clerc, Jean, *Négociations secrètes touchant la paix de Munster et d'Osnabrug*, The Hague, 1725–26. 4 vols.

Lehrndorfer, Gustav, *Die Souveränität in ihrer Beziehung zur völkerrechtlichen Rechts- und Handlungs-fähigkeit*, Münster, 1912.

Leibnitz, G. W., *Codex juris gentium diplomaticus*, Hanover, 1693.

Leibnitz, G. W., *Mantissa codicis juris gentium diplomatici*, Hanover, 1700.

Levi, Leone, *International Law*, New York, 1887.

Lippmann, Karl, *Die Konsularjurisdiktion im Orient*, Leipzig, 1898.

Liszt, Franz, *Das Völkerrecht systematisch dargestellt*, 7th ed., Berlin, 1911.

Littlejohn, J. M., *The Political Theory of the Schoolmen and Grotius*, New York, 1896.

Lorimer, James, *The Institutes of the Law of Nations*, Edinburgh and London, 1883–84. 2 vols.

Luden, Heinrich, *Hugo Grotius nach seinen Schicksalen und Schriften*, Berlin, 1806.

Lutfi, K. O., *Die völkerrechtliche Stellung Bulgariens und Ostrumeliens*, Erlangen, 1903.

Mably, G. B. de, *Le droit public de l'Europe, fondé sur les traités*, Geneva, 1776. 3 vols.

Macdonell, John, and Manson, Edward, *Great Jurists of the World*, ed. by Macdonell and Manson, Boston, 1914.

Mackintosh, James, *A Discourse on the Study of the Law of Nature and Nations*, 3d London ed., Boston, 1843.

Maine, H. S., *Ancient Law*, 10th ed. by Sir Frederick Pollock, London, 1906.

Maine, H. S., *International Law*, London, 1888.

Markby, William, *Elements of Law Considered with Reference to Principles of General Jurisprudence*, 6th ed., Oxford, 1905.

Martens, F. de, *Traité de droit international*, transl. by Alfred Léo, Paris, 1883–87. 3 vols.

Martens, G. F. von, *Précis du droit des gens moderne de l'Europe*, ed. by Charles Vergé, 2d ed., Paris, 1864. 2 vols.

Martens, G. F. von, *Summary of the Law of Nations*, transl. by William Cobbett, Philadelphia, 1795.

Maurel, Marius, *De la declaration de guerre; étude d'histoire diplomatique, de droit constitutionnel*, Toulouse, 1907.

Mazarin, Cardinal, *Lettres du Cardinal Mazarin pendant son ministère, 1642–50*, ed. by M. A. Chéruel, Paris, 1872–83. 3 vols.

Mead, E. D., *The Great Design of Henry IV*, ed. by E. D. Mead, Boston, 1909.

Meier, Ernst, *Über den Abschluss von Staatsverträgen*, Leipzig, 1874.

Mérignhac, Alexandre, *La conférence internationale de la paix*, Paris, 1900.

Mérignhac, Alexandre, *Traité de droit public international*, Paris, 1905–12. 3 vols.

Merriam, C. E., *History of the Theory of Sovereignty Since Rousseau*, Columbia University Studies in History, Economics and Public Law, XII, No. 4, New York, 1900.

Metternich, Fürst von, *Mémoires, documents et écrits divers*, Paris, 1880–84. 8 vols.

Meulen, J. T., *Der Gedanke der internationalen Organisation in seiner Entwicklung*, The Hague, 1917.

Michaud, J., *Le droit d'asile en Europe et en Angleterre*, Paris, 1858.

Michon, Louis, *Les traités internationaux devant les chambres*, Paris, 1901.

Milanowitch, M., *Les traités de garantie au XIXe siècle*, Paris, 1888.

Minor, R. C., *A Republic of Nations*, New York, 1918.

Mitteis, Ludwig, *Römisches Privatrecht bis auf die Zeit Diokletians*, Leipzig, 1908.

Moore, J. B., *A Digest of International Law*, Washington, 1906. 8 vols.

Moore, J. B., *Extradition and Interstate Rendition*, Washington, 1891. 2 vols.

Moore, J. B., *Principles of American Diplomacy*, New York and London, 1918.

Moser, J. J., *Beyträge zu dem neuesten europäischen Völckerrecht in Fridens-Zeiten*, Tübingen, 1778–80. 5 vols.

Moser, J. J., *Versuch des neuesten europäischen Völker-rechts in Friedens- und Kriegs-Zeiten*, Frankfort-on-the-Main, 1777–80. 10 vols in 6.

Moulin, H. A., *La doctrine de Drago*, Paris, 1908.

Muirhead, James, *Historical Introduction to the Private Law of Rome*, revised and ed. by Henry Goudy, 3d ed. by Alexander Grant, London, 1916.

Myers, D. P., *Non-Sovereign Representation in Public International Organs*, a pamphlet reprinted from pp. 753–802 of *Actes du Congrès Mondial*, 2e Session, 1913.

Neumann, Leopold von, *Éléments du droit des gens moderne européen*, 3d ed., transl. by M. A. de Riedmatten, Paris, 1886.

Nys, Ernest, *Études de droit international et de droit politique*, Brussels and Paris, 1896–1901. 2 vols.

Nys, Ernest, *Le droit de la guerre et les précurseurs de Grotius*, Brussels and Leipzig, 1882.

Nys, Ernest, *Le droit international; les principes, les théories, les faits*, 2d ed., Brussels, 1912. 3 vols.

Nys, Ernest, *Les origines du droit international*, Brussels and Paris, 1894.

396   BIBLIOGRAPHY

Oakes, Sir Augustus, and Mowat, R. B., *The Great European Treaties of the Nineteenth Century*, Oxford, 1918.

Ompteda, D. H. L. von, *Litteratur des gesammten sowohl natürlichen als positiven Völkerrechts*, Regensburg, 1785. 2 vols. in 1.

Oppenheim, Lassa, *International Law*, 2d ed., London, 1912. 2 vols.

Pélissié du Rausas, G., *Le régime des capitulations dans l'Empire ottoman*, '2d ed., Paris, 1910–11. 2 vols.

Philippi, *Der Westphälische Friede*, Münster, 1898.

Phillimore, Robert, *Commentaries Upon International Law*, 3d ed., London, 1879–89. 4 vols.

Phillips, W. A., *The Confederation of Europe; A Study of the European Alliance, 1813–23, as an Experiment in the International Organization of Peace*, London and New York, 1914.

Phillipson, Coleman, *Termination of War and Treaties of Peace*, New York, 1916.

Phillipson, Coleman, *The International Law and Custom of Ancient Greece and Rome*, London, 1911. 2 vols.

Piédelièvre, Robert, *Précis de droit international public ou droit des gens*, Paris, 1894–95. 2 vols.

Piggot, F. T., *Exterritoriality. The Law Relating to Consular Jurisdiction and to Residence in Oriental Countries*, new ed., London, 1907.

Pillet, Antoine, *Recherches sur les droits fondamentaux des états*, Paris, 1899.

Pillet, Antoine, *Les fondateurs du droit international*, ed. by A. Pillet, Paris, 1904.

Pitisteano, A. G., *La question du Danube*, Paris, 1914.

Planiol, M. F., *Traité élémentaire de droit civil*, 6th ed., Paris, 1911–13. 3 vols.

Pomeroy, J. N., *Lectures on International Law in Time of Peace*, ed. by T. S. Woolsey, Boston and New York, 1886.

Pradier-Fodéré, Paul, *Traité de droit international public européen & américain*, Paris, 1885–1906. 8 vols.

Pradt, M. de, *Du Congrès de Vienne*, Paris, 1815. 2 vols.

Pradt, M. de, *L'Europe après le Congrès d'Aix-la-Chapelle*, Paris, 1819.

Pufendorf, Samuel von, *De jure naturæ et gentium, libri octo*, Amsterdam, 1704.

Pufendorf, Samuel von, *De officio hominis et civis juxta legem naturalem*, London, 1673.

Pufendorf, Samuel von, *Law of Nature and Nations, abridged from the original*, by J. Spavan, London, 1716. 2 vols.

Pufendorf, Samuel von, *Le droit de la nature & des gens*, transl. by Jean Barbeyrac, Leyden, 1759. 2 vols.

Pufendorf, Samuel von, *The Law of Nature and Nations*, transl. by Basil Kennett, 5th ed., London, 1749.

Pütter, J. S., *Geist des westphälischen Friedens*, Göttingen, 1795. 2 vols.

Rachel, Samuel, *De jure naturæ et gentium dissertationes*, ed. by Ludwig von Bar, with transl. by J. P. Bate, Classics of International Law, Washington, 1916. 2 vols.

Reinsch, P. S., *Public International Unions; Their Work and Organization, a Study in International Administrative Law,* Boston, 1911.
Rey, Francis, *De la protection diplomatique et consulaire dans les échelles du Levant et de Barbarie,* Paris, 1899.
Rioche, Yves, *Les juridictions consulaires anglaises dans les pays d'Orient, Turquie, Perse, Mascate, Maroc,* Paris, 1904.
Ritchie, D. G., *Natural Rights,* 2d ed., London, 1903.
Rivier, Alphonse, *Principes du droit des gens,* Paris, 1896. 2 vols.
Root, Elihu, *Addresses on International Subjects,* ed. by Robert Bacon and J. B. Scott, Cambridge, Mass., 1916.
Root, Elihu, *Latin America and the United States,* ed. by Robert Bacon and J. B. Scott, Cambridge, Mass., 1917.
Rutherforth, Thomas, *Institutes of Natural Law: Being the Substance of a Course of Lectures on Grotius De jure belli et pacis,* Cambridge, 1754-56. 2 vols.
Rutherforth, Thomas, *Institutes of Natural Law;* etc., 2d Am. ed., Baltimore, 1832.
Saint-Pierre, Abbé de, *A Project for Settling an Everlasting Peace in Europe,* transl. into English, London, 1714.
Saint-Pierre, Abbé de, *L'abrégé du projet de paix perpetuelle,* in *Ouvrages de politiques,* I, Paris, 1738.
Sanger, C. P., and Norton, H. T. J., *England's Guarantee to Belgium and Luxemburg, With the Full Text of the Treaties,* London, 1915.
Sarüvanoff, *La Bulgarie est-elle un état mi-souverain ?,* Paris, 1907.
Satow, Ernest, *A Guide to Diplomatic Practice,* London, 1917. 2 vols.
Sayre, F. B., *Experiments in International Administration,* New York, 1919.
Scott, J. B., *American Addresses at The Second Hague Peace Conference,* ed. by J. B. Scott, Boston and London, 1910.
Scott, J. B., *An International Court of Justice; Letter and Memorandum of January 12, 1914, to the Netherland Minister of Foreign Affairs, in Behalf of the Establishment of an International Court of Justice,* New York, 1916.
Scott, J. B., *Instructions to the American Delegates to The Hague Peace Conferences and Their Official Reports,* ed. by J. B. Scott, New York, 1916.
Scott, J. B., *The American Institute of International Law: Its Declaration of the Rights and Duties of Nations,* Washington, 1916.
Scott, J. B., *The Hague Peace Conferences of 1899 and 1907,* Baltimore, 1909. 2 vols.
Scott, J. B., *The Status of the International Court of Justice,* New York, 1916.
Selden, John, *Opera omnia,* London, 1726. 3 vols.
Serkis, Charles, *La Roumélie orientale et la Bulgarie actuelle,* Paris, 1898.
Sohm, Rudolph, *The Institutes, A Text-book of the History and System of Roman Private Law,* transl. by J. C. Ledlie, 3d ed., Oxford, 1907.
Sorel, Albert, *L'Europe et la révolution française,* Paris, 1885-1904. 8 vols.
Sorel, Albert, *Le Traité de Paris du 20 novembre 1815,* Paris, 1872.
Stallybrass, W. T. S., *A Society of States: Sovereignty, Independence and Equality in a League of Nations,* New York, 1919.
Stapleton, A. G., *The Political Life of the Right Honorable George Canning,* London, 1831. 3 vols.

Suarez, Franciscus, *Tractatus de legibus ac Deo legislatore in decem libros distributus*, Mayence, 1619.

Sully, Duc de, *Mémoires de Sully*, Paris, 1814. 6 vols.

Talleyrand, C. M. de, *Memoirs of the Prince of Talleyrand*, ed. by the Duc de Broglie, transl. by R. L. de Beaufort, New York and London, 1891–92. 5 vols.

Taylor, Hannis, *A Treatise on International Public Law*, Chicago, 1901.

Taylor, John, *A Summary of the Roman Law*, from the same author's *Elements of the Civil Law*, London, 1772.

Textor, J. W., *Synopsis juris gentium*, ed. by Ludwig von Bar, with transl. by J. P. Bate, Classics of International Law, Washington, 1916. 2 vols.

Thomasius, Christian, *Institutionum jurisprudentiæ divinæ libri tres, in quibus fundamenta juris naturalis secundum hypotheses illustris Pufendorffii perspicue demonstrantur*, etc., 3d ed., Halle, 1702.

Tobar y Borgoño, C. M., *L'asile interne devant le droit international*, Barcelona and Paris, 1911.

Todd, Alpheus, *Parliamentary Government in the British Colonies*, London, 1880.

Torres, Alberto, *Vers la paix; études sur l'établissiment de la paix générale et sur l'organisation de l'ordre international*, Rio de Janeiro, 1909.

Tucker, H. St. G., *Limitations on the Treaty-Making Power Under the Constitution of the United States*, Boston, 1915.

Twiss, Travers, *The Law of Nations Considered as Independent Political Communities*, 2d ed., Oxford, 1884.

Tyau, M. T. Z., *The Legal Obligations Arising Out of Treaty Relations Between China and Other States*, Shanghai, 1917.

Ullman, Emanuel von, *Völkerrecht*, Tübingen, 1908.

Urusov, A. M., *Résumé historique des principaux traités de paix conclus entre les puissances européennes depuis le Traité de Westphalie (1648) jusqu'au Traité de Berlin (1878)*, Evreux, 1884.

Vaclick, *La souveraineté du Monténégro et le droit des gens moderne de l'Europe*, Paris, 1858.

Vasquez, Ferdinand, *Controversiarum illustrium aliarumque usu frequentium libri tres*, Venice, 1564.

Vattel, Emmerich de, *Le droit des gens, ou, Principes de la loi naturelle, appliqués à la conduite & aux affaires des nationes & des souverains*, text of 1758, with transl. by C. G. Fenwick, Classics of International Law, Washington, 1916. 3 vols.

Vaunois, A., *De la notion du droit naturel chez les Romains*, Paris, 1884.

Victoria, Franciscus de, *De Indis et de iure belli relectiones*, ed. by Ernest Nys, with transl. by J. P. Bate, Classics of International Law, Washington, 1917.

Voigt, Moritz, *Das jus naturale, æquum et bonum und jus gentium der Römer*, Leipzig, 1856–75. 4 vols.

Vreeland, Hamilton, *Hugo Grotius*, New York, 1917.

Walker, T. A., *A History of the Law of Nations*, Cambridge, 1899.

Walker, T. A., *A Manual of Public International Law*, Cambridge, 1895.

Walker, T. A., *The Science of International Law*, London, 1893.

Ward, Robert, *An Enquiry Into the Foundation and History of the Law of Nations in Europe From the Time of the Greeks and Romans to the Age of Grotius*, London, 1795. 2 vols.

Weber, Ottocar, *Der Friede von Utrecht; Verhandlungen zwischen England, Frankreich, dem Kaiser und den Generalstaaten, 1710–13*, Gotha, 1891.

Westlake, John, *The Collected Papers of John Westlake on Public International Law*, ed. by L. Oppenheim, Cambridge, 1914.

Westlake, John, *International Law*, 2d ed., Cambridge, 1910–13. 2 vols.

Wharton, Francis, *The Revolutionary Diplomatic Correspondence of the United States*, Washington, 1889. 6 vols.

Wheaton, Henry, *Elements of International Law*, 2d annotated ed. by W. B. Lawrence, Boston, 1863.

Wheaton, Henry, *History of the Law of Nations in Europe and America; From the Earliest Times to the Treaty of Washington, 1842*, New York, 1845.

White, A. D., *Autobiography of Andrew Dickson White*, New York, 1905. 2 vols.

White, A. D., *Seven Great Statesmen in the Warfare of Humanity with Unreason*, New York, 1910.

Wildman, Richard, *Institutes of International Law*, London, 1849–50. 2 vols.

Wilson, G. G., *Handbook of International Law*, St. Paul, 1910.

Wilson, G. G., *The Hague Arbitration Cases*, Boston and London, 1915.

Wolff, Christian von, *Institutiones du droit de la nature et des gens*, transl. by E. Luzac, Leyden, 1772.

Wolff, Christian von, *Institutiones juris naturæ et gentium*, Halle, 1750.

Wolff, Christian von, *Jus gentium methodo scientifica pertractatum*, Frankfort and Leipzig, 1764.

Wolff, Christian von, *Jus naturæ methodo scientifica pertractatum*, Frankfort and Leipzig, 1764. 8 vols.

Woolf, L. S., *International Government*, New York, 1916.

Woolsey, T. D., *Introduction to the Study of International Law*, 6th ed. by T. S. Woolsey, New York, 1908.

Wright, H. F., *Francisci de Victoria De iure belli relectio*, Washington, 1916.

Zorn, Albert, *Grundzüge des Völkerrechts*, Leipzig, 1903.

Zouche, Richard, *Iuris et iudicii fecialis, sive, iuris inter gentes, et quaestionum de eodem explicatio, qua quae ad pacem & bellum inter diversos principes, aut populos spectant, ex praecipuis historico-jure-peritis, exhibentur*, ed. by T. E. Holland, with transl. by J. L. Brierly, Classics of International Law, Washington, 1911. 2 vols.

INDEX

INDEX

Abd-ul-Messih *v.* Farra, 238 n. 3.

Abdy, comment on naturalists, 89 n. 2.

Abyssinia, protection of, 245; excluded from League, 347, 360.

Act, legal, 4.

Administrative unions, 125, 280, 310–321; constitution of, 310–311, 361; representation, 201, 311–313, 321, 333, 367; voting, 311, 313–319, 321, 333, 369, 371; financial support, 311, 319–321, 333, 376.

Adrianople, Treaty of, 233 n. 1.

Aeneas Sylvius, state of nature, 28.

Agidir incident, cited in Salvador *v.* Nicaragua, 172.

Agriculture. *See* International Institute of.

Air navigation, Convention of 1919, 337 n. 2, 361; International Commission, 361, 369, 371, 375, 375 n. 6, 376.

Aix-la-Chapelle, Congress of, 174, 296–299, 366.

Aix-la-Chapelle — Maastricht Railroad Co. *v.* Thewis and Royal Dutch Government, 262 n. 4.

Algeciras, Act of, 242, 317 n. 1; Conference of, 282.

Aliens, admission, exclusion, expulsion, 212–213, 219, 228–229; status, 213–214, 219; protection, 214–216, 219, 227–228.

American Conferences, International. *See* International American Conferences.

American Institute of International Law, Declaration of Rights of Nations, 154–155, 175, 187.

American republics, state equality, 154, 175; constitutional limitations on treaty power, 198–200, 207–209, on war power, 203, 204, 210, 211; other

constitutional limitations, 205, 206, 211, 212–216; United States guardianship, 246; protest against forcible collection of public debts, 272–274; representation at international conferences, 282, 285, 285 n. 2; international bureaus, 319; at Conference of Paris, 349, 355 n. 1.

American Society of International Law, state equality discussed, 113 n. 1, 134, 135, 135 n. 1, 136 n. 1.

Amos, laws of status and organization distinguished, 137.

Analogy between natural persons and states, source of principle of state equality, 6, 29–31, 32, 33; in Grotian system, 35, 49–50; forerunners of Grotius, 37, 39; Hobbes, 73; naturalists, 79, 80, 83, 84, 86, 87, 88; positivists, 90, 93, 94; eclectics, 96, 97, 98; justification of state equality, 99, 111–113, 113 n. 1, 149.

Andorra, vassalage, 239.

Anson, treaty power under English Constitution, 195.

Antelope, The, 24 n. 1, 155, 160–162.

Antoine, state equality, ideal character of, 122; primacy of great powers, 139.

Argentine, delegate to Hague Conference, remarks on equality, 181, 285; treaty power, 198; war power, 203; admission of foreign troops, 205; sending abroad of national troops, 205; navigation of interior rivers, 212, 212 n. 1; admission of aliens, 213; status of aliens, 214; neutralization of Straits of Magellan, 255; Drago's despatch, 272; reservation in regard to forcible collection of contract debts, 273; composition of proposed Arbitral Court, 327. *See* American republics, and Constitutions.

independence 233–234, 237, 303; vassalage, 236–237; guaranty of independence, 250; servitudes, 266; participation in Congress of Berlin, 303; abstained on *Vœu* in regard to proposed Arbitral Court, 331; at Conference of Paris, 349, 350, 355 n. 1; represented on Reparation Commission, 354, on Danube Commission, 367. *See* Constitutions.

Roumelia, autonomy and union with Bulgaria, 234, 304; European Concert and affairs in, 305.

Rufinus, natural equality, 24.

Russia, equality of, 109, 113, 115, 116, 134, 161; a great power, 130; treaty power, 193; war power, 202; autonomy of Danubian principalities, 233; diplomatic representation in Bulgaria, 238; agreements in regard to Mongolia, 239; protection of Cracow, 241, of Persia, 243; recognition of Korean independence, 243, of Japanese interests in Korea, 244; protection of Mongolia, 245; guaranty of independence of Greece, 250, of integrity of Norway, 251, of neutralization of Switzerland, Belgium, and Luxemburg, 252–254; neutralization of Black Sea, 255, 265, 266, 266 n. 1; representation at international conferences, 281–282; initiative in calling Hague Conferences, 290; Congress of Vienna, 294–296; Congress of Aix-la-Chapelle, 296–299; Holy Alliance, 299; proposed conference on affairs in Greece, 300; affairs in Greece, 301; war with Turkey, 303; opposed coercion of Holland, 306; dependencies represented in Wireless Telegraph Union, 313; merchant marine tonnage, 323 n. 3; representation on proposed Prize Court, 324; excluded from League, 347, 360. *See* Concert of Europe, Constitutions, and Great powers.

Rutherforth, life and works, 85 n. 4; law of nations and state equality, 85–86, 86 n. 4.

Saar, cession of mines, 344, 353, 372; government, 345, 352, 354, 356, 370, 372,373.

St. Augustine, natural equality, 18, 19; the Fall, 19.

St. Germain, Treaty of, 337 n. 1.

St. Gregory, natural equality, 18.

St. Isidore of Seville, natural law, 20; natural equality, 24.

St. Paul, universal law, 17; quoted by Grotius, 60.

St. Thomas Aquinas, natural law, 20, 21, 22; natural equality, 25; theory developed by Suarez, 36.

Saint-Pierre, l'abbé de, 75 n. 2.

Salisbury, European Concert, 309.

Salvador, protest against Bryan-Chamorro Treaty, 174; treaty power, 198, 207, 208, 209; war power, 203; extradition, 211; status of aliens, 214; protection of aliens, 215; Salvador *v.* Nicaragua, 172. *See* American republics, and Constitutions.

Salvador *v.* Nicaragua, 172, 276 n. 2.

Salvian, natural equality, 18.

Sanitary Conference. *See* International Sanitary Conference.

Sanitary Convention, International, 316.

San Marino, equality of, 89, 113; protection of, 242.

Sardinia, neutralization of Savoy, 265; proposed conference on Italian affairs, 305, 306. *See* Italy.

Savoy, neutralization, 255; servitude of neutrality, 265; neutralization terminated, 342.

Sayre, equality of votes, 145 n. 2; unanimity, 318; Sugar Commission, majority decisions, 318 n. 1.

Schooner Exchange *v.* M'Faddon, 156, 157.

Scotia, The, 162 n. 1.

Scott, J. B., state equality, and inequalities of fact, 120; nature of Hague Conferences, 290 n. 1; influence of great powers at Hague Conferences, 290 n. 2; composition of proposed Arbitral Court, 328.

Scott, Sir William (Lord Stowell), state equality, Le Louis, 155, 159, 161, 172, 187, inequality, The Madonna Del Burso, 163, The Helena, 163 n. 1.

Secretary of State v. Charlesworth, Pilling and Co., 224 n. 2.

Seneca, natural law, 9; natural equality, 14; state of nature, 14, 26, 27, 28; influence on patristic thought, 18; cited by Grotius, 39.

Serb-Croat-Slovene State, represented on Klagenfurt Commission, 353, on Reparation Commission, 354; at Conference of Paris, 355 n. 1. *See* Servia.

Servia, limitations incident to geographical situation, 163, 222, 222 n. 2; equality of, 186; treaty power, 196, 207; war power, 202; autonomy and independence, 234, 303; vassalage, 237; guaranty of independence, 250; financial control of, 256; excluded from Congress of Berlin, 303; participation in Conference of London, 304; at Conference of Paris, 349, 349 n. 2, 350, 355 n. 1. *See* Constitutions, and Serb-Croat-Slovene State.

Servitudes, in Grotian system, 58; limitations incident to, 168–171, 264–268, 278, 343–345, 377.

Shimonoseki, Treaty of, 243.

Siam, at Conference of Paris, 349, 355 n. 1.

Sorel. *See* Funck-Brentano.

Slave trade, court decisions, 159–162, 162 n. 1; suppression of, 295, 319.

Slavery, Aristotle, 13; Seneca, 14; Roman Law, 15, 27, 46; the early Church, 17; patristic writings, 18, 27; civilians, 23; canonists, 24; St. Thomas Aquinas, 25; other mediaeval sources, 28, 28 n. 1; Grotius, 48, 51, conquered states compared, 50, 59, 60.

Snow, primacy of great powers, 141 n. 2.

Socrates, natural right, 6.

Sophists, natural right, 6.

South Africa, at Conference of Paris, 349.

South African Republic, vassalage, 239.

South America. *See* American republics.

Sovereignty, universal rejected, 37, 57; in Grotian system, 50, 53, 55–60, 61, 66–67; part-sovereign states, 50, 55, 58, 91, 92 n. 6, 93, 93 n. 6, 119, 133, 169; early development of idea, 56, 57; relation to origin of principle of state equality, 56, 74, 79, 84 n. 6, 90, 93, 99; justification for state equality, 114, 115, 150; supernatural organization, 138; Pillet's alternative principle, 146; servitudes, 168–171; Gray's comment on Austinian theory, 191 n. 1; internal limitations on capacity distinguished, 191; effect of incapacity to make treaties, 210; effect of intervention, 261 n. 3.

Spain, equality of, 89; The Antelope, 160; Venezuelan Arbitration, 166, 167; treaty power, 196, 198 n. 1; war power, 202; admission of foreign troops, 205; admission of aliens, 212; representation at international conferences, 281, 282; signed Treaty of Paris, 294; revolution in, 299; dependencies represented in Wireless Telegraph Union, 313. *See* Constitutions.

Spectator, The, criticism of Hague Conference, 287.

Spheres of influence, limitation on equality, 121 n. 4.

State, equality, general principles, 3–5; legal personality, 31, 111, 150, 189; society of states, 32; conception of the state, 37, 57, 71, 79, 80, 87, 97; legal capacity as international person, 190; internal capacity, 191 n. 1; effect of constitutional amendment, 191, 200. *See* Analogy between natural persons and states, Equality, political, Equality before the law, Equality of capacity for rights, Equality of states, and Sovereignty.

State, inland. *See* Inland state.

State of nature, source of principle of state equality, 6, 14, 18, 26–29, 31–33; in Grotian system, 35, 47–49, 52; forerunners of Grotius, 36, 37; identified with international society, 69, 77,

WORLD AFFAIRS: National and International Viewpoints
An Arno Press Collection

Angell, Norman. **The Great Illusion, 1933.** 1933.

Benes, Eduard. **Memoirs:** From Munich to New War and New Victory. 1954.

[Carrington, Charles Edmund] (Edmonds, Charles, pseud.) **A Subaltern's War.** 1930. New preface by Charles Edmund Carrington.

Cassel, Gustav. **Money and Foreign Exchange After 1914.** 1922.

Chambers, Frank P. **The War Behind the War, 1914-1918.** 1939.

Dedijer, Vladimir. **Tito.** 1953.

Dickinson, Edwin DeWitt. **The Equality of States in International Law.** 1920.

Douhet, Giulio. **The Command of the Air.** 1942.

Edib, Halidé. **Memoirs.** 1926.

Ferrero, Guglielmo. **The Principles of Power.** 1942.

Grew, Joseph C. **Ten Years in Japan.** 1944.

Hayden, Joseph Ralston. **The Philippines.** 1942.

Hudson, Manley O. **The Permanent Court of International Justice, 1920-1942.** 1943.

Huntington, Ellsworth. **Mainsprings of Civilization.** 1945.

Jacks, G. V. and R. O. Whyte. **Vanishing Lands:** A World Survey of Soil Erosion. 1939.

Mason, Edward S. **Controlling World Trade.** 1946.

Menon, V. P. **The Story of the Integration of the Indian States.** 1956.

Moore, Wilbert E. **Economic Demography of Eastern and Southern Europe.** 1945.

[Ohlin, Bertil]. **The Course and Phases of the World Economic Depression.** 1931.

Oliveira, A. Ramos. **Politics, Economics and Men of Modern Spain, 1808-1946.** 1946.

O'Sullivan, Donal. **The Irish Free State and Its Senate.** 1940.

Peffer, Nathaniel. **The White Man's Dilemma.** 1927.

Philby, H. St. John. **Sa'udi Arabia.** 1955.

Rappard, William E. **International Relations as Viewed From Geneva.** 1925.

Rauschning, Hermann. **The Revolution of Nihilism.** 1939.

Reshetar, John S., Jr. **The Ukrainian Revolution, 1917-1920.** 1952.

Richmond, Admiral Sir Herbert. **Sea Power in the Modern World.** 1934.

Robbins, Lionel. **Economic Planning and International Order.** 1937. New preface by Lionel Robbins.

Russell, Bertrand. **Bolshevism:** Practice and Theory. 1920.

Russell, Frank M. **Theories of International Relations.** 1936.

Schwarz, Solomon M. **The Jews in the Soviet Union.** 1951.

Siegfried, André. **Canada:** An International Power. [1947].

Souvarine, Boris. **Stalin.** 1939.

Spaulding, Oliver Lyman, Jr., Hoffman Nickerson, and John Womack Wright. **Warfare.** 1925.

Storrs, Sir Ronald. **Memoirs.** 1937.

Strausz-Hupé, Robert. **Geopolitics:** The Struggle for Space and Power. 1942.

Swinton, Sir Ernest D. **Eyewitness.** 1933.

Timasheff, Nicholas S. **The Great Retreat.** 1946.

Welles, Sumner. **Naboth's Vineyard:** The Dominican Republic, 1844-1924. 1928. Two volumes in one.

Whittlesey, Derwent. **The Earth and the State.** 1939.

Wilcox, Clair. **A Charter for World Trade.** 1949.